exploring

TYPOGRAPHY

exploring

TYPOGRAPHY

Tova Rabinowitz

THOMSON

DELMAR LEARNING   Australia   Canada   Mexico   Singapore   Spain   United Kingdom   United States

DESIGN
EXPLORATION
SERIES

THOMSON
™
DELMAR LEARNING

Exploring Typography
Tova Rabinowitz

Vice President, Technology and Trades SBU:
Dave Garza

Director of Learning Solutions:
Sandy Clark

Senior Acquisitions Editor:
James Gish

Product Manager:
Jaimie Weiss

Editorial Assistant:
Niamh Matthews

Channel Manager:
William Lawrensen

Marketing Coordinator:
Mark Pierro

Production Director:
Mary Ellen Black

Senior Production Manager:
Larry Main

Senior Production Editor:
Thomas Stover

Technology Project Manager:
Kevin Smith

Art and Design Coordinator
Francis Hogan

Cover Design:
Steven Brower

Cover image and Selected Art Direction:
Tim Jonas

Cover Production:
David Arsenault

ISBN: 1-4018-1505-7

NOTICE TO THE READER

contents

CONTENTS

contents

CONTENTS

Self-promotional wrapping paper design
by Greg Lamarche of SPONE, 2003.

PREFACE

preface

INTENDED AUDIENCE

Exploring Typography offers a thorough study of the use and design of type in the field of Graphic Design. It is geared toward the needs of college students and professionals who seek an accessible and practical introduction to this complex subject matter, in an image-dominant format.

EMERGING TRENDS

Recent evolution of computer technologies has provided designers with new opportunities to challenge the boundaries of what fonts are and how they may be used. While presenting exciting possibilities for growth in this area of design, these advances also have created new challenges for those who wish to master the use of type as a tool for communication. As improved technologies have increased accessibility of type design and use, so too has the need grown for clear methodologies and focused strategies to guide their use and creation.

BACKGROUND OF THIS TEXT

As a college instructor, I discovered that students often found this rich subject matter dry and confusing. Few available textbooks seemed to present an accurate and clear structure to ease understanding and facilitate practice while presenting a compelling case for the importance of this topic to designers. My goal in writing this book was to present typography in an accessible way that would emphasize practical uses and organized systems. My research included a vast amount of readings on the subject matter, the viewing of a huge amount of typographic images, and the detailed examination of a multitude of typefaces. I investigated historical and contemporary theories and practices, from which I extruded the most predominant and essential concepts; I then found sensible ways to explain this complex topic in user-friendly and logical fashion, relying heavily on visual aids. No prior knowledge of typography or design is needed to enjoy this book. However, any previous design-related experiences and insights the reader can bring to the readings will allow for a deeper and richer understanding of the concepts offered within this text.

TEXTBOOK ORGANIZATION

Chapter 1: History of Type presents an overview of the history of type, structured as a timeline to help readers grasp the developmental progression of design in relation to history and technological innovations. This chapter traces the development and use of type from its earliest beginnings in prehistoric times to the present.

Illustration by Dave McKean of Hourglass from Neil Gaiman's book *The Day I Swapped My Dad for Two Goldfish* for HarperCollins, 1997.

Chapter 2: Physical Attributes of Type facilitates a technical understanding of type, providing language for discussion of the physical qualities that make each typeface unique. This chapter addresses the structural elements that are used to build letterforms, as well as type measurement, and the terminology associated with typography.

Chapter 3: Type Family Classification discusses the strategy and methods used in classifying type into type families, providing an extensive collection of historically significant type specimens for readers to study and use. This chapter attempts to dispel the confusion expressed by so many readers about this subject by providing a logical organizational system based in both history and common sense.

Chapter 4: Legibility and Readability presents an examination of the factors that can affect the legibility and the readability of a design. This chapter addresses how designers can manipulate controllable factors, catering to the user's experience and physiology, and improving communication.

Chapter 5: Layout Design Aspects asks readers to examine the relationship between form and content, and the role of each in the layout of designs. This chapter addresses the Laws of Gestalt and concepts of visual hierarchy, emphasis, and reading gravity as tools for effective layout of type and imagery.

Chapter 6: Using Grids discusses the use and applications of the grid as a tool for bringing consistency to multipage documents and layouts. This chapter explains what a grid is, and explores the variety of ways a grid may be used to facilitate and guide the design process.

Chapter 7: Type in a Digital Environment explores issues that are specific to type in a digital environment. This chapter addresses font formats and display resolution, as well as legibility and readability issues as they pertain to screen typography.

Chapter 8: Designing Type walks readers through the process of designing an original font. This chapter provides a thorough guide for the novice type designer, including tips that can help readers undertake the challenge of type design in an organized fashion.

Chapter 9: Creative Uses of Type presents a survey of recent designs in which type has been used uniquely and successfully. This chapter provides analyses of outstanding designs, focusing on how the typographic standards that were established in previous chapters have been followed, and broken, to create designs that are both innovative and effective.

Glossary
Selected Bibliography, including web site addresses
List of Contributors
Index

FEATURES

The following list provides some of the salient features of the text:

Pennsylvania Festival of the Arts: Kids Day poster by Lanny Sommese of Sommese Design for the Central Pennsylvania Festival of the Arts, 1997.

- Image-dominant format, including a timeline presentation of the history of type, drawing relationships between the development of design and technological innovations throughout history

- Coverage looks at how choices in type can affect a reader's ability to "receive" information

- Illustrative examples, imagery, and charts support each idea and bring clarity to typographic concepts

- Simple and concise explanations that are based on the practical concerns of working designers help readers organize the information and make important connections

- Detailed guide walks readers through the process of designing their own typefaces

- Study questions, exercises, and assignments enable readers to sharpen their skills and put key principles to work as they design their own visual projects

- Interviews of prominent working designers, who share their own experiences and opinions about the field of design

SPECIAL FEATURES

objectives
- Understand type terminology
- Learn about the historical evolution of type family categories
- Recognize how the structural elements of letterforms differ for each type family category
- Understand how type is classified
- Make educated decisions when choosing typefaces for designs

introduction

You have probably noticed that there are an enormous number of fonts available for use in your designs—so many that it can be overwhelming and difficult to choose sometimes. On one hand, the abundance of available font styles can help you to make your designs expressive and unique. On the other hand, with such a wide selection, it's easy to fall into the trap of using fonts inappropriately—that is, based on enthusiasm for the font itself, rather than the appropriateness of its qualities for the design's message. The way a typeface looks may suggest a certain time period or cultural phenomenon to viewers. It can also set a mood or suggest an association to a remembered experience. To gain insight into the connotations of various typeface designs, it is necessary to become familiar with the ways that typefaces are classified and the related terminology.

TYPE FAMILY CLASSIFICATION

73

▶ Objectives

Learning objectives start off each chapter. They describe the competencies readers should achieve upon understanding the chapter material.

▶ New Vocabulary

Key terms for each chapter are defined in these boxes, appearing throughout the text.

▶ The Typographer at Work

These career profiles are interspersed throughout the text. Each features a successful designer who has contributed innovative and dynamic typographic works to the field of design.

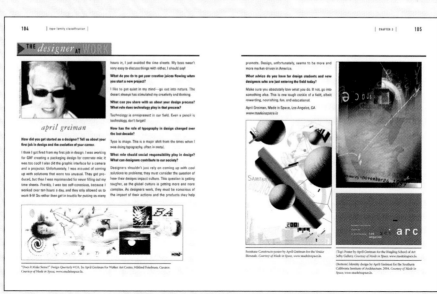

104 | type family classification |
CHAPTER 3 | 105

▶ Notes

Notes provide
special hints,
practical tips,
and information
to the reader.

Sidebars

Sidebars appear
throughout the text,
offering additional
valuable information
on specific topics.

▶ Review Questions and Exercises

Review questions and exercises are located at the end
of each chapter and allow the reader to assess their
understanding of the chapter. Exercises are intended to
reinforce the chapter material through practical application.

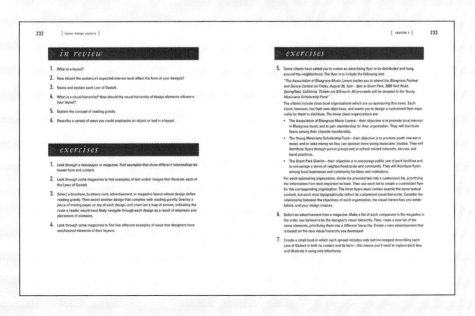

ABOUT THE AUTHOR

Tova Rabinowitz is an educator and an artist. Renowned among those who know her for being particularly creative and inventive, she has worked in a range of artistic mediums from pencil to paint to pixels, and has enjoyed teaching students ranging from preschool age to college undergraduates. Tova worked at Westwood College of Technology for three years, first as a Graphic Design instructor and later as Graphic Design Program Director, where she was heavily involved in developing programming and curriculum. She has also worked as a dishware designer, a display artist, and has owned and operated a small business specializing in custom fiber-arts design. She holds degrees in both art and education.

E.RESOURCE

This guide on CD was developed to assist instructors in planning and implementing their instructional programs. It includes sample syllabi for using this book in both 11-week and 15-week semesters. It also provides chapter review questions and answers, exercises, PowerPoint slides highlighting the main topics, and additional instructor resources.

ISBN: 1-4018-1506-5

Block book, *Apocalypsis Sancti Johannis*, Germany, 1470 CE.
© *Lessing J. Rosenwald Collection, Library of Congress,*
Washington, D.C. Used with permission.

ACKNOWLEDGMENTS

Thank you for kindly sharing your helpfulness, your time, your patience, your expertise, your insights, your resources, and your support throughout this process:

Heather and Bobby Rabinowitz, Heidi Estrin, Dru and Al Simon, Tim Jonas, Aaron Hawkins, Elizabeth Nevin (of Briar Press), David Jury, Brad Knapp, Paul Ruffino, Clifford Deer, Tamar Cordover, Jill Cordover, Malcolm Lubliner and Monica Maass, Ethan Dyer, Rachel Charson, Angie Reichert-Hester and Tom Hester, Fred Klein, Kanako Takeda, Carol Meegan, Kathy Moran, Melissa Unzicker, Peter Schoewe, David Peters, Leslie Cabarga, Art Chantry (of Art Chantry Design), Nick Curtis (of Nick's Fonts), Ryan Pescatore Frisk and Catelijne van Middelkoop (of Strange Attractors), Joyce Gorrell (of Core11), April Greiman (of Made in Space), Eduardo Recife (of Misprinted Type), Joe Freedman (of Sarabande), Dave Parmley (of 13thFloor), Jan Maarten de Booij (of Koninklijke Bibliotheek), Jovaney Hollingsworth (of CSA Images), Linda McCurdy (of Rare Book, Manuscript, and Special Collections Library, Duke University), Fabrice Ruth Dissieux (of Linotype Library GmbH), Bob Alonso (of BA Graphics), Melissa M. Hunt (of Berthold Types Limited), Veronika Elsner (of Elsner-Flake GbR), Simon Daniels (of Microsoft Corp.), Richard Kegler (of P22 Type Foundry, Inc.), Sergey Kochin (of ParaType, Ltd.), Kurt Koepfle (of Pentagram Design), Thierry Puyfoulhoux (of Presence Typo), and Peter Rosenfeld (of URW++ Design & Development GmbH).

A special thanks to the Delmar team, who guided me through this enormous process with great patience, flexibility, and wisdom, and whose hard work and support made this all possible: Jaimie Weiss, Product Manager, James Gish, Senior Acquisitions Editor, Francis Hogan, Art and Design Coordinator, and Tom Stover, Senior Production Editor.

And great thanks to Delmar affiliates, whose great talents and attention to detail proved essential to the quality outcome of this work: Anne Majusiak, Mardelle Kunz, and Liz Kingslien.

Screenshots from web site containing artwork and photos by Erykah Badu, *www.erykahbadu.com*, produced by Dan Petruzzi and Afra Amir Sanjari and designed by Kirsten O'Loughlin and Chris Ro of *Okayplayer.com*. *Used by permission of Motown Records, a division of UMG Recordings, Inc, 2004.*

Art Deco packaging design, *Rhum*, 1928. *Courtesy of Rikuyosha Co., Ltd.*

Thomson Delmar Learning and the author would also like to thank the following reviewers for their valuable suggestions and expertise:

Scott Carnz
Assistant Dean of Academic Affairs
The Art Institute of Seattle
Seattle, Washington

Cece Cutsforth
Visual & Performing Arts Department
Portland Community College
Portland, Oregon

Rebecca Gallagher
Chair, Digital Media Communications
Katharine Gibbs School
New York, New York

Kathrena Halsinger
Art Department
Clark College
Vancouver, Washington

Lindsey Rush Heuwetter
Graphic Design Department
Westwood College of Technology
Atlanta, Georgia

Therese LeMelle
Visual Communications Department
Katharine Gibbs School
New York, New York

Janine Wong
University of Massachusetts – Dartmouth
Graphic Design Department
College of Visual and Performing Arts
Dartmouth, Massachusetts

Tova Rabinowitz
2006

QUESTIONS AND FEEDBACK

Thomson Delmar Learning and the author welcome your questions and feedback. If you have suggestions that you think others would benefit from, please let us know and we will try to include them in the next edition.

To send us your questions and/or feedback, you can contact the publisher at:

Thomson Delmar Learning
Executive Woods
5 Maxwell Drive
Clifton Park, NY 12065
Attn: Media Arts and Design Team
800-998-7498

Or the author at:
tovayeah@yahoo.com

dedication

Ma, Dad, Heidi, Dru, Al, Tim, and Aaron, you made this book possible through your kind generosity, your helpfulness, your patience, and your support. But especially you, Ma. Your hard work made all the difference. Working with you has been a special honor and treat.

Block book, *Apocalypsis Sancti Johannis*, Germany, 1470 CE.
© *Lessing J. Rosenwald Collection, Library of Congress,*
Washington, D.C. Used with permission.

CHAPTER 1

objectives

- Recognize the interdependent relationship between design, technology, and social forces
- Understand how type has impacted human culture
- Trace the evolution of typography and printing processes through history
- Learn the historical significance of a variety of type design styles
- Contemplate a variety of artistic ideologies and their typographic implications
- Synthesize innovative designs using ideas and images from the past for inspiration

introduction

Written language has been a powerful agent of change for the cultures of human civilizations for thousands of years. Political, social, academic, artistic, musical, scientific, religious, and technological forces have been guided and transformed by written language, just as written language has evolved out of the scope of these human experiences and institutions.

Throughout history, the development of technological advancements has been instrumental in the progression of typography as a tool and as a design form. New technologies have always inspired designers to explore new capabilities and challenge the boundaries of existing visual language structures, in order to express their unique experiences and differentiate themselves from their predecessors.

Typography has traditionally been defined as the study, use, and design of sets of identical repeated letterforms. Though typography evolved from one-of-a-kind handwritten scripts, the development of printing technologies so drastically changed the nature of written communication, that the term typography was coined to describe it. Whether the typefaces look formal or informal, geometric or organic, messy or clean, their typographic quality has been based in their reproducibility. However, even this definition has been challenged with recent digital typographic innovations that push the boundaries of type use and design.

10,000 BCE — 400 CE **THE BEGINNINGS OF WRITTEN LANGUAGE**
3000 BCE: Early Writing Systems

We begin to explore the history of type by examining humankind's earliest remaining communicative markings—cave art. **Petroglyphs** (rock engravings) and **pictographs** (cave paintings) were left behind over ten thousand years ago by early humans, who used what they had available to record their experiences. They mixed natural pigments with animal fat to make paints, or they carved images into stone. Prehistoric people made marks ranging from representative images to abstract symbols (Figure 1-1). Sometimes these markings were in the form of **pictograms** (simplified images illustrating specific words), and other times they were in the form of **ideograms** (images that stand for concepts or ideas). How these prehistoric visual communications were used and how common they were cannot be determined because all that remains are the few most sturdy and remote specimens.

3000 BCE: Early Sumerian Writing

Sometime before 3000 BCE, Sumerian people living in Mesopotamia used pointed styluses to draw pictograms on clay tablets to create permanent records of business transactions. Some of these clay tablets have survived, providing glimpses of the nature of the visual communications of their creators. By around 2500 BCE, the Sumerians had adopted technological and conceptual innovations that made writing quicker and easier. They developed a writing system, called cuneiform, in which a wedge-shaped stylus was pressed into the clay using small strokes (Figure 1-2); the marks had become ideograms instead of pictograms. This allowed for a smaller list of symbols to memorize and practice writing. By studying Sumerian written language, archeologists are able to trace an evolution from pictograms to ideograms, and eventually to **phonograms** (symbols that represent sounds).

3000 BCE: Egyptian Hieroglyphics

At the same time that Sumerians were developing their writing system, Egyptians were developing their own. Egyptian hieroglyphics (Figure 1-3) also started as pictograms before 3000 BCE and eventually evolved into a complex combination of pictographs, ideograms, and phonograms over the next three thousand years or so.

figure | 1-2 |

A Sumerian clay tablet with cuneiform characters tallying sheep and goats, from Tello in ancient southern Mesopotamia. © *Gianni Dagli Orti/CORBIS.*

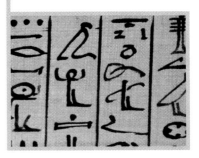

figure | 1-3 |

Egyptian hieroglyphics, detail from the Book of the Dead. © *Sandro Vannini/CORBIS.*

figure | 1-1 |

Paleolithic cave painting at Lascaux. © *Bettmann/CORBIS.*

1800 BCE: Chinese Calligraphy

In ancient China, people were also developing written language and technologies to support their use. Chinese legend tells us that around the year 1800 BCE, a man named Ts'ang Chieh was inspired by the footprints and claw marks of animals and birds to develop his own written marks. The result was Chinese calligraphy. Ts'ang Chieh's symbols were abstracted pictographs and **logograms** (a symbol that represents a whole word, like @ or $ or #). The oldest surviving examples of Chinese calligraphy are oracle bone writings (Figure 1-4), which were carved into bones and tortoise shells to communicate with dead ancestors and tell fortunes. There is also evidence that Chinese people wrote on bronze objects like coins, containers, and weapons. They also used bamboo pens to write on silk cloth and on wooden and bamboo slats.

figure | 1-5 |

Gold sheet with Phoenician inscription, sixth century BCE. © *Archivo Iconografico, S.A./CORBIS.*

figure | 1-4 |

Shang Dynasty inscribed oracle bone. © *Royal Ontario Museum/CORBIS.*

1500 BCE: Phoenician Alphabet

Around 1500 BCE, Phoenician people were also using an abstract phonogram-based alphabet of twenty-two characters (Figure 1-5). Since Phoenicia was an important center of trade, the Phoenician language was dispersed to various lands by merchants and other travelers. Other phonogram-based written languages came into use around the same time and developed into Semitic languages: Hebrew, Aramaic, Demotic, and Arabic.

1000 BCE: Greeks Adopt Phoenician Alphabet

Around 1000 BCE, the Greeks adopted the Phoenician alphabet. Over time, they adapted it into Greek by changing some consonants and adding vowels (Figure 1-6).

figure | 1-6 |

Ancient Greek writing on a tablet in Delphi, Greece. © *David Elfstrom / iStockphoto.*

2000 BCE: Papyrus

Egyptians wrote hieroglyphics using chisels on stone, but they also used brushes made of plant stems to paint hieroglyphic characters on more portable materials. Egyptians used the Cyperus Papyrus plant to make a paper-like material called papyrus (Figure 1-7). Although it is unclear when the earliest use of papyrus was, the oldest surviving papyrus documents were created around 2000 BCE.

figure | 1-7 |

Papyrus sample from Apollonios, a civil official in the region of the Apollonopolites Heptakomias, ca. 120 CE. *Courtesy of Duke University Rare Book, Manuscript, and Special Collections Library.*

100 BCE: Roman Letterforms Develop

Around 100 BCE, the Romans invaded Greece. Among the riches taken by the Romans were the contents of entire Grecian libraries. The Greek influence on Roman culture was substantial because the Greek cultural artifacts taken by the Romans were studied, revered, adapted, and dispersed throughout the Roman Empire. The Latin alphabet that we use today was used by the Romans, but is believed to have grown out of a combination of Greek, Semitic, and southern Italian (Etruscan) influences. By the first century CE, there were two common Roman scripts: square capitals (Figure 1-8) and rustic capitals (Figure 1-9). Square capitals had only square capital letterforms, while rustic capitals were less formal. Because rustic capitals were slightly narrower and more rounded, they were faster and easier to write. Both square and rustic capitals had serifs (extensions added to the endpoints of letter strokes), which gave an air of stability and strength to the letterforms. Typically, words were not set apart by space, although sometimes a centered dot separated words.

figure | 1-8 |

Roman square capitals from a section of the inscription on the Trajan Column in Rome, 114 CE.

figure | 1-9 |

Rustic capitals, detail of Bede manuscript, eighth century.
© David Reed/CORBIS.

100 CE: Uncials

By 100 CE, the Greeks had developed rounded letterforms called uncials (Figure 1-10). Uncials required fewer strokes and so could be written more quickly and easily than square Greek letters.

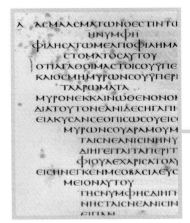

figure | 1-10 |

Greek uncials, Codex Sinaiticus Petropolitanus, 350 CE, by permission of The British Library [1701.d.1].

190 BCE: Invention of Parchment

Legend has it that around 190 BCE an embargo on papyrus led an innovative shepherd, living in what is now Turkey, to develop a paper-like writing surface made of leather, called parchment. To make parchment, animal skins were washed, stretched, scraped clean of hair, whitened with chalk, and pumiced smooth. Parchment became popular because of its flexibility, availability, and portability.

105 CE: Invention of Paper

In 105 CE, Ts'ai Lun of China reported having invented paper to the emperor. Ts'ai Lun soaked rags and bark, and beat them to a pulp. Then he spread the fibers on a mold, pressed them flat, and peeled the resulting sheet of paper from the mold so it could be hung to dry. For thousands of years, paper continued to be made in this way.

200 CE: Half-Uncials

Half-uncials, which are shorter with ascenders and descenders, were first used in Greece during the third century, but didn't gain popularity until the late sixth century (Figure 1-11). (Ascenders and descenders are parts of letters that extend vertically above and below the traditional guidelines.) Half-uncials are the precursors to lowercase letters.

figure | 1-11 |

Half-uncials, Msc.Patr.87, fol.79v, Hieronymus und Gennadius: De Viris Illustribus. Augustinus: De Haeresibus. De Cura Pro Mortuis Gerendaenchiridion De Fide, Spe et Caritate. Staatsbibliothek, Bamberg.

300 CE: Roman Literate Class and Libraries

By 300 CE, Rome had a literate class of merchants, scholars, priests, and governmental officials, and thirty public libraries to support their reading and reference needs. Literacy was growing.

200 CE: Pens with Nibs

By the third century CE, Greeks were writing on papyrus, parchment, metal, leather, wood, and wax and clay tablets using pens made from reeds with metal nibs attached to the ends to better regulate the flow of the ink. Around the seventh century, people started using goose quills as pens, with the hollow end split and shaped to act as a nib for more precision. In the twelfth century, people started cutting the quill pens at a greater angle. Later, pen nibs of different widths and shapes were introduced as attachments to quill pens. Each change in pen technology has drastically altered the shape of the pen's strokes, and therefore has affected the evolution of handwritten scripts.

New Vocabulary

ideogram: an image that stands for a concept or idea

logogram: a symbol that represents a whole word, like @ or $ or #

petroglyph: a rock engraving

phonogram: a symbol that represents a spoken sound

pictogram: a simplified image illustrating a specific word

pictograph: a prehistoric rock painting; also known as a pictogram

typography: the study, use, and design of type

The early medieval period was marred by Feudalism, a political structure in which wealthy landowning noblemen exercised dictatorial rule over the poor masses in their regions, whom they worked, taxed, and exploited at will. Most common folk in Europe had little self-determination and few resources. The early Christian arts of that period were luxuriant religious works intended for a wealthy or clerical audience. The late medieval period saw relative political stability, economic prosperity, and a growing population in Europe. Art was still ornate and religiously themed, but art forms were now extended to the common people as a means of religious indoctrination and propaganda. The Byzantine and Gothic arts of the fifth to sixteenth centuries in Europe were both highly decorative and based on Christian themes. Monumental architectural elements, frescoed wall murals, rich textiles, and liturgical texts were created to satisfy the needs of the rites and ceremonies of the priestly class and of communal worship.

400 CE: Illuminated Manuscripts in Europe

Sometime during the fifth century, people started creating illustrated and illuminated books. Around 600 CE, Pope Gregory the Great's statement that "in images, the illiterate read" popularized book illumination among Christians as a method for preaching to the illiterate. Illuminations are illustrations and flourishes that decorate the pages of handwritten texts to illuminate, or reveal, their meanings. Often illuminated manuscripts were adorned with gold leaf and rich colors that gave each page a majestic and holy presence. The practice of creating illuminated manuscripts was popular in Europe until the fifteenth century CE when movable type was first used in Europe (Figure 1-12).

figure | 1-12 |

Illuminated manuscript, *The Book of Hours*, Valencia, c. 1460, collection of the Koninklijke Bibliotheek.

550 CE: Celtic Half–Uncials and Word Spacing

In the late sixth century CE, half-uncials began to gain popularity, particularly in Ireland among the Celts. Celtic half-uncials (also called insular half-uncials) were economical to use because they took up less space than uncials, and they were easier to read because of the increased differentiation between letter shapes (Figure 1-13). The Celtic scribes also initiated another practice that increased legibility: they began to add spaces between words, making it easier for readers to recognize where words began and ended.

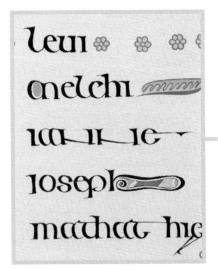

figure | 1-13 |

Insular half-uncials from *The Book of Kells*.
© Stapleton Collection/CORBIS.

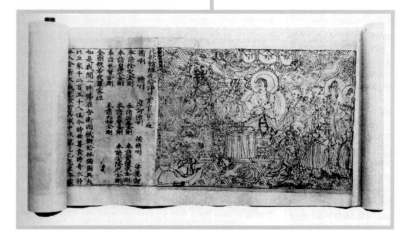

figure | 1-14 |

Carolingian minuscules, MS 28 Folio 5 (verso), by permission of the President and Fellows of Saint John Baptist College in the University of Oxford.

789 CE: Carolingian Minuscules

Charlemagne, the first emperor of the Holy Roman Empire, gathered a posse of scribes in 789 CE to create new copies of important religious texts, to be disseminated throughout Europe. Charlemagne's cadre of scribes worked at his direction to set standards that would ensure the quality of the books they would produce. This process included devising a standardized alphabet, which was derived by combining characteristics of Celtic half-uncials with traditional Latin majuscules, or capital letters. Carolingian minuscules were the result—direct ancestors to the lowercase letters that we commonly use today (Figure 1-14).

700 CE: Woodblock Printing in China

By the eighth century CE, the Chinese had developed a woodblock printing process, or **xylography**, that is still used today. Raised images and calligraphy were cut onto wooden slabs, which were then inked. The printer would transfer the ink to the paper by placing a piece of paper on the raised inked surface and rubbing the back. A fast printer could pull two hundred prints of a design in an hour. Xylography is an example of **relief printing**—any printing process in which the ink sits on a raised surface. Early uses of this printing technology included paper money and playing cards, so the public quickly became exposed to printed materials like currency. Eventually, whole books were also created this way, which at first were in scroll form. The first woodblock printed book was a Buddhist text called the *Diamond Sutra* (Figure 1-15), published by Wang Jie of China in 868 CE.

figure | 1-15 |

First printed book, the *Diamond Sutra*, by permission of The British Library [fp Or.8210p2].

1200 CE: Development of Medieval Scripts

1200 CE: Blackletter Scripts

Over time, the costliness of parchment led scribes to economize by using narrower and narrower lettering styles. By the thirteenth century, European Gothic designs had taken on a heavy, rigid, tall, narrow appearance that seemed to stretch upward toward the heavens. These rhythmic, narrow, sharp, rigid Textura scripts of the Gothic period are commonly referred to as blackletter because of their visual heaviness (Figure 1-16).

figure | 1-16 |

Textura blackletter script.
© *Historical Picture Archive/CORBIS.*

1040 CE: Movable Type Used in China

Around 1040 CE, a Chinese man named Pi Sheng became renowned as a master of movable type, and he may have been its inventor. Pi Sheng affixed individual clay stamps, each bearing a relief of a Chinese character, in sequence on a waxed iron plate that could then be used like a woodblock to print an entire page at once. The stamps could be removed afterwards and reused for future designs. This technology didn't gain much popularity in China because the large number of Chinese characters made sorting stamps for reuse impractical.

figure | 1-17 |

Watermark, 1484, Netherlands, collection of the Koninklijke Bibliotheek.

1276 CE: First Watermark

In 1276 CE, the first paper mill in Europe was established in Fabriano, Italy. Arab soldiers in Samarkand had learned how to make paper from Chinese war prisoners in 751 CE, and knowledge of the handmade papermaking process spread from Samarkand to Italy by the twelfth century. The mill used water-powered machines to pound rags into pulp to be made into paper, making paper a lot cheaper to produce. That year, Fabriano Mills became the first to use a watermark to distinguish its papers from those of its competitors, though other mills were quick to pick up on the idea and produce their own watermarks (Figure 1-17). A **watermark** is a kind of a trademark that is built into fine papers by including raised designs in the paper molds. These raised designs create areas of varying density in the paper that are visible when held up to the light. Watermarks, along with goldsmith's marks, were among the first trademarks ever used to promote commercial brand recognition. Many paper mills still use watermarks today in their finer papers.

> *fiue ad inutile fit et otiofum . fiue*
> *m, fed orationi et operi diftribuei*
> *Quod manifefte docuit ifq mag*
> *diuit angeluf. Probat quidem ʒ*
> *ed ftudium et caritatem in deui*
> *probat orationif intentiffime qu*
> *it graduf x viii. Incipit De c*

1300 CE: Whiteletter Scripts

In fourteenth century Italy and southern Europe, a style of script called whiteletter was emerging (Figure 1-18). These scripts evolved from Carolingian minuscule scripts, and were significantly lighter, rounder, and less ornate than blackletter scripts of the era.

figure | 1-18 |

Whiteletter script from *Epistola ad Acaceum* by Cyril of Alexandria, 1488 CE. *Courtesy of The Pierpont Morgan Library, New York [MS M 496, f.168V].*

1300 CE: Block Printing Industry Flourishes

By the 1300s, woodblock printing technology had made its way from China to Europe by way of travelers, most of whom were merchants or soldiers. Within a hundred years, gaming and tourism had become driving factors in the spread of woodblock printing throughout Europe. Printers saw that it was profitable to produce souvenir devotional prints for tourists who were visiting shrines and playing cards for the general population, and so the block printing industry flourished.

1440 CE: First Printed Books in Europe

In the mid-1400s, printers in Europe started using the woodblock printing process to print whole books of thirty to fifty pages (Figure 1-19). Text and images were generally cut into the same block of wood for printing, often in a format resembling modern day comic books. Usually the books were religious in theme, intended to teach religious stories and values to illiterates, but soon became a tool for increasing literacy.

> ### New Vocabulary

relief printing: any printing process in which the ink sits on a raised surface

watermark: a kind of trademark that is built into fine papers by including raised designs in the paper molds; these marks are visible when the paper is held up to the light

xylography: a relief printing process in which raised images and calligraphy are cut onto wooden slabs and inked

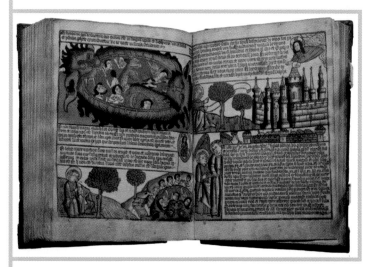

figure | 1-19 |

Block book, *Apocalypsis Sancti Johannis,* Germany, 1470 CE. © *Lessing J. Rosenwald Collection, Library of Congress, Washington, D.C. Used with permission.*

The Renaissance of the fourteenth and fifteenth centuries was a time of great growth in the arts and the sciences in Europe. This growth was partially fueled by the invention of printing technologies whose effects were wider literacy and cultural awareness. Renaissance literally means "rebirth," and it truly was a time of rebirth for the people of Europe—from a predominating worldview based on superstition to a new one based on scientific rationalism. It was also a period of rebirth for the arts and the study of Greek and Roman classical ideals and love of learning. Renewed public interest in ancient Greek and Roman art and design spurred a growing use of whiteletter scripts throughout Europe.

1470 CE: Humanist Type

In 1470, Nicolas Jenson cut a highly legible typeface based on the whiteletter scripts that scribes were currently using in Italy (Figure 1-20). Jenson's typeface and others like it are referred to as Humanist typefaces because they are based on the handwriting of Italian scribes. Digital revivals of Humanist typefaces can be found on pages 83–90 of this book.

figure | 1-20 |

Humanist type printed by Nicolas Jenson, 1470 CE, Eusebius Pamphili, *De evangelica praeparatione*, Venice. *Courtesy of the Library of Congress, Washington, D.C.*

1455 CE: Movable Type Used in Europe

Johannes Gutenberg's 42-line Bible became the first book printed in Europe using movable type technology in 1455 (Figure 1-21). Gutenberg, who lived in Mainz, Germany, had toiled for over two decades to invent a functional printing press with interchangeable reusable letters and the appropriate inks for the process. Gutenberg's printing press was based on the technology of existing wine presses (Figure 1-22). With only slight modifications and improvements, this technology was used for printing during the next four hundred years.

figure | 1-22 |

Gutenberg's printing press.

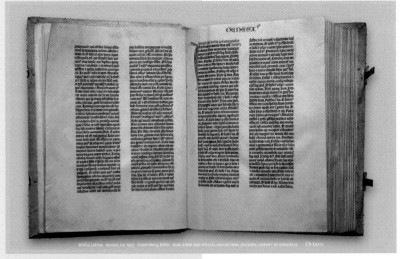

figure | 1-21 |

Gutenberg's 42-line Bible, by permission of The British Library [C.9.d.3].

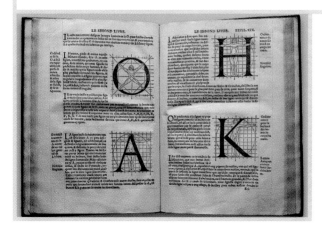

figure | 1-23 |

Champs Fleury by Geofroy Tory, 1529. © 2004 from the Lessing J. Rosenwald Collection, Library of Congress. Imaged by Octavo (www.octavo.com). *Used with permission.*

1500 CE: Old Style Typefaces and the First Independent Foundry

During the sixteenth century, new lighter, more legible typefaces that were based on Humanist typefaces were being designed and widely used in France. These typefaces, called Old Style typefaces, would eventually become the standard in Europe and in the New World. Two designers who were instrumental in the development and popularization of these typefaces were Geofroy Tory and Claude Garamond. Tory was a designer, author, engraver, and letterpress printer—a multitalented, true "Renaissance man." He designed and helped to popularize Old Style typefaces by using them extensively in his own printshop. Tory's widely read book of 1529, *Champs Fleury,* asserted that roman capitals should be based on the proportions of the idealized human body (Figure 1-23). Claude Garamond established the first independent type foundry that was not affiliated with any printshop in 1530. He popularized Old Style typefaces by selling his typefaces to printshops all over Europe. See pages 93–101 to view digital revivals of Old Style typefaces.

1455 CE: Broadsides and Broadsheets

One of the earliest uses of movable type was the printing of single-page journalistic broadsides that could be posted or distributed like flyers, and broadsheets, which had news items printed on both sides and might even be folded. Broadsides and broadsheets were printed irregularly, but were the ancestors to newspapers, posters, flyers, and brochures.

1461 CE: Growth of Printing Industry in Europe

The period between 1455 and 1500 marked a shift from handwritten manuscripts to printed books all across Europe. Books produced during this era are called **incunabula** (Latin for "cradle" or "swaddling cloth") because these books were produced during the infancy of printing. Until 1461, there were few printshops outside of Mainz, Germany. However, in that year, Mainz was sacked and burned by soldiers in a rivalry between two archbishops, and many townspeople, including printers, fled to other parts of Europe. This quickened the spread of movable type printing technology across Europe. In 1470, there were only fourteen printshops in all of Europe; only thirty years later, there were printshops in over two hundred European towns, and more were being established all over the world.

1465 CE: Intaglio Printing Processes Developed

Around 1465 CE, people in France started using intaglio printing processes. **Intaglio** refers to any printing process in which the ink sits below the surface of the plate. At first, people made drypoint engravings—that is, they would scratch an image into a sheet of copper, rub ink into the grooves, and then press paper against the plate to transfer the ink. Scratching grooves into metal was hard work, so people soon started developing easier engraving methods. For instance, the etching process involved coating a metal plate with a wax resist, scratching a design into the wax, and then placing the plate into an acid bath. The acid would bite grooves into the metal wherever the resist was missing. Etching and other engraving methods would become important to the development of type design, because finer lines could be achieved with engraving than with relief printing.

1500 CE: First Italic Typeface

Around 1500, the first italic typeface was cut by Francesco Griffo at the commission of printer Aldus Manutius (Figure 1-24). Its purpose was to emulate Italian vernacular handwriting, and to take up less space on the page so that its publisher could market a new pocket-sized book. This italic was not a type style of another existing typeface, but a separate, independent typeface.

figure | 1-24 |

The first italic, page from *Juvenal and Persius*, commissioned by Aldus Manutius, cut by Francesco Griffo, 1501 CE, Staatliche Museen. *Courtesy of Bildarchiv Preussischer Kulturbesitz / Art Resource, New York.*

1557 CE: Script Typefaces

In 1557, the first script typeface to be based on a cursive handwriting style was cut by Robert Granjon of France, who called the typeface *lettre francoise d'art de main*. However, this graceful script style came to be known as *Civilité* because of its early use in a book of children's etiquette called *La Civilité puerile*. Granjon intended the typeface to be a French version of the Italian italic styles that had become popular in Europe. *Civilité* type eventually fell out of use, however, because it couldn't compete with the superior legibility of italics.

The eighteenth century is called the "Age of Enlightenment" because people were embracing progress, logic, and scientific reasoning. They were also questioning the veracity of existing institutions, traditions, and authorities. The new ideas and philosophies that were emerging regarding conceptions of human nature and society set the stage for the democratization and globalization that were to come. In the art and design of this era, we see a shift away from the production of religiously themed art, toward themes of human nature, lifestyles, and cultural experience.

1692 CE: The Beginning of Transitional Typefaces

In 1692, King Louis XIV commissioned a new typeface to be cut that would be meant for only the court's royal use. The result was Roman du Roi, cut by Philippe Grandjean and first used in 1700 in *Medailles de Louis XIV*. This typeface was designed using drafting tools and a mathematical grid system (Figure 1-25). Introduction of this typeface marks the beginning of the use of Transitional typefaces, which showed increased precision, higher contrast between the thick and thin parts of characters, and a new symmetry and vertical stress that reflected improvements and changes in technology. Engraving, which had become a popular medium for production of documents like broadsheets and posters, had started a trend toward greater refinement of hairline strokes (secondary strokes). Developments in type casting allowed finer relief forms to be printed without breaking, and changes in the shaping of pen nibs were causing more vertical angles of stress in handwritten letterforms. (Strokes and angles of stress will be discussed further in Chapter 2.)

figure | 1-25 |

Roman du Roi by Philippe Grandjean, 1700 CE, from *Printing Types* by Alexander Lawson. *Copyright ©1971 by Alexander Lawson. Reprinted by permission of Beacon Press, Boston.*

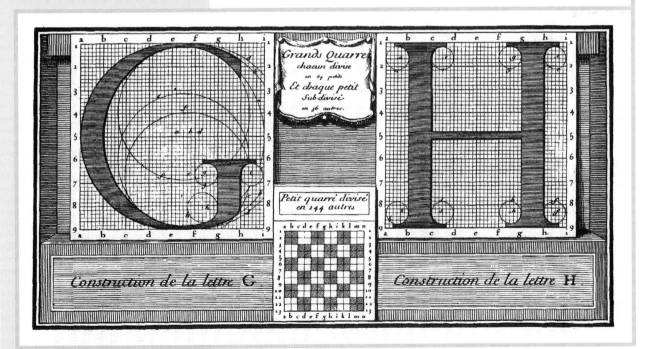

figure | 1-26 |

Rococo typefaces by Fournier le Jeune, *Manuel Typographique*, 1764.

figure | 1-27 |

Caslon's first specimen sheet, 1734 CE, by permission of the British Library [C.180 ff.4(2)].

1720 CE: Rococo Style

The Rococo style was popular in France from about 1720 to 1770. It was an ornate lavish style, full of flourishes and ornamentation, that reflected the taste of the privileged class for elegance, comfort, and a worry-free lifestyle. Rococo's influence on type and print can be seen in the decorative layouts and typefaces of Pierre Simon Fournier le Jeune (Figure 1-26).

1720 CE: William Caslon Establishes a Type Foundry in England

William Caslon started a type foundry in England in 1720, around the same time that Transitional typefaces were all the rage in Europe. Despite the fact that Caslon's Old Style type designs weren't particularly innovative or fashionable for his time, they were widely used in England because there were very few punchcutters there due to the strict censorship laws of the 1600s. English colonialism helped to spread the use of his typefaces to countries all over the world, establishing them as a standard worldwide. Caslon's first specimen sheet, produced in 1734, is pictured in Figure 1-27.

1737 CE: Type Measurement Systems

As printers increasingly bought fonts from type founders rather than self-producing them, the need developed for some sort of standardization of type sizes. In 1737, Pierre Simon Fournier le Jeune was the first to propose and publish a standardized system of measuring type, referred to as the Fournier Type Measurement System. He then went on to apply this method by developing the first type family—a set of characters of an individual typeface, cut in a variety of sizes. These differing sizes of the same typeface could be used together to create type layouts with a consistent feel. To promote acceptance of his system, Fournier based the type sizes on colloquially used sizes of the day, rather than on any established scale of measurement. As use of the French foot became dominant, this lack of compatibility became a source of frustration for printers.

1757 CE: John Baskerville Develops Transitional Typefaces

A key designer in the development of Transitional typefaces from 1757 to 1775 was John Baskerville of England. He loved and participated in all aspects of bookmaking; he designed and cut type, printed books, and improved printing and papermaking processes. His typeface designs extended the trends set by the Transitional typeface Roman du Roi of increased refinement and mechanization of typefaces, and higher contrast between thick and thin letter parts (Figure 1-28). Digitally revived type styles of Baskerville's typefaces can be found on pages 106–107.

figure | 1-28 |

Latin Virgil, printed by John Baskerville, 1757 CE, from *Printing Types* by Alexander Lawson.
Copyright ©1971 by Alexander Lawson. Reprinted by permission of Beacon Press, Boston.

Another problem was the naming convention Fournier had used to identify type sizes; often named for the works in which they had first appeared, the names seemed arbitrary and confusing, sharing no clear relationship with each other.

In 1785, Françoise Ambroise Didot improved Fournier's Type Measurement System by adapting the standard point size to correlate with the French Royal inch (which is slightly larger than an English inch). This made reconciling the standard sizes of type with the standard sizes of paper, which was measured in French feet and inches, much easier for printers. Didot's system was also more user-friendly than Fournier's because the subjective common names given by Fournier for type sizes were replaced with numbers that indicated actual point size. The Didot Point System quickly gained popularity, and is still in use throughout most of Europe.

English-speaking countries like Britain and America use the English foot as a standard measure, instead of the slightly larger French foot. The American Point Scale, which was adopted in 1886 by the U.S. Type Founders Association, is based on the English foot rather than the French foot, and also correlates to the metric system. The American Point Scale redefined a point as being 1/72.27 of an English inch.

A more recent development in type measurement has been the adaptation of the American Point Scale to the PostScript Point Scale. Most computer programs use the PostScript Point Scale, in which the size of a point has been rounded to *exactly* 1/72 of an inch for simpler conversions between points and inches. Because the PostScript scale is used in computer applications internationally, this type measurement scale has become prevalent worldwide.

1750 CE: The Hot Press Paper Finishing Process

Sometime in the 1750s, John Baskerville developed the Hot Press process for finishing paper to make it extra smooth. Baskerville wanted his publications to look pristinely refined and elegant, and so he developed a secret process in which he was able to smooth the surface of papers, probably by pressing them between heated polished copper plates or between copper rollers. Baskerville also developed a new deeper, more lustrous black ink for his printings, by adding lampblack to a linseed oil and resin mixture.

In 1765, the invention of the first efficient steam engine by James Watt of Scotland marked the beginning of the Industrial Revolution, a time when mechanization and industrialization were rapidly occurring in Europe and America. New technologies like the steam engine, the electric light, the telephone, and the power loom were causing enormous upheaval in many countries. Production of goods was becoming increasingly mechanized, and the world saw a great shift from agriculturally based economies to industrially based ones. People were moving from rural areas to cities, seeking employment in factories where mass production and assembly-line division of labor were lowering prices and making products widely available. Economies were shifting power from monarchies and landowners to capitalists and corporations, and as a result, many countries were experiencing increased democratization. Common people suddenly had buying power, and there were many products to choose from. People were empowered by their newly increased spending power and mobility, and they revolted against the hoarding of wealth, resources, and power that had been celebrated by the lavish Rococo, Gothic, and Baroque aesthetics. In addition, archeological excavations in and around Rome during the 1790s renewed a public taste for the simple classical elegance of ancient Rome and Greece. Around the globe, people were establishing a new vision for the future and a new mechanized typographic aesthetic to express it. Although the industrial revolution initially reduced literacy rates because the increased demand for child labor in factories meant fewer children attending school, the enactment of child labor laws and mandatory school attendance helped to turn around falling literacy rates.

The technological advances of the Industrial Revolution brought about a new modern age, full of new conveniences and innovations. In the visual arts, new production methods and materials were influencing the look, quantity, and quality of commercial products, which were increasingly mass-produced. However, people who lived at that time had to adjust to enormous economic, social, environmental, and aesthetic changes in a relatively short period of time. Some people welcomed and celebrated these changes, while others mourned the loss of quality and individuality that had been sacrificed in the name of progress. The design styles that emerged around the turn of the century were symptomatic of people trying to cope with and assimilate the new industrialized landscape into their lives.

1784 CE: Modern Typefaces, Firmin Didot, and Giambattista Bodoni

Firmin Didot of France cut the first Modern typeface in 1784—a dramatic font with thin serifs, extreme contrast, and a vertical angle of stress. Soon after, in Italy, a talented perfectionist named Giambattista Bodoni began to produce typefaces that revealed his admiration for Didot's work. The simple mechanized typefaces that Bodoni designed were made of interchangeable parts, reflecting the machine age of that day. They were dramatically vertical in stress and high in contrast between thick and thin letter parts and between short and long letter parts, leaving large proportions of open space. Bodoni also set his text with wide margins and ample spacing for an open, airy modern feel.

Both Bodoni and Didot were associated with the courts of their respective countries, and had achieved some fame in their lifetimes. Their typefaces were widely recognized and emulated. Typefaces like Bodoni's and Didot's, with their increased drama and contrast of thick to thin parts and short to long parts, are referred to as Modern typefaces. This can be confusing for students, because the word "modern" is often used in reference to the Modern Art movement of the twentieth century. However, when we speak of the Modern family of typefaces, we are referring to the sparse, dramatic roman typefaces, like Bodoni's and Didot's, that initiated the Modern age of the early nineteenth century. After Bodoni's death in 1813, his widow published his *Manuale Tipografico* in 1818 (Figure 1-29). This volume included the 300 typefaces he had designed. Digital revivals of Modern typefaces can be viewed on pages 115–122 of this book.

I

GIAMBATTISTA BODONI

A CHI LEGGE.

Eccovi i saggi dell'industria e delle
fatiche mie di molti anni consecrati
con veramente geniale impegno ad
un'arte, che è compimento della più
bella, ingegnosa, e giovevole inven-
zione degli uomini, voglio dire dello
scrivere, di cui è la stampa la mi-
glior maniera, ogni qual volta sia
pregio dell'opera far a molti copia
delle stesse parole, e maggiormente
quando importi aver certezza che

figure | 1-29 |

Manuale Tipografico by Giambattista Bodoni, 1818.

figure | 1-31 |

Selection of lithographed brand tins, nineteenth and twentieth
centuries. Private collection, Bridgeman Art Library.

figure | 1-30 |

Lithography stone with image, from
Michael Twyman, *Early Lithographed
Books*, 1990.

1796 CE: Invention of Lithography Printing Process

In 1796, Aloys Senefelder of Bavaria developed an entirely new printing process called
lithography, which was based on treating a limestone so that it would attract ink in some
places and repel it in others (Figure 1-30). Lithography is a **planographic printing** process,
which means that the ink rests on top of a smooth surface rather than on raised areas like
in relief printing, or in sunken grooves as with intaglio. Lithography allowed new freedom
for designers, who could now easily reproduce drawn images and letterforms in a full
range of tones, without concern for the structures of the letterpress or the cost or incon-
veniences of engraving. Continued development of the lithographic process eventually allowed colored and even photographic lithographs to be made (chromolithography). Offset
lithography, which was patented in 1875 by Robert Barclay and John Doyle Fry of
England, was used at first for printing onto tin for production of packaging containers
(Figure 1-31). By the early 1900s, offset printing presses for paper were developed that
could print full-color images using process colors, quickly and cheaply. These machines
became the standard for commercial printing, and are widely used today.

1810 CE: Display Typefaces

Because of increased industrialization in the late eighteenth and early nineteenth centuries, there was suddenly an abundance of products to buy, and since automated papermaking had made paper commonly affordable, advertising boomed like never before. To make their advertisements stand out from all the others, advertisers wanted to use bold, large, and decorative typefaces for display. Among these novelty faces were the first Fat faces, the first three-dimensional faces, the first Egyptian faces, and the first sans-serif faces. Printers tended to use these pioneering novelty typefaces in centered cluttered eclectic compositions (Figure 1-32).

figure | 1-32 |

Victorian theatrical poster showing display type, 1842.

1810 CE: First Fat Faces

In 1810, Bower, Bacon, and Bower of Sheffield issued a type specimen book that included the first Fat faces, which were quickly emulated by other foundries. Fat faces were exaggeratedly heavy typefaces that were intended for display, but some were barely legible even for display purposes. A digital typeface called Bodoni No2 EF Ultra (see page 116) was closely based on an early Fat face design.

1814 CE: Invention of the First Steam-Powered Printing Press

Friedrich König mechanized the printing industry by inventing the first commercial steam-powered printing press for *The Times* of London. *The Times* became automated on November 29, 1814, and on that day, the new technology that had printed the newspaper was also featured as the cover story (Figure 1-33). Other newspapers soon followed *The Times* example. Mechanization of the printing industry dramatically decreased the price of newspapers and books, and increased readership.

figure | 1-33 |

The Times of London, November 29, 1814.

1815 CE: First Three-Dimensional Typefaces

A typeface designed to look three-dimensional was first introduced as a novelty face in 1815. Advertisers were quick to pick up on the idea, and soon there was an abundance of three-dimensional typefaces being used in advertisements (Figure 1-34). You can find a digital font called Vineta that is reminiscent of early to mid-nineteenth-century three-dimensional typefaces on page 157.

1816 CE: First Sans-Serif Typefaces

The first sans-serif typeface was introduced by William Caslon in 1816, as a variation on the Egyptian-style display typeface that had become prevalent (Figure 1-35). Although sans-serif typefaces weren't tremendously popular at first, several foundries did pick up on the idea and offer some. Each foundry that designed typefaces without serifs named them differently, originally calling them names like Dorics, Grotesques, Gothics, Sans-surryphs, and Sans-serifs. It wasn't until the twentieth century that sans-serif typefaces became widely used for purposes other than display.

figure | 1-34 |

First three-dimensional and Egyptian typefaces, printed by Vincent Figgins, 1815. *Courtesy of the estate of Berthold Wolpe.*

1816 CE: First Egyptian Typefaces

Egyptian typefaces initially emerged as novelty typefaces for display in the early nineteenth century (Figures 1-34 and 1-37). Egyptian typefaces are easy to recognize by their distinctive squared, slab-like serifs and the low contrast between their thick and thin letter parts. The name "Egyptian" may have been selected to draw a reference to the blocky horizontal look of Egyptian hieroglyphics, which were in the public eye at the time, due to the recent excavation of the Rosetta Stone by Napoleon's troops. An Egyptian typeface that has enjoyed enormous popularity and is still widely used today is Clarendon, designed by Robert Besley in 1845. A digital revival of Clarendon can be viewed on pages 124–125.

W CASLON JUNR   LETTERFOUNDER

figure | 1-35 |

First sans-serif typeface, printed by William Caslon, 1816. *Courtesy of the estate of Berthold Wolpe.*

1822 CE: Early Development of Photography

The first photographic image was created in 1822 by Joseph Niepce of France, paving the way for photolithographic and phototypesetting processes to come. The growth of photography over the years had profound effects—not only on the definition and role of traditional illustration in design, but also on the compositional approaches to type and image layout that designers would employ.

1827 CE: Wood Used for Type

Advertisers wanted bigger and bigger typefaces for display, but large metal type was impractical because it was expensive and heavy to work with and transport. In 1827, an American named Darius Wells invented a machine that could cheaply mass-produce large, light-weight type out of wood (Figure 1-36), and in 1934, William Leavenworth invented a lateral router that worked with Wells's machine to produce highly decorative typeface designs. Novelty typefaces became even more outrageous and abundant, making for even more chaotic and esoteric designs. Some current digital typefaces that are based closely on early decorative designs, called Victorian, Bearded Lady, Kismet, and Playbill, can be found on pages 158–159.

figure | 1-36 |

Wood type at the Hamilton Wood Type and Printing Museum. *Photograph by Brad Knapp of the Karma Group.*

1830 CE: Victoriana

From the 1830s until the turn of the twentieth century, the Victorian style was popular. Named for Queen Victoria, the overly decorated appearance reflected the optimistic sentiment that anywhere the eye would fall, it should find beauty. Highly decorative and detailed imagery of flowery vines, happy people enjoying comforts, and idealized classical scenes of antiquity adorned just about everything—printed materials from fine menus to professional trade cards to lowly invoice forms—were embellished with flowery borders and fantastic type. To Victorians, these abundant decorations represented the comforts that were newly available to the burgeoning middle class. Untrained in arts and design, Victorian manufacturers drew on the ornate styles of the past, including Gothic, Baroque, and Rococo, using copious jumbled amalgamations of visuals and type, without regard for any relationship between form and content. Consumerism was on the rise; there was an increasing variety of products being produced and sold, due to industrialization, and regular people now had buying power. A whole new industry of chromolithographed children's toys and books was emerging, based on a new modern notion of childhood as a time for nurturance and whimsy (as opposed to the previously accepted conception of children as "little adults"). Technological advances in papermaking techniques, lithographic printing, and wooden type allowed manufacturers and advertisers to flood the market with bold and ornate announcements, advertisements, illustrations, and documents (Figure 1-37).

figure | 1-37 |

Victorian trade card by John McGahey. *Courtesy of Michael Twyman.*

1833 CE: The Penny Press and the Rise of Advertising

Initially, most American newspapers were run by political parties or commercial interests, and were sold by subscription at about six cents per issue to an elite audience of wealthy businessmen. Ben Day of Manhattan changed all that when he established the first "penny press" in 1833—an independent newspaper that was sold on the streets to the masses for only a penny per issue. Enabled by new inexpensive production methods and revenue from advertisers, the "penny press" democratized the nature of news reporting. More people could now afford to read the news, and content was now geared toward its expanding audience. This shift birthed a new journalistic ethic: that news reporting should be objective, rather than based on the biases of the paper's ownership. Of course, newspapers had new pressures to contend with from their advertisers, whose biases and interests sometimes became overly represented editorially. Nonetheless, this evolution of the press enabled the growth of literacy and the further development of printing technologies that positively impacted private presses and magazine publishers. In this way, advancements in news reporting catalyzed the increasing popularity of magazines and serial novels during the 1800s.

1867 CE: Ukiyo-e Design Style

Political change in Japan caused a lifting of the restrictive policy of seclusion in 1867, and contact was resumed between the Japanese people and the rest of the world. National seclusion had became state policy in 1635, as proclaimed by the Shogun in response to fears of colonial expansion. Foreign trade, travel, and tourism were severely restricted. The artistic style that developed during the period of isolation is called Ukiyo-e, which means "pictures of the floating world." Images with painterly outlines and flat areas of color and pattern illustrated sensual erotic, theatrical, and natural themes. Text was often integrated into the imagery by being stamped, block-printed, or hand-calligraphed right into the image space (Figure 1-38). Once Japan's policy of seclusion was lifted, the visual characteristics and themes of Ukiyo-e and its integrated type-image dynamic were studied and emulated by Western artists of the late nineteenth and early twentieth centuries.

figure | 1-38 |

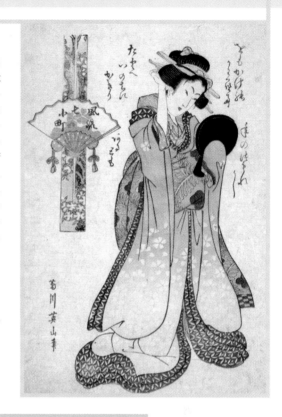

Ukiyo-e print, *The Modern Seven Komachi,* by Kikugawa Eizan, pre-1867. *Courtesy of the Library of Congress, Washington, D.C, Prints and Photographs Division [LC-USZC4-8486].*

figure | 1-39 |

Linotype Model 26, Linotype Library, GmbH, Bad Homburg, Germany *(www.linotype.com).*

1838 CE: Typesetting Technologies

David Bruce of New York invented the first effective type-casting machine in 1838, which could set type ten times faster than a person could do by hand. However, this machine could only cast individual type sorts, which then needed to be filed and set. Other inventors experimented with ways to make type casting more efficient, but the two major type-casting machines that captured and dominated the market until the 1950s were invented in 1886 and 1894. The first was the Linotype machine (Figure 1-39), invented by a German mechanic named Ottmar Mergenthaler. His machine could assemble and space lines of type matrices and cast them in complete spaced lines. The original matrices could then be reused. The second dominating machine was the Monotype machine, invented by Tolbert Lanston of Washington. This machine cast individual letters according to the sequence punched into a perforated tape using a keyboard.

1875 CE: Arts & Crafts Movement

By 1875, William Morris of England found himself disillusioned with what he considered soulless designs and low-quality products that had resulted from the mechanization of the industrial revolution. Morris longed for the integrity of design that artisans imbue into fine workmanship. In an effort to reinvent society as one that valued quality in production, he founded the Arts & Crafts movement, which emphasized individual workmanship and high-quality artisanship for all crafts, including typography. Morris has been credited with reviving typography as an art form, and elevating the crafts to a status equal to the arts.

figure | 1-40 |

Cover of *Hobby Horse,* the first fine visual arts magazine.

1882 CE: The Century Guild

Artists influenced by William Morris established the Century Guild in 1882, which was a group of artisans, poets, and designers whose common purpose was to elevate the status of the decorative arts to that of the fine arts. In 1884, the Century Guild published the first fine visual arts magazine, *Hobby Horse,* which was printed on handmade paper using elaborate woodblock illustrations (Figure 1-40). Publication of *Hobby Horse* helped to spread the philosophy of the Arts & Crafts movement throughout Europe and America.

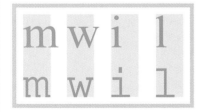

figure | 1-41 |

Regular type (top) compared to monospace type (bottom).

1873 CE: Typewriter Invented

The invention by Christophe Latham Sholes and Carlos Glidden of the typewriter with the universal keyboard arrangement that we use today made it possible for individuals and small businesses to produce printed materials. Because typewriters had equal spacing for every letter, monospace typefaces had to be developed that had wider *i* and *l* characters, and narrower *w* and *m* characters, in order to maintain optical balance of typewritten materials (Figure 1-41). The Shoals and Glidden typewriter changed the way that offices all over the world conducted their business operations, and expanded career options for women, who previously had not been welcome in office environments.

1883 CE: Art Nouveau Movement

The flowing organic Art Nouveau movement originally grew out of the Arts & Crafts movement around 1883, when Arthur Mackmurdo of England published *Wren's City Churches*, (Figure 1-42). As with the Arts & Crafts movement, Art Nouveau artists and designers were reacting to industrialization by seeking individuality in the face of mass production and by celebrating natural themes in a decorative style. However, their designs were also heavily influenced by the Japanese Ukiyo-e aesthetic, which had only recently become unveiled to the West when the Japanese policy of seclusion ended in 1867. From Ukiyo-e, Art Nouveau artists and designers borrowed asymmetrical composition, painterly outlining, curvilinear biomorphic shapes, and natural and supernatural themes, which often included imagery of sensual female figures. Freed from the structures of the letterpress by new lithographic technologies, designers took new liberties in integrating organic type and imagery. Art Nouveau type was designed to look almost alive, the characters imitating sinewy vines and plump invertebrates that looked like they might crawl away if given the chance (Figure 1-43). Art Nouveau typefaces that have been revived as digital fonts, including Arnold Boecklin, Eckmann, and Mucha, are shown on pages 161–162.

figure | 1-44 |

Advertising poster, *Kassama*, by the Brothers Beggarstaff, 1900.

figure | 1-42 |

Title page for *Wren's City Churches*, designed by Arthur Heygate Mackmurdo, 1883. *Courtesy of V&A IMAGES / Victoria & Albert Museum [CT57843].*

figure | 1-43 |

Art Nouveau poster advertising the 'Salon des Cent' Mucha Exhibition, 1897 (color litho), by Alphonse Marie Mucha (1860-1939), Mucha Trust, Bridgeman Art Library. *© 2005 Artists Rights Society (ARS), New York / ADAGP, Paris.*

1890 CE: First Modernist Art Posters

In 1890, the first posters began to appear in which elements were reduced to include only what was essential to create a specific impression; Figure 1-44 shows a poster by James Pryde and William Nicholson of England who called themselves "the Brothers Beggarstaff." However, their static flat images weren't thought by advertisers to have persuasive selling power, and so they failed to get much recognition or many commissions. Ironically, the simple, direct graphic style of the Brothers Beggarstaff foreran the tremendously popular German advertising poster style called Plakatstil, which proved their shared directness to have tremendous selling power.

1890 CE: Regional Variations of Art Nouveau

By 1890, regional variations of Art Nouveau had developed throughout Europe. In Germany, designers of the Jugendstil (or "Youth Style") movement integrated the sinewy lines of Art Nouveau with German precision to create distinctive type and layouts (Figure 1-45). In Scotland, Glasgow style designers used linear forms and symmetrical balance in combination with gentle curvilinear biomorphic forms and botanical themes (Figure 1-46). In Austria, designers of the Vienna Secession used flat organic shapes and patterning to create organic compositions emphasizing harmonious balance (Figure 1-47). The digital typefaces called Arts & Crafts and Mojo on pages 161 and 162 are based on the typefaces of the Glasgow and Vienna Secession Art Nouveau styles.

figure | 1-45 |

Advertisement for *Jugend* magazine by Josef Rudolf Witzel, 1896. *Courtesy of Von Zezschwitz: Art and Design Auctions, Munich.*

figure | 1-46 |

(Left) Glasgow style poster, *The Scottish Musical Review,* by Charles Rennie Mackintosh, 1896. *Courtesy of Glasgow City Council (Museums) [PR. 1977.13.ar].*

figure | 1-47 |

(Right) Vienna Secession poster by Alfred Roller, 1902.

New Vocabulary

lithography: a planographic printing process which is based on treating a limestone to attract ink in some places and repel it in others

planography: any printing process in which the ink sits on top of a smooth surface

1891 CE   **1900 CE**

1891 CE: The Private Presses: Kelmscott, Ashendene, and Doves

William Morris founded the Kelmscott Press in 1891, a small private press that embraced the traditional craft of bookmaking and rejected the low-quality monotony of mass production. The Kelmscott Press emphasized quality in every aspect of each book; he used handmade papers and original typefaces, and printed his books manually using a letterpress. Each element of his books—including the papers, the inks, and the bindings—was attended to with care. He designed his own typefaces for his books; Chaucer and Troy were based on blackletter scripts, and Golden was based on the first whiteletter typefaces originally cut by Jenson in the 1470s. Morris referenced the medieval aesthetic of fine craftsmen, illuminating his books according to the medieval tradition (Figure 1-48). Other designers and private presses were soon to follow Morris's example. The Ashendene Press, founded in 1894, and the Doves Press, founded in 1900, emphasized high-quality, meticulous design and hand production. The Kelmscott, Ashendene, and Doves presses led the ensuing movement of small private presses that emphasized quality production of printed works. You can see digital revivals of Morris's typefaces called Kelmscott and True Golden on pages 80 and 90.

1900 CE: Sans-Serif Typefaces As Running Text

As early as 1900, Peter Behrens of Germany was advocating the use of sans-serif typefaces to express the modern experience. During that year, Behrens published a book called *Feste des Lebens und der Kunst* (Figure 1-49), which was very likely the first use of a sans-serif typeface for running text in a publication. Two years earlier, the Berthold Foundry had offered the first family of sans-serif typefaces to include an array of type styles, called Akzidenz-Grotesk (Standard in the U.S.). The first designers to embrace sans-serif type had few faces aside from Akzidenz-Grotesk to choose from, until the late 1920s, when Paul Renner's Futura, and Eric Gill's Gill Sans became available.

figure | 1-48 |

Book page designed by William Morris, from Geoffrey Chaucer, *Works*, Hammersmith, 1896 CE. *Courtesy of The Pierpont Morgan Library, New York [PML 23121].*

figure | 1-49 |

The first book with running sans-serif text, *Feste des Lebens und der Kunst*, Peter Behrens, Germany, 1900.

The first part of the twentieth century birthed a number of art and design movements, all of which are considered to be members of the Modern Art movement. Although each has its own visual style and political impetus, they all took part in reinventing art and design in a voice that spoke to the common people, as opposed to the rich and powerful elite. In creating an aesthetic that spoke to the working man and woman, each movement rejected the elaborate ornamentation that represented the old world order for a simpler, more straightforward visual language that grew out of the modern experience. Together they represented a wide range of reactions to a newly industrialized world.

1905: Expressionism

From 1905 to 1923, German Expressionists made art and designs that expressed raw emotional cries for individuality in the face of growing monotony, and later expressed anger and pain in reaction to World War I. Early Expressionists rejected conventional beauty and instead embraced a primitive aesthetic of rough, distorted woodcut figures and text (Figure 1-50). Later Expressionists featured nonobjective compositions that communicated emotion and message through color, shape, proportion, and symbols. The commercial world took no interest in Expressionism, but the self-published rough, bold, emotive aesthetic of Expressionist type and imagery laid the groundwork for future design movements that would purposefully defy typographic conventions. Nonobjective Expressionists Paul Klee and Wassily Kandinsky later became extremely influential in the design world, as instructors at the Bauhaus. The digital font Neuland, shown on page 165, is a revival of Rudolph Koch's Expressionist display face from 1923 that has a bold woodcut feel.

figure  1-50

Expressionist title page for *Der Kampf mit dem Engel*, by Conrad Felixmuller, 1917. ©2005 Artists Rights Society (ARS), New York / VG Bild-Kunst, Bonn.

1905: Plakatstil: Early Modern Posters

With the invention of offset lithography, industrialists could now afford to produce advertising posters to promote their wares. Previously, posters had been used mostly to advertise performances or literary events and products. Common retail products generally weren't considered to be poster subject matter. This changed with the development of Plakatstil, German for "poster style." People were searching for a new visual language that would reflect their own modern experience as citizens of an industrialized society. The flowery ornate styles that had represented the leisurely lifestyles of the rich were being discarded.

1905: Art Posters for Advertising

In 1905, Lucian Bernhard of Germany entered an advertising poster competition for Priester matches (Figure 1-51). His entry won the competition, and started a whole new wave of advertising posters that reflected the new modern style called Plakatstil. Based on the successful advertising power of Bernhard's first poster, many advertisers adopted the graphic formula of reducing an illustration to its simplest form, placing it against a flat background, and adding abrupt text to the composition. Short, concise messages were conveyed using simple, direct imagery and highly legible serif and sans-serif typefaces.

figure | 1-51 |

Advertising poster for Priester Match Company by Lucian Bernhard, 1905. *© 2005 Artists Rights Society (ARS), New York / VG Bild-Kunst, Bonn.*

1906: Art Posters for Propaganda

One highly influential poster artist was Ludwig Hohlwein of Germany. Hohlwein's direct, stylized subject matter with bold, concise text floating against flat backgrounds was very successful, and helped to revolutionize the poster as something to be collected and displayed for aesthetic purposes. However, Hohlwein worked for many years for the Nazi political party, helping their rise to power with his designs for many evocative propaganda posters (Figure 1-52). The power of persuasion inherent to this direct advertising style was evident, and artists all over the world adopted it to promote their own promotional, social, and political messages.

1906: Halftone Printing Process Goes Commercial

Frederick Ives of Philadelphia adapted the halftone photogravure process in 1885 by using filters to make color-separated halftone plates in red, yellow, and blue that made full color prints when printed in register. However, it wasn't until 1906, when suitable plates and filters became more readily available, that the process began to pick up commercial interest. The eventual addition of black to Ives's tricolor halftone printing process resulted in the four-color printing process which is widely used today, and has allowed the inexpensive printing of detailed colored photographs in countless magazines, newspapers, and books.

figure | 1-52 |

Early modern propaganda poster, *LUFTSCHUTZ!*, by Ludwig Hohlwein, 1917, courtesy of Miscellaneous Man: Rare original Posters and vintage Graphics, *www.miscman.com. © 2005 Artists Rights Society (ARS), New York / VG Bild-Kunst, Bonn.*

figure | 1-53 |

Futurist book cover for *Les Mots en Liberte Futuristes* by Filippo Tommaso Marinetti, 1919. © 2005 Artists Rights Society (ARS), New York /SIAE, Rome.

1909: Futurism

In 1909, a major Paris newspaper published Italian poet Filippo Marinetti's passionate *Manifesto of Futurism*, which called for a reinvention of poetry and art based on the new sounds, smells, and materials of the new machine age. Marinetti encouraged the destruction of what he considered to be outdated and bourgeois cultural and social institutions, like museums and libraries, asserting that only new and wholly original artistic and poetic works were legitimate and all art of the past had grown irrelevant and should be discarded. Marinetti and his followers exalted speed, noise, aggression, fearlessness, technology, and war, while disdaining sentimentality, moralism, feminism, and immobility with an almost religious fervor: these Futurist designs were typically dynamically composed, using sharp shapes and letters to imply aggressive movement and noise (Figure 1-53). Futurist designers used type in new exciting ways that provided the world with an alternative outlook on industrialization. However, because the Futurists aligned themselves with Mussolini's fascist political movement, their contributions to design have been discredited in the eyes of some art historians. Futurists published a series of manifestos from 1910 to 1919, declaring inflexible philosophies on everything from painting and poetry to lust and war. Marinetti's manifesto on typography, called *Destruction of Syntax—Imagination without Strings—Words-in-Freedom,* asserted that type and images should be used to visually express poetry and emotion without the constraints of grammar, spelling, or punctuation.

1917

1917: Dadaism

Dadaism—Dada meaning "nothing"—was an "anti-art" movement, begun in Switzerland by a group of disillusioned expatriate artists and writers around 1917, who felt disgusted with the hypocrisy of "civilized" societies allowing the atrocities of World War I to take place. Dadaists expressed their anger by creating paintings, sculpture, literature, plays, and designs that mocked and defied the traditional arts; their goal was to create things without purpose, to protest the banality of war. The movement lasted only until 1922, but ironically, this "anti-art" was incredibly influential upon the world of design. Dadaists took unprecedented liberties with typographic use and page composition, liberating future designers to use type in nontraditional ways. Dada designs broke as many typographic rules as possible, with no concern for legibility (Figure 1-54). Type was used in expressive angry compositions in which letters of many sizes and typefaces were overlapped, collaged, distorted, and oriented in all directions, in order to evoke emotion more than communicate content.

figure | 1-54 |

Dada poster, *Kleine Dada Soiree*, by Theo van Doesburg and Kurt Schwitters, 1923. © *2005 Artists Rights Society (ARS), New York / Beeldrecht, Amsterdam / VG Bild-Kunst, Bonn.*

1917: De Stijl

In 1917, Theo van Doesburg of Holland led Piet Mondrian and a group of other artists in making purely abstract geometric art, composed of horizontals, verticals, flat areas of primary colors, and black and white. De Stijl, meaning "the style," was a spiritual search for compositional harmony through the asymmetrical balance of unequal elements and the exclusion of representations and subjective values and emotions. Van Doesburg published an arts journal from 1917 to 1931 called *de Stijl,* in which he proposed that through a search for structural harmony in art, structural harmony in society could be achieved. De Stijl type was set in strong horizontal and vertical structures, using mostly squarish sans-serif typefaces (Figure 1-55). The digital font DeStijl, on page 165, is a revival of the type used by members of this movement.

figure | 1-55 |

Cover of *de Stijl* magazine by Vilmos Huszar, 1917. © *2005 Artists Rights Society (ARS), New York / Beeldrecht, Amsterdam.*

figure | 1-56 |

Constructivist magazine cover, *Novy Lef,* by Alexander Rodchenko, 1928. *Courtesy of David King Collection, London.*

1919: El Lizzitsky Spreads Constructivism

El Lizzitsky (Lazar Markovich) met Kasmir Malevich in 1919, and was influenced by his ideas. Lizzitsky came to be instrumental in the development and spread of Constructivism, experimenting with a variety of mediums including photomontage and printmaking, and expanded Constructivism's international exposure by affiliating with leading artists of other modern art movements, and by designing layouts for a variety of European publications in the Constructivist style. Lizzitsky designed and co-edited a book called *The Isms of Art: 1914-1924,* which was highly influential in its creative and innovative use of grid structures, asymmetrical layouts, sans-serif type, and bold rules (Figure 1-57).

figure | 1-57 |

The Isms of Art: 1914–1924 by Hans (Jean) Arp and El Lizzitsky. © *2005 Artists Rights Society (ARS), New York / VG Bild-Kunst, Bonn.*

1918: Constructivism

When the Czar of Russia was overthrown in 1918, and the Soviet Union was in its formative stage, a new politically driven art and design movement began to emerge that was based on the use of abstract geometric shapes, bold rules, and text set at right angles. This simple aesthetic was a giant departure from the luxurious tastes of Czarist Russia, and so was meant to embody the vision of the new social order. Its pioneer, Kasmir Malevich, called it Suprematism. Materials were course, and colors were used sparingly, due to the limited resources and supplies available in a post-war economy. As the new Soviet Union began to recover from World War I, artists inspired by patriotism decided that they must use their artistic skills in the service of helping to construct a healthy social order for their country by creating a truly Soviet art. The style they created was called Constructivism. Born out of the Suprematist aesthetic, Constructivism was based on the use of simple geometric shapes, sans-serif typefaces, asymmetrical balance (Figure 1-56), photomontage, and a primary color palette. Using this artistic vocabulary, bold visual statements were designed to evoke emotions and incite participation in patriotic and community-building activities.

1925

1919: Bauhaus

In 1919, Walter Gropius of Germany became the director of a new state-sponsored school that was created by merging the Weimar Art Academy and the Weimar Arts & Crafts School. Gropius instated the name Das Staatlich Bauhaus, which means The State Home for Building, and published the Bauhaus manifesto, which advocated a union of art and technology. Gropius modeled his pedagogy after William Morris's Arts & Crafts workshops, in which the teacher/student relationship was more of a master/apprentice relationship, students worked in workshops rather than studios, and fine and applied arts held equal status. Gropius created a graphic design department and hired prominent artists from modern art movements including Expressionism, Constructivism, and De Stijl as instructors. These instructors helped set the tone for the style of work that emerged from the Bauhaus. Under their tutelage, students created asymmetrical, geometric compositions composed of sans-serif typefaces, photography, and photomontage that presented clear, direct messages (Figure 1-58).

figure | 1-58 |

Bauhaus poster, *Bauhaus*, by Joost Schmidt, 1923. © *2005 Artists Rights Society (ARS), New York / VG Bild-Kunst, Bonn.*

1925: Herbert Bayer's Universal Type

Bauhaus faculty member Herbert Bayer created a typeface in 1925 called Universal, which reduced the alphabet to one set of sans-serif lowercase letterforms constructed of geometric shapes (Figure 1-59). He also experimented with flush-left, ragged-right text alignment and the use of visual elements like bars, rules, type size, and bullets to indicate visual hierarchy (the order of importance of elements). Although Universal was never widely used, Bayer's other contributions had a profound effect on common page layout methodology. Books printed in a flush-left, ragged-right orientation are now commonplace.

abcdefghi jklmnopqr stuvwxyz

figure | 1-59 |

Universal type by Herbert Bayer, 1925. © *2005 Artists Rights Society (ARS), New York / VG Bild-Kunst, Bonn.*

1925: Bauhaus Moves to Dessau

The Bauhaus moved from Weimar to a small German town called Dessau in 1925 because of political tensions with the Weimar government. The political situation only worsened, though; by 1931, the Nazi party was a powerful political force in Dessau. Nazi persecution and harassment finally caused the Bauhaus faculty to dissolve the school in 1933. Many of the instructors, including Walter Gropius, Herbert Bayer, and Laszlo Moholy-Nagy, fled Nazi Germany for the United States, where they continued to be influential figures in the design world and design education. In 1937, Moholy-Nagy established the New Bauhaus in Chicago, which has since been renamed the Illinois Institute of Technology.

As technology has evolved, the world has seemed a smaller and smaller place. Improvements in transportation and communication technologies have created a globalized economy, characterized by increased advertising, political, and social messages being distributed over air waves, radio waves, telephone lines, and later, by computer networks and satellites. The barrage of information that is familiar to us today started after World War I and really took off after World War II, when many of the technological developments innovated by armies were applied to civilian uses. The impact of post-war growth upon design was a collective effort to adjust to the new busier, more confusing and diverse world through a visual language that emphasized structure, objectivity, legibility, simplicity, and internationalism.

1925: Art Deco

Art Deco was introduced at the 1925 Exposition Internationale des Arts Decoratifs et Industrials Modernes in Paris. Like other Modern Art movements, Art Deco was based on simplified geometric shapes. However, it differed in that its purpose was elegant embellishment of commercial products, as opposed to expression of any social or political ideology. Art Deco was very popular, perhaps because it was more accessible to the general public than some of the more abstract and ideological Modern Art movements. Art Deco designs conveyed an image of glamour and affluence, beautifying the world of consumerism with exotic stylized Egyptian, Asian, and Aztec motifs and geometric patterns. Dramatic alluring typefaces and layouts were created using strong contrasts between thicks and thins, lights and darks, and rectilinear and curvilinear shapes (Figure 1-60). The Art Deco style remained popular until around 1940, when World War II shortages and wartime austerity caused a general shift away from playful exuberant consumerism. Many elegant and opulent Art Deco display fonts that were designed during that period have since been digitally revived. Three of them—Parisian, Broadway, and Day Tripper NF—are on pages 162 and 163 of this book.

figure | 1-60 |

Art Deco packaging design, *Rhum*, 1928. *Courtesy of Rikuyosha Co., Ltd.*

Allies

USA , British Empire France, Belgium, Italy, Serbia, Romania, Russia, Japan u. s.o.

Central Powers

Germany, Austria-Hungary, Bulgaria, Turkey

Great War 1914-18

Each figure 1 million soldiers (killed, wounded, others returning home)

ISOTYPE

figure | 1-61 |

ISOTYPE chart, *The Great War of 1914-18*, 1933. *Courtesy of the Otto & Marie Neurath Isotype Collection, Department of Typography & Graphic Communication,* © *University of Reading.*

1928: ISOTYPE Movement

In 1928, Otto Neurath of Austria led a team of designers to develop ISOTYPE (International System of Typographic Picture Education). These highly functional and straightforward elementary pictographs were designed to be used on signage and in graphs and charts depicting statistical data (Figure 1-61).

1928: The New Typography

Jan Tschichold of Germany was so impressed by a visit to the Bauhaus 1923 exhibition at Weimar that he published an article two years later called "elementaire typographie," which described the new typographic style he saw evolving. Tschichold asserted that a "new typography" was necessary for the new age of industrialism, in which people had less time to read, but more reading materials than ever competing for their attentions. He proposed that the basis of type design for the modern age should be clarity, rather than beauty, and that type stripped of ornamentation was most effective for this purpose. In 1928, he published a book called *The New Typography*, which read like a manual, setting forth rules for type use and page composition. In his later years, Tschichold mellowed, acknowledging the merits of traditional typography and expressing regret at having tried to codify creativity. However, the extensive influence of his widely read publications had already spurred the spread of a functional design approach throughout Europe and America, in which form grew from function and clarity was paramount.

1932: Soviet Governmental Accusations

The Soviet government had at first welcomed the Constructivists' contributions to the cause, but Stalin didn't welcome the international direction in which the movement was headed. In 1932, Stalin announced that the only acceptable artistic style was to be Social Realism, which featured realistic imagery depicting Soviet life and Communist values. Stalin had decided that Social Realism would be more useful for propaganda, so he accused the Constructivists of "antipatriotic bourgeois cosmopolitanism" (meaning capitalist globalization) and withdrew support for the movement. Without governmental support, the movement withered in the Soviet Union, but by then its effects had influenced the world, where its traditions were carried on throughout the 1930s.

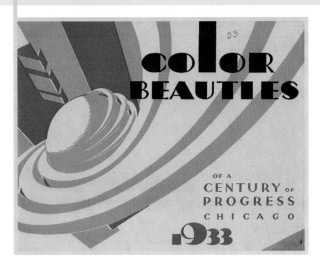

figure | 1-62 |

Streamline Art Deco pamphlet, *Color Beauties of a Century of Progress*, Chicago, 1933. *Courtesy of Special Collections Research Center, University of Chicago Library, http://century.lib.uchicago.edu/.*

1933: Streamline

An Art Deco style called Streamline was introduced at the 1933 Chicago World's Fair. Streamline designs and fonts were less decorative, though equally as elegant as other Art Deco designs. The design was based on an aerodynamic vocabulary of motion lines and speed (Figure 1-62). The digital fonts called Streamline, Red Star Line NF, and Ambient seen on pages 150 and 164 are based on the simple sophisticated Art Deco Streamline typefaces of the 1930s.

figure | 1-63 |

International Typographic Style poster, *Büro*, by Théo Ballmer, Switzerland, 1928.

1945: International Typographic Style

Around 1945, two former Bauhaus students, Théo Ballmer and Max Bill of Switzerland, recognized that increasing globalization was creating a need for a visual language that would be suitable for international communication. The style they developed—which was based on a clear arrangement of elements, photography, abstract designs, and sans-serif typefaces—came to be called the International Typographic Style (also called Swiss International Style), shown in Figure 1-63. Any elements that might be confusing to an international audience were excluded. Unemotional layouts were composed that relied heavily on mathematical modular grids and a hierarchical organization of information. All elements were selected and sized to create direct informative layouts. The calm objectivity of the International Typographic Style gained popularity, especially among corporate interests, and was dominant in America and Europe throughout the 1950s. International Typographic Style typefaces were sans serifs, based on geometric shapes. Helvetica, designed by Max Miedinger in 1952 and shown on page 137, became one of the most widely used typefaces in history. Univers, designed by Adrian Frutiger in 1957, shown on page 144, gained immense popularity because of its extensive range of type styles. Instead of naming each Univers type style, Frutiger devised an innovative numbering system that indicated type weights and widths, and he used the chart pictured on page 133 to organize and exhibit the Univers type family.

figure | 1-64 |

Advertising billboard,
*Look Ahead—
Paint with Pabco,*
by Saul Bass. *Courtesy
of Saul Bass Estate.*

1945: American Corporate Style

During the 1950s and 1960s, a distinctly American style of layout and type use emerged from the United States. Flourishing American corporations were attracted to the simple and airy layouts and direct communicative texts of the International Typographic Style. They hired designers like Paul Rand, Saul Bass, and Otto Storch, who added an American flavor to this formula by creating witty and conceptual designs to sell corporate products and personas. Using vernacular visual cues to encourage a sense of humility and accessibility to its audience, they solved design problems concisely without sacrificing personal expression in the process. They created direct, friendly layouts by integrated text and imagery through collage, wordplay, distortion, illustration, and photography (Figure 1-64).

1949: Photocomposition Goes Digital

The first photocompositor to use digital technology, called the Photon-Lumitype, was debuted in 1949 by Rene Higonnet and Louis Moyrund of France. This machine had a primitive computer that connected a keyboard to the photographic unit. It could produce up to 28,000 characters per hour. A book published in 1964 has been considered a landmark in phototypesetting, comparable to what Gutenberg's 42-line Bible was to printing. The *Index Medicus* was over six hundred pages long, and was phototypeset in approximately twelve hours; production of the same materials using a type-casting machine would have taken about a year! Invention of the Photon-Lumitype set a new course for typesetting in the direction of digital imaging, but it would be decades before this evolution fully occurred.

1946: Phototypesetting and Photocomposition

The Intertype Fotosetter was installed in the Governmental Printing Office in Washington in 1946 and became widely popular within a few years. Although phototypesetting technologies had been in development since 1925, World Wars I and II had interrupted its adoption, so the Fotosetter was the first one to be widely used. The Fotosetter worked by exposing letters on a circulating matrix in the sequence recorded on a tape using a keyboard. The system worked similarly to the Monotype machine, only with a photographic unit replacing the caster. Major benefits of phototypesetting were that one matrix of type negatives could produce a full array of type sizes, and characters could easily be made to overlap, giving designers new compositional freedom. Photocomposition made it easy to combine words and pictures for lithographic printing. At first, it was mostly used for display and children's book layouts, but inventors continued to experiment with new machines and photographic processes to set type and compose layouts efficiently and cheaply.

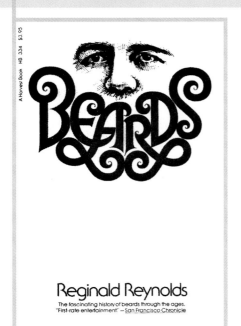

1950: Figurative Typography

During the 1950s, 1960s, and 1970s, designers like Gene Federico, Herb Lubalin, and others extended the Corporate Style's playful approach to type use by experimenting with new ways of integrating type and image, which helped to further break down the boundaries that traditionally divided them. Images became words, and vice versa. Anthropomorphic type physically interacted with imagery and other type (Figure 1-65). Developments in phototypesetting technologies made new creative possibilities for overlapping and size variation of type forms possible, and these new options were explored to create designs that communicated content while expressing values, emotions, and individuality.

figure | 1-65 |

Figurative book cover design, *Beards*, by Herb Lubalin, 1975. *Courtesy of the Herb Lubalin Study Center of Design and Typography at The Cooper Union School of Art.*

1954: Revivalism and Eclecticism

Both Revivalism and Eclecticism were popularized by Push Pin Studios designers Milton Glazer, Seymour Chwast, and Edward Sorel, and by the Push Pin Studios magazine *Push Pin Graphics*, starting in the 1950s. Revivalism refers to the reintroduction of outdated typefaces, while Eclecticism refers to a mix-and-match approach to combining typefaces in design. Glazer and Chwast had started reviving the decorative typefaces of the past, which had lost favor during the first half of the century, and mixing them with newer typefaces and drawings in a fusion of illustration and design. Older styles that had been chaotically mixed by inexperienced printers in the 1800s were adeptly recombined with the addition of newer typefaces and a more sophisticated understanding of design (Figure 1-66). By the 1960s, it was common to see designs composed of many assorted typefaces. Mike Salisbury of California applied similar design concepts when he reinvented the format of *Rolling Stone* magazine in 1974. Salisbury varied his type usage widely from one article to the next, giving the magazine an eclectic, energetic sense of unconstrained spontaneity that was well received by *Rolling Stone's* rock'n'roll audience.

figure | 1-66 |

Revival/Eclectic poster. *Courtesy of Seymour Chwast, Push Pin Studios.*

1966

figure | 1-67 |

Poster, *Psychedelic,* by Victor Moscoso, 1967.
© *Chester Helms, DBA Family Dog Productions.*

1966: Psychedelic Art

Instead of breaking typographic "rules," the Psychedelic Art movement of the 1960s set out to reverse them. Instead of delivering clear messages, psychedelic posters advertising drug culture dances and rock'n'roll concerts often had to be deciphered by audiences. The designers' goals were not to deliver messages as succinctly and efficiently as possible, but rather, to engage the viewers for as long as possible—to tease them with hard-to-read feasts for the senses. Vibrant hallucination-like color combinations, wild Victorian type, and heavy swirling, fluid hand-drawn letters were typically used with complex line drawings, optically challenging photographs, and East Indian iconography (Figure 1-67). The movement was centered in San Francisco, where Milton Glazer, Seymour Chwast, Lee Conklin, Rick Griffin, Alton Kelley, Bonnie Maclean, Victor Moscoso, Stanley Mouse, David Singer, Wes Wilson, and other designers created posters, record album covers, broadsides, and newspapers—often for clients in the music industry. Psychedelic type was well received locally, but due to its low legibility, remained marginal nationally until the 1969 introduction of "Psychedelitype" phototypesetting fonts. Subsequently, it lost favor with its originators. Digital fonts that are based on the optically challenging typefaces of the Psychedelic Art movement include Hendrix, Elephant Bells, and Macrame Super Triline, which can be found on page 166 of this book.

1955: Kinetic Type

Kinetic type was pioneered in the 1950s by Saul Bass, with his innovative film title sequence for *The Man with the Golden Arm*. Before that time, film titles and credits were mostly based on a theatrical model—static or scrolling. Throughout the 1960s, designers used incredibly creative animated line art, claymation, and photographic techniques to create daring, funny, and expressive kinetic type for hundreds of movie titles. However, the 1974 stock market crash and ensuing recession caused most moviemakers to cut exceptionally designed title sequences out of their budgets, and the field of kinetic type stagnated.

The first commercial computer was introduced in 1951, and computer technologies had been combined with photocomposition since the 1960s, but it was the introduction of the first personal computers in 1977 that marked the beginning of the Digital Revolution. As soon as computer technologies became available to the mass market, their popularity skyrocketed. Information from the U.S. Census Bureau indicates that between the years 1984 and 2000, the number of American households with home computers rose from 8.2 percent to 51 percent. As computer technologies have advanced, so have the quality of type resolution and the ease of use. Graphics software has made design and production of professional-quality fonts, print materials, and screen interfaces attainable for both designers and hobbyists. The traditionally separate roles of compositor, editor, type founder, designer, printer, and reader have been merged and mixed, producing a revolutionary boom in creative output that has included groundbreaking uses of type and font design, as well as an abundance of poorly designed materials and fonts. The profusion of new font designs that have emerged in recent years echoes the design productivity of the Industrial Revolution.

1970: International Typeface Corporation (ITC)

An organization was established in 1970, with the mission of protecting type designers from plagiarism. Its founders—Herb Lubalin, Edward Rondthaler, and Aaron Burns—called it the International Typeface Corporation, or ITC. Because of the development of new phototypesetting technologies, type production had become much less expensive and much easier to pirate, too. Designers were having difficulty protecting their copyrighted designs, and getting paid for the use of the typographic fruits of their labors. By collaborating with designers to market and license their fonts, ITC was able to encourage innovations in type design by building a market for them while protecting the legal interests of their designers. During that decade, the fonts ITC showcased tended to have tall x-heights, wide set widths, and short ascenders and descenders (Figure 1-68), which will be discussed in Chapter 2. ITC's fonts were widely used, and helped to established the distinctive look that is now associated with that era. Edward Benguiat's ITC Souvenir of 1972 was one of the most popular typefaces during the 1970s (see page 89).

figure | 1-68 |

Cover for *U&lc*, by Herb Lubalin, 1974. *Courtesy of the Herb Lubalin Study Center of Design and Typography at The Cooper Union School of Art.*

```
Chicago                          Geneva
ABCDEFGHIJKLMNOPQRSTU            ABCDEFGHIJKLMNOPQRSTU
UVWXYZabcdefghijklmnop           VWXYZabcdefghijklmnopqr
qrstuvwxyz1234567890             stuvwxyz1234567890

Monaco                           New York
ABCDEFGHIJKLMNOPQRSTUV           ABCDEFGHIJKLMNOPQRST
WXYZabcdefghijklmnopqr           UVWXYZabcdefghijklmno
stuvwxyz1234567890               pqrstuvwxyz1234567890
```

1970: Dot-Matrix Printers Invented

In 1970, the first dot-matrix printer was introduced by Centronics; these were the first printers to be used with computers. Dot-matrix printers composed letters using a series of printed dots. The dotted letters were generally somewhat difficult to read because of their uneven texture. In 1983, Susan Kare designed Chicago, Geneva, Monaco, and New York, the first font families designed especially to have high legibility

figure | 1-69 |

Screen fonts by Susan Kare.

on-screen and when printed at the low resolution of a dot-matrix printer (Figure 1-69). These fonts set the course for type designers who were faced with the challenge of designing fonts for the new medium of computer screen interfaces and computer printing.

1984: Font Formats

The PostScript font format was first released by Adobe in 1984. This scalable, universal printing language was revolutionary in that it was device independent, meaning it could be used with a range of compatible devices produced by a variety of manufacturers. Before PostScript, fonts were developed for individual brand machines and could only work with the specified hardware. PostScript (Type 1) fonts were introduced with Aldus Pagemaker, the first desktop publishing program. Pagemaker used PostScript to output type to a laser printer so that it looked professionally printed. In 1991, a new scalable font format called TrueType was released by Apple Computer, which was compatible with both Macintosh and Windows platforms. Microsoft licensed the software, adapted, and adopted it. An explosion of font development ensued, and use of the Windows platform for desktop publishing grew. Around 1996, Adobe and Microsoft joined in a collaborative effort to introduce a new font format called OpenType, which combines the best aspects of the PostScript and TrueType font formats.

Postmodern Design

Postmodern design styles were expressive, energetic rebounds from the geometric, calm legibility of the Modern Art movement. A shift away from communal values toward individualism was occurring in industrialized societies, which were becoming faster paced than ever. The introduction of cable television, video games, and computers produced a generation of designers whose collective world experiences could not be expressed by the cool objective functionalism of Modern Art. Each of the design movements that emerged during this period were highly energetic, bold, and individualistic. By the 1990s, evolving societal perspectives celebrating diversity catalyzed design movements that questioned the legitimacy of accepted visual structures and dominant values. As viewers were bombarded with increasing numbers of simultaneous messages, they were also growing accustomed to the new speed and nonlinear variety of input, due to trends in popular television programming, video gaming, and Web surfing. Designers started creating for an audience with a short attention span and well-developed multitasking abilities. In addition, digital capabilities for interactivity and motion graphics provided a new multidimensional landscape that drew the roles of designer and viewer closer together and offered a whole new realm of design for exploration. People began to question the precepts upon which prevailing design theories had been based, including clarity, legibility, objectivity, and the assumption that symbols could have fixed meanings; this dialogue continues today.

1976: Punk

Around 1976, a youth-oriented movement in art, music, and fashion emerged from London called Punk. Punk was the expression of a philosophy celebrating youth, individuality, nihilism, aggression, nonconformism, free self-expression, and rebellion against the establishment. Disillusioned youth felt the previous generation had hypocritically sold out their liberal idealism to conservative corporate interests, and they expressed their contempt through loud harsh music, shocking fashion statements, and aggressively irreverent self-published designs. Punk designs were often seen in music show flyers, record album covers, and fashion magazines. Because of this movement's strong emphasis on autonomy, people avoided using production equipment to create their designs. Instead, they used whatever tools were readily accessible and inexpensive, like typewriters, photocopiers, stencils, found type and images, and their own hand-lettering. Collages of found and drawn type and images were composed in chaotic arrangements (Figure 1-70). Punk's rejection of the dominant typographic rules in favor of free expression paved the way for more mainstream design movements that would react against the rigidity of the prevailing modern trends.

figure | 1-70 |

Punk poster, *The Humans.*
© 1980 Su. Suttle, NekoStudios.com.

figure | 1-71 |

New Wave poster, *18. Didacta Eurodidac,*
by Wolfgang Weingart, 1981.

1976: New Wave

One of the first influential designers to make the departure into New Wave design was Wolfgang Weingart of Switzerland. In the 1970s, Weingart rejected the clean precision, right angles, and high legibility of the International Typographic Style, and began to create more intuitive and playful work. He challenged existing traditional layout systems by changing stroke weights mid-word, extending and eliminating indentations at the start of paragraphs, and experimenting with letterspacing. He also started a trend of using the shape of text passages to create geometric compositional elements (Figure 1-71). An American named April Greiman studied under Weingart in Europe, and was instrumental in bringing early New Wave design to San Francisco. Greiman extended New Wave's basic vocabulary, using photomontage, digital techniques, overlapping, bright colors, stepped shapes, and bold patterning. By 1980, a New Wave backlash against the functional designs of Modernism had erupted in San Francisco and Milan by designers who were influenced by the spirited designs of Weingart and Greiman and the nonconformist chaotic aesthetic of the Punk movement, and who were inspired by the fresh capabilities of computer graphics. Instead of discarding the geometric styling of Modern Art, New Wave designers made their departure by unhinging geometric forms from their grids and incorporating them into lively, dynamic compositions that expressed whimsy and individuality. Text and layouts were often energized by creating visual tension through the contrast of loud, overlapped geometric and organic patterns, textures, and shapes, combined with diagonal and unusually spaced text.

1981: MTV (Music Television)

In 1981, a cable network dedicated to twenty-four-hour music videos called MTV, or Music Television, went on the air. The network's logo revolutionized corporate identity and motion graphics, because the large flat-faced three-dimensional sans-serif *M* with the scrawled script *TV* were the only constants in the brand image. A series of animated station identification clips that were aired hourly featured hundreds of variations of the MTV logo using combinations of illustration, photography, video manipulation and animation techniques, and a range of colors, textures, sequential narratives, and decorative elements.

1984: *Emigre* Magazine

Emigre is a magazine that started in 1984 as a cultural arts journal, but evolved into a showcase and foundry for innovative and experimental digital font designs and expressive layouts (Figure 1-72). Founder Rudy VanderLans and Zuzana Licko of San Francisco were among the first designers to explore computer technology as a tool for type design and magazine layout, and their foundry, Emigre Inc., was one of the first independent digital type foundries established. Although the magazine initially met with harsh criticism for its unconventionality, it soon became a paradigm of typographic innovation for the design industry.

figure | 1-72 |

Table of contents page from *Emigre* magazine, by Rudy VanderLans of Emigre, 1986.

1985: Digital Composition

By the mid-1980s, a growing number of people were beginning to understand and use fonts in ways that only founders, printers, and typesetters would have in the past. Apple's use of Susan Kare's user-friendly Macintosh WYSIWIG, or "what-you-see-is-what-you-get," graphical user interface made digital composition practicable for the average person. Also, graphics software became commercially available that let people manipulate and even originate typefaces digitally—and at terrific speeds compared to traditional typefounding! In 1985, AltSys released a font design software program called Fontographer, at the same time Aldus released the first user-friendly desktop publishing program called Pagemaker. These software packages led to the development of a multitude of user-friendly graphics programs, with a wide variety of growing capabilities, by Aldus Corporation, Adobe Systems Incorporated, Corel Corporation, and others. By the early 1990s, digital composition had almost entirely replaced photocomposition for commercial printing, and digital type foundries had become standard.

Book cover, *Advertising Cuts from A to Z*, designed by Charles Anderson, 1989. Anderson's book of clip art is a visual dictionary of 1950s nostalgia.

1985: Vernacular Style

Around 1985, a vernacular style of design emerged in America that used familiar visual cues and symbols from popular culture and history to appeal to the audience through a sense of shared experience and inclusion. Clichéd advertising elements, kitsch packaging designs, and blatant references to outdated early modern styles were all recycled to create a new witty visual language that celebrated lowbrow folk art by playfully evoking fond memories of simpler times using tongue-in-cheek voice. This movement picked up steam in the 1990s and into the new millennium, as designers continued to explore vernacular themes and sources in the "high" and "low" arts, and in outmoded cultural artifacts and phenomenon (Figure 1-73).

figure | 1-73 |

Vernacular style book cover for *Old Advertising Cuts A-Z*, by Charles Anderson of Charles S. Anderson Design Company for AIGA/Colorado (self-promotion).

figure | 1-74 |

Rave concert flyer by Trevor Jackson of Bite It! for the Stereo MC's.

1986: Rave Design

The Rave design style emerged around 1986 in the form of promotional flyer art, advertising massive all-night dance party events called Raves (Figure 1-74). By 1989, this energetic, surrealistic techno style was already being appropriated by commercial interests as a tool for advertising products to youth markets. This style celebrates streamlined action and computer precision. Rave designs incorporate futuristic dimensional, outlined, and bitmapped fonts into escapist surrealistic dreamscapes based on the youthful visual language of videogames, comics, and virtual reality. Some examples of digital fonts based on the Rave aesthetic include New Nerd Shadowed and Automatic AOE, shown on page 167.

1990

1990: Deconstruction

Around 1990, a movement called Deconstruction (or Post-structuralism) emerged from academic and alternative circles and entered the mainstream design world. Deconstruction is an interactive process in which both designer and viewer are asked to take apart messages, in order to recognize the precepts behind them and expose the social forces that hold them together. In this way, established social institutions, power structures, and prevailing concepts of "truth" can be critically reevaluated. Although the philosophy of Deconstruction was first proposed as a literary theory in 1967 by Jacques Derrida, it was introduced into design theory in 1978 when Katherine McCoy, co-chair at Cranbrook Academy of Art, infused this methodology into the Graphic Design department's academic approach. By 1990, Deconstruction had become a part of mainstream visual language. The roles of designer and viewer were being redefined, as those in the design industry became concerned with the audience's active role in selecting and interpreting messages according to their own belief systems. In appreciation of this diversity of perspectives, designers like David Carson and Neville Brody created designs that attempted to reveal the complexity of issues and project many voices simultaneously by layering and fragmenting information. Rather than sending a clear message that would dictate a specific response, viewers were invited to decipher, interpret, and critically evaluate messages according to their own scope of knowledge and experiences. David Carson's magazines *RayGun* and *Beach Culture* helped to popularize this visual approach (Figure 1-75).

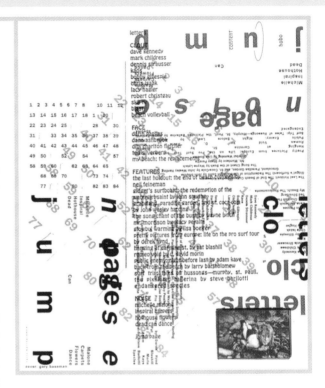

figure | 1-75 |

Table of contents page, *Beach Culture* magazine by David Carson, Art Director/Designer, 1989.

1990: Grunge Style

The Grunge design style grew out of the disheveled aesthetic of the Seattle music scene around 1990. Grunge designs extended the work of Deconstruction by featuring distressed, decomposing, and messy type and imagery in chaotic, multilayered emotive compositions (Figure 1-76). Grunge designers questioned the veracity of common assumptions about legibility by designing demonstratively dingy and erosive typefaces and using them in expressive compositions that were purposefully mucky and cluttered. Carlos Segura and Jim Marcus were among the pioneering Grunge designers. Grunge fonts Viscosity, Bokonon, and Zapped can be seen on pages 168–169.

figure | 1-76 |

Grunge style postcard, *Glue*, by Carlos Segura of Segura, Inc. / T-26.

1991: *Fuse* Magazine and Experimental Typography

Some designers have been inspired to push the capabilities of the digital medium to explore and redefine the boundaries of what type can be. Legibility is rarely a major concern for these designers and artists; instead, their priority is developing fonts that expressively utilize the digital medium and comment on the new socioeconomic environment in uncharted ways. Neville Brody's magazine *Fuse* promoted creative typographic experimentation from 1991 to 2001 by inviting designers to address social issues artistically through the creation and application of experimental typefaces. This magazine encouraged and inspired designers to push the limits of typography's definition and role (Figure 1-77).

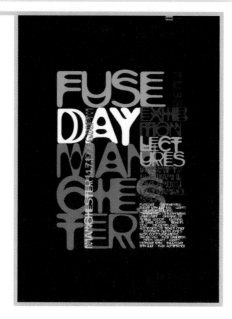

figure | 1-77 |

Experimental *Fuse* magazine font Ritual by Neville Brody of Research Studios, 1995.

The New Millennium

Predominant American values in the new millennium include increasing national pride in diversity and continued veneration of individualism over communalism. These values are reflected in the diversely individualistic and expressive qualities of current design. In addition, the merging of roles of designer, type founder, printer, and consumer has meant more personal control for designers, resulting in more nonconformist and individualistic designs (Figure 1-78). Of course, amidst the chaotic and busy designs that are prevalent today, one can still find visually simple designs that provide a soothing resting place for the eye to linger. However, even the simpler designs that are being created today tend to express personality, individuality, and sophisticated themes. Some of these designs are neo-classical in nature, emphasizing symmetrical balance and historical visual references. Others are minimalist designs in which the designer attempts to communicate effectively using a minimum of elements and symbols, trusting the viewer to actively fill in the missing pieces. Others touch upon vernacular and retro themes by reintroducing simple aesthetics reminiscent of the past. Still others take the form of icons or digital pictographs—simplified, iconographic computer-generated images that reveal personal meanings by inventing a new visual vocabulary (Figure 1-79).

1991: Kinetic Typography

Kinetic typographic designs of today have departed from their Futurist and cinematic roots and passed through a pubescence of relying only on two-dimensional visual cues to indicate speed and motion (such as overlaps, blurs, trails, and wiggle lines). Now kinetic typography is entering an adolescence of ever-expanding digital capabilities for interactivity and movement through the fourth dimension (time). Motion graphics have been a part of the film and television industry for years, and until recently, an elite group of highly trained designers, funded by mainstream commercial interests, has developed the vocabulary of kinetic typography. However, as with motionless typography, the emergence of evolving computer technologies has allowed a wider range of trained and untrained designers to experiment with kinetic typography. The 1991 introduction of the World Wide Web particularly triggered new growth in typographic exploration of motion and interactivity, as diverse individuals have extended kinetic typography in ways that expressed their own contemporary experiences as members of today's fast-paced global community.

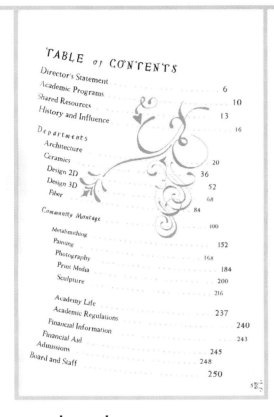

figure | 1-78 |

Table of contents page, *Cranbrook Academy of Art catalog,* 2002, by Catelijne van Middelkoop and Dylan Nelson.

figure | 1-79 |

Wedding invitation by Karanya Aksornkoae and Panya Chittaratlert, 2003.

CHAPTER SUMMARY

In a way, the history of the written word has come full circle, in that people today are sharing the experiences of the earliest humans who made purposeful personalized markings, and who devised picture-based, written language systems that were relevant and meaningful to their own lives. Humans continue to define and redefine these visual systems of written language. From the creation of cave paintings to the synthesis of digital pictographs, we have constantly striven to invent new personalized symbols to express our unique experiences, and new modes of visual communication to help us share our thoughts, feelings, and beliefs with other human beings. The widespread participation in typography's recent evolution and its vibrant and experimental nature present an optimistic outlook for the continuation of type as a vehicle for expression and a democratizing cultural force for social justice.

in review

1. What are pictograms? What are ideograms? What are phonograms?

2. What are the origins of the uppercase and lowercase letters we use today?

3. When and where was paper invented? What are three surfaces people used for writing before paper was available?

4. Explain the difference between woodblock printing and printing that uses movable type.

5. What were the effects of Gutenberg's (re)invention of movable type?

6. Explain the difference between relief printing, intaglio, and planographic printing. How does each of these printing methods affect the way that the printed type will look?

7. How do Transitional typefaces look different from Humanist and Old Style typefaces? How do Modern typefaces differ from Transitional ones?

8. Compare and contrast the ways that the Industrial Revolution and the digital revolution have influenced typography.

9. What role has advertising played in the historical development of type?

10. How did private presses like Kelmscott, Ashendene, and Doves revitalize typography?

11. Briefly describe the way that type was utilized by designers of the Modern Art movements (Futurism, Dada, De Stijl, and Constructivism).

12. How did the "New Typography" graphically represent the voice of its generation? What social connotations were implied by its use?

13. What was the International Typographic Style? How did Postmodern Art movements rebel against it?

14. What is Deconstruction? What is the Deconstructionist view of the audience's role?

exercises

1. Create a typographic composition for a cookbook cover by using homemade relief printing letter stamps (type sorts). To make your stamps, carve backward letterform reliefs out of at least five different household objects (suggestions: a potato, a candle, a cardboard box, a piece of wood, an old tennis ball, etc.—be creative!). Ink your stamps using an inked stamp pad or paints, or experiment with other pigments. Consider how your choice of materials influenced the characteristics of your marks.

2. Create a collage using only found type that expresses your conceptions of sensory overload and solitude in the "Information" age.

3. Create a purely typographic layout of a favorite children's poem that expresses its content through its form by the creative use—and misuse—of selection, distortion, scaling, treatment, and arrangement of characters.

4. Create an artistic poster in the Plakatstil style that advertises your favorite kind of candy.

5. Create a calendar design (you choose the month) using figurative typography to add humor, personality, narrative, and/or conceptual content to your layout.

6. Select one of the art movements discussed in this chapter and create a design for a one-page magazine advertisement that uses the stylistic qualities of that movement for one of the following clients: Suck-It-Up Vacuum Cleaner Co., Around the World Travel Agency, or Juicy Burgers Frozen Entrees. Read real ads, packaging, and promotional materials from your client's "competitors" to determine appropriate text to include in your ad.

Photograph courtesy of David Jury from his book
About Face, Reviving the Rules of Typography.

CHAPTER 2

objectives

- Become fluent in the terminology of typography
- Understand the different kinds of typographic guidelines and their purposes
- Recognize and name the different kinds of strokes, junctions, and negative spaces that are used to create letterforms
- Identify the structural aspects of type
- Identify a variety of differently shaped terminals and serifs
- Learn how to measure type using points and picas

introduction

Letterforms are built of combinations of straight and curved strokes. Sounds simple, right? Not quite so! As you can see from the vast variety of available typefaces, the way strokes are physically rendered can vary widely; the way these strokes look and relate to one another gives a typeface its sense of identity. Recognizing the subtle differences between the shapes of letter parts can help you to differentiate one typeface from another. Studying typographic terminology and the measurement system will help you to become familiar with these physical differences, and will let you communicate effectively about type with printers, production houses, other designers, and clients. An awareness of the structural aspects of type can also provide useful insights for making informed design decisions.

PHYSICAL ATTRIBUTES OF TYPE

ELEMENTS OF LETTERFORMS

Because much of the terminology describing letter parts is based on human anatomy, the terminology of typography isn't difficult, but there is a lot of it to remember. It is important to first understand how guidelines are used with letterforms; then it is essential to learn about all the parts that make up letterforms.

Guidelines

When you write in a ruled notebook, you probably write the words so they appear to rest along the evenly spaced horizontal lines that are printed onto the notebook paper. When you do this, you are using the lines as baselines. Even if your notebook is unruled, your letters probably line up fairly evenly along an imaginary baseline. A **baseline** is a real or imaginary line that the letters of a word rest upon so that the characters appear to line up evenly.

Remember when you were first learning to draw the letters of the alphabet? Your teacher may have given you special paper with additional guidelines printed on it to help you know how tall to make your capital and lowercase letters. In Figure 2-1, you see a similar set of typographic guidelines. The line that the letters rest upon is called the baseline. The line that shows how tall to make capital letters is called the **cap height**. The center dotted line that shows how tall to make the lowercase letters is called the **x-height**. For tall lowercase letters like b, d, f, h, k, and l, the x-height marks their **waistline** (the top of the body of the letter) instead of their full height.

> ## New Vocabulary
>
> **ascender line:** a real or imaginary line that marks the proper height for the tall lowercase letters of a typeface like b, d, f, h, k, and l; for some typefaces, this line is the same as the cap height
>
> **baseline:** a real or imaginary horizontal line upon which the letters of a word rest so that the characters appear to line up evenly
>
> **cap height:** a real or imaginary horizontal line that marks the height of the capital letters of a typeface
>
> **descender line:** a real or imaginary horizontal line that marks the proper length for the lowercase g, j, p, q, and y of a typeface
>
> **waistline:** a real or imaginary horizontal line that marks the height of the body of a tall lowercase letter (often is the same as the x-height)
>
> **x-height:** a real or imaginary horizontal line that shows how tall to make the lowercase letters of a typeface

The x-height is so named because it marks the proper optical height for the lowercase letter x. The optical size or shape of a letter (the size or shape we perceive) isn't always the same as the actual size or shape. Because characters are differently shaped, optical illusions sometimes occur that can make evenly sized and spaced characters look uneven. Designers compensate for these optical illusions by making slight adjustments. For example, in some typefaces, you'll notice that the rounded letters like c and e may be ever so slightly taller than the x-height. They were designed that way so that they would appear to be the same height as the other letters since their rounded shape creates an illusion that they are smaller than their actual size.

The dotted line that shows how long to make a lowercase g, j, p, q, and y is called the **descender line**. Sometimes tall lowercase letters like b, d, f, h, k, and l are the same height as the capital letters, but if they aren't, an **ascender line** can mark their proper height (Figure 2-1).

Expand

ascender line
cap height
x-height (and waistline)
baseline
descender line

figure | 2-1 |

Typographic guidelines are used to align type.

Counters and Counterforms

The word "counter" literally means "opposite," so it makes sense that the white (or negative) spaces inside and around letterforms are called **counterforms**. The counterforms of letterforms are just as important to letter recognition as the letter shapes themselves. The positive space (the letterforms) and the negative space (the counterforms) exist in relation to each other to produce distinctive characters, as you can see in Figure 2-2.

Sometimes characters contain, or even enclose, areas of white space; these areas, like the ones shown in Figure 2-3, are called **counters**. Counters can be open or closed. As you can see in Figure 2-4, an open counter is a space that is

contained, but not enclosed by a character. For example, a **crotch**, the pointed space where two parts of a character meet, is an open counter. A closed counter is a space that is enclosed by a character. For example, an **eye**, the small upper space in the lowercase letter e, is a closed counter.

> ## New Vocabulary
>
> **counter:** area where space is contained or enclosed by a letterform
>
> **counterforms:** the negative spaces inside and around letterforms
>
> **crotch:** the pointed counter where two strokes of a character meet
>
> **eye:** the small counter of a lowercase letter e

ABCD
letterforms (positive spaces)

ABCD
counterforms (negative space)

figure | 2-2 |

Letterforms and counterforms (shown in blue).

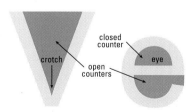

figure | 2-3 |

Counters (shown in blue).

closed counter
crotch
open counters
eye

figure | 2-4 |

Open and closed counters (shown in blue).

Ascenders and Descenders

The section of a tall lowercase character that extends above the x-height is called an **ascender**, as shown in Figure 2-5. Most ascenders are as tall as the ascender line, which varies from typeface to typeface. There are exceptions, though. For instance, part of the lowercase letter t ascends above the x-height, but usually it is shorter than the ascender line.

Some letters like g, j, p, q, y, and Q have parts that descend below the baseline (Figure 2-5). The section of a character that falls below the baseline is called a **descender**. Like ascenders, descenders can be long or short, depending on the specific typeface design.

figure | 2-5 |

Ascenders and descenders.

Strokes

Each line that is used to build a character is called a **stroke**. The word "stroke" recalls the calligraphic origins of letters—the stroke of a pen. Strokes can be straight or curved, thick or thin. The straight main stroke of a character is called a **stem stroke**; these strokes can be vertical or diagonal, and are often thicker than the other strokes of the letter. The thinner, secondary strokes of a character are called **hairline strokes**. You can see examples of stem strokes and hairline strokes in Figure 2-6.

figure | 2-6 |

Stem strokes and hairline strokes (shown in blue).

LAF LAF

stem strokes   hairline strokes

A hairline stroke that intersects the stem stroke of a letterform, like in the letters T, t, X, and x, is called a **cross stroke**. A horizontal hairline stroke that connects two main strokes, as in the letters A, e, and H, is called a **crossbar**, as shown in Figure 2-7.

figure | 2-7 |

Cross strokes and crossbars (shown in blue).

cross strokes   crossbars

When we talk about stem and hairline strokes, we are referring to whether the stroke is primary or secondary, fat or thin. Other names for strokes describe their shapes and orientations. For example, the main stroke of the letter S has a unique double-curved shape called a **spine**, as shown in Figure 2-8.

figure | 2-8 |

S

Spine (shown in blue).

A secondary stroke, extending from a stem stroke and ending freely, is called an **arm**. You can see in Figure 2-9, arms can extend horizontally as in the letter E, or they can extend upward diagonally as in the letter K. The letters E, F, K, k, L, V, v, W, w, Y, y, Z, and z have arms.

figure | 2-9 |

E K

Arms (shown in blue).

A secondary stroke that extends downward from a stem to the baseline and ends freely, is called a **leg**. You can see in Figure 2-10 that the letters K, k, and R have legs.

The diagonal or curved cross stroke at the base of the capital Q, that differentiates it from a capital O, is called a **tail**. The descenders on lowercase j, p, q, and y are sometimes also called tails. See Figure 2-11 for examples of tails.

K k R

j p Q q y

New Vocabulary

arm: a secondary stroke, extending horizontally or upward from a stem stroke and ending freely

bowl: a curved stroke that encloses a counter

cross stroke: a secondary stroke that intersects a stem stroke

crossbar: a horizontal secondary stroke that connects two main strokes

hairline stroke: a secondary stroke of a character, often is thinner than the stem

leg: a secondary stroke that extends downward from a stem to the baseline and ends freely

spine: the curved main stroke of a letter S

stem stroke: a character's main vertical, diagonal, or curved stroke, which is often thicker than the other strokes of the letter

stroke: an individual straight or curved line that is used to build a character

tail: the small stroke at the base of a capital Q that differentiates it from a capital O; the descenders on lowercase j, p, q, and y are sometimes also called tails

figure | 2-10 |

Legs (shown in blue).

figure | 2-11 |

Tails (shown in blue).

Bdp

figure | 2-12 |

Bowls (shown in blue).

A curved stroke that encloses a counter is called a **bowl**. The letters a, B, b, D, d, g, O, o, P, p, Q, q, and R have bowls. You can see some examples of bowls in Figure 2-12.

Junctions of Strokes

When two strokes angle upward toward each other, as in the letter A, the outermost point where they meet is called the **apex**. When two strokes angle downward toward each other, as in the letter V, the outermost point where the two strokes meet is called the **vertex**. So, for example, the letter W has two vertexes and an apex. Apexes and vertexes can be pointed, flat, rounded, oblique, hallowed, or extended, as shown in Figures 2-13 and 2-14.

figure | 2-13 |

Apexes (shown in blue).

figure | 2-14 |

Vertexes (shown in blue).

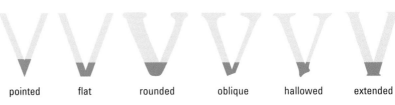

pointed flat rounded oblique hallowed extended

pointed flat rounded oblique hallowed extended

New Vocabulary

apex: the point at which two upward slanting strokes of a letterform meet

shoulder: the transitional area of a stroke that goes from curved to straight

vertex: the point at which two downward slanting strokes of a letterform meet

Some letters have curved strokes that transition into straight ones, as in Figure 2-15; the transitional section of the letter is called the **shoulder**. An abrupt transition results in squarish looking letterforms, while a longer transition gives letterforms a rounder appearance.

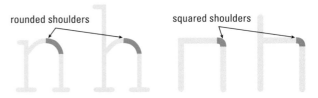

rounded shoulders squared shoulders

figure | 2-15 |

Shoulders (shown in blue).

Special Strokes of the Letter G

Spurs, loops, links, and ears are all specific to the letter G. A **spur** is the small stroke that is sometimes found at the right side of the base of a capital letter G. A **loop** is the lower curved portion of a lowercase g, and a **link** is the small connecting stroke that joins the upper and lower parts of a lowercase letter g. An **ear** is a small stroke that sometimes extends from the top of a lowercase g. Examples of spurs, loops, links, and ears, in a variety of shapes and sizes, are pictured in Figures 2-16 through 2-19.

New Vocabulary

ear: a small stroke that sometimes extends from the top of a lowercase letter g

link: a small connecting stroke between the loop and the upper bowl of a lowercase letter g

loop: lower curved stroke or bowl of a lowercase g

spur: a small stroke sometimes found on the right side of the base of a capital letter G

figure | 2-16 |

Spurs (shown in blue).

figure | 2-17 |

Loops (shown in blue).

figure | 2-18 |

Links (shown in blue).

figure | 2-19 |

Ears (shown in blue).

SHAPES OF TYPE

The consistency of stroke shapes is what makes the characters of a typeface seem to "go together." Throughout history, these aspects have experienced a wide range of interpretations due to technological advancements, social and political shifts, and the influence of popular tastes. Some of the aspects of type that help define the sameness of typefaces are the terminals and serifs of strokes, the contrast between thick and thin strokes, the angle of stress used, and the x-height ratio and the set width.

figure | 2-20 |

Terminals (shown in blue).

horizontal

vertical

rounded

cupped

sheared

oblique

teardrop shaped

ball shaped

pointed

Terminals and Serifs

A **terminal** is an endpoint of a stroke. Strokes can end in a variety of shapes, as shown in Figure 2-20. When letters have extensions at their terminals, we call those extensions **serifs**. A typeface that has serifs is referred to as a serif typeface, and a typeface without serifs is called a **sans-serif** typeface. (Sans is the French word for "without" so sans serif literally means "without serifs.") The origin of using serifs at the terminals of letters is widely thought to be the ancient Roman texts, in which the chisels used to carve letterforms into stone walls and tablets left such extensions at the terminals of letterforms, as can be seen in Figure 1-8. For this reason, upright (non-italic) letters which have serifs are often referred to as **roman**.

The shapes of serifs can vary widely, as shown in Figure 2-21. They can be cupped (arched like a foot) or flat, rounded, straight, squared, oblique (angled), splayed (widens gradually like a bell-bottom pant leg), or pointed. They can be thick or thin.

figure | 2-21 |

Serifs (shown in blue).

Often, serifs are bracketed. A **bracketed serif** has a curved wedge connecting the serif to the stem stroke, easing the transition between them. Serifs can be bracketed heavily, lightly, or not at all, as you can see in Figure 2-22.

no bracketing   light bracketing   heavy bracketing

figure | 2-22 |

Bracketing (shown in blue).

Sometimes horizontal strokes may end in half-serifs, which are called **beaks**. You can see examples of beaks in Figure 2-23.

barb: a serif that is shorter on one end, found on the terminal of a curved stroke

beak: a half-serif on the terminal of a straight stroke

bracketed serif: a serif that has a curved wedge connecting the serif to the stem stroke, easing the transition between them

roman: an upright, non-italic typeface with serifs

sans serif: a typeface that has no serifs (often used in the adjective form: sans-serif)

serif: an extension at a terminal of a letterform; also refers to a typeface that has serifs

swash: a decorative extended stroke that some-times projects from a terminal, often found on script letterforms

terminal: an endpoint of a stroke, which may or may not have a serif

figure | 2-23 |

Beaks (shown in blue).

Curved strokes sometimes have serifs that are shorter on one end than on the other, called **barbs**. See examples of barbs in Figure 2-24.

figure | 2-24 |

Barbs (shown in blue).

Sometimes the terminals end with a decorative extended stroke called a **swash**, as shown in Figure 2-25. Most often swashes are found on script typefaces, but not always.

figure | 2-25 |

Swashes (shown in blue).

Contrast Between Thick and Thin Strokes

Another important aspect of type is **contrast**—that is, the variation in thickness between a character's thickest and thinnest stroke weights. The **stroke weight** refers to the thickness of the individual strokes of a character. If the stem stroke is much thicker than the hairline strokes of a character, we say the typeface has high contrast, and if there is little variation in the thickness of the strokes, we say it has low contrast. A typeface with no variation in the optical weight of its strokes is said to have no contrast. Examples of letters with high, low, and no contrast are pictured in Figure 2-26.

figure | 2-26 |

Contrast (shown in blue).

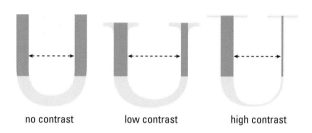

no contrast   low contrast   high contrast

Angle of Stress

The concept of angle of stress is based in the calligraphic ancestry of print—a wide-nibbed pen makes a varying mark depending on the angle at which the pen is held. As you can see from Figure 2-27, strokes that flow in the same direction share a consistent stroke weight. The **angle of stress** describes the angle to which the main strokes of a typeface aim, in relation to their baseline. You can identify any font's angle of stress by drawing an imaginary line through the thinnest membranes of a curved letterform like the letter O, as in Figure 2-28.

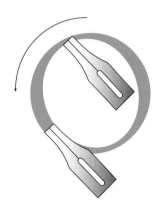

figure | 2-27 |

A wide-nibbed pen draws varying stroke weights when held at varying angles in relation to the paper (shown in blue).

figure | 2-28 |

Angle of stress.

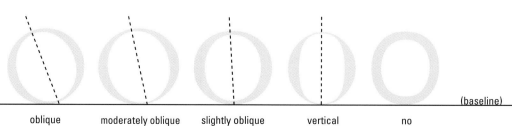

oblique angle of stress   moderately oblique angle of stress   slightly oblique angle of stress   vertical angle of stress   no angle of stress

(baseline)

x-height Ratio and Set Width

The proportions of a typeface are defined mainly by the x-height ratio and the set width. The **x-height ratio** of a typeface describes the height of regular lowercase letters (those without ascenders) in relation to the typeface's cap height. The term "x-height" is so named because the letter x provides a good standard for making this measurement. As you can see from Figure 2-29, the x-height ratio can vary from typeface to typeface. Some typefaces have tall x-heights, while others have short ones.

The **set width** of a letter describes how wide the character is, relative to its cap height. If a letter appears short and squat, we say it has a wide set. If it appears thin and lanky, we say it has a narrow set. Figure 2-30 shows letters of varying set widths.

New Vocabulary

angle of stress: the angle to which the main strokes of a typeface aim, in relation to their baseline

contrast: 1. a difference among compared elements; 2. to exhibit dissimilar qualities when compared; 3. to compare differences; and 4. in type, the variation in thickness between a character's thickest and thinnest stroke weights

set width: the width of a character, relative to its cap height

stroke weight: the thickness of the individual strokes of a character

x-height ratio: the height of regular lowercase letters of a typeface (those without ascenders) in relation to the typeface's cap height, generally measured using the lowercase x as a standard

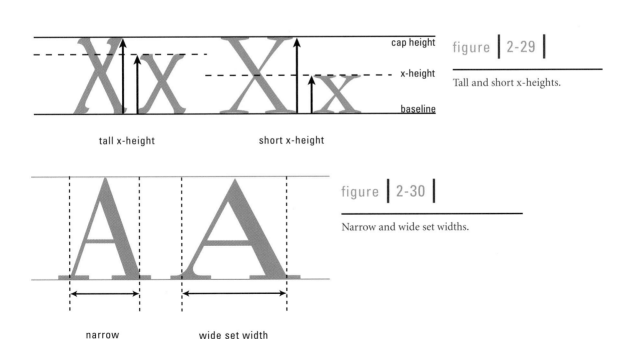

tall x-height   short x-height

cap height
x-height
baseline

figure | 2-29 |

Tall and short x-heights.

narrow set width   wide set width

figure | 2-30 |

Narrow and wide set widths.

THE *designer* AT WORK

art chantry

How did you get started as a designer? Tell us about your first job in design and the evolution of your career.

I started doing graphic design after seeing a copy of *Graphis* magazine in a library in 1972. Before that, I had been collecting psychedelic posters, comic books, and records (for their covers), and trying to duplicate them. It wasn't until I saw that *Graphis* magazine that I knew what my goal career was actually called.

After that, I began reading everything I could on the subject and looking at schools with design programs. By the time I got my first real job doing graphics, I was attending a community college. Prior to that, I had been hired by friends to do logos and stuff as far back as high school.

I took what I had done and gathered a sort of portfolio together. It was a pathetic collection of doodles and crazy lettering, really embarrassing even then. I went to the community college in-house design department and talked to a woman named Rebecca Nolte, and I think she felt sorry for me. Anyway, she hired me as part of a work/study pro-

gram. I ended up doing Photostats, Leroy lettering, and other odd items. She knew I loved posters, so she let me do some for the local college theater department. That's where I created my first silkscreen posters in 1974 and 1975.

I transferred to a graphic arts program at a local four-year state school, which turned out to be a technical program where I learned to run a printing press. I ended up taking many classes in the fine arts department, and found out that the departments were "at war" with each other. The result was that I had to conceal my work in each department from the other department, in order to create my own graphic design program.

Eventually, I was hired by that school's in-house department through yet another work/study program to do Leroy lettering, etc. I also began to pick up freelance work—mostly posters for campus events. So, I was able to support myself doing graphic design and get a college degree. Because of the departmental feud, I couldn't declare a major until my very last quarter of school; I ended up with an art degree by default, which I earned in spite of the teachers doing everything possible to eliminate me from both programs. This was my training.

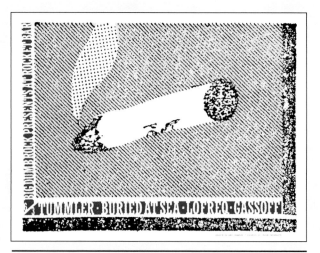

Rocket Bar poster by Art Chantry for BigDumbRock. *Courtesy of Art Chantry Design*, www.artchantry.com.

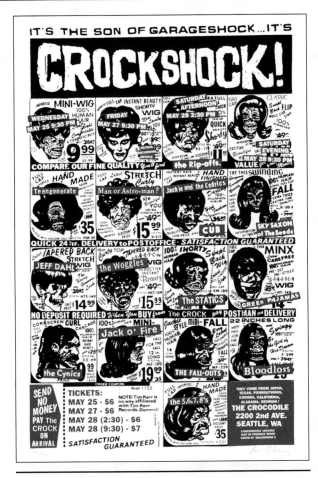

Crockshock! poster by Art Chantry for the Crocodile Cafe.
Courtesy of Art Chantry Design, www.artchantry.com.

When I went into the "real" world trying to do graphic design, I couldn't get hired to save my life, so I struggled with what freelance work I could acquire. Over the next thirty years, I was able to build a career out of it. To this day, I've never been offered a real salaried position in graphic design.

What do you do to get your creative juices flowing when you start a new project? What can you share with us about your design process? What role does technology play in that process?

I see the creative process as occurring in a part of the brain that is not a conscious part. In other words, creativ-

ity is like driving a car: when you drive a car, you don't consciously think about driving that car while you are driving. Actually, you are listening to the radio, or thinking about dinner, or thinking about what you should have said to the boss, or whatever.

The creative process works in the same way. We think about the solutions and then magically kick fully realized, finished ideas onto the paper. The trick is to learn how to let that part of your brain send the information you've developed far enough into the conscious part of your brain that it comes out through your hands. I have several techniques that I've developed over the years that seem to work, but they all boil down to distraction. I need something going on around me to distract the controlling conscious part of me, so that the creative unconscious other part of me can move freely without interference. To do that (these days), I simply fill my head with as much information as I can about the problem at hand, then I wait a week and let my mind do its thing. I seldom think about it. Then I turn on the radio and start listening while I get to work. The ideas simply flow out while I work, distracted by the radio.

This sounds strange, I know, but I've read many accounts of other creative and artistic people doing some version of the same thing. Andy Warhol used massive amounts of distraction to do his work. Others simply take a nap and use that semi-conscious state that happens just before you wake (that strange period when you're not asleep, but not quite awake yet). It seems that for them, that moment is when their minds are free enough and uninhibited by the conscious part of the brain to allow the ideas to develop.

At any rate, I never ever suffer for ideas. I can come up with them effortlessly.

How has the role of typography in design changed over the last decade? Where do you see it going in the future?

The development of typography as a craft and art form in the late nineteenth and early twentieth centuries sparked the advent of graphic design as we know it today. If you

► THE *designer* AT WORK   *art chantry, continued*

The Ventures poster by Art Chantry for the Crocodile Cafe.
Courtesy of Art Chantry Design, www.artchantry.com.

study the basic rules of the modern period of design, you'll quickly see that the rules of typography are what they are based upon. Never mind that commercial art, in all of its many guises, has been around since the days of cave paintings. Actual graphic design is a modern invention based upon a set of rules. Those rules emerged from the art of typography.

Since the advent of the computer, the world of typography has ceased to be one of the craftsman and artist, and has been placed into the hands of the everyman. Anybody can buy a computer and become at least a C-level designer/typographer almost immediately. With time, anyone can master the basic necessary rules and create competent graphic design. So, where does that leave the art of graphic design? In a quandary, that's where.

My response to the onslaught of DIY (do-it-yourself) designers, created by the dawn of the easy access computer design programs over the era, has been to step back. I've been forced to rely upon skills that I have—that I can market—that a computer does NOT have. So, I find myself getting rougher and cruder and more stylized as time goes on. I'm almost an artist now, and not a graphic designer. That being said, I no longer do typography as it used to be defined. I now do lettering—a skill that is entirely defined by the author's hand. So, I am no longer a typographer. I may no longer be a graphic designer. The terms have become deeply muddied and so vague that they may no longer apply to what I do.

What role should social responsibility play in design? What can designers contribute to our society?

We are propagandists for a technological marketing culture. The base act of our society is selling. We, as designers of items created to promote sales, often do so without any consideration as to what or who we are helping. If, indeed, we are a service industry, we need to ask the question: who do we serve?

I, for one, have become very sensitive over time to who I help sell things. I use my many skills to help a client change the way people think about something—buy this product, go to this event, vote for this candidate—and I do it for money. So, just who am I willing to help to trick people? These are questions I ask myself with every new project I take on. Sometimes the answers to these questions conflict with the way I feel and think about my place in society. As a result, I feel the need to turn down work on occasion. I made a pact with myself years ago that I won't help jerks just for the money. Money only lasts so long, and then it's gone. But the causes you helped will still be there, working along. When I'm offered work, I have to ask myself if I really want to help that cause/product/client.

Kustom Kulture poster by Art Chantry for the Center on Contemporary Art. *Courtesy of Art Chantry Design,* www.artchantry.com.

What advice do you have for design students and new designers who are just entering the field today?

Expect it to be tough. It was always tough, and it will always be tough. The real reason to do graphic design for a living is because you love it. Without that, it's a terrible and difficult choice for a career. So, if you plan to do it for money or power or fame or fashion, you need to rethink your goals.

Art Chantry, Art Chantry Design, St. Louis, Missouri
www.artchantry.com

(Top) Concert poster by Art Chantry for the 3B Tavern. (Bottom) Mondo Bizarre Anniversary poster by Art Chantry for *Mondo Bizarre* magazine. *Both images courtesy of Art Chantry Design,* www.artchantry.com.

TYPE MEASUREMENTS

Because we generally use type at such a small scale, tiny units of measure are needed for designing and laying out type. At present, the most commonly used type measurement system is the PostScript Point Scale, adapted from the American Point Scale, whose units of measure include the inch, the pica, and the point. The inch is, of course, a standard unit of measure in the United States. The **pica**, usually used for measuring lines of type, is exactly ⅙ of an inch, as you can see from Figure 2-31; a pica can be further subdivided into 12 **points**, which are most often used to measure character sizes and spacing.

figure | 2-31 |

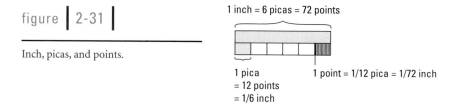

Inch, picas, and points.

The typefaces used for letterpress printing are cast onto a rectangular lead **sort**, as you can see in Figure 2-32. When we talk about the point size of a typeface, we are usually referring to the **body size** of the type. The body size must include enough space to accommodate any capital and lowercase letter in full, plus extra room to prevent adjacent printed characters from touching each other. Even though letterpresses are rarely used today, the concept of the type's body size has been transferred to the virtual environment (Figure 2-32).

figure | 2-32 |

Lead typeface with its digital equivalent.
Photograph courtesy of Elizabeth Nevin of the Briar Press.

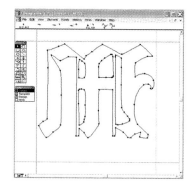

You can determine the point size of a typeface by using a rule like the one pictured in Figure 2-33 to measure from the baseline of one line of text to the baseline of the next. For example, notice that in Figure 2-33, the baselines of the text align with the 12-point gauge on the rule.

Sometimes extra space is added between lines of type. In letterpress printing, this was done by placing thin strips of lead between lines of type, as in Figure 2-34. These strips of lead are called **leading** (pronounced led-ing). Again, the concept of leading has been transferred to the virtual environment. Even though we no longer use lead to separate lines of text, we still refer to line spacing as leading.

figure | 2-33 |

Pica scale.

figure | 2-34 |

Leading being inserted between lines of metal type. *Photograph courtesy of David Jury from his book* About Face, Reviving the Rules of Typography.

When leading is added to the body size of a typeface, both measurements are added together to determine the type's point size, as shown in Figure 2-35. So for instance, 35-point type with 13 points of leading would be expressed as 48 points, or 35/48.

point size = 48 points

leading = 13 points

type size = 35 points

figure | 2-35 |

Point size.

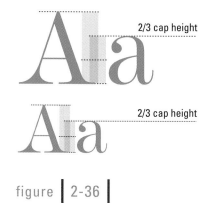

2/3 cap height

2/3 cap height

figure │ 2-36 │

Relative point size.

Because type can be rendered at so many different point sizes, it is also useful to use relative units of measurement to measure type. Relative units help us discuss the sizes of letterforms in relation to one another within a specific typeface at a specific point size. For instance, the exact height and width of a capital letter A and a lowercase letter a vary depending upon their point size, but the relationship between the two characters remains the same whether they are printed at 48 points or at 72 points, and so on. That is, if a is ⅔ the height of A at one point size, it will also be ⅔ its height at any other point size, as shown by Figure 2-36.

The relative units we use to compare type dimensions within a point size are called **ems (em squares)** and **ens (en squares)**, shown in Figure 2-37. An em (or em square) is a relative unit of measurement used for making comparisons between sizes of characters and spaces within a typeface of a particular point size. An em is always a square unit equal in height and in width to the point size of a given typeface. Usually, an em square is about the same as the advance width of the capital letter M. An en is always half the width of the em square, and is usually about the same as the advance width of a lowercase n. So for example, the em square of a 12-point typeface would be 12 points wide and 12 points tall. The en square of the same typeface would be 6 points wide, but would still be 12 points tall.

Once the em and en of a typeface have been established, the widths of characters, indentations, and spaces between words can be discussed as fractions or units of the em and en.

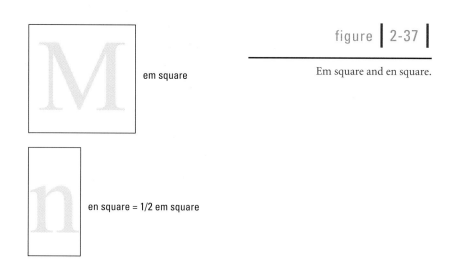

em square

en square = 1/2 em square

figure │ 2-37 │

Em square and en square.

New Vocabulary

body size: the height of the face of a type sort, or its digital equivalent

em or **em square:** a relative unit of measurement used for making comparisons between sizes of characters and spaces within a typeface of a particular point size; an em is always a square unit equal in height and in width to the point size of a given typeface

en or **en square:** a relative unit of measurement used for making comparisons between sizes of characters and spaces within a typeface of a particular point size; an en is always half the width of the em

leading: (pronounced led-ing) thin strips of lead placed between lines of type in letterpress printing; the space between two consecutive measures of type on a page or layout (line spacing)

pica: measurement of type that equals 1/6 of an inch

point: measurement of type that equals 1/72 of an inch

sort: a rectangular metal piece of type for use in letterpress printing

CHAPTER SUMMARY

The straight and curved strokes of characters can be physically rendered and combined in a wide variety of ways to suggest a full range of meanings and associations, independent of the type's content. The physical attributes of these strokes create a sense of identity within a typeface, making the characters seem to "go together." These attributes are defined by the strokes, junctions, and counterforms. Terminals and serifs, contrast between thick and thin stokes, angle of stress, x-height ratio, and set width help define sameness in typefaces. The variations among these shapes are measured using a special typographic scale made up of units called picas and points. Also, relative units based on the em square are used for measuring type within a point size of a given typeface, so that size relationships can be extrapolated from one point size to another.

Learning to recognize and compare the intricacies and nuances of letterforms is an important step in learning how to effectively identify, select, and use type. This knowledge is also essential for any designer who plans to create a new typeface. Studying typographic terminology related to type anatomy and structure not only increases awareness of these subtle physical differences, but also facilitates effective communication about type and supports informed design decision-making.

in review

1. Name five types of typographic guidelines associated with letterforms.

2. What is an ascender? What is a descender?

3. What is the difference between a stem stroke and a hairline stroke?

4. What is a counter?

5. What is a serif?

6. What does sans serif mean?

7. What special strokes are particular to the capital letter G and lowercase letter g?

8. What are the structural elements of letterforms? Name each structural element, and explain what it is.

9. How is the point size of a typeface measured?

10. How many points are in an inch? How many picas are in an inch? How many points are in a pica?

exercises

1. Visit a free font web site on the Internet. (You can find one easily by typing the query "free fonts" into your web browser's search engine.) Find and print examples of the differently shaped terminals and serifs discussed in this chapter. (You can do this either by downloading and installing fonts to your computer, or by using the web site's "type test-drive" function and copy/pasting the results into a Word document.) Label each kind of terminal that you find.

2. Look through a magazine to find examples that illustrate each of the vocabulary words presented in this chapter. Label each example.

3. Find a typeface with a vertical angle of stress and high contrast, and one with an oblique angle of stress and low contrast. Use samples of both typefaces to create a dynamic composition that accents the physical differences between the two typeface designs.

4. Select a letter of the alphabet. Create a composition that collages that letter in a minimum of five different typefaces. Label the parts of the letters in smaller text as a component of the design. Elements of your design may overlap if you wish.

Courtesy of Elizabeth Nevin of the Briar Press.

CHAPTER 3

objectives

- Understand type terminology
- Learn about the historical evolution of type family categories
- Recognize how the structural elements of letterforms differ for each type family category
- Understand how type is classified
- Make educated decisions when choosing typefaces for designs

introduction

You have probably noticed that there are an enormous number of fonts available for use in your designs—so many that it can be overwhelming and difficult to choose sometimes. On one hand, the abundance of available font styles can help you to make your designs expressive and unique. On the other hand, with such a wide selection, it's easy to fall into the trap of using fonts inappropriately—that is, based on enthusiasm for the font itself, rather than the appropriateness of its qualities for the design's message. The way a typeface looks may suggest a certain time period or cultural phenomenon to viewers. It can also set a mood or suggest an association to a remembered experience. To gain insight into the connotations of various typeface designs, it is necessary to become familiar with the ways that typefaces are classified and the related terminology.

!	"	#	$	%	&	'	(	
)	*	+	,	-	.	/	0	1
2	3	4	5	6	7	8	9	:
;	<	=	>	?	@	A	B	C
D	E	F	G	H	I	J	K	L
M	N	O	P	Q	R	S	T	U
V	W	X	Y	Z	[	\	]	^
_	`	a	b	c	d	e	f	g
h	i	j	k	l	m	n	o	p
q	r	s	t	u	v	w	x	y
z	{	|	}	~		€	,	ƒ
,,	…	†	‡	^	‰	Š	‹	Œ
Ž	'	'	"	"	•	—	—	~
™	š	›	œ	ž	Ÿ		¡	¢
£	€	¥	¦	§	¨	©	ª	«
¬	-	®	¯	°	±	2	3	´
µ	¶	·	,	1	º	»	¼	²⁄₄
³⁄₄	¿	À	Á	Â	Ã	Ä	Å	Æ
Ç	È	É	Ê	Ë	Ì	Í	Î	Ï
Ð	Ñ	Ò	Ó	Ô	Õ	Ö	×	Ø
Ù	Ú	Û	Ü	Ý	Þ	ß	à	á
â	ã	ä	å	æ	ç	è	é	ê
ë	ì	í	î	ï	ð	ñ	ò	ó
ô	õ	ö	÷	ø	ù	ú	û	ü
ý	þ	ÿ						

TYPE TERMINOLOGY

As a graphic designer, you will be using a lot of new terminology specific to type. You will need to incorporate these terms correctly into your vocabulary so that you can discuss your designs with other designers, and so that you can explain them to your clients. The term **type** refers to typeset text or any specifically shaped reproducible characters (and even the metal sorts used for printing letterforms, as discussed in Chapter 2), but you've probably also heard the terms "typeface," "font," "type style," and "type family." Because they can be confusing, it's important to differentiate between these terms.

Typeface

Let's say that you are hired by Mr. Smith to design a logo for Smith's Country Cookin' Cottage. He wants the logo to include new and original letterforms that you will design just for his logo. In this case, you might not even design all the letters of the alphabet for him—only the ones he will need to spell out his business name. When you design the original letterforms for Mr. Smith's logo, you are designing a new *typeface*. The term **typeface** refers to a collection of letterforms that have been especially designed to go together. It is a broad term that can refer to just a few letters in a logo or a whole font.

Font

Let's say that Mr. Smith loves the typeface you designed for his logo. Now he wants you to design all the rest of the characters that he will need to create all of his brochures, menus, stationery, and annual reports using this typeface. He will need both the capital and the lowercase forms of each letter of the alphabet, as well as numbers, symbols, and punctuation marks. He might also need fractions, ligatures, accents, and other special characters, like ™.

figure | 3-1 |

A character map of the complete font Times New Roman. *Courtesy of Bitstream, Inc. type foundry*, www.bitstream.com, www.myfonts.com.

What you are doing for Mr. Smith is developing your typeface into a *font*. You may already be familiar with fonts. When you use a word processing program on a computer, you can usually select the font that you'd like your text to appear in. The term **font** refers to a collection of all the characters of a specific typeface that are necessary for typesetting. The characters of a particular font usually share specific characteristics that make them seem to belong together. Figure 3-1 shows a character map for the complete font Times New Roman.

Type Style

Mr. Smith loves the font you designed for him. Now he has decided that he would like you to modify the font to create an italic version, a bold version, a light version, an expanded version, and a condensed version; Mr. Smith is asking you to develop a variety of *type styles* of your font. A **type style** refers to a modified version of the typeface. When you are using a word processing program on a computer, and you make the text bold or italic, you are applying a type style to your text.

When purchasing fonts, you will often see type styles packaged as separate font files and sold separately. These type styles will always be superior to the type styles that your word processing software can generate. This is because your computer generates type styles by applying a set mathematical formula to each letterform, while a designer considers the optical balance of where visual weight should be added, subtracted, or adjusted when designing a type style. Figure 3-2 shows the difference between the designed and computer-generated bold and italic type styles of the font Times New Roman.

figure | 3-2 |

AaBbCc
Times New Roman regular

AaBbCc   *AaBbCc*
AaBbCc   **AaBbCc**

Designed type styles   Computer-generated type styles

Designed and computer-generated type styles of the font Times New Roman.

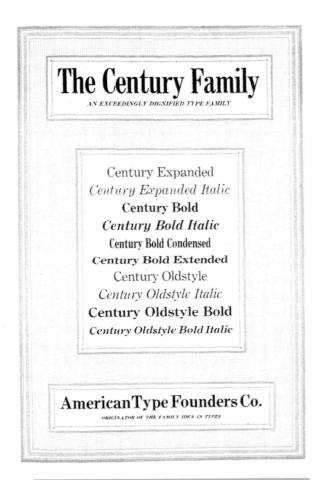

figure | 3-3 |

Type specimen of the Century type family. *Courtesy of American Type Founders.*

Type Family

If you group all of the type styles of the font that you developed for Mr. Smith together, including the original unmodified font, this collection would be called a **type family**. The term type family can refer to a collection of type that includes a specific typeface and all the type styles of that typeface. In Figure 3-3, you can see a specimen chart of the Century type family.

Unfortunately, the term *type family* can be confusing because it can be correctly used to describe *two different concepts*; type family can also refer to the categories that we classify type into, based on the historical origin and physical characteristics of the letterforms. For the sake of clarity, we will refer to this sort of type family as a type family category.

There are a number of type families that designers should be familiar with because they are standards that have withstood the test of time. These classics are exceptional in design and usability, both for display purposes and for longer passages of text. Some noteworthy examples include:

- Baskerville
- Bodoni
- Caslon
- Futura
- Helvetica
- Optima
- Times New Roman
- Univers

New Vocabulary

font: a collection of all the characters of a specific typeface that are necessary for typesetting

type: 1. metal sorts used for printing letterforms; 2. typeset text; and 3. printed characters

typeface: a collection of letterforms that have been especially designed to go together

type family: 1. a collection of type that includes a specific typeface and all the type styles of that typeface; 2. a category that type is classified into, based on the historical origin and physical characteristics of the letterforms

type style: a modified version of a typeface

TYPE FAMILY CATEGORIES

Typefaces are classified into categories that reflect their historical origins and their stylistic qualities. Understanding how typefaces are classified can help you to make better decisions about when and how to use them, and can guide your decisions when creating new typeface designs. Designers who make educated choices about font usage can create stronger, more successful designs.

Unfortunately, there is no one accepted system for classifying type; the variety of books on typography describe several different approaches to classification. The common thread that you will find in these books, though, is that classification of typefaces is useful and necessary for understanding and applying type effectively. In each classification system, typefaces are classified based on a combination of the historical evolution of type and stylistic characteristics of the letterforms.

Luckily, the differences between these systems is superficial. They really only differ in the names that are used for each category, and how extensively the categories are subdivided.

For the purposes of this book, we will use the most commonly accepted classifications, and explore several conventional subdivisions. The common (and alternate) names for these type family categories are:

- Blackletter
- Humanist (or Venetian)
- Old Style (or Old Face, Garalde)
- Transitional (or Réales)
- Modern (or Didone)
- Egyptian (or Slab Serif, Square Serif, Mécanes, Antiques)
- Sans Serif
  - Grotesque sans serif
  - Geometric sans serif
  - Humanist sans serif
- Script
- Display

figure | 3-4 |

Image of lead letterpress sorts. *Courtesy of Elizabeth Nevin of the Briar Press.*

When designing a new letterform, the designer makes decisions about specific structural elements of the letters, including the x-height, the contrast, the angle of stress, and the terminals. Generally, these elemental decisions are repeated in most or all of the characters, as the typeface is developed into a font. This commonality of structural elements is what makes the different characters of a font seem to go together.

As we discuss each of the following historical type family categories, take note of how these structural elements tended to vary from one to the next during different time periods. Recognizing the variations in these elements is key to differentiating between the type family categories.

The Blackletter Type Family Category

When Johannes Gutenberg invented movable type in 1455 in Mainz, Germany, he fashioned his type after the popular local scribal handwriting style of the day. German scribes used wide-nibbed pens that gave the letters a sharp angular look. To conserve parchment, scribes drew very narrow letters with narrow counters. The lack of negative space gave pages an overall dark appearance, and so this lettering style came to be known as blackletter (sometimes also called Old English).

Gutenberg cast letterforms on slugs of lead called sorts, like the ones pictured in Figure 3-4. The first fonts used in Europe were designed to emulate blackletter scribal calligraphy. The Blackletter type family category includes all fonts that were designed to emulate Gothic medieval scripts. It also includes all the revival fonts that were designed to look like early blackletter fonts. Also included in this category are fonts based on the more rounded medieval Irish uncial lettering style that was contemporary to Gothic blackletter.

Blackletter Typeface

Tendencies

(Gothic & celtic)

↳	**Terminals**	**Terminals:** the ends of strokes are often sharp and may include flourishes **Serifs:** terminals may or may not have serifs
	Angle of Stress	Usually oblique (rises from the baseline, aiming strongly toward the left)
	Contrast	Often there is high contrast between thick and thin strokes
	Proportions	**x-height:** often relatively tall in relation to the cap height **Set width:** Gothic styles often appear narrow, Celtic styles often appear wide **Positive/Negative space:** closely spaced letters with small counterforms give an overall dark appearance
	Additional Features	• Based on handwriting styles of Gothic (German) and Celtic (Irish) medieval scribes • Highly decorative • Heavy vertical stems cause a strong vertical presence

figure | 3-5 |

Blackletter typeface tendencies.

BLACKLETTER TYPE FAMILY CATEGORY AND EXAMPLES

The design of Johannes G, a digital blackletter revival font (shown below), was based on the letterforms cut by Gutenberg for his 42-line Bible. You can compare the digital typeface to the original, which is pictured in Figure 3-6; other digital blackletter revivals are also shown. Keep in mind as you examine them that revivals generally are not exact copies of preexisting fonts—new designers usually add their own interpretations to revival typefaces, hopefully to improve them in some way.

figure | 3-6 |

Close-up of text from Gutenberg's 42-line Bible of 1455,
by permission of the British Library [C.9.d.3].

ﬀﬀ Johannes G
26 pt

ﬀﬀ Johannes G was designed by Manfred Klein in 1991, based on original designs created by Johannes Gutenberg in 1455. ﬀﬀ Johannes G, courtesy of FSI FontShop International type foundry, www.fontshop.com, www.fontfont.com.
8/12 pt

FF Johannes G – 28 pt

abcdefghijklmnopqrſtuvwxyz
ABCDEFGHIJKLMNOPQRSTU
VWXYZ ‹1234567890◎'!?:;""›

american uncial
24 pt

american uncial was designed By victor hammer in 1953, Based on celtic scripts and typefaces of the thirteenth to the sixteenth centuries. american uncial d, courtesy of urw++ type foundry, www.urwpp.de/english/home.htm.
8/10 pt

American Uncial – 24 pt

abcdefghijklmnopqrstuvwxyz
abcdefghijklmnopqrstu
vwxyz (1234567890$%&*@'!?:;"")

Cloister Black
32 pt

Cloister Black is a revival of original designs created by Morris Fuller Benton and Joseph W. Phinney in 1904. Cloister Black, courtesy of Bitstream Inc. type foundry, www.myfonts.com.

10/12 pt

Cloister Black – 28 pt

abcdefghijklmnopqrstuvwxyz
ABCDEFGHIJKLMNOPQRSTU
VWXYZ (1234567890$%&*@'!?:;"")

Duc de Berry
32 pt

Duc de Berry was designed by Gottfried Pott in 1990, based on Gothic scripts and typefaces of the thirteenth to the sixteenth centuries. It is part of the "Type before Gutenberg" series from Linotype. Duc de Berry, courtesy of Linotype type foundry, Linotype Library GmbH, www.linotype.com.

8/10 pt

Duc de Berry – 28 pt

abcdefghijklmnopqrstuvwxyz
ABCDEFGHIJKLMNOPQRSTU
VWXYZ (1234567890$%&*@'!?:;"")

Fette Fraktur
28 pt

Fette Fraktur is a revival of Gothic scripts and typefaces of the thirteenth to the sixteenth centuries. Fette Fraktur, courtesy of Linotype type foundry, Linotype Library GmbH, www.linotype.com.

8/10 pt

Fette Fraktur – 26 pt

abcdefghijklmnopqrstuvwxyz
ABCDEFGHIJKLMNOPQRSTU
VWXYZ (1234567890$%&*@'!?:;"")

BLACKLETTER TYPE FAMILY CATEGORY EXAMPLES

Goudy Text
30 pt

The Goudy Text type family was designed by Frederic Goudy in 1928, based on Gothic and Celtic type-faces of the thirteenth to the sixteenth centuries. Goudy Text MT and Goudy Text MT Lombardic Capitals, courtesy of Linotype type foundry, Linotype Library GmbH, www.linotype.com.

8/12 pt

Goudy Text – 28 pt

abcdefghijklmnopqrstuvwxyz
ABCDEFGHIJKLMNOPQRSTU
VWXYZ (1234567890$%&*@'!?:;"")

Kelmscott
32 pt

Kelmscott was designed by David Nalle in 1993, based on original designs created by William Morris in 1892. Kelmscott, courtesy of Scriptorium type foundry, www.fontcraft.com.

8/10 pt

Kelmscott – 28 pt

abcdefghijklmnopqrstuvwxyz
ABCDEFGHIJKLMNOP
QRSTVWXYZ
(1234567890$%&*@'!?:;"")

The Humanist (or Venetian) Type Family Category

In 1461, Mainz was sacked and burned by soldiers. That drove many people, including printers, from Germany. This event hastened the spread of movable type printing to locations all over Europe. Within a decade of the onslaught, Venice, Italy, had become an important center of the printing industry.

Scribes in Italy did not use the blackletter handwriting style. Italian scribes wrote in a more open airy style that was based on the lettering style of the ancient Romans, who were revered by Italians. The Italian scribal handwriting was called whiteletter, because the additional negative space made for an overall lighter aesthetic. The ancient Roman influence also resulted in the addition of an important new feature: the serif. Whiteletter scripts looked very much like the types that are most widely used today.

By 1470, movable type based on the Italian scribal whiteletter handwriting style became available. At first, the Italians tried to closely emulate their scribes' handwriting style, like the Germans did before them, so the whiteletter fonts that were first produced looked very calligraphic. These early whiteletter types are called Humanist, because they look like they were lettered by a human hand.

Many people found whiteletter typefaces easier to read than the heavy, ornate blackletter styles that were popular in Germany, so Roman typefaces quickly gained popularity throughout Europe. Today, we continue to use the term roman to describe upright, non-italic typefaces that have serifs.

The Humanist type family category includes these early roman typefaces and the newer ones that share their structural elements. The term Humanist comes from the humanistic qualities of the letters, which tend to have a soft, handwritten, organic feel. Letterforms appear heavy and rounded, and have low contrast. They tend to have a very oblique angle of stress. Serifs are also oblique, and are usually cupped (arched like a foot). The crossbar on the lowercase **e** is always slanted in Humanist typefaces, as shown in Figure 3-7. The Humanist type family category is sometimes called the Venetian type family category because the first Humanist typefaces emerged from Venice.

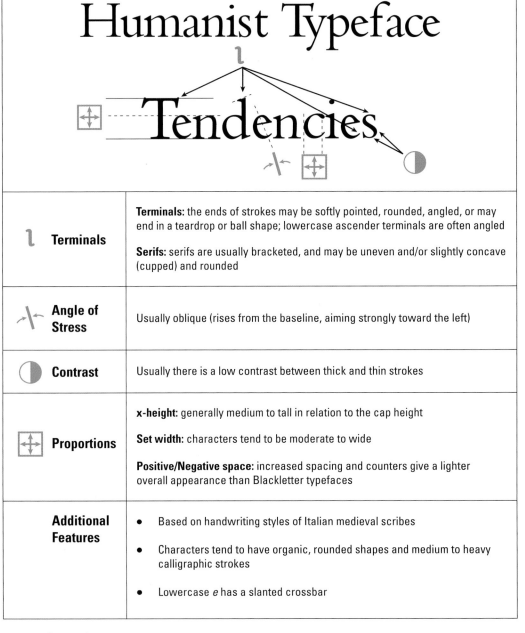

Terminals	**Terminals:** the ends of strokes may be softly pointed, rounded, angled, or may end in a teardrop or ball shape; lowercase ascender terminals are often angled **Serifs:** serifs are usually bracketed, and may be uneven and/or slightly concave (cupped) and rounded
Angle of Stress	Usually oblique (rises from the baseline, aiming strongly toward the left)
Contrast	Usually there is a low contrast between thick and thin strokes
Proportions	**x-height:** generally medium to tall in relation to the cap height **Set width:** characters tend to be moderate to wide **Positive/Negative space:** increased spacing and counters give a lighter overall appearance than Blackletter typefaces
Additional Features	• Based on handwriting styles of Italian medieval scribes • Characters tend to have organic, rounded shapes and medium to heavy calligraphic strokes • Lowercase *e* has a slanted crossbar

figure │ 3-7 │

Humanist typeface tendencies.

HUMANIST TYPE FAMILY CATEGORY AND EXAMPLES

One of the earliest Humanist typefaces was cut by Nicolas Jenson in 1470, pictured in Figure 3-8. The typefaces that Jenson cut were pivotal in setting the course that type design would take for centuries to come. His designs, which were based on the proportions of ancient Roman letterforms, catalyzed the European conversion from blackletter to whiteletter typefaces as the standard. Jenson's direct influence on type design has been far-reaching. Humanist type designs have been revived in the nineteenth and twentieth centuries, and continue to experience new digital revivals today. A digital Humanist revival that emulates Jenson's work, called Jenson Classico, and some of its related type styles are shown here. Other digitally revived Humanist fonts are on the pages that follow.

figure | 3-8 |

Close-up of Jenson's type from *Institutiones Oratoriae* by Marcus Fabius Quintilianus, of 1471.

Jenson Classico

36 pt

The Jenson Classico type family was designed by Franko Luin, based on original designs created by Nicolas Jenson in 1470. Jenson Classico, Jenson Classico Bold, Jenson Classico Italic, Jenson Classico Bold Italic, and Jenson Classico Small Caps, courtesy of Linotype type foundry, Linotype Library GmbH, www.linotype.com.

9/12 pt

Jenson Classico – 46 pt

abcdefghijklmnop
qrstuvwxyz
ABCDEFGHIJKLM
NOPQRSTUVWXYZ
(1234567890$%&
*@'!?:;"")

HUMANIST TYPE FAMILY CATEGORY EXAMPLES

Jenson Classico Italic – 28 pt

abcdefghijklmnopqrstuvwxyz
ABCDEFGHIJKLMNOPQRSTU
VWXYZ (1234567890$%&*@'!?:;"")

Jenson Classico Bold – 28 pt

abcdefghijklmnopqrstuvwxyz
ABCDEFGHIJKLMNOPQRSTU
VWXYZ (1234567890$%&*@'!?:;"")

Jenson Classico Bold Italic – 28 pt

abcdefghijklmnopqrstuvwxyz
ABCDEFGHIJKLMNOPQRSTU
VWXYZ (1234567890$%&*@'!?:;"")

Jenson Classico Small Caps – 28 pt

ABCDEFGHIJKLMNOPQRSTUVWXYZ
ABCDEFGHIJKLMNOPQRSTU
VWXYZ (1234567890$%&*@'!?:;"")

Centaur

32 pt

The Centaur type family is a revival of original designs created by Bruce Rogers in 1914. Centaur MT, Centaur MT Italic, and Centaur MT Bold, courtesy of Linotype type foundry, Linotype Library GmbH, *www.linotype.com*.

8/10 pt

Centaur MT – 28 pt

abcdefghijklmnopqrstuvwxyz
ABCDEFGHIJKLMNOPQRSTU
VWXYZ (1234567890$%&*@'!?:;"")

Centaur MT Italic – 28 pt

abcdefghijklmnopqrstuvwxyz
ABCDEFGHIJKLMNOPQRSTU
VWXYZ (1234567890$%&@'!?:;"")*

Centaur MT Bold – 28 pt

abcdefghijklmnopqrstuvwxyz
ABCDEFGHIJKLMNOPQRSTU
VWXYZ (1234567890$%&*@'!?:;"")

Cloister
32 pt

The Cloister type family was designed by Phil Martin, based on original designs created by Morris Fuller Benton in 1913. Cloister URW T Regular, Cloister URW T Regular Italic, and Cloister URW T Bold, courtesy of URW++ type foundry, *www.urwpp.de/english/home.htm*.
8/10 pt

Cloister URW T Regular – 28 pt

abcdefghijklmnopqrstuvwxyz
ABCDEFGHIJKLMNOPQRSTU
VWXYZ (1234567890$%&*@'!?:;"")

Cloister URW T Regular Italic – 28 pt

abcdefghijklmnopqrstuvwxyz
ABCDEFGHIJKLMNOPQRSTU
VWXYZ (1234567890$%&@'!?:;"")*

Cloister URW T Bold – 28 pt

abcdefghijklmnopqrstuvwxyz
ABCDEFGHIJKLMNOPQRSTU
VWXYZ (1234567890$%&*@'!?:;"")

Deepdene

30 pt

The Deepdene type family is a revival of original designs created by Frederic Goudy in 1927. Deepdene URW T Roman, Deepdene URW T Roman Italic, and Deepdene URW T Bold, courtesy of URW++ type foundry, *www.urwpp.de/english/home.htm.*

8/10 pt

Deepdene URW T Roman – 28 pt

abcdefghijklmnopqrstuvwxyz
ABCDEFGHIJKLMNOPQRSTU
VWXYZ (1234567890$%&*@'!?:;"")

Deepdene URW T Roman Italic – 28 pt

abcdefghijklmnopqrstuvwxyz
ABCDEFGHIJKLMNOPQRSTU
VWXYZ (1234567890$%&@'!?:;"")*

Deepdene URW T Bold – 28 pt

abcdefghijklmnopqrstuvwxyz
ABCDEFGHIJKLMNOP
QRSTUVWXYZ
(1234567890$%&*@'!?:;"")

Stratford
30 pt

The Stratford type family was designed by Adrian Williams and Freda Sack in 1979. Stratford T Roman, Stratford T Italic, and Stratford T Bold, courtesy of URW++ type foundry, www.urwpp.de/english/home.htm.

7/10 pt

Stratford T Roman – 28 pt

abcdefghijklmnopqrstuvwxyz
ABCDEFGHIJKLMNOPQRSTU
VWXYZ (1234567890$%&*@'!?:;"")

Stratford T Italic – 28 pt

abcdefghijklmnopqrstuvwxyz
ABCDEFGHIJKLMNOPQRSTU
VWXYZ (1234567890$%&@'!?:;"")*

Stratford T Bold – 28 pt

abcdefghijklmnopqrstuvwxyz
ABCDEFGHIJKLMNOP
QRSTUVWXYZ
(1234567890$%&*@'!?:;"")

Souvenir

32 pt

The ITC Souvenir type family was designed by Ed Benguiat in 1971, based on original designs created by Morris Fuller Benton in 1914. ITC Souvenir Medium, ITC Souvenir Medium Italic, and ITC Souvenir Bold, courtesy of Linotype type foundry, Linotype Library GmbH, *www.linotype.com*.

8/10 pt

ITC Souvenir – 28 pt

abcdefghijklmnopqrstuvwxyz
ABCDEFGHIJKLMNOPQRSTU
VWXYZ (1234567890$%&*@'!?:;"")

ITC Souvenir Medium Italic – 28 pt

abcdefghijklmnopqrstuvwxyz
ABCDEFGHIJKLMNOPQRSTU
VWXYZ (1234567890
$%&@'!?:;"")*

ITC Souvenir Bold – 28 pt

abcdefghijklmnopqrstuvwxyz
ABCDEFGHIJKLMNOPQRSTU
VWXYZ (1234567890
$%&*@'!?:;"")

True Golden

36 pt

The True Golden type family is a revival of original designs created by William Morris in 1891. True Golden, True Golden Italic, and True Golden Bold, courtesy of Scriptorium type foundry, *www.fontcraft.com*.

8/10 pt

True Golden – 28 pt

abcdefghijklmnopqrstuvwxyz
ABCDEFGHIJKLMNOPQRSTU
VWXYZ (1234567890$%&*@'!?:;"")

True Golden Italic – 28 pt

abcdefghijklmnopqrstuvwxyz
ABCDEFGHIJKLMNOPQRSTU
VWXYZ (1234567890$%&@'!?:;"")*

True Golden Bold – 28 pt

abcdefghijklmnopqrstuvwxyz
ABCDEFGHIJKLMNOPQRSTU
VWXYZ (1234567890$%&*@'!?:;"")

The Old Style (or Old Face, Garalde) Type Family Category

At first, many people were disdainful of printed books, thinking them inferior to hand-lettered ones. The printing industry also met with resistance from the scribal trade because people feared for their jobs and were slow to accept change. However, public opinion shifted as publishers began to see how profitable printed books could be, and as consumers saw increased affordability and availability of books. The Catholic Church saw that printed books and materials could help spread Christianity to the European masses, and so endorsed printed books. Soon, it had become culturally accepted to collect printed books, and prestigious to own a private library.

By 1500, new Old Style fonts became available that looked slightly less calligraphic. Although they retained some of the organic feel of Humanist typefaces, Old Style letterforms were more precise, appeared lighter, and had more contrast. Serifs were also lighter, and often sharper and straighter. Another new feature was that the ascenders of lowercase letters like **b**, **d**, **f**, and **l** extended above the cap height. Also, the slanted crossbar of the Humanist lowercase **e** gave way to the horizontal crossbar of the Old Style lowercase **e**, as shown in Figure 3-9.

This stylistic shift was partly because punchcutters had improved their precision and skills at cutting letterforms into the slugs of metal used for printing. It was also partly due to a cultural acceptance of printed books—publishers no longer felt the need to make their books appear to have been hand-lettered. The introduction of Old Style fonts marked a subtle, but important shift of the printed word away from its calligraphic origins.

| NOTE |

In some classification systems, you will see Humanist typefaces appear as a subset of the Old Style type family category. This is because the two are so closely linked in style, and because Humanist typefaces were prevalent for only a few decades.

Old Style Typeface

Tendencies

∫ **Terminals**		**Terminals:** the ends of strokes may be pointed, rounded, angled, or may end in a teardrop or ball shape, but generally are lighter, sharper, and straighter than Humanist terminals; lowercase ascender terminals are often angled **Serifs:** serifs are usually more lightly bracketed and straighter than Humanist serifs
Angle of Stress		Usually moderately oblique (rises from the baseline, aiming moderately toward the left)
Contrast		Usually there is a low to medium contrast between thick and thin strokes
Proportions		**x-height:** x-height is generally tall in relation to the cap height **Set width:** characters tend to be moderate to wide **Positive/Negative space:** increased spacing and counters give a slightly lighter overall appearance than Humanist typefaces
Additional Features		• Still somewhat organic, but more precise than Humanist type • Ascenders of lowercase letters are usually taller than cap height • Lowercase *e* has a horizontal crossbar

figure | 3-9 |

Old Style typeface tendencies.

OLD STYLE TYPE FAMILY CATEGORY AND EXAMPLES

One of the most widely used Old Style typefaces was designed by William Caslon. Caslon started a foundry in England in 1720, just as strict censorship laws, which had discouraged local printing and punchcutting, were being revoked. Caslon's fonts were very popular in England, largely because of a lack of competition; Caslon's was one of a very few British foundries, so his fonts were readily available and inexpensive in England. Caslon's typefaces were exported from England to countries all over the world, by way of British colonialism, and were used in globally important documents, including the Declaration of Independence of the United States of America. In Figure 3-10, you see an example of an original typeface specimen by William Caslon.

Old Style typefaces remained popular throughout the sixteenth, seventeenth, and early eighteenth centuries; during the twentieth century, many Old Style typeface designs were revived. Many of these revivals have since been digitally revived, and remain popular today. A digital Old Style revival that emulates Caslon's work, called Caslon Classico, and some of its related type styles are shown here. Other digitally revived Old Style fonts are on the pages that follow.

figure | 3-10 |

Close-up of type from William Caslon's first specimen sheet, 1734 C.E., by permission of the British Library [C.180 ff.4(2)].

Caslon Classico

30 pt

The Caslon Classico type family was designed by Franko Luin in 1993, based on original designs created by William Caslon in 1725. Caslon Classico, Caslon Classico Italic, Caslon Classico Bold, Caslon Classico Bold Italic, and Caslon Classico Small Caps, courtesy of Linotype type foundry, Linotype Library GmbH, *www.linotype.com.*

8/10 pt

Caslon Classico – 46 pt

abcdefghijklmnop
qrstuvwxyz
ABCDEFGHIJKLMN
OPQRSUVWXYZ
(1234567890$
%&*@'!?:;"")

Caslon Classico Italic – 28 pt

abcdefghijklmnopqrstuvwxyz
ABCDEFGHIJKLMNOPQRSTU
VWXYZ(1234567890$%&@'!?:;"")*

Caslon Classico Bold – 28 pt

abcdefghijklmnopqrstuvwxyz
ABCDEFGHIJKLMNOP
QRSTUVWXYZ
(1234567890$%&*@'!?:;"")

Caslon Classico Bold Italic– 28 pt

abcdefghijklmnopqrstuvwxyz
ABCDEFGHIJKLMNOPQRSTU
VWXYZ (1234567890$%&@'!?:;"")*

Caslon Classico Small Caps– 28 pt

ABCDEFGHIJKLMNOPQRSTUVWXYZ
ABCDEFGHIJKLMNOPQRSTU
VWXYZ (1234567890$%&*@'!?:;"")

OLD STYLE TYPE FAMILY CATEGORY EXAMPLES

Bembo

32 pt

The Bembo type family was designed by Stanley Morison in 1929, based on original designs created by Francesco Griffo in 1496. Bembo, Bembo Italic, and Bembo Bold, courtesy of Linotype type foundry, Linotype Library GmbH, *www.linotype.com.*

8/10 pt

Bembo – 28 pt

abcdefghijklmnopqrstuvwxyz
ABCDEFGHIJKLMNOPQRSTU
VWXYZ (1234567890$%&★@'!?:;"")

Bembo Italic – 28 pt

abcdefghijklmnopqrstuvwxyz
ABCDEFGHIJKLMNOPQRSTU
VWXYZ (1234567890$%&★@'!?:;"")

Bembo Bold – 28 pt

abcdefghijklmnopqrstuvwxyz
ABCDEFGHIJKLMNOP
QRSTUVWXYZ
(1234567890$%&★@'!?:;"")

Caxton

The Caxton type family was designed by Leslie Usherwood in 1981. Caxton Book, Caxton Book Italic, Caxton Bold, courtesy of Linotype type foundry, Linotype Library GmbH, *www.linotype.com*.

32 pt

8/10 pt

Caxton Book – 26 pt

abcdefghijklmnopqrstuvwxyz
ABCDEFGHIJKLMNOPQRSTU
VWXYZ (1234567890$%&*@'!?:;"")

Caxton Book Italic – 26 pt

*abcdefghijklmnopqrstuvwxyz
ABCDEFGHIJKLMNOP
QRSTUVWXYZ
(1234567890$%&*@'!?:;"")*

Caxton Bold – 26 pt

**abcdefghijklmnopqrstuvwxyz
ABCDEFGHIJKLMNOP
QRSTUVWXYZ
(1234567890$%&*@'!?:;"")**

OLD STYLE TYPE FAMILY CATEGORY EXAMPLES

Goudy Old Style
32 pt

The Goudy Old Style type family is a revival of original designs created by Frederic Goudy in 1915. Goudy Old Style, Goudy Old Style Italic, and Goudy Old Style Bold, courtesy of Bitstream Inc. type foundry, *www.myfonts.com*.   8/10 pt

Goudy Old Style – 28 pt

abcdefghijklmnopqrstuvwxyz
ABCDEFGHIJKLMNOPQRSTU
VWXYZ (1234567890$%&*@'!?:;"")

Goudy Old Style Italic – 28 pt

abcdefghijklmnopqrstuvwxyz
ABCDEFGHIJKLMNOPQRSTU
VWXYZ (1234567890$%&@'!?:;"")*

Goudy Old Style Bold – 28 pt

abcdefghijklmnopqrstuvwxyz
ABCDEFGHIJKLMNOP
QRSTUVWXYZ
(1234567890$%&*@'!?:;"")

Original Garamond

24 pt

The PT Original Garamond type family was designed by Gayaneh Bagdasaryan in 2002, based on designs produced by the Stempel Foundry in 1925, which were based on original designs created by Claude Garamond in 1592. PT Original Garamond, PT Original Garamond Italic, and PT Original Garamond Bold, courtesy of Paratype type foundry, *www.paratype.com*.

8/10 pt

PT Original Garamond – 28 pt

abcdefghijklmnopqrstuvwxyz
ABCDEFGHIJKLMNOPQRSTU
VWXYZ (1234567890$%&*@'!?:;"")

PT Original Garamond Italic – 28 pt

abcdefghijklmnopqrstuvwxyz
ABCDEFGHIJKLMNOPQRSTU
VWXYZ (1234567890$%&@'!?:;"")*

PT Original Garamond Bold – 28 pt

abcdefghijklmnopqrstuvwxyz
ABCDEFGHIJKLMNOP
QRSTUVWXYZ
(1234567890$%&*@'!?:;"")

Palatino

32 pt

The Palatino type family was designed by Hermann Zapf in 1950. (Today, a revived version is available as Palatino Nova.) Palatino Roman, Palatino Italic, and Palatino Bold, courtesy of Linotype type foundry, Linotype Library GmbH, *www.linotype.com.*

8/10 pt

Palatino Roman – 28 pt

abcdefghijklmnopqrstuvwxyz
ABCDEFGHIJKLMNOPQRSTU
VWXYZ (1234567890$%&*@'!?:;"")

Palatino Italic – 28 pt

abcdefghijklmnopqrstuvwxyz
ABCDEFGHIJKLMNOPQRSTU
VWXYZ (1234567890$%&@'!?:;"")*

Palatino Bold – 28 pt

abcdefghijklmnopqrstuvwxyz
ABCDEFGHIJKLMNOP
QRSTUVWXYZ
(1234567890$%&*@'!?:;"")

Times New Roman

24 pt

The Times New Roman type family was designed by Stanley Morison in 1931, for *The Times* of London. Times New Roman, Times New Roman Italic, and Times New Roman Bold, courtesy of Linotype type foundry, Linotype Library GmbH, *www.linotype.com.*

8/10 pt

Time New Roman – 28 pt

abcdefghijklmnopqrstuvwxyz
ABCDEFGHIJKLMNOPQRSTU
VWXYZ (1234567890$%&*@'!?:;"")

Time New Roman Italic – 28 pt

*abcdefghijklmnopqrstuvwxyz
ABCDEFGHIJKLMNOPQRSTU
VWXYZ (1234567890$%&*@'!?:;"")*

Time New Roman – 28 pt

**abcdefghijklmnopqrstuvwxyz
ABCDEFGHIJKLMNOP
QRSTUVWXYZ
(1234567890$%&*@'!?:;"")**

▶ THE *designer* AT WORK

'Ray' Greiman portrait by Made in Spacers, www.madeinspace.la.

april greiman

How did you get started as a designer? Tell us about your first job in design and the evolution of your career.

I think I got fired from my first job in design. I was working for GAF creating a packaging design for concrete mix; it was too cool! I also did the graphic interface for a camera and a projector. Unfortunately, I was accused of coming up with solutions that were too unusual. They got produced, but then I was reprimanded for never filling out my time sheets. Frankly, I was too self-conscious, because I worked over ten hours a day, and they only allowed us to work 9-5! So rather than get in trouble for putting so many hours in, I just avoided the time sheets. My boss wasn't very easy to discuss things with either, I should say!

What do you do to get your creative juices flowing when you start a new project?

I like to get quiet in my mind—go out into nature. The desert always has stimulated my creativity and thinking.

What can you share with us about your design process? What role does technology play in that process?

Technology is omnipresent in our field. Even a pencil is technology, don't forget!

How has the role of typography in design changed over the last decade?

Type is image. This is a major shift from the times when I was doing typography, often in metal.

What role should social responsibility play in design? What can designers contribute to our society?

Designers shouldn't just rely on coming up with cool solutions to problems; they must consider the question of how their designs impact culture. This question is getting tougher, as the global culture is getting more and more complex. As designers work, they must be conscious of the impact of their actions and the products they help

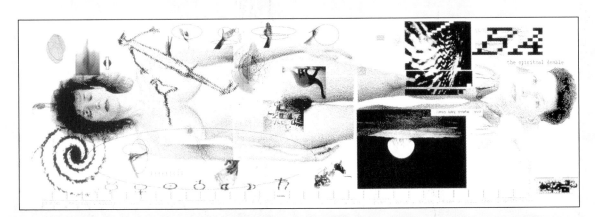

"Does it Make Sense?" *Design Quarterly #133,* by April Greiman for Walker Art Center, Mildred Friedman, Curator. *Courtesy of Made in Space,* www.madeinspace.la.

promote. Design, unfortunately, seems to be more and more market-driven in America.

What advice do you have for design students and new designers who are just entering the field today?

Make sure you absolutely love what you do. If not, go into something else. This is one tough cookie of a field, albeit rewarding, nourishing, fun, and educational.

April Greiman, Made in Space, Los Angeles, California
www.madeinspace.la

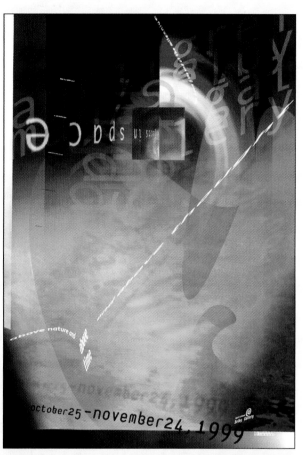

Samitaur Constructs poster by April Greiman for the Venice Biennale. *Courtesy of Made in Space*, www.madeinspace.la.

(Top) Poster by April Greiman for the Ringling School of Art Selby Gallery. *Courtesy of Made in Space*, www.madeinspace.la.

(Bottom) Identity design by April Greiman for the Southern California Institute of Architecture, 2004. *Courtesy of Made in Space*, www.madeinspace.la.

The Transitional (or Réales) Type Family Category

Old Style typefaces dominated the international printing industry for a long time, about two hundred years. Then, in the eighteenth century, popular styles of type began to change again, in response to technological advancements in printing. Type designs from this period began a stylistic transition from the Old Style typefaces of the sixteenth and seventeenth centuries to the Modern ones of the nineteenth century—hence, the type family category name Transitional.

The first Transitional typeface was called *Roman du Roi*, meaning "typeface of the King." It was designed in 1693 by Philip Grandjean, at the commission of Louis XIV (an example of Grandjean's Roman du Roi can be viewed in Chapter 1 on page 13). In response to complaints of declining production quality in trade items, the king had set up a committee to establish new national standards for a number of crafts, one of which was typography. As a part of this effort, a new typeface design was commissioned for the exclusive use of the court. This new typeface was to be based on technical, scientific, and mathematical principles, rather than on scribal calligraphy. A more vertical angle of stress and higher contrast reflected the distancing of Transitional fonts from their calligraphic origins. Finer, more precise shapes and increased contrast were made possible by newly emerging technologies like engraving and improvements in type casting. Although it was illegal for anybody outside the court of Louis XIV to use Roman du Roi, contemporary designers emulated the more vertical angle of stress, the narrower letter set widths, and the higher contrast anyway.

Transitional Typeface

Tendencies

ℓ	**Terminals**	**Terminals:** the ends of strokes may be pointed, rounded, angled, or may end in a teardrop or ball shape, but generally are lighter, sharper, and straighter than Old Style terminals; lowercase ascender terminals are often horizontal or very slightly angled
		Serifs: serifs usually are lightly bracketed and straighter and shaper than Old Style serifs
	Angle of Stress	Usually vertical (perpendicular to the baseline) or slightly oblique (aiming slightly toward the left)
	Contrast	Usually there is medium contrast between thick and thin strokes, generally higher contrast than Old Style typefaces
	Proportions	**x-height:** generally of medium height in relation to the cap height
		Set width: characters tend to be narrower than Old Style typefaces
		Positive/Negative space: increased spacing and counters give a slightly lighter overall appearance than Old Style typefaces
	Additional Features	• More precise than Old Style type • Ascenders of lowercase letters may be slightly taller than cap height

figure | 3-11 |

Transitional typeface tendencies.

TRANSITIONAL TYPE FAMILY CATEGORY AND EXAMPLES

An important contributor to the development of Transitional typeface designs was John Baskerville. He not only designed typefaces that extended the trend toward a more technical aesthetic, he also invented smoother papers and improved tools and inks that could produce more delicate and precise letterforms. Figure 3-12 shows an example of Baskerville's work.

Many digital revivals of Transitional typefaces exist, including some based on the work of John Baskerville. One such font, called John Baskerville, and some of its related type styles appear below; other digitally revived Transitional fonts are on the pages that follow.

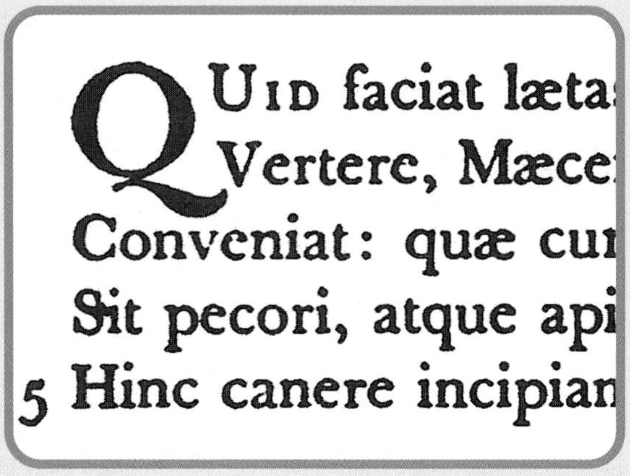

figure | 3-12 |

Close-up of type from *Latin Virgil*, printed by John Baskerville, 1757 C.E., from *Printing Types* by Alexander Lawson. *Copyright ©1971 by Alexander Lawson, reprinted by permission of Beacon Press, Boston.*

John Baskerville

24 pt

The John Baskerville type family was designed by Frantisek Storm, based on original designs created by John Baskerville in 1757. John Baskerville, John Baskerville Italic, John Baskerville Bold, and John Baskerville Bold Italic, courtesy of Storm type foundry, *www.stormtype.com*.

8/10 pt

John Baskerville – 38 pt

abcdefghijklm
nopqrstuvwxyz
ABCDEFGHIJKLM
NOPQRSTUVWXYZ
(1234567890$%&*@'!?:;"")

John Baskerville Italic – 28 pt

abcdefghijklmnopqrstuvwxyz
ABCDEFGHIJKLMNOPQRSTU
VWXYZ (1234567890$%&*@'!?:;"")

John Baskerville Bold – 28 pt

abcdefghijklmnopqrstuvwxyz
ABCDEFGHIJKLMN
OPQRSTUVWXYZ
(1234567890$%&*@'!?:;"")

John Baskerville Bold Italic – 28 pt

abcdefghijklmnopqrstuvwxyz
ABCDEFGHIJKLMNOPQRSTU
VWXYZ (1234567890$%&*@'!?:;"")

Cheltenham

32 pt

The Cheltenham type family was designed by Morris Fuller Benton, Hannibal Ingalls Kimball, and Bertram Grosvenor Goodhue in 1904. Cheltenham, Cheltenham Italic, and Cheltenham Bold, courtesy of Bitstream Inc. type foundry, *www.myfonts.com*.

8/10 pt

Cheltenham – 28 pt

abcdefghijklmnopqrstuvwxyz
ABCDEFGHIJKLMNOPQRSTU
VWXYZ (1234567890$%&*@'!?:;"")

Cheltenham Italic – 28 pt

*abcdefghijklmnopqrstuvwxyz
ABCDEFGHIJKLMNOPQRSTU
VWXYZ (1234567890$%&*@'!?:;"")*

Cheltenham Bold – 28 pt

**abcdefghijklmnopqrstuvwxyz
ABCDEFGHIJKLMNOP
QRSTUVWXYZ
(1234567890$%&*@'!?:;"")**

Cochin

The Cochin type family was expanded by Matthew Carter in 1975, based on original designs created by Georges Peignot in 1914. Cochin, Cochin Italic, and Cochin Bold, courtesy of Linotype type foundry, Linotype Library GmbH, *www.linotype.com*.

32 pt

8/10 pt

Cochin – 28 pt

abcdefghijklmnopqrstuvwxyz
ABCDEFGHIJKLMNOPQRSTU
VWXYZ (1234567890$%&*@'!?:;"")

Cochin Italic – 28 pt

abcdefghijklmnopqrstuvwxyz
ABCDEFGHIJKLMNOPQRSTU
VWXYZ (1234567890$%&³@'!?:;"")*

Cochin Bold – 28 pt

abcdefghijklmnopqrstuvwxyz
ABCDEFGHIJKLMNOPQRSTU
VWXYZ (1234567890$%&*@'!?:;"")

TRANSITIONAL TYPE FAMILY CATEGORY EXAMPLES

Corona

32 pt

The Corona type family is a revival of original designs created by Chauncey H. Griffith in 1941. Corona, Corona Italic, and Corona Bold Face No. 2, courtesy of Linotype type foundry, Linotype Library GmbH, *www.linotype.com.*

8/10 pt

Corona – 28 pt

abcdefghijklmnopqrstuvwxyz
ABCDEFGHIJKLMNOP
QRSTUVWXYZ
(1234567890$%&*@'!?:;"")

Corona Italic – 28 pt

*abcdefghijklmnopqrstuvwxyz
ABCDEFGHIJKLMNOP
QRSTUVWXYZ
(1234567890$%&*@'!?:;"")*

Corona Bold Face No. 2 – 28 pt

**abcdefghijklmnopqrstuvwxyz
ABCDEFGHIJKLMNOP
QRSTUVWXYZ
(1234567890$%&*@'!?:;"")**

Electra

32 pt

The Electra type family was created by W. A. Dwiggins in 1935. In 1988 Linotype expanded this type family with four different weights, true italics, and display versions. Electra LH Regular, Electra LH Cursive, and Electra LH Bold, courtesy of Linotype type foundry, Linotype Library GmbH, *www.linotype.com.*

8/10 pt

Electra LH Regular – 28 pt

abcdefghijklmnopqrstuvwxyz
ABCDEFGHIJKLMNOPQRSTU
VWXYZ (1234567890$%&*@'!?:;"")

Electra LH Cursive – 28 pt

abcdefghijklmnopqrstuvwxyz
ABCDEFGHIJKLMNOPQRSTU
VWXYZ (1234567890$%&@'!?:;"")*

Electra LH Bold – 28 pt

abcdefghijklmnopqrstuvwxyz
ABCDEFGHIJKLMNOPQRSTU
VWXYZ (1234567890$%&*@'!?:;"")

TRANSITIONAL TYPE FAMILY CATEGORY EXAMPLES

Mrs. Eaves

32 pt

The Mrs. Eaves type family was designed by Zuzana Licko in 1996, based on original designs created by John Baskerville in 1757. Mrs. Eaves Roman, Mrs. Eaves Italic, and Mrs. Eaves Bold, courtesy of Emigre type foundry, *www.emigre.com*.

9/10 pt

Mrs. Eaves Roman – 30 pt

abcdefghijklmnopqrstuvwxyz
ABCDEFGHIJKLMNOPQRSTU
VWXYZ (1234567890$%&*@'!?:;"")

Mrs. Eaves Italic – 30 pt

abcdefghijklmnopqrstuvwxyz
ABCDEFGHIJKLMNOPQRSTU
VWXYZ (1234567890$%&@'!?:;"")*

Mrs. Eaves Bold – 30 pt

abcdefghijklmnopqrstuvwxyz
ABCDEFGHIJKLMNOPQRSTU
VWXYZ (1234567890$%&*@'!?:;"")

Versailles

30 pt

The Versailles type family was designed by Adrian Frutiger in 1984. Versailles Roman, Versailles Italic, and Versailles Bold, courtesy of Linotype type foundry, Linotype Library GmbH, *www.linotype.com.*

8/10 pt

Versailles Roman – 28 pt

abcdefghijklmnopqrstuvwxyz
ABCDEFGHIJKLMNOP
QRSTUVWXYZ
(1234567890$%&*@'!?:;"")

Versailles Italic – 28 pt

abcdefghijklmnopqrstuvwxyz
ABCDEFGHIJKLMNOP
QRSTUVWXYZ
(1234567890$%&@'!?:;"")*

Versailles Bold – 28 pt

abcdefghijklmnopqrstuvwxyz
ABCDEFGHIJKLMNOP
QRSTUVWXYZ
(1234567890$%&*@'!?:;"")

The Modern (or Didone) Type Family Category

The word "modern" can be confusing because it has many common uses. Of course, it can refer to something that is contemporary or new. Sometimes when we say modern, we are referring to the Modern Art movement of the early twentieth century, even though art from that time period isn't new (modern) anymore. Ironically, the typefaces which are categorized into the Modern type family category are NOT the same ones that we associate with the Modern Art movement of the twentieth century. This is an important differentiation.

When classifying type, the term modern refers to the roman typefaces developed in the late eighteenth and nineteenth centuries that ushered in the "Modern age." These typefaces tend to have narrow set widths, high contrast, lightly bracketed or unbracketed serifs, short x-height ratios, and a vertical angle of stress. They look very precise and mechanical. They reflect the advancing technical capabilities of societies undergoing industrialization, and so are almost completely stylistically divorced from their calligraphic origins.

figure | 3-13 |

Modern typeface
tendencies.

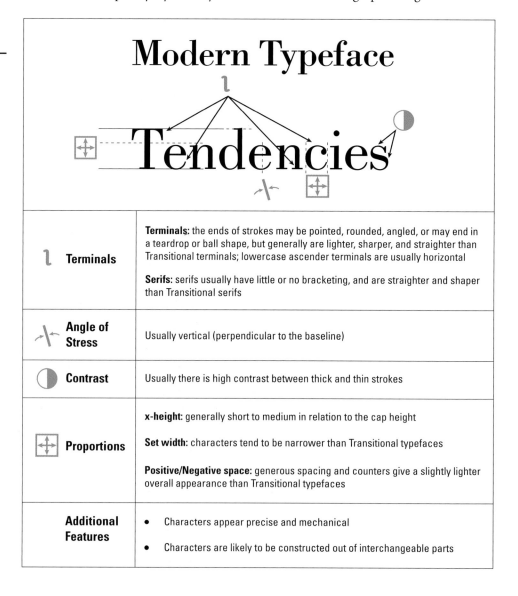

𝟙 **Terminals**	**Terminals:** the ends of strokes may be pointed, rounded, angled, or may end in a teardrop or ball shape, but generally are lighter, sharper, and straighter than Transitional terminals; lowercase ascender terminals are usually horizontal	
	Serifs: serifs usually have little or no bracketing, and are straighter and shaper than Transitional serifs	
Angle of Stress	Usually vertical (perpendicular to the baseline)	
Contrast	Usually there is high contrast between thick and thin strokes	
Proportions	**x-height:** generally short to medium in relation to the cap height	
	Set width: characters tend to be narrower than Transitional typefaces	
	Positive/Negative space: generous spacing and counters give a slightly lighter overall appearance than Transitional typefaces	
Additional Features	• Characters appear precise and mechanical	
	• Characters are likely to be constructed out of interchangeable parts	

MODERN TYPE FAMILY CATEGORY AND EXAMPLES

Two of the most notable designers of Modern typefaces were Firmin Didot of France and Giambattista Bodoni of Italy. Both men used opposition of visual elements (like thick vs. thin and short vs. tall) to create a high level of drama in their typefaces. The fonts they cut had a mechanized aesthetic—they were very precise, and featured a vertical angle of stress and interchangeable parts, as you can see in the example of Bodoni's work, pictured in Figure 3-14. The typefaces that Bodoni and Didot designed were widely emulated during their own time, and have experienced many revivals since. One example of a digital revival based on Bodoni's designs, called Bodoni EF, appears below, along with some of its related type styles. Other digitally revived Modern fonts are on the pages that follow.

figure | 3-14 |

Close-up of text from Giambattista Bodoni's *Manuale Tipografico* of 1818.

Bodoni EF
32 pt

The Bodoni EF type family and the Bodoni No 2 type family are revivals of original designs created by Giambattista Bodoni in 1798. Bodoni EF Regular, Bodoni EF Regular Italic, Bodoni EF Bold, Bodoni EF Bold Italic, and Bodoni No 2 EF Ultra, courtesy of Elsner + Flake type foundry, *www.elsner-flake.com*.

8/10 pt

Bodoni EF Regular – 46 pt

abcdefghijklmnop
qrstuvwxyz
ABCDEFGHIJKLMNO
PQRSTUVWXYZ
(1234567890$%
&*@'!?:;"")

MODERN TYPE FAMILY CATEGORY EXAMPLES

Bodoni EF Regular Italic – 24 pt

abcdefghijklmnopqrstuvwxyz
ABCDEFGHIJKLMNOPQRSTU
VWXYZ (1234567890$%&@'!?:;"")*

Bodoni EF Bold – 24 pt

abcdefghijklmnopqrstuvwxyz
ABCDEFGHIJKLMNOPQRSTU
VWXYZ (1234567890$%&*@'!?:;"")

Bodoni EF Bold Italic – 24 pt

abcdefghijklmnopqrstuvwxyz
ABCDEFGHIJKLMNOPQRSTU
VWXYZ (1234567890$%&*@'!?:;"")

Bodoni No 2 EF Ultra – 24 pt

abcdefghijklmnopqrstuvwxyz
ABCDEFGHIJKLMNOP
QRSTUVWXYZ
(1234567890$%&*@'!?:;"")

Bernhard Modern

30 pt

The Bernhard Modern type family is a revival of original designs created by Lucian Bernhard in 1937. Bernhard Modern, Bernhard Modern Italic, and Bernhard Modern Bold, courtesy of Bitstream Inc. type foundry, *www.myfonts.com*.

8/10 pt

Bernhard Modern – 28 pt

abcdefghijklmnopqrstuvwxyz
ABCDEFGHIJKLMNOPQRSTU
VWXYZ (1234567890$%&*@'!?:;"")

Bernhard Modern Italic – 28 pt

*abcdefghijklmnopqrstuvwxyz
ABCDEFGHIJKLMNOPQRSTU
VWXYZ (1234567890$%&*@'!?:;"")*

Bernhard Modern Bold – 28 pt

**abcdefghijklmnopqrstuvwxyz
ABCDEFGHIJKLMNOP
QRSTUVWXYZ
(1234567890$%&*@'!?:;"")**

MODERN TYPE FAMILY CATEGORY EXAMPLES

Craw Modern

22 pt

The Craw Modern type family is a revival of original designs created by Freeman Craw in 1964. Craw Modern URW T Regular, Craw Modern URW T Regular Italic, and Craw Modern URW T Bold, courtesy of URW++ type foundry, *www.urwpp.de/english/home.htm.*

7/10 pt

Craw Modern URW T Regular – 20 pt

abcdefghijklmnopqrstuvwxyz
ABCDEFGHIJKLMNOPQRSTU
VWXYZ (1234567890$%&*@'!?:;"")

Craw Modern URW T Regular Italic – 20 pt

abcdefghijklmnopqrstuvwxyz
ABCDEFGHIJKLMNOPQRSTU
VWXYZ (1234567890$%&@'!?:;"")*

Craw Modern URW T Bold – 20 pt

abcdefghijklmnopqrstuvwxyz
ABCDEFGHIJKLMNOPQRSTU
VWXYZ (1234567890$%&*@'!?:;"")

De Vinne

36 pt

The De Vinne type family is a revival of original designs created by Gustav F. Schroeder in 1890. De Vinne Roman, De Vinne Italic, and De Vinne Text, courtesy of Bitstream Inc. type foundry, *www.myfonts.com*.

8/10 pt

De Vinne Roman – 28 pt

abcdefghijklmnopqrstuvwxyz
ABCDEFGHIJKLMNOPQRSTU
VWXYZ (1234567890$%&*@'!?:;"")

De Vinne Italic – 28 pt

abcdefghijklmnopqrstuvwxyz
ABCDEFGHIJKLMNOPQRSTU
VWXYZ (1234567890$%&@'!?:;"")*

De Vinne Text – 28 pt

abcdefghijklmnopqrstuvwxyz
ABCDEFGHIJKLMNOP
QRSTUVWXYZ
(1234567890$%&*@'!?:;"")

Linotype Didot
24 pt

The Linotype Didot type family was created by Adrian Frutiger and the Linotype Studio based on original designs created by Firmin Didot in 1784. Linotype Didot Roman, Linotype Didot Italic, and Linotype Didot Bold, courtesy of Linotype type foundry, Linotype Library GmbH, *www.linotype.com*. 7/10 pt

Linotype Didot Roman – 28 pt

abcdefghijklmnopqrstuvwxyz
ABCDEFGHIJKLMNOPQRSTU
VWXYZ (1234567890$%&*@'!?:;"")

Linotype Didot Italic – 28 pt

abcdefghijklmnopqrstuvwxyz
ABCDEFGHIJKLMNOPQRSTU
VWXYZ (1234567890$%&@'!?:; "")*

Linotype Didot Bold – 28 pt

abcdefghijklmnopqrstuvwxyz
ABCDEFGHIJKLMNOP
QRSTUVWXYZ
(1234567890$%&*@'!?:;"")

Modern No 216

20 pt

The ITC Modern No 216 type family was designed by Edward Benguiat in 1982. Modern No 216 Medium, Modern No 216 Medium Italic, and Modern No 216 Bold, courtesy of Linotype type foundry, Linotype Library GmbH, *www.linotype.com.*

8/10 pt

Modern No 216 Medium – 24 pt

abcdefghijklmnopqrstuvwxyz
ABCDEFGHIJKLMNOPQRSTU
VWXYZ (1234567890$%&*@'!?:;"")

Modern No 216 Medium italic – 24 pt

*abcdefghijklmnopqrstuvwxyz
ABCDEFGHIJKLMNOPQRSTU
VWXYZ (1234567890$%&*@'!?:;"")*

Modern No 216 Bold – 24 pt

**abcdefghijklmnopqrstuvwxyz
ABCDEFGHIJKLMNOP
QRSTUVWXYZ
(1234567890$%&*@'!?:;"")**

Walbaum

30 pt

The Walbaum type family is a revival of original designs created by Justus Erich Walbaum in 1919. Walbaum Roman, Walbaum Italic, and Walbaum Bold, courtesy of Linotype type foundry, Linotype Library GmbH, *www.linotype.com.*

8/10 pt

Walbaum Roman – 28 pt

abcdefghijklmnopqrstuvwxyz
ABCDEFGHIJKLMNOP
QRSTUVWXYZ
(1234567890$%&*@'!?:;"")

Walbaum Italic – 28 pt

*abcdefghijklmnopqrstuvwxyz
ABCDEFGHIJKLMNOPQRSTU
VWXYZ (1234567890$%&*@'!?:;"")*

Walbaum Bold – 28 pt

**abcdefghijklmnopqrstuvwxyz
ABCDEFGHIJKLMNOP
QRSTUVWXYZ
(1234567890$%&*@'!?:;"")**

The Egyptian Type Family Category (or Slab Serif, Square Serif, Mécanes, Antiques)

Egyptian typefaces emerged as display type in Victorian advertisements in the nineteenth century. Because the new offset lithography technology made it easier and cheaper than ever to print advertisement posters and flyers, designers were quickly developing bold and decorative typefaces meant to grab the attention of their audience. Egyptian typefaces are easy to recognize by their heavy, squared serifs and their chunky appearance. The name Egyptian refers to the heavy, horizontal aesthetic of ancient Egyptian art, architecture, and hieroglyphics; the typeface gained popularity at about the time of Napoleon's conquest of Egypt. The Egyptian type family category is also called the Slab Serif or Square Serif type family category because of its characteristic heavy, unbracketed serifs. Egyptian typefaces are generally heavy, have low contrast, and often have a vertical angle of stress, as shown in Figure 3-15.

figure | 3-15 |

Egyptian typeface
tendencies.

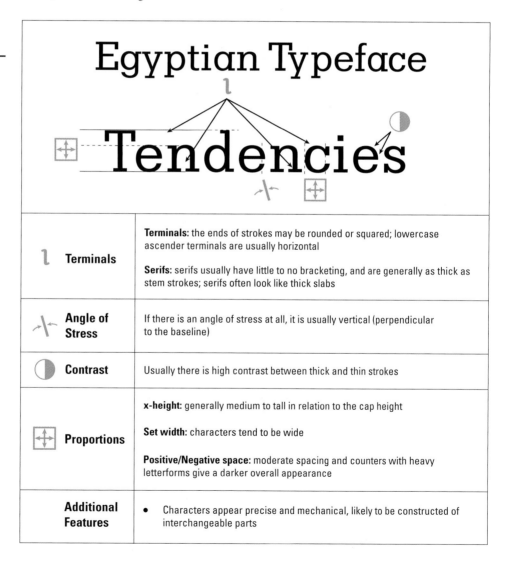

ʅ	**Terminals**	**Terminals:** the ends of strokes may be rounded or squared; lowercase ascender terminals are usually horizontal **Serifs:** serifs usually have little to no bracketing, and are generally as thick as stem strokes; serifs often look like thick slabs
	Angle of Stress	If there is an angle of stress at all, it is usually vertical (perpendicular to the baseline)
	Contrast	Usually there is high contrast between thick and thin strokes
	Proportions	**x-height:** generally medium to tall in relation to the cap height **Set width:** characters tend to be wide **Positive/Negative space:** moderate spacing and counters with heavy letterforms give a darker overall appearance
	Additional Features	• Characters appear precise and mechanical, likely to be constructed of interchangeable parts

EGYPTIAN TYPE FAMILY CATEGORY AND EXAMPLES

In 1845, Robert Besley designed the first Clarendon typeface—a highly legible, bold Egyptian typeface, with lightly bracketed slab serifs and low contrast, pictured in Figure 3-16. Because so many fonts mimicked Besley's design, the name Clarendon is sometimes used to describe any Egyptian typeface that has slight contrast and bracketing. Egyptian typefaces, including Clarendon, remained popular until the 1920s, then experienced a revival in the 1950s. A digital font based on Besley's Clarendon, called Clarendon, is shown here, along with some of its associated type styles. Other digital revivals of Egyptian typefaces follow.

uousque tandem abutere Catilina, patientia nostra
uamdiu nos etiam furor iste tuus eludet ? quem
nem sese effrenata jactabit audacia ? nihilne te no
rnum præsidium palatii, nihilne urbis vigiliæ, nil
mor populi, nihil consensus bonorum omnium, nil
ic munitissimus habendi senatus locus, nihil horu
£1234567890
SALES BY PUBLIC AUCTION.

figure | 3-16 |

Type specimen of an early Clarendon by Robert Besley.

Clarendon

28 pt

The Clarendon type family is a revival of original designs by Robert Besley of the Fann Street Foundry in 1845. URW Clarendon T Regular, URW Clarendon T Regular Oblique, URW Clarendon T Extra Bold, URW Clarendon T Extra Bold Oblique, and URW Clarendon T Light, courtesy of URW++, type foundry, *www.urwpp.de/english/home.htm*. 6/10 pt

URW Clarendon T Regular – 42 pt

abcdefghijklmnop
qrstuvwxyz
ABCDEFGHIJKLMN
OPQRSTUVWXYZ
(1234567890$%
&*@'!?:;"")

URW Clarendon T Regular Oblique – 24 pt

abcdefghijklmnopqrstuvwxyz

ABCDEFGHIJKLMNOPQRST

VWXYZ (1234567890$%&*@'!?:;"")

URW Clarendon T Extra Bold – 24 pt

abcdefghijklmnopqrstuvwxyz

ABCDEFGHIJKLMNOPQRST

VWXYZ (1234567890$%&*@'!?:;"")

URW Clarendon T Extra Bold Oblique – 24 pt

abcdefghijklmnopqrstuvwxyz

ABCDEFGHIJKLMNOPQRST

VWXYZ (1234567890$%&*@'!?:;"")

URW Clarendon T Light – 24 pt

abcdefghijklmnopqrstuvwxyz

ABCDEFGHIJKLMNOPQRSTU

VWXYZ (1234567890$%&*@'!?:;"")

EGYPTIAN TYPE FAMILY CATEGORY EXAMPLES

American Typewriter

24 pt

The ITC American Typewriter type family was designed by Joel Kaden and Tony Stan in 1974. ITC American Typewriter Light, ITC American Typewriter Medium, and ITC American Typewriter Bold, courtesy of Linotype type foundry, Linotype Library GmbH, www.linotype.com.

6/10 pt

ITC American Typewriter Light – 28 pt

abcdefghijklmnopqrstuvwxyz
ABCDEFGHIJKLMNO
PQRSTUVWXYZ
(1234567890$%&*@'!?:;"")

ITC American Typewriter Medium – 28 pt

abcdefghijklmnopqrstuvwxyz
ABCDEFGHIJKLMNO
PQRSTUVWXYZ
(1234567890$%&*@'!?:;"")

ITC American Typewriter Bold – 28 pt

abcdefghijklmnopqrstuvwxyz
ABCDEFGHIJKLMNO
PQRSTUVWXYZ
(1234567890$%&*@'!?:;"")

PT Courier

28 pt

The PT Courier type family was designed by Tagir Safayev and Alexander Tarbeev in 1990, based on the original Courier typewriter face of International Business Machines, designed by Howard Kettler in 1956. PT Courier, PT Courier Oblique, and PT Courier Bold, courtesy of ParaType type foundry, *www.paratype.com.*

8/10 pt

PT Courier – 28 pt

abcdefghijklmnopqrstuvwxyz
ABCDEFGHIJKLMNOPQRSTUVWXYZ
(1234567890$%&*@'!?:;"")

PT Courier Oblique – 28 pt

*abcdefghijklmnopqrstuvwxyz
ABCDEFGHIJKLMNOPQRSTUVWXYZ
(1234567890$%&*@'!?:;"")*

PT Courier Bold – 28 pt

**abcdefghijklmnopqrstuvwxyz
ABCDEFGHIJKLMNOPQRSTUVWXYZ
(1234567890$%&*@'!?:;"")**

EGYPTIAN TYPE FAMILY CATEGORY EXAMPLES

Egyptienne F

24 pt

The Egyptienne F type family is the text face design created by Adrian Frutiger in 1956. Egyptienne F 55 Roman, Egyptienne F 56 Italic, and Egyptienne F 65 Bold, courtesy of Linotype type foundry, Linotype Library GmbH, *www.linotype.com*.

8/10 pt

Egyptienne F 55 Roman – 28 pt

abcdefghijklmnopqrstuvwxyz
ABCDEFGHIJKLMNOPQRSTU
VWXYZ (1234567890$%&*@'!?:;"")

Egyptienne F 56 Italic – 28 pt

*abcdefghijklmnopqrstuvwxyz
ABCDEFGHIJKLMNOPQRSTU
VWXYZ (1234567890$%&*@'!?:;"")*

Egyptienne F 65 Bold – 28 pt

**abcdefghijklmnopqrstuvwxyz
ABCDEFGHIJKLMNOP
QRSTUVWXYZ
(1234567890$%&*@'!?:;"")**

Memphis

The Memphis type family was designed by Emil Rudolf Wolf in 1929. Memphis Medium, Memphis Medium Italic, and Memphis Bold, courtesy of Linotype type foundry, Linotype Library GmbH, *www.linotype.com.*

8/10 pt

Memphis Medium – 28 pt

abcdefghijklmnopqrstuvwxyz
ABCDEFGHIJKLMNOPQRSTU
VWXYZ (1234567890$%&*@'!?:;"'")

Memphis Medium Italic – 28 pt

abcdefghijklmnopqrstuvwxyz
ABCDEFGHIJKLMNOPQRSTU
VWXYZ (1234567890$%&@'!?:;"'")*

Memphis Bold – 28 pt

abcdefghijklmnopqrstuvwxyz
ABCDEFGHIJKLMNOPQRSTU
VWXYZ (1234567890$%&*@'!?:;"'")

Stymie

32 pt

The Stymie type family is a revival of original designs created by Morris Fuller Benton, Sol Hess, and Gerry Powell in 1931. Stymie Medium, Stymie Medium Italic, and Stymie Bold, courtesy of Bitstream Inc. type foundry, *www.myfonts.com.*

8/10 pt

Stymie Medium – 28 pt

abcdefghijklmnopqrstuvwxyz
ABCDEFGHIJKLMNOPQRSTU
VWXYZ (1234567890$%&*@'!?:;"")

Stymie Medium Italic – 28 pt

*abcdefghijklmnopqrstuvwxyz
ABCDEFGHIJKLMNOPQRSTU
VWXYZ (1234567890$%&*@'!?:;"")*

Stymie Bold – 28 pt

**abcdefghijklmnopqrstuvwxyz
ABCDEFGHIJKLMNOPQRSTU
VWXYZ (1234567890$%&*@'!?:;"")**

Volta

32 pt

The Volta type family is a revival of original designs created by Konrad F. Bauer and Walter Baum 1955. Volta T Medium, Volta T Medium Italic, and Volta T Bold, courtesy of URW++ type foundry, *www.urwpp.de/english/home.htm*.

8/10 pt

Volta T Medium– 24 pt

abcdefghijklmnopqrstuvwxyz
ABCDEFGHIJKLMNOP
QRSTUVWXYZ
(1234567890$%&*@'!?:;"")

Volta T Medium Italic – 24 pt

abcdefghijklmnopqrstuvwxyz
ABCDEFGHIJKLMNOP
QRSTUVWXYZ
(1234567890$%&@'!?:;"")*

Volta T Bold – 24 pt

abcdefghijklmnop
qrstuvwxyz
ABCDEFGHIJKLMNOP
QRSTUVWXYZ
(1234567890$%&*@'!?:;"")

The Sans-Serif Type Family Category

Up until now, all of the type family categories we have discussed have included only roman, or serif, typefaces. Until the twentieth century, typefaces without serifs (sans serif) weren't very popular. Although there were some sans-serif typefaces designed in the nineteenth century, they were mostly used as display type and were considered to be ugly—or grotesque—by the fashion standards of the day. The sans-serif types that were designed before the twentieth century, like Akzidenz-Grotesk for example, are therefore referred to as Grotesque sans serifs.

| NOTE |

Sans is the French word for "without"; so, the literal translation of sans serif is "without serifs" (often used in the adjective form: sans-serif).

Sans-serif typefaces gained popularity in the early twentieth century. Designers were searching for typefaces that could express their experiences as members of fast-paced industrialized societies, unique from any human civilizations that had come before. Industrialization had changed the world drastically, in only a short period of time. New technologies had changed the nature of whole industries, resulting in a wide-scale shift from agriculturally based economies to industrially based ones. This caused an enormous shift in wealth and power, as people swarmed to the cities where work in factories had become available. Human cultures were experiencing tremendous growing pains, as people tried to adjust to their new fast-paced and automated world. Advances in transportation and communication technologies started the process of globalization; advances in the technologies of war made World War I more devastating in scale and scope than any before it.

Democratic and Communist political movements that rebuffed the traditional power structures of royalty and wealth were gaining popularity worldwide. Designers wished to create an aesthetic that would reject the concept of class, and instead reflect emerging egalitarian values. They sought a new typographic and artistic voice that could differentiate their work from that of the previous generations.

The Modern Art movement emerged as artists and designers began to strip away the excessive decorations that had been popular with the rich and powerful classes. Now, more reading materials and advertisements than ever before became available to more people than ever before; but ironically, people had less time for reading. The sans-serif typefaces that were designed in conjunction with the Modern Art movement symbolized the voice of a new generation that was living in an industrialized world.

Some sans-serif fonts designed in the twentieth century, like Gill Sans for example, were based on the proportions of the first Humanist roman fonts, and so these sans serifs are referred to as Humanist sans serifs. Other twentieth-century sans-serif fonts were based on geometric proportions, to pay tribute to the mechanization of modern life that had come with the industrial revolution and the "machine age." These fonts, like Futura for example, are referred to as Geometric sans serifs.

So, sans-serif typefaces are divided into three categories: Grotesques, Geometrics, and Humanists. To differentiate between these three kinds of sans-serif fonts, a quick trick is to inspect the capital **A** and **G** and the lowercase **a** and **g** of each typeface. The forms of these letters can give you information about how the typeface is classified.

GROTESQUE SANS-SERIF TYPE FAMILY CATEGORY AND EXAMPLES

Grotesques include all sans-serif type-faces designed before the twentieth century, and all the revivals based on them. These typefaces usually feature a tall x-height and a narrow to moderate set width, and a slightly squarish appearance. The Grotesque capital G usually has a spur, as shown in Figure 3-20, and lowercase g is usually open-tailed. The capital A is usually squared off at the apex, and the lowercase a is usually double story. Helvetica, Akzidenz-Grotesk, and Univers, all shown below, are prototypical Grotesque sans-serif typefaces. You can compare the digital version of Univers to the original type family chart, which was developed by Adrian Frutiger in 1957, pictured in Figure 3-17.

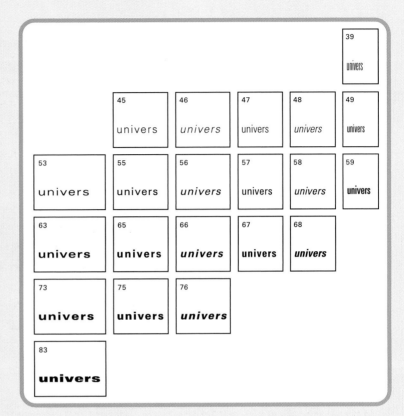

figure | 3-17 |

Chart of the Univers type family by Adrian Frutiger in 1957. Univers™ is a trademark of Heidelberger Druckmaschinen AG, which may be registered in certain jurisdictions, exclusively licensed through Linotype Library GmbH, a wholly owned subsidiary of Heidelberger Druckmaschinen AG.

GROTESQUE SANS-SERIF TYPE FAMILY CATEGORY EXAMPLES

Univers

32 pt

The Univers type family was designed by Adrian Frutiger in 1957. A revived version with 63 different weights and improved letterforms is also available as Linotype Univers. Univers 55 Roman, Univers 55 Oblique, Univers 65 Bold, Univers 65 Bold Oblique, and Univers 45 Light, courtesy of Linotype type foundry, Linotype Library GmbH, *www.linotype.com.*

8/10 pt

Univers 55 Roman – 44 pt

abcdefghijklmnop
qrstuvwxyz
ABCDEFGHIJKLM
NOPQRSTUVWXYZ
(1234567890$%
&*@'!?:;"")

Univers 55 Oblique– 28 pt

abcdefghijklmnopqrstuvwxyz
ABCDEFGHIJKLMNOP
QRSTUVWXYZ
(1234567890$%&@'!?:;"")*

Univers 65 Bold– 28 pt

abcdefghijklmnopqrstuvwxyz
ABCDEFGHIJKLMNOP
QRSTUVWXYZ
(1234567890$%&*@'!?:;"")

Univers 65 Bold Oblique– 28 pt

abcdefghijklmnopqrstuvwxyz
ABCDEFGHIJKLMNOP
QRSTUVWXYZ
(1234567890$%&@'!?:;"")*

Univers 45 Light – 28 pt

abcdefghijklmnopqrstuvwxyz
ABCDEFGHIJKLMNOP
QRSTUVWXYZ
(1234567890$%&*@'!?:;" ")

GROTESQUE SANS-SERIF TYPE FAMILY CATEGORY EXAMPLES

Akzidenz-Grotesk
24 pt

The Akzidenz-Grotesk type family was created by the Berthold Foundry in 1896. Akzidenz-Grotesk Regular, Akzidenz-Grotesk Italic, and Akzidenz-Grotesk Bold, courtesy of Berthold Types Limited, *www.bertholdtypes.com.*

8/10 pt

Akzidenz-Grotesk Regular – 28 pt

abcdefghijklmnopqrstuvwxyz
ABCDEFGHIJKLMNOPQRSTU
VWXYZ (1234567890$%&*@'!?:;"")

Akzidenz-Grotesk Italic – 28 pt

abcdefghijklmnopqrstuvwxyz
ABCDEFGHIJKLMNOPQRSTU
VWXYZ (1234567890$%&@'!?:;"")*

Akzidenz-Grotesk Bold – 28 pt

abcdefghijklmnopqrstuvwxyz
ABCDEFGHIJKLMNOP
QRSTUVWXYZ
(1234567890$%&*@'!?:;"")

Helvetica

The Helvetica type family was created by Max Miedinger in 1957. In 1983 Helvetica was revived and expanded by Linotype as Neue Helvetica. Helvetica, Helvetica Oblique, and Helvetica Bold, courtesy of Linotype type foundry, Linotype Library GmbH, *www.linotype.com*.

32 pt

8/10 pt

Helvetica – 28 pt

abcdefghijklmnopqrstuvwxyz
ABCDEFGHIJKLMNOPQRSTU
VWXYZ (1234567890$%&*@'!?:;"")

Helvetica Oblique – 28 pt

abcdefghijklmnopqrstuvwxyz
ABCDEFGHIJKLMNOPQRSTU
VWXYZ (1234567890$%&@'!?:;"")*

Helvetica Bold – 28 pt

abcdefghijklmnopqrstuvwxyz
ABCDEFGHIJKLMNOP
QRSTUVWXYZ
(1234567890$%&*@'!?:;"")

GEOMETRIC SANS-SERIF TYPE FAMILY CATEGORY AND EXAMPLES

Geometrics include sans-serif type-faces whose letterforms are based on geometric shapes like circles, rectangles, and triangles, and all the revivals based on them. They are fairly wide in their set width, due to the prevalent use of geometric shapes like circles and squares. Since these typefaces were designed to reflect the increasing mechanization of society, letterforms appear highly mechanized and precise. Although the easiest way to recognize Geometric sans serifs is by their distinctively geometric look, there are other clues you can look for. The Geometric capital A generally has a pointed apex, the lowercase a is often single story, and the lowercase g is usually open-tailed, as shown in Figure 3-20. Futura, Kabel, and Eurostile, all shown below, are prototypical Geometric sans-serif typefaces. You can compare the digital version of Futura to the initial type specimen of 1930 by Paul Renner, which is pictured in Figure 3-18.

figure | 3-18 |

Initial version of Futura designed by Paul Renner in 1930, type specimen called Europe, from Deberny & Peignot type foundry. *Courtesy of V&A Images / Victoria & Albert Museum.*

Futura

32 pt

The Futura type family was created by Paul Renner in 1928. Futura Light, Futura Light Oblique, Futura Book, Futura Book Oblique, and Futura Extra Bold, courtesy of Linotype type foundry, Linotype Library GmbH, *www.linotype.com.*

8/10 pt

Futura Light – 36 pt

abcdefghijklmnop
qrstuvwxyz
ABCDEFGHIJKLMNOP
QRSTUVWXYZ
(1234567890$%&*@'!?:;"")

Futura Light Oblique – 26 pt

abcdefghijklmnopqrstuvwxyz
ABCDEFGHIJKLMNOPQRSTU
VWXYZ (1234567890$%&*@'!?:;"")

Futura Book – 26 pt

abcdefghijklmnopqrstuvwxyz
ABCDEFGHIJKLMNOPQRSTUVWXYZ
(1234567890$%&*@'!?:;"")

Futura Book Oblique – 26 pt

abcdefghijklmnopqrstuvwxyz
ABCDEFGHIJKLMNOPQRSTU
VWXYZ (1234567890$%&*@'!?:;"")

Futura Extra Bold – 26 pt

abcdefghijklmnopqrstuvwxyz
ABCDEFGHIJKLMNOP
QRSTUVWXYZ
(1234567890$%&*@'!?:;"")

Kabel

32 pt

The Kabel type family was created by Rudolf Koch in 1928. Kabel Light, Kabel Book, and Kabel Heavy, courtesy of Linotype type foundry, Linotype Library GmbH, www.linotype.com.

10/12 pt

Kabel Light – 28 pt

abcdefghijklmnopqrstuvwxyz
ABCDEFGHIJKLMNOPQRST
VWXYZ (1234567890$%&*@'!?:;"")

Kabel Book – 28 pt

abcdefghijklmnopqrstuvwxyz
ABCDEFGHIJKLMNOPQRSTU-
VWXYZ (1234567890$%&*@'!?:;"")

Kabel Heavy – 28 pt

abcdefghijklmnopqrstuvwxyz
ABCDEFGHIJKLMNOP
QRSTUVWXYZ
(1234567890$%&*@'!?:;"")

Eurostile

32 pt

The Eurostile type family was created by Aldo Novarese in 1962. Eurostile, Eurostile Oblique, and Eurostile Bold, courtesy of Linotype type foundry, Linotype Library GmbH, *www.linotype.com.*

8/10 pt

Eurostile – 28 pt

abcdefghijklmnopqrstuvwxyz
ABCDEFGHIJKLMNOP
QRSTUVWXYZ
(1234567890$%&*@'!?:;"")

Eurostile Oblique – 28 pt

*abcdefghijklmnopqrstuvwxyz
ABCDEFGHIJKLMNOP
QRSTUVWXYZ
(1234567890$%&*@'!?:;"")*

Eurostile Bold – 28 pt

**abcdefghijklmnopqrstuvwxyz
ABCDEFGHIJKLMNOP
QRSTUVWXYZ
(1234567890$%&*@'!?:;"")**

HUMANIST SANS-SERIF TYPE FAMILY CATEGORY AND EXAMPLES

Humanist sans-serif typefaces were designed based on the proportions of the original Humanist typefaces of Jenson and his contemporaries. They have a more organic feel than Grotesques and Geometrics. In the Humanist sans-serif typeface, the lowercase a and lowercase g are usually double story, as shown in Figure 3-20 (like the double story a and g of any Humanist roman type). The capital A generally has a squared-off apex, and the capital G usually has no spur. Gill Sans, Frutiger, and Optima are prototypical Humanist sans-serif typefaces. You can compare the digital version of Gill Sans to Eric Gill's original drawings of 1929, shown in Figure 3-19.

figure | 3-19 |

Original drawings of Gill Sans for the Monotype Corporation by Eric Gill in 1929. *Courtesy of Monotype Imaging Ltd, U.K.*

Gill Sans

32 pt

The Gill Sans type family was designed by Eric Gill in 1927. Gill Sans, Gill Sans Italic, Gill Sans Bold, Gill Sans Bold Italic, and Gill Sans Ultra-Bold, courtesy of Linotype type foundry, Linotype Library GmbH, *www.linotype.com.*

8/10 pt

Gill Sans – 38 pt

abcdefghijklmnopqrstuvwxyz
ABCDEFGHIJKLMNOP
QRSTUVWXYZ
(1234567890$%
&*@'!?:;"")

Gill Sans Italic – 26 pt

abcdefghijklmnopqrstuvwxyz
ABCDEFGHIJKLMNOPQRSTU
VWXYZ (1234567890$%&@'!?:;"")*

Gill Sans Bold – 26 pt

abcdefghijklmnopqrstuvwxyz
ABCDEFGHIJKLMNOPQRSTU
VWXYZ (1234567890$%&*@'!?:;"")

Gill Sans Bold Italic – 26 pt

abcdefghijklmnopqrstuvwxyz
ABCDEFGHIJKLMNOPQRSTU
VWXYZ (1234567890$%&*@'!?:;"")

Gill Sans Ultra-Bold – 24 pt

abcdefghijklmnop
qrstuvwxyz
ABCDEFGHIJKLMNOP
QRSTUVWXYZ
(1234567890$%&*@'!?:;"")

HUMANIST SANS-SERIF TYPE FAMILY CATEGORY EXAMPLES

Frutiger

32 pt

The Frutiger type family was created by Adrian Frutiger in 1976. The Frutiger type family was revived in 1999 by Adrian Frutiger and is called Frutiger Next. Frutiger 55 Roman, Frutiger 56 Italic, and Frutiger 65 Bold, courtesy of Linotype type foundry, Linotype Library GmbH, *www.linotype.com*.

7/10 pt

Frutiger 55 Roman — 28 pt

abcdefghijklmnopqrstuvwxyz
ABCDEFGHIJKLMNOP
QRSTUVWXYZ
(1234567890$%&*@'!?:;"")

Frutiger 56 Italic — 28 pt

abcdefghijklmnopqrstuvwxyz
ABCDEFGHIJKLMNOP
QRSTUVWXYZ
(1234567890$%&@'!?:;"")*

Frutiger 65 Bold — 28 pt

abcdefghijklmnopqrstuvwxyz
ABCDEFGHIJKLMNOP
QRSTUVWXYZ
(1234567890$%&*@'!?:;"")

Optima
The Optima type was designed by Hermann Zapf in 1958. Today, a revived version is available as Optima Nova. Optima, Optima Italic, and Optima Bold, courtesy of Linotype type foundry, Linotype Library GmbH, *www.linotype.com*.

32 pt

8/10 pt

Optima – 28 pt

abcdefghijklmnopqrstuvwxyz
ABCDEFGHIJKLMNOPQRSTU
VWXYZ (1234567890$%&*@'!?:;"")

Optima Italic – 28 pt

abcdefghijklmnopqrstuvwxyz
ABCDEFGHIJKLMNOPQRSTU
VWXYZ (1234567890$%&@'!?:;"")*

Optima Bold – 28 pt

abcdefghijklmnopqrstuvwxyz
ABCDEFGHIJKLMNOPQRSTU
VWXYZ (1234567890$%&*@'!?:;"")

figure | 3-20 |

Sans-serif typeface
tendencies.

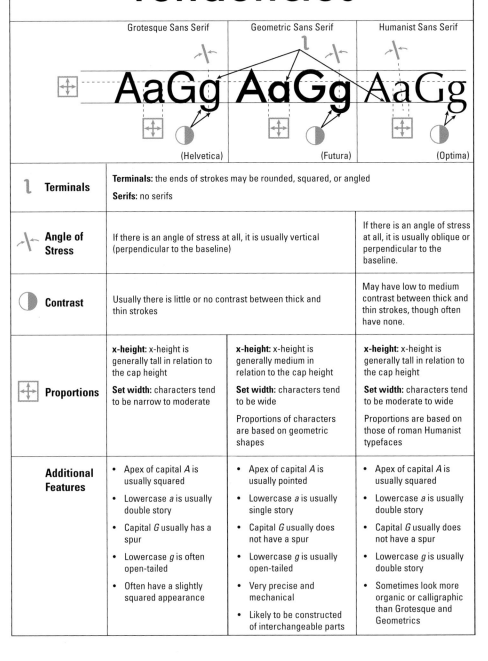

Sans-serif Typeface
Tendencies

		Grotesque Sans Serif	Geometric Sans Serif	Humanist Sans Serif
		AaGg	AaGg	AaGg
		(Helvetica)	(Futura)	(Optima)
	Terminals	**Terminals:** the ends of strokes may be rounded, squared, or angled **Serifs:** no serifs		
	Angle of Stress	If there is an angle of stress at all, it is usually vertical (perpendicular to the baseline)		If there is an angle of stress at all, it is usually oblique or perpendicular to the baseline.
	Contrast	Usually there is little or no contrast between thick and thin strokes		May have low to medium contrast between thick and thin strokes, though often have none.
	Proportions	**x-height:** x-height is generally tall in relation to the cap height **Set width:** characters tend to be narrow to moderate	**x-height:** x-height is generally medium in relation to the cap height **Set width:** characters tend to be wide Proportions of characters are based on geometric shapes	**x-height:** x-height is generally tall in relation to the cap height **Set width:** characters tend to be moderate to wide Proportions are based on those of roman Humanist typefaces
	Additional Features	• Apex of capital *A* is usually squared • Lowercase *a* is usually double story • Capital *G* usually has a spur • Lowercase *g* is often open-tailed • Often have a slightly squared appearance	• Apex of capital *A* is usually pointed • Lowercase *a* is usually single story • Capital *G* usually does not have a spur • Lowercase *g* is usually open-tailed • Very precise and mechanical • Likely to be constructed of interchangeable parts	• Apex of capital *A* is usually squared • Lowercase *a* is usually double story • Capital *G* usually does not have a spur • Lowercase *g* is usually double story • Sometimes look more organic or calligraphic than Grotesque and Geometrics

The Script Type Family Category

Script typefaces are those designed to look like they were hand-rendered, even though they were not. Scripts can look like printed or cursive handwriting; they can appear hand-lettered, brushed, or calligraphic. Scripts include typefaces with letters that connect to each other, and some that do not. Because blackletter fonts are based on scribal scripts, some people consider them to be members of this type family category. However, it is generally agreed that the first true script typeface was cut in 1557 by Robert Granjon of France. Granjon called his script typeface *lettre francoise d'art de main*, but it came to be known as Civilité because it was used to print a popular children's etiquette book called *La Civilité puerile*.

SCRIPT TYPE FAMILY CATEGORY EXAMPLES

In 1928, Hermann Zapf revived Robert Granjon's Civilité when he designed a typeface also called Civilité. This has since been digitally revived as St. Augustin Civilité, which is shown below. You can compare the digital version of Civilité to the close-up of the title page of Granjon's *La Civilité puerile*, pictured in Figure 3-21. Digital fonts and revivals of other popular script typefaces follow.

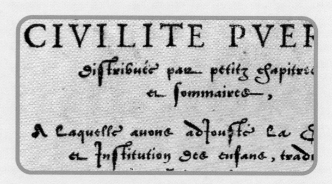

figure | 3-21 |

Civilité typeface from Robert Granjon's *La Civilité puerile* of 1558. *Courtesy of Zentralbibliothek Zürich.*

St. Augustin Civilité

24 pt

The HTF Historical St. Augustin Civilité typeface was designed by Jonathan Hoefler, based on original designs created by Robert Granjon in 1557. Copyright © 1994 The Hoefler Type Foundry, Inc., www.typography.com.

10/14 pt

St. Augustin Civilité – 24 pt

abcdefghijklmnopqrstuvwxyz

ABCDEFGHIJKLMNOPQ

RSTUVWXYZ (1234567890$%&*@'!?:;"")

SCRIPT TYPE FAMILY CATEGORY EXAMPLES

Tekton
36 pt

Tekton was designed by David Siegel and Jim Wasco in 1989. Tekton, courtesy of Adobe Systems Inc., www.adobe.com/type, and Microsoft Corporation, www.microsoft.com.
9/11 pt

Tekton – 30 pt

abcdefghijklmnopqrstuvwxyz

ABCDEFGHIJKLMNOP

QRSTUVWXYZ

(1234567890$%&*@'!?:;"")

Brush Script
32 pt

Brush Script is a revival of original designs created by Robert E. Smith in 1942. Brush Script, courtesy of Bitstream Inc. type foundry, www.myfonts.com.
10/12 pt

Brush Script – 30 pt

abcdefghijklmnopqrstuvwxyz

ABCDEFGHIJKLMNOP

QRSTUVWXYZ

(1234567890$%&*@'!?:;"")

Dom Casual

32 pt

Dom Casual is a revival of original designs created by Peter Dombrezian in 1952. Dom Casual, courtesy of Bitstream Inc. type foundry, www.myfonts.com.

10/12 pt

Dom Casual – 30 pt

abcdefghijklmnopqrstuvwxyz

ABCDEFGHIJKLMNOP

QRSTUVWXYZ

(1234567890$%&*@'!?:;"")

Shelley Script

32 pt

Shelley Script was designed by Matthew Carter in 1972, based on the hand-writing of early eighteenth-century English writing master, George Shelley. Shelley Allegro Script, courtesy of Linotype type foundry, Linotype Library GmbH, www.linotype.com.

10/11 pt

Shelley Script – 30 pt

abcdefghijklmnopqrstuvwxyz

ABCDFGHIJKLMNOP

QRSTUVWXYZ

(1234567890$%&*@'!?:;"")

SCRIPT TYPE FAMILY CATEGORY EXAMPLES

Streamline
24 pt

Streamline was designed by Leslie Cabarga in 1995, based on typographic scripts of the 1940s. Streamline Light, courtesy of Font Bureau type foundry, www.fontbureau.com.
8/10 pt

Streamline – 26 pt

abcdefghijklmnop
qrstuvwxyz
ABCDEFGHIJKL
MNOPQRSTVWX
YZ (1234567890$7.&*@'!?.:;"")

Typo Upright
32 pt

Typo Upright is a revival of original designs created by Morris Fuller Benton in 1915. Typo Upright, courtesy of Bitstream Inc. type foundry, www.myfonts.com.
12/14 pt

Typo Upright – 36 pt

abcdefghijklmnopqrstuvwxyz
ABCDEFGHIJKLMNOP
QRSTUVWXYZ
(1234567890$%&*@'!?.:;"")

Zapfino

32 pt

The Zapfino type family was designed by Hermann Zapf in 1998. An enhanced version called Zapfino Extra allows the usage of features in the OpenType format. Zapfino One, courtesy of Linotype type foundry, Linotype Library GmbH, www.linotype.com.

6/18 pt

Zapfino – 30 pt

abcdefghijklmnopqr
stuvwxyz

ABCDEFGHIJ
KLMNOP
QRSTUVWXYZ
(1234567890$%@ *
@'!?:;"")

adventures
IN **DESIGN**

PIXEL FONTS

Pixel fonts are a new category of type that has evolved in response to the demands of new technologies. Pixel fonts are those that were designed specifically to optimize legibility on a low-resolution computer screen. Many pixel fonts are designed especially for viewing at small sizes, since reading small type on a computer screen is particularly challenging for most readers. Stylistically, they can be cross-listed with any of the type family categories.

Pixel font proportions are based on the grid of tiny squares, or pixels, that compose the screen. Since pixels are square, so are the building blocks that are used to construct pixel fonts, which tends to give these typefaces a blocky, jagged look. However, that's where the similarities end. Pixel fonts can be sans serif or serif, and include typefaces that cross-reference all other type family classifications. Among of the first pixel fonts were Chicago, New York, Geneva, Lucida, Monaco, and Charcoal.

Chicago
32 pt

Chicago was designed by Susan Kare in 1983 as a bitmap font, and was later converted to a scalable TrueType font by Charles Bigelow and Kris Holmes in 1990. Chicago, courtesy of Apple type foundry, http://fonts.apple.com, and Microsoft Corporation, www.microsoft.com.

6/10 pt

Chicago – 28 pt

abcdefghijklmnop
qrstuvwxyz
ABCDEFGHIJKLMNOP
QRSTUVWXYZ
(1234567890$%
&*@'!?:;"")

Geneva

32 pt

Geneva was designed by Susan Kare in 1983 as a bitmap font, and was later converted to a scalable TrueType font by Charles Bigelow and Kris Holmes in 1991. Geneva, courtesy of Apple type foundry, http://fonts.apple.com, and Microsoft Corporation, www.microsoft.com.

7/10 pt

Geneva – 28 pt

abcdefghijklmnopqrstuvwxyz
ABCDEFGHIJKLMNOP
QRSTUVWXYZ
(1234567890$%&*@'!?:;"")

Lucida Sans

32 pt

The Lucida Sans type family was designed by Charles Bigelow and Kris Holmes in 1985. Lucida Sans EF Roman, courtesy of Elsner + Flake type foundry, www.elsner-flake.com.

10/12 pt

Lucida Sans – 28 pt

abcdefghijklmnopqrstuvwxyz
ABCDEFGHIJKLMNOP
QRSTUVWXYZ
(1234567890$%&*@'!?:;"")

PIXEL TYPE FAMILY CATEGORY EXAMPLES

Monaco

32 pt

Monaco was designed by Susan Kare in 1983 as a bitmap font, and was later converted to a scalable TrueType font by Charles Bigelow and Kris Holmes in 1991. Monaco, courtesy of Apple type foundry, http://fonts.apple.com, and Microsoft Corporation, www.microsoft.com.

6/10 pt

Monaco – 28 pt

abcdefghijklmnopqrstuvwxyz
ABCDEFGHIJKLMNOP
QRSTUVWXYZ
(1234567890$%&*@'!?:;"")

New York

32 pt

New York was designed by Susan Kare in 1983, as a bitmap font, and was later converted to a scalable TrueType font by Charles Bigelow and Kris Holmes in 1991. New York, courtesy of Apple type foundry, http://fonts.apple.com, and Microsoft Corporation, www.microsoft.com.

6/10 pt

New York – 28 pt

abcdefghijklmnop
qrstuvwxyz
ABCDEFGHIJKLMNOP
QRSTUVWXYZ
(1234567890$%&*@'!?:;"")

Charcoal

30 pt

Charcoal was designed by David Berlow in 1995. Charcoal, courtesy of Apple type foundry, http://fonts.apple.com, and Microsoft Corporation, www.microsoft.com.

8/10 pt

Charcoal – 28 pt

abcdefghijklmnopqrstuvwxyz
ABCDEFGHIJKLMNOP
QRSTUVWXYZ
(1234567890$%&*@'!?:;"")

FixSys

36 pt

FixSys was designed by Alexander Tarbeev in 1995. FixSys, courtesy of Paratype type foundry, www.paratype.com.

10/12 pt

FixSys – 36 pt

abcdefghijklmnopqrstuvwxyz
ABCDEFGHIJKLMNOPQRSTUVWXYZ
(1234567890$%&*@'!?:;"")

PIXEL TYPE FAMILY CATEGORY EXAMPLES

Lo Res

32 pt

The Lo Res type family was designed by Zuzana Licko in 2001. Low Res 12 Regular, courtesy of Emigre type foundry, www.emigre.com.

8/10 pt

Lo Res – 28 pt

abcdefghijklmnopqrstuvwxyz

ABCDEFGHIJKLMNOP

QRSTUVWXYZ

(1234567890$%&*@'!?:;""")

The Display Type Family Category

The first Display typefaces were designed in the early nineteenth century, for use in advertising posters. The social shifts, advancing technologies, and mass production of the Industrial Revolution had resulted in enormous quantities of competing products to be bought and sold, and a larger working class with more money to spend. The invention of automated papermaking made it affordable to advertise these new products to these new consumers. The invention of wooden type made these novelty faces even cheaper to produce—and at larger sizes, too. Soon fat, bold, three-dimensional, sans serif, and decorative typefaces were being produced at faster rates than ever before to fill the demand of advertisers.

History repeated itself when the "digital revolution" of the 1990s caused a similar flood of new and novel typefaces. For classification purposes, both old and new typefaces that don't fit into any of the other categories are grouped into one Display type family category. Typefaces in this category can often be cross-classified with any of the other type family categories because members of this family do not necessarily share a common aesthetic.

What many of these typefaces do share, though, is a low level of legibility when set as body text. Sometimes they have ornate flourishes and unusual shapes that make them difficult to read; other times, their proportions are too extreme for easy reading. Display typefaces are better suited for decorative and attention-grabbing purposes, such as headlines. Often a font is categorized into the Display type family category because its appearance departs considerably from the general audience's realm of familiarity, diminishing its legibility and making it suitable only for display purposes.

DISPLAY TYPE FAMILY CATEGORY EXAMPLES

The Display typefaces shown below include digital designs and revivals
based on a wide range of historically significant typefaces.

Vineta

24 pt

Vineta was designed by Ernst Volker in 1973, based on late
nineteenth-century display letterforms. Vineta, courtesy of
Bitstream Inc. type foundry, www.myfonts.com.

6/10 pt

Vineta – 36 pt

abcde
fghijklmnop
qrstuvwxyz
ABCDE
FGHIJKLMN
OPQRSTU
VWXYZ
(1234567890
$%&*@'!?:;"")

DISPLAY TYPE FAMILY CATEGORY EXAMPLES

Victorian LT
32 pt

Victorian LT was designed by Freda Sack in 1980, based on late nineteenth-century display letterforms. Victorian LT, courtesy of Linotype type foundry, Linotype Library GmbH, www.linotype.com.
10/12 pt

Victorian LT – 32 pt

abcdefghijklmnopqrstuvwxyz
ABCDEFGHIJKLMNOPQRSTU
VWXYZ (1234567890$%&*@'!?:;"")

Bearded Lady BB
32 pt

Bearded Lady BB was designed by Nate Piekos in 2004, based on late nineteenth-century display letterforms. Bearded Lady BB, courtesy of Blambot type foundry, www.blambot.com.
9/10 pt

Bearded Lady BB – 36 pt

ABCDEFGHIJKLMNOPQRSTUVWXYZ
ABCDEFGHIJKLMNOPQRSTU
VWXYZ (1234567890$%&*@'!?:;"")

Kismet

32 pt

Kismet is a revival of original designs created by John F. Cumming in 1879. Kismet, courtesy of Linotype type foundry, Linotype Library GmbH, www.linotype.com.

10/12 pt

Kismet – 28 pt

abcdefghijklmnopqrstuvwxyz

ABCDEFGHIJKLMNOPQRSTU

VWXYZ (1234567890$%&°*'!?:;"")

Playbill

32 pt

Playbill was designed by Robert Harling in 1938, based on late nineteenth-century display letterforms of the American West. Playbill, courtesy of Bitstream Inc. type foundry, www.myfonts.com.

10/12 pt

Playbill – 36 pt

abcdefghijklmnopqrstuvwxyz

ABCDEFGHIJKLMNOPQRSTU

VWXYZ (1234567890$%&*@'!?:;"")

DISPLAY TYPE FAMILY CATEGORY EXAMPLES

Arnold Boecklin
28 pt

Arnold Boecklin is a revival of original designs created by Otto Weisert in 1904. Arnold Boecklin, courtesy of Linotype type foundry, Linotype Library GmbH, www.linotype.com.
8/10 pt

Arnold Boecklin – 28 pt

abcdefghijklmnopqrstuvwxyz
ABCDEFGHIJKLMNOPQRSTU
VWXYZ (1234567890$%&*@'!?:;"")

Eckmann
32 pt

Eckmann was designed by Otto Eckmann in 1900. Eckmann, courtesy of Linotype type foundry, Linotype Library GmbH, www.linotype.com.
10/12 pt

Eckmann – 30 pt

abcdefghijklmnopqrstuvwxyz
ABCDEFGHIJKLMNOPQRSTU
VWXYZ (1234567890$%&*'!?:;"")

P22 Mucha
28 pt

P22 Mucha was designed by Christina Torre in 2001, based on original designs created by Alphonse Mucha in 1900. P22 Mucha, courtesy of P22 Type Foundry, Inc., www.p22.com.
10/12 pt

P22 Mucha – 30 pt

abcdefghijklmnopqrstuvwxyz
ABCDEFGHIJKLMNOPQRSTU
VWXYZ (1234567890$%&*@'!?:;"")

ARTS AND CRAFTS GS
24 pt

ARTS AND CRAFTS GS WAS DESIGNED BY TODD HALLOCK, BASED ON ORIGINAL DESIGNS CREATED BY CHARLES RENNIE MACKINTOSH AND OTHER MEMBERS OF THE GLASGOW SCHOOL, CIRCA 1900. ARTS AND CRAFTS GS, COURTESY OF BANNIGAN ARTWORKS TYPE FOUNDRY, WWW.CELTICARTWORKS.COM.
8/10 pt

Arts and Craft GS – 28 pt

ABCDEFGHIJKLMNOP
QRSTUVWXYZ
ABCDEFGHIJKLMNOPQRSTU
VWXYZ (1234567890$%&*@'!?:;"")

DISPLAY TYPE FAMILY CATEGORY EXAMPLES

MOJO

46 pt

MOJO WAS DESIGNED BY JIM PARKINSON, BASED ON ORIGINAL DESIGNS CREATED BY ALFRED ROLLER IN 1902. MOJO, COURTESY OF LINOTYPE TYPE FOUNDRY, LINOTYPE LIBRARY GMBH, WWW.LINOTYPE.COM.

14/14 pt

Mojo – 60 pt

ABCDEFGHIJKLMNOP

QRSTUVWXYZ

(1234567890$%&*@'!?:;"")

Parisian

40 pt

Parisian is a revival of original designs created by Morris Fuller Benton in 1928. Parisian, courtesy of Bitstream Inc. type foundry, www.myfonts.com.

12/14 pt

Parisian – 28 pt

abcdefghijklmnopqrstuvwxyz

ABCDEFGHIJKLMNOPQRSTU

VWXYZ (1234567890$%&*@'!?.:;"")

Broadway
24 pt

Broadway is a revival of original designs created by Morris Fuller Benton in 1929. Broadway, courtesy of Bitstream Inc. type foundry, www.myfonts.com.
8/12 pt

Broadway– 28 pt

**abcdefghijklmnop
qrstuvwxyz
ABCDEFGHIJKLMNOP
QRSTUVWXYZ
(1234567890$%&*@'!?:;""")**

Day Tripper NF
26 pt

Day Tripper NF was designed by Nick Curtis, based on original designs created by Alphonso E. Tripp in the 1930s. Day Tripper NF, courtesy of Nick's Fonts type foundry, www.nicksfonts.com.
9/12 pt

Day Tripper NF – 28 pt

abcdefghijklmnopqrstuvwxyz
ABCDEFGHIJKLMNOP
QRSTUVWXYZ
(1234567890$%&*@'!?:;"")

DISPLAY TYPE FAMILY CATEGORY EXAMPLES

RED STAR LINE NF

20 pt

RED STAR LINE NF WAS DESIGNED BY NICK CURTIS IN 2003, BASED ON TYPE FROM A 1926 TRAVEL BROCHURE FOR A STEAMSHIP LINE. RED STAR LINE NF, COURTESY OF NICK'S FONTS TYPE FOUNDRY, WWW.NICKSFONTS.COM.

6/10 pt

Red Star Line NF – 24 pt

ABCDEFGHIJKLMNOP
QRSTVWXYZ
(1234567890$%&*@'!?;""')

AMBIENT

32 pt

AMBIENT WAS DESIGNED BY GABÓR KÓTHAY IN 2002. AMBIENT, COURTESY OF P22 TYPE FOUNDRY, INC., WWW.P22.COM.

10/12 pt

Ambient – 30 pt

ABCDEFGHIJKLMNOPQRSTUVWXYZ
ABCDEFGHIJKLMNOPQRSTU
VWXYZ (1234567890$%&*@'!?;"")

26 pt

NEULAND WAS DESIGNED BY RUDOLF KOCH IN 1923 FOR KLINGSPOR TYPE FOUNDRY. NEULAND, COURTESY OF LINOTYPE TYPE FOUNDRY, LINOTYPE LIBRARY GMBH, WWW.LINOTYPE.COM.

8/10 pt

Neuland – 28 pt

ABCDEFGHIJKLMNOP
QRSTUVWXYZ
(1234567890$%&*@'!?:;"")

P22 DESTIJL

24 pt

THE P22 DESTIJL TYPE FAMILY WAS DESIGNED BY RICHARD KEGLER AND MICHAEL WANT IN 1995, BASED ON ORIGINAL DESIGNS CREATED BY THEO VAN DOESBURG IN 1919. P22 DESTIJL REGULAR, COURTESY OF P22 TYPE FOUNDRY, INC., WWW.P22.COM.

8/10 pt

P22 DeStijl – 40 pt

ABCDEFGHIJKLMNOP
QRSTUVWXYZ
[1234567890$£&*@]!?;;'""]

DISPLAY TYPE FAMILY CATEGORY EXAMPLES

32 pt

HENDRIX WAS DESIGNED BY DAVID NALLE IN 1994, BASED ON LETTERING STYLES FROM ROCK POSTERS OF THE 1960S. HENDRIX, COURTESY OF SCRIPTORIUM TYPE FOUNDRY, WWW.FONTCRAFT.COM.

9/12 pt

Hendrix – 28 pt

ABCDEFGHIJKLMNOPQRSTUVWXYZ
(1234567890$¢£*!?:.;)

Macrame Super Triline
24 pt

Macrame super triline was designed by Jess Latham in 2002 based on designs from the 1960s and 1970s. Macrame super triline, courtesy of blue vinyl fonts type foundry, www.bvfonts.com.

9/12 pt

Macrame Super Triline – 28 pt

abcdefghijklmnopqrstuvwxyz
abcdefghijklmnopqrstu
vwxyz (1234567890$%&*(@"!?:;"")

Elephant Bells Heavy
21 pt

Elephant Bells Heavy was designed by Bob Alonso. Elephant Bells Heavy, courtesy of BA Graphics type foundry, www.myfonts.com.

10/12 pt

Elephant Bells Heavy – 28 pt

abcdefghijklmnopqrstuvwxyz
ABCDEFGHIJKLMNOPQRSTUVWXYZ
(1234567890$%&*@'!?:;"")

New Nerd Shadowed 22 pt

The New Nerdish type family was designed by Robert Schenk in 1994. New Nerd Shadowed, courtesy of Ingrimayne Type foundry, http://ingrimayne.saintjoe.edu/fonts/. 9/14 pt

New Nerd Shadowed – 28 pt

abcdefghijklmnopqrstuvwxyz
ABCDEFGHIJKLMNOPQRSTU
VWXYZ (1234567890$%&*@'!?:;"")

Automatic AOE 28 pt

Automatic AOE was designed by Brian J. Bonislawsky in 2000. Automatic AOE, courtesy of Astigmatic One Eye Typographic Institute, www.astigmatic.com. 12/14 pt

Automatic AOE – 36 pt

ABCDEFGHIJKLMNOPQRSTUVWXYZ
ABCDEFGHIJKLMNOPQRSTU
VWXYZ (1234567890$%¢*@'!?:;"")

DISPLAY TYPE FAMILY CATEGORY EXAMPLES

Viscosity 32 pt

Viscosity was designed by Bob Aufuldish and Kathy Warinner in 1996. Viscosity, courtesy of FontBoy type foundry, www.fontboy.com. 12/14 pt

Viscosity – 28 pt

abcdefghijklmnopqrstuvwxyz
ABCDEFGHIJKLMNOPQRSTU
VWXYZ (1234567890$%&*@'!?:;"''")

Bokonon 32 pt

Bokonon was designed by Todd Dever in 1997. Bokonon, courtesy of Cool Fonts type foundry, www.cool-fonts.com. 12/14 pt

Bokonon – 28 pt

abcdefghijklmnopqrstuvwxyz
ABCDEFGHIJKLMNOPQRSTU
VWXYZ (1234567890$%&*@'!?:;"")

Zapped — 28 pt

CHAPTER SUMMARY

Over time, printed letterforms have undergone physical changes that reflected improvements in technological capabilities, socio-political shifts, and changing popular tastes. We classify typefaces into families according to their physical characteristics and historical significance in order to help us identify and use them appropriately. The nine type family categories into which fonts are most often classified are Blackletter, Humanist, Old Style, Transitional, Modern, Egyptian, Sans Serif, Script, and Display. Variations in the structure of elements—including terminals, angle of stress, stroke weight, contrast, set width, and x-height—make each type family category distinctive from the others.

Designers need to make educated decisions when choosing typefaces for their designs because the look of a typeface can contribute a mood, invoke a memory, or suggest a historical era to the audience. Designers who understand how type is classified can create stronger designs. Understanding the terminology that describes type is also important in order for designers to communicate effectively about their designs, whether with other designers or with their clients.

in review

1. What is a typeface? What is a font? What is a type style?

2. What are the two possible meanings of type family?

3. Name the nine type family categories.

4. Describe how the terminals, angle of stress, contrast, stroke weights, set widths, and x-heights look for each type family category.

5. Why did Gutenberg use a blackletter typeface to print his 42-line Bible?

6. Where did Humanist typefaces originate, and why did printers start to use them?

7. What's the difference between Humanist and Old Style typefaces?

8. What elements changed from Old Style to Transitional typefaces? From Transitional to Modern?

9. Why did Display typefaces become popular in the nineteenth century?

10. Why did Sans-Serif typefaces become popular in the twentieth century?

exercises

1. Look through magazines to find three examples of typefaces from each type family category. Think about why you classified each typeface into the type family category that you did.

2. Find a web site that offers free font downloads. Look through the choices of free fonts and identify three fonts that are difficult to classify because they have characteristics from more than one type family category. List which structural elements lead you to classify them in different ways.

3. Select a typeface from each type family category. Using a photocopier, enlarge a single letterform of each typeface to the size of a full page. Compare the structural elements of each, including the terminals and serifs, angle of stress, contrast, stroke weight, set width, and x-height. Label your observations. Consider how the structural elements varied from typeface to typeface.

4. Use the letters of your first name to design a new typeface that would be classified into the Modern type family category.

5. Use the letters of your last name to design a new typeface that would be classified into the Sans-serif type family category. Decide why your typeface would best be described as a Grotesque, Geometric, or Humanist sans-serif typeface.

6. Your favorite band of musicians has hired you to create cover art for a reissue of your favorite CD. Using only typefaces sampled in this chapter, design front and back cover art, and a sticker design for the CD. Your designs may include as many letterforms as you wish. You may make the letterforms large or small, any color, overlapping, etc.

Courtesy of Jeff Louviere of Louviere + Vanessa.

CHAPTER 4

objectives

- Understand the difference between legibility and readability
- Gain an appreciation for the importance of legibility and readability to visual communication
- Consider how a variety of factors—including style, color, size, shape, and background—can influence the legibility of a design
- Learn how the arrangement of letterforms and negative spaces can affect the readability of a design
- Contemplate ways a designer can increase readability by catering to the viewer's experience and physiology

introduction

Creating a design that is readable is essential to keeping a reader engaged; creating words for the design that are legible is essential to transmitting the design's message effectively. **Legibility** refers to the ease with which a reader can recognize and differentiate between letterforms. For example, when you have difficulty reading a handwritten note from your friend, you might say his handwriting is illegible. When the shapes of printed characters vary too far from their simplest forms, readers may experience confusion, frustration, and less comprehension.

Readability refers to how easily a page of text can be read and navigated. The legibility of the text on the page certainly affects readability, but so do many other factors. Even if text is legible, a reader may find a layout to be unreadable if it is jumbled, crowded, or difficult to navigate. On the other hand, if a layout looks visually appealing, and elements are placed in such a way that they are easy to locate, the reader will find the layout to be readable and will be more likely to read and comprehend the entire message.

In this day and age when there are so many competing media messages constantly bombarding us and vying for our attention, creating designs that are both readable and legible can make a big difference in whether a message reaches its audience!

New Vocabulary

legibility: the ease with which a reader can recognize and differentiate between letterforms

readability: how easily a page of text can be read and navigated

FACTORS THAT INFLUENCE LEGIBILITY

You want your text to be legible, so what choices can you make to increase the legibility of your designs? A variety of factors can influence the legibility of print on a page or on a computer screen; understanding them will allow you to make informed choices that will result in more effective and successful designs. Considering these issues as you create layouts will help you to balance legibility concerns with stylistic demands in ways that will ultimately contribute to the readability of your designs.

Style of a Typeface

Now more than ever, there is a vast selection of typefaces to choose from when creating a design. Your typeface choices will directly affect the legibility of your design. However, some typefaces may be legible when used as **display type** (larger and/or decorative type used to attract attention; generally used for titles, headings, or headlines), but illegible when used for **body type** (textual passages longer than a few words, also called **text type**, or **body text**).

Familiarity

Familiarity plays a big part in whether your audience will be able to read your text. Typefaces that are more familiar can be read more quickly and easily than unfamiliar ones. The sentence shown in Figure 4-1 illustrates this key idea. The blackletter typeface that it is set in (Johannes G) would have been considered highly legible in Gutenberg's time, but to a modern audience, this is not so. Obscure and unusual typefaces should not be used for body text, although they can be used as display type to add style and interest to a design.

figure | 4-1 |

Text block set in an unfamiliar typeface, FF Johannes G, designed by Manfred Klein in 1991, based on original designs created by Johannes Gutenberg in 1455. *Courtesy of FSI FontShop International type foundry,* www.fontshop.com, www.fontfont.com.

Typefaces that are more familiar can be read more quickly and easily than unfamiliar ones.

Serif vs. Sans Serif

Research has shown that for body text, serif typefaces are easier to read than sans-serif typefaces—those without (sans) serifs. Research participants exhibited comprehension levels that were as much as five times higher when reading body type passages set in serif typefaces compared to those set in sans-serif typefaces. (For display text, there was no difference in comprehension.)

There are two reasons why serif typefaces are easier to read; the first reason is that serifs help the reader to differentiate letters from one another. For example, in Figure 4-2, the letters of the word *Illinois* are much easier to differentiate in the serif typeface (Times New Roman) than in the sans-serif typeface (Arial). This is because the serifs actually change the shape of the letters to provide additional visual cues that can aid in character recognition. If you had never heard of the state of Illinois, you might not even be sure how to read the sans-serif example.

The second reason serifs increase legibility of body type is that the horizontal orientation of the serifs help the reader's eyes to flow smoothly along the horizontal lines of text. Most sans-serif typefaces have a more vertical appearance because of the dominant vertical stems of our alphabet's letterforms which can conflict with eye flow, slowing it down slightly.

Optima, a sans-serif font designed with splayed terminals, is more legible than most sans-serif fonts because the splayed terminals in this typeface create a more horizontal appearance, easing eye flow in the same way serifs would.

Type Styles

A type style refers to a modified version of a typeface. For instance, text could be set in *italic*, **bold**, ALL CAPS, or <u>underlined</u> type styles. Most type styles are very useful for emphasis, and work well for display types; however, long passages of body type should rarely be set in one of these type styles.

For example, long passages of bolded letterforms are less legible than regular ones because the thickening of the letters diminishes the size of the counters. This concept also applies to any heavy typeface. Remember, the negative spaces inside the letterforms are just as important to reader recognition as the strokes of the letters.

Illinois
Illinois

figure | 4-2 |

The word "Illinois" set in a serif font (top) and a sans-serif font (bottom).

figure | 4-3 |

Text block set in a sans-serif typeface, Helvetica, designed by Max Miedinger in 1957. *Courtesy of Linotype type foundry, Linotype Library GmbH,* www.linotype.com.

figure | 4-4 |

Text block set in a san-serif typeface with splayed terminals, Optima, designed by Hermann Zapf in 1958. *Courtesy of Linotype type foundry, Linotype Library GmbH,* www.linotype.com.

figure | 4-5 |

Text block set in a bold type style.

figure | 4-6 |

Text block set in an all caps type style.

LONG PASSAGES OF BODY TYPE SET IN ALL CAPS ARE ALSO DIFFICULT TO READ. IN THIS CASE, LEGIBILITY IS DECREASED BECAUSE THERE IS LESS VARIATION BETWEEN THE CAPITAL LETTERS (WHICH ARE ALL THE SAME HEIGHT) THAN THERE IS BETWEEN THE LOWERCASE LETTERS (WHICH SOMETIMES HAVE ASCENDERS AND DESCENDERS).

Readers can become familiar with the shapes of whole words, and this speeds up reading; however, words printed in all caps are always the same shape: rectangular. Most legible is the standard combination of capital and lowercase letters that can be found in most printed materials, partly because of the variation in character shapes and partly because of the audience's familiarity with this style of presentation.

figure | 4-7 |

Text block set in an underlined type style.

<u>For printed materials, underlined text should be used sparingly, if at all. Long passages of underlined text can be difficult to read. Although underlining does add to the horizontal flow of the text, it also competes visually with the letterforms.</u>

In digital environments, underlining has come to signal the presence of hyperlinks. However, alternate methods of indicating links, like highlighting or color variation, can be just as effective and less visually disruptive. On-screen, underlines should never be used for words without hyperlinks, since this will confuse and frustrate viewers.

figure | 4-8 |

Text block set in an italic type style.

Available research provides conflicting information about the legibility of body type set in italics. Some research results have shown italics to be more difficult to read, while other research has shown no difference in legibility of italics as compared to regular text. So, what's the truth of the matter? The truth is that nobody is completely sure. However, the knowledge that some research has shown italics to lessen legibility should make you careful in your usage of italics for long passages of body text.

Color and Value

Color and value are great stylistic tools that can help set a mood, suggest an association, and grab the attention of your audience. As a designer, you will be making decisions about both the color of text and the color of the background that surrounds the text.

Research on legibility issues regarding color has provided some very clear results. Black text on a white background is by far the most legible combination. In one study, even the slight difference of a darkly colored body type on a white background resulted in a significantly reduced comprehension rate among participants.

However, black text on lightly tinted backgrounds has proved to be highly legible and can improve readability as well; studies have shown that most people find tinted backgrounds attractive. Background tints should generally not exceed a 10-percent grayscale value though, because at that point legibility starts to diminish rapidly.

According to the same research, white body type on a black background proved to be a highly illegible combination. Of the combinations tested, reader comprehension proved lowest for white text on a black background. This is because white text on a black background can produce an optical dazzle effect, making reading difficult and tiring to the eyes of the readers.

Another problem with white text on a black background is that our eyes tend to perceive the black as "spilling over" into the white areas. Sometimes, the black ink does literally spill over, or bleed, into white areas—especially if the paper is highly absorbent.

Does this mean you should never use white text on a black background? No. As a designer, you must negotiate an appropriate balance between legibility and style for each design. Sometimes you will compromise one somewhat for the other. However, you must always be aware of the compromises you are making, so that you can make informed choices. For example, when using white text on a black background, the dazzle effect can be somewhat reduced by choosing fonts with lower contrast, and the effects of bleeding can be reduced by thickening the strokes of the white characters. Taking these steps will help reduce eye strain and improve legibility for your readers. Figure 4-10 shows two examples of white text on black backgrounds; note the effects of the typeface selections on legibility.

figure | 4-9 |

Text block set against a lightly tinted background.

(Left) High-contrast text block set in white on a black background, Linotype Didot Roman, created by Adrian Frutiger and the Linotype Studio based on original designs created by Firmin Didot in 1784. *Courtesy of Linotype type foundry, Linotype Library GmbH, www.linotype.com.*

(Right) Low-contrast text block set in white on a black background, Cloister URW T Bold, designed by Phil Martin, based on original designs created by Morris Fuller Benton in 1913. *Courtesy of URW++ type foundry, www.urwpp.de/english/home.htm.*

White text on a black background can produce an optical dazzle effect, making reading difficult and tiring to the eyes of readers.

The dazzle effect can be somewhat reduced by choosing fonts with lower contrast, and the effects of bleeding can be reduced by thickening the strokes of the white characters.

Typographic Color

We've talked about color in terms of the hue of the text and the background. Now we need to discuss **typographic color**, which refers to the overall tonal value of a block of type on a page, as perceived when the eye combines the positive and negative shapes in the layout. For example, when your eyes see the combination of black letters and white negative space, your brain combines them so that you perceive the typographic color of the text block to be some specific value of grey. The size and weight of the characters affect typographic color, but so do the sizes of the negative shapes—the spacing. So, heavy text sparsely spaced could conceivably produce the same typographic color as lighter text spaced very tightly, as shown in Figure 4-11.

A tightly spaced text block of a smaller typeface can share a typographic color similar to a widely spaced text block of a larger, heavier typeface.

This light text spaced very tightly is perceived to have a typographic color similar to the next sentence. This light text spaced very tightly is perceived to have a typographic color similar to the next sentence. This light text spaced very tightly is perceived to have a typographic color similar to the next sentence. This light text spaced very tightly is perceived to have a typographic color similar to the next sentence. This light text spaced very tightly is perceived to have a typographic color similar to the next sentence. This light text spaced very tightly is perceived to have a similar

This heavy text, sparsely spaced, is perceived to have a typographic color similar

New Vocabulary

body type (text type, body text): type used for long passages or the main body of a text

display type: larger and/or decorative type used to attract attention; generally used for titles, headings, or headlines

typographic color: the overall tonal value of a block of type on a page, as perceived when the eye combines the positive and negative shapes of the layout

Texture of Type

When we talk about texture, we are discussing how smooth, rough, soft, or sharp we perceive a surface to be. We may perceive a texture using our sense of touch, as we do when we hold a smooth stone or a piece of rough sandpaper. We may perceive texture using our sense of taste, as we do when we eat smooth or chunky peanut butter. We hear textures as rhythms in music and noise. We can also use our sense of sight to perceive texture, as we do when we look at a wallpaper pattern, a sheet of music—or an image of a smooth stone, a piece of sandpaper, or a dollop of chunky or smooth peanut butter.

Just as with a sheet of music or a wallpaper pattern, text on a page or screen also has a texture. If the texture of the typographic color is very smooth—as a result of consistent letterform sizes, weights, shapes, type styles, and spacing—the passage will be easier to read than one with a rough or choppy texture built using inconsistent elements. However, there may be times when you'll find a rough texture to be appropriate. For example, in Figure 4-12, the designer added a sense of excitement to the layout by using a variety of textured text blocks in areas where legibility wasn't essential.

Size and Shape of Type

Several components contribute to the size and shape of letterforms, including stroke weight, contrast, set width, and point size. The size and shape of letterforms have a strong effect on legibility, so each of these elements must be considered. As with the typeface styles discussed above, text with unusual sizes and shapes can be very effective when used as display type, but will become difficult to read when used as body text.

figure | 4-12 |

This poster, *Zero 7* by Jeff Kleinsmith of Patent Pending Industries for House of Blues, includes areas of text with rough textures.

Stroke Weight

The stroke weight of the characters of a typeface also influences legibility. As you can guess by looking at Figure 4-13, a moderate stroke weight will usually be the most legible choice.

The same phenomenon we saw with bolded typefaces is true for any typeface with a heavy stroke weight. The thick strokes begin to fill in the characters' counters, making the letters more difficult to recognize.

On the other hand, when a typeface has a very thin stroke weight, the strokes can become difficult for a reader's eyes to see at all, compromising legibility in long passages of text.

Contrast

Sometimes one letterform will have strokes of varying thickness. For example, the stem stroke of a character is often thicker than its hairline strokes. The level of contrast between the thickest and the thinnest strokes of a character can affect legibility.

Body type, set in a typeface with very high contrast, has a dazzle effect that tires the eyes, much like we witnessed earlier with the white text on a black background.

On the other hand, typefaces with very low contrast can be difficult to read in long passages because there is less variation to help readers recognize one letterform from another.

Set Width

A particularly narrow column may call for a typeface with a narrow set width. However, be aware that typefaces with letters that are unusually narrow or wide can be difficult to read in long passages.

In the case of narrow (or condensed) letterforms, the relationship between the strokes and the counters is modified in a way that makes the letters more difficult to recognize. In addition, the narrow set width gives the typeface a vertical appearance that contrasts with our horizontal reading flow.

WIDE (OR EXPANDED) TYPE-FACES MAY BE USEFUL WHEN LINE LENGTH MUST BE PAR-TICULARLY LONG. HOWEVER, KEEP IN MIND THAT WIDE TYPE-FACES CAN REDUCE LEGIBIL-ITY; WHEN LETTERFORM WIDTH IS SO EXTREME THAT THE READER'S EYES CANNOT READ WORDS IN REGULAR EYE SWEEPS, THE PHYSICAL EXPE-RIENCE OF READING IS DIS-RUPTED AND SLOWED.

figure | 4-15 |

(Top) Text block set in a typeface with a narrow set width, Reforma Grotesk Light, designed by Albert Kapitonov in 1999. *Courtesy of Paratype type foundry,* www.paratype.com.

(Bottom) Text block set in a typeface with a wide set width, Cavalero AOE, designed by Brian J. Bonislawsky in 1999. *Courtesy of Astigmatic One Eye Typographic Institute,* www.astigmatic.com.

Point Size

If you've ever written a paper using a word processing program, you probably noticed that you can manipulate the page length of your paper by simply choosing a different typeface. Without changing the point size, the same text takes up more or less room depending on the typeface that you apply to it. This is because typefaces of the same point size can vary in set width, cap height, and x-height ratio. Since the point size of a type-face is based on a measurement from baseline to baseline (as discussed in Chapter 2), the actual cap height and x-height sizes might not be the same for different typefaces of the same point size.

Try this short exercise: start a new document in your word processing program. Increase the width of your margins, and type the letter **A** enough times to fill several four-inch measures. Now select each **A**, one at a time, and change the font so that no two letters share a typeface. Next, select all the letters, and assign them a font size of 36 points.

Examine the results closely. Notice that although the letters on each measure share a baseline, many probably vary in height and in set width—yet all of these letters are 36 points, from baseline to baseline.

The point size of a character affects its legibility. For display text, most typefaces will be optimal at 14 points or larger, but because of the variety of typeface qualities, you will need to use your best judgment. For body text, optimal point sizes range from 8 points to 12 points (again, the range is due to the variations in width, cap height, and x-height ratio among typefaces of the same point size). A typeface with a tall cap height and/or x-height will probably be easier to read in long passages than one with a small cap height and/or x-height at the same point size.

However, if the x-height of a typeface is extremely tall, the letterforms may become difficult to distinguish also, because the variation between letters with and without ascenders (like a and d) can be diminished.

An extremely short x-height tends to make a typeface appear to be small for its point size, which can diminish legibility because readers may have difficulty focusing on and reading very small letters. Even if readers are able to recognize letterforms at a small point size, their eyes are likely to become tired quickly.

figure | 4-16 |

(Top) Text block set in a typeface with a tall x-height, Seagull, designed by Adrian Williams and Bob McGrath in 1978. *Courtesy of Bitstream Inc. type foundry,* www.myfonts.com.

(Bottom) Text block set in a typeface with a short x-height, Koch Antiqua, designed by Rudolf Koch in 1922. *Courtesy of Linotype type foundry, Linotype Library GmbH,* www.linotype.com.

When you must use a very small point size for body text, try increasing the leading to optimize your reader's experience. The text blocks in Figure 4-17, set in a point size of 6, illustrate this concept.

figure | 4-17 |

Text blocks set in a small point size (6 points) with extra leading (left) and without (right).

(Opposite page) Text block set at a large point size (68 points).

It was Toto that made Dorothy laugh, and saved her from growing as gray as her other surroundings. Toto was not gray; he was a little black dog, with long silky hair and small black eyes that twinkled merrily on either side of his funny, wee nose. Toto played all day long, and Dorothy played with him, and loved him dearly. Today, however, they were not playing. Uncle Henry sat upon the doorstep and looked anxiously at the sky, which was

It was Toto that made Dorothy laugh, and saved her from growing as gray as her other surroundings. Toto was not gray; he was a little black dog, with long silky hair and small black eyes that twinkled merrily on either side of his funny, wee nose. Toto played all day long, and Dorothy played with him, and loved him dearly. Today, however, they were not playing. Uncle Henry sat upon the doorstep and looked anxiously at the sky, which was grayer than usual. Dorothy stood in the door with Toto in her arms, and looked at the sky too. Aunt Em was washing the dishes.

Body type set at a very large point size (shown opposite) can also be problematic for readers. If the size of the letters is so big that the reader cannot read the text using normal eye sweeps, the physiology of reading will be disrupted and slowed, as is also true for typefaces with extremely wide set widths.

If the size of the letters is so big that the reader cannot read the text using normal eye sweeps, the physiology of reading will be disrupted and slowed.

You must consider your intended audience when selecting a point size for the body text. Older readers in particular, whose eyesight may be waning, might find small point sizes difficult to read. Likewise, younger audiences who are just learning to read may have a difficult time distinguishing very small letterforms from one another.

Background

Since the negative space of a letterform is as important to legibility as the shapes of the character strokes, it should be no surprise that a text's background can also affect legibility. Whether your text will be appearing in print or on a computer screen, there are some important factors that you must keep in mind about the background.

Contrast Between Text and Background

We have discussed the typographic term contrast, which refers to the difference between the thickest and thinnest parts of a letterform. However, you have probably also heard the term contrast used as a broader term meaning difference. To promote legibility, you must always make sure that there is adequate contrast (or difference) between the text and the background.

figure | 4-18 |

Text block that has low contrast to its background.

When the contrast between the text and the background is too low, your audience will have a difficult time distinguishing the letterforms from the background.

For designs composed using a computer, this adds a special challenge. The colors that you see on your monitor may look different on other monitors, and could also look different when printed. For this reason, use extra caution when selecting a background that is close in value to your text. If your design will appear in print, you'll also need to make test prints to verify how the printed piece will look, and you may need to convert the RGB colors used by your monitor to the equivalent CMYK colors used for printing.

Texture of Background

If the texture of the background surrounding characters is rough or choppy, as shown in Figure 4-19a, it may distract the reader's eyes from the text, decreasing legibility. For example, you may have noticed that if you used a wallpaper with a busy pattern on your computer desktop, it becomes harder to see your desktop icons.

Cool-looking papers and digital backgrounds can be exciting, but you should always make your design decisions based on a well-considered combination of style and legibility concerns. When a busy background is necessary, providing a smoother background for blocks of text can aid legibility, as is shown in Figure 4-19b.

From the far north they heard a low wail of the wind, and Uncle Henry and Dorothy could see where the long grass bowed in waves before the coming storm. There now came a sharp whistling in the air from the south, and as they turned their eyes that way they saw ripples in the grass coming from that direction also.

From the far north they heard a low wail of the wind, and Uncle Henry and Dorothy could see where the long grass bowed in waves before the coming storm. There now came a sharp whistling in the air from the south, and as they turned their eyes that way they saw ripples in the grass coming from that direction also.

figure | 4-19a |

figure | 4-19b |

Text block set against a textured background.

Text block set against a desaturated textured background.

Surface

The surface of the media the reader is viewing also affects legibility. When your design is meant to be seen on a computer screen, the glare of the monitor can tire your reader's eyes prematurely so passages should be kept short, with plenty of negative space. If your design is to be printed on glossy paper, there will be a similar effect.

The absorbency of the paper on which your design will be printed can also affect legibility. Have you ever used a magic marker to fill in a precise area of a shape or picture? Probably you did as a child when you colored in a coloring book.

If you have a marker and a pencil handy, try this simple exercise: Draw a small shape on a piece of paper using a pencil, and then try to fill it in using your marker. Notice that if you place the marker at the edge of the shape, the ink bleeds past your pencil line. Try it on a piece of notebook paper and on a piece of newspaper. The more absorbent your paper, the more the ink will bleed. If your design is intended to be printed on very absorbent paper, you must take this phenomenon into account because the bleeding of the ink will diminish the counters of your letterforms, making them less legible.

FACTORS THAT INFLUENCE READABILITY

We've established that letters which are easy to recognize are legible, and that legibility is very important to visual communication. However, simply making sure your text is legible won't guarantee that your message will be successfully conveyed to your audience. Legibility describes only how easily readers can recognize specific characters or words; it does not address the additional factors that affect how readers perceive and draw meaning from a page of text.

Good designs can help readers understand how to organize, navigate, and assign meaning to the information presented to them. Designers are able to do this by manipulating the arrangement of both positive and negative spaces within their compositions. The way a designer physically places letterforms in relation to one another can contribute to or detract from the readability of the design. Considering the effects your choices will have on your audience's reading experience will help you to make smart design decisions. After all, the readability of a design is so important, readers will be likely to turn away if a design isn't readable, even if it is legible.

Typeface Selection

figure | 4-20 |

Guinea Pig: High Performance Anxiety monkey CD cover by Jeff Louviere of Louviere + Vanessa uses varied type styles of one typeface to create a sense of diversity and interest while maintaining a sense of unity.

Using too many typefaces in one design can produce a chaotic effect that decreases readability. A safe bet is to select two typefaces that are different enough that a reader can differentiate between them at a glance. A good solution is often to choose one serif typeface and one sans-serif typeface, and then limit yourself to using only those two typefaces. However, if you use this strategy, you can use all of the type styles, sizes, and colors that are available. See how the designer who created the CD cover pictured in Figure 4-20 was able to use one typeface in many ways to create a sense of diversity and interest in the design, while retaining a cohesive thread and a sense of unity.

Arrangement of Letterforms

For any design involving text, there are several decisions a designer must make regarding the way the text should be arranged on the page. The choices you make regarding *alignment, measure, widows*, and *orphans* will influence the readability of your designs.

Alignment

Alignment refers to how text on a page relates to its margins. If you've ever typed a document using a word processing program, then you are probably already familiar with the most popular ways to align text. How text is aligned on a page can have a big effect on the readability of a design. The following are some of the most commonly used alignments.

Left-aligned text, also called **flush left/ragged right**, aligns flush against the left margin but is uneven on the right, as in this paragraph. This is widely considered to be the most readable text alignment because a moderately ragged right edge gives readers a point of reference to find the next line. Since it is the most common alignment used today, it is also familiar to readers, and the consistent word spacing produces a smooth typographic color.

Alignment Tip

When you use a left-aligned/ragged right alignment, keep an eye on how "ragged" the right margin is. An extreme raggedness can reduce readability, but can easily be avoided by manually inserting strategic line breaks to make the line lengths more consistent.

Justified text aligns to the margins on the left and on the right. This sort of text alignment is also highly readable and is very commonly used. The straight-edged margins present a very tidy, clean appearance. However, in order to create those edges, extra spaces must be inserted between words or letters. This can make for a choppy texture with **white rivers** of negative space flowing through it, as in this paragraph. These white rivers can be distracting, because they draw the reader's eyes in a vertical direction, away from the intended horizontal path of the text. You can look for the white rivers in this paragraph by squinting, or look at Figure 4-21 to see this paragraph's white rivers highlighted.

Justified text aligns to the margins on the left and on the right. This sort of text alignment is also highly readable and is very commonly used. The straight edged margins present a very tidy, clean appearance. However in order to create those edges, extra spaces must be inserted between words or letters. This can make for a choppy texture with "white rivers" of negative space flowing through it, as in this paragraph. These white rivers can be distracting, because they draw the reader's eyes in a vertical direction, away from the intended horizontal path of the text. You can look for the white rivers in this paragraph by squinting, or look at Figure

figure | 4-21 |

An example of justified text alignment, with highlighted white rivers.

Right-aligned text, or **flush right/ragged left**, aligns flush against
the right margin, but is uneven on the left, as in this paragraph.
It is not a very readable alignment because readers must search for each
new line of text. However, this alignment can add style for shorter or
more poetic passages.

Centered text aligns along the center
so that left and right margins
are symmetrical, as in this paragraph. This alignment isn't
highly readable in long passage for the same reason that right-
aligned text is difficult to read—
finding the next line of text
can be difficult.
Again, for smaller
or poetic passages,
it is often useful,
and provides a very formal, classical tone.

Other types of alignment, like *runaround, asymmetrical, shaped, contoured,* and *concrete,* are less commonly used, but can be valid solutions
to design problems.

Runaround text alignment wraps around graphics or textual elements
in a layout, as illustrated in Figure 4-22. This can be readable and can act
to nicely integrate images with text.

Asymmetrical text alignment references neither the left nor the right
margin, as shown in Figure 4-23. This alignment can be very artistically
applied, though it is not highly readable. Asymmetrical alignment is
most appropriate for short or poetic passages.

Shaped text alignment flows along a curved or irregular line or shape,
as seen in Figure 4-24. How readable the text is will depend on the shape
of the text's path and the amount of text. Generally, only a small amount
of shaped text is readable. However, when used properly, shaped text can
add style and help readers to navigate through a layout.

Contoured text alignment fills a shape. One or more words can be distorted to create a shape, or a whole passage of text can fill a shape by
aligning measures of type to the edges. **Concrete text alignment** is a
special kind of contoured text alignment, in which the shape of the text
illustrates the content, as seen in Figure 4-25.

figure ┃ 4-22 ┃

This ad, *How to Hold a Saw When
Removing a Limb* by Michael Ashley of
Arnika for Harper Hardware, uses
runaround text alignment.

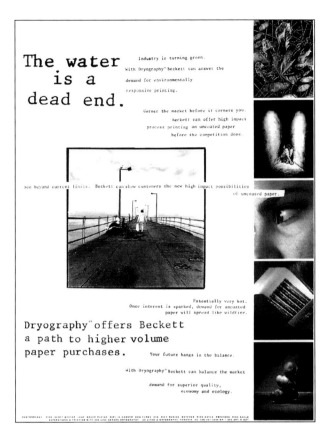

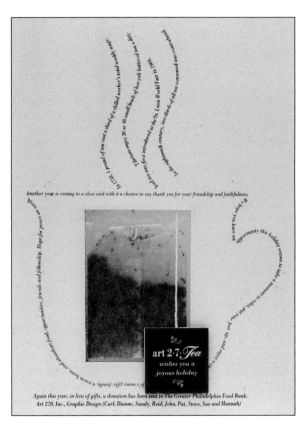

figure | 4-23 |

This promotional poster, *Dryography™* by Mike Campbell of Campbell Fisher Design for Beckett, uses asymmetrical text alignment.

figure | 4-24 |

This greeting card, by Carl Mill of Art 270, Inc., uses shaped text alignment.

figure | 4-25 |

This editorial spread, *Diamonds are Forever* by J. R. Arebalo, Jr. of American Airlines Publishing for Southwest Airlines, uses concrete text alignment.

Measure

Measure is also called line length, and that's what it is—the length of a line of text. The ideal measure for a line of printed body type is usually around 60 to 70 characters per line, or 18 to 24 picas. For digital environments, the ideal measure for body type is even shorter—about 40 characters per line.

figure | 4-26a |

Text block with very long measure.

If a passage of text has an extremely long measure (as illustrated in this paragraph), readability will decrease. This happens because as readers finish one line of text, they have difficulty finding the next line. If you find yourself in a situation in which you must use a very long measure, using a typeface with a wide set width can help improve the readability of the passage.

When a passage has a very short measure, as in a narrow column like this one, readability also decreases because the readers must pause to locate the next line so often. This not only slows down the readers but also tires their eyes. Using a typeface with a narrow set width can help improve the readability of a very narrow passage of text.

When a narrow. column of text has a justified a l i g n m e n t, there can be the added problem of severe white rivers flowing through the passage. This not only makes for a very u n e v e n texture, it also can actually force word spaces to e n o r m o u s l y inappropriate widths.

figure | 4-26b |

Text blocks with very short measures, left aligned and justified.

Widows and Orphans

When a paragraph ends in a single last line at the top of a new column or page, that isolated line is called a **widow**. However, this term is also commonly used to describe any very short last line of a paragraph that is only one or two words long, as you can see in Figure 4-27a. When a paragraph begins with a single first line at the bottom of a column or page, as in Figure 4-27b, that isolated line is called an **orphan**.

Widows and orphans are problematic because they reduce readability by disrupting reading rhythm and creating awkward negative spaces on the page. Both widows and orphans can be avoided by changing the line length, or by manually breaking other longer lines to redistribute the text.

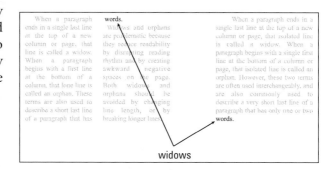

widows

figure | 4-27a |

Widows.

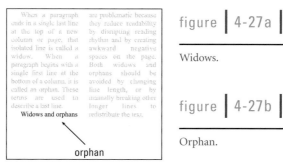

orphan

figure | 4-27b |

Orphan.

New Vocabulary

alignment: refers to how text on a page relates to its margins

asymmetrical text alignment: text that is not aligned to either margin

centered text alignment: aligns evenly between the left and right margins of the text block

concrete text alignment: text shaped to illustrate the idea or word that the text describes

contoured text alignment: text placed so that it creates or fills a specific shape

justified text: aligns flush against the left and right margins of the text block

left-aligned text (flush left/ragged right): aligns flush against the left margin of the text block, but is uneven on the right

measure (line length): the length of a line of text

orphan: the first line of a paragraph, isolated at the bottom of a column or page

right-aligned text (flush right/ragged left): aligns flush against the right margin of the text block, but is uneven on the left

runaround text alignment: text wraps around graphics or textual elements in a layout

shaped text alignment: text flows along a curved or irregular line or shape

white rivers: negative white space seeming to flow down a page within a block of text, usually due to inconsistent word spacing

widow: the last one or two words of a paragraph, isolated at the bottom of a page or at the top of a new column or page

Use of Negative Spaces in a Layout

When arranging elements in a layout, a designer must consider not only the objects to be placed, but also the negative spaces that will surround those objects. Creating attractive negative spaces can give a design a sense of airiness and make it more inviting.

On the other hand, a design with awkward negative spaces will convey a sense of disharmony and can result in a less readable design. This doesn't mean that negative spaces always have to be attractive. Sometimes designers purposely use awkward negative spaces to evoke discomfort in their viewers. As always, the designer must negotiate an appropriate balance between readability and style, based on the goals and intended audience of the specific design.

When a designer is arranging letterforms, the shapes and sizes of negative spaces become particularly important to both legibility and readability. Decisions regarding *letterspacing, tracking, kerning, word spacing,* and *leading* heavily affect the readability of any design that includes text.

Letterspacing, Tracking, and Kerning

A **letterspace** is the space between two letters in a word. The terms tracking and kerning describe specific ways that letterspaces can be modified. The term **letterspacing** is often used to generally describe the collective letterspaces within a string or block of text, but can also be used interchangeably with the term tracking.

Tracking happens when letterspaces are consistently increased or decreased within a string of text. Typefaces can be tracked to have wide letterspacing or narrow letterspacing. Moderately widening and shortening letterspacing can be useful to adapt typefaces to accommodate very long or short measures of text. However, both can be difficult to read in long passages.

figure | 4-28a |

Text block set with excessive letterspacing.

W i d e n e d   l e t t e r s p a c i n g s u c h   a s   t h i s   c a n   b e   d i f -f i c u l t   t o   r e a d   b e c a u s e w h e n   l e t t e r s   a r e   t o o   f a r a p a r t ,   w o r d   r e c o g n i t i o n b e c o m e s   a   c h a l l e n g e .

figure | 4-28b |

Text block set with cramped letterspacing.

Shortened letterspacing is also difficult to read because the diminished negative spaces between the letters may strain the eyes and make word recognition more difficult.

Usually an average amount of letterspacing will be most readable and the most legible, but most important is that letterspacing be consistent. Inconsistent letterspacing will confuse readers as to which letters are in which words, and will create an inconsistent visual texture. However, sometimes it is necessary to track or kern adjacent letters to make the letterspacing appear more even.

Kerning happens when the letterspace between two specific characters is altered. Kerning is necessary when adjacent letterforms fit together poorly, creating an awkwardly large or small letterspace. For example, in Figure 4-29 the dotted and dashed boxes show how the letters on the right have been moved closer together and are actually in each other's space. Note how the word **To** looks more awkward when it is not kerned (on the left). This is because the shapes of those particular letters leave a great deal of negative space between them. Kerning them so the letters invade each other's space actually makes them easier to read as one word.

To To
To To

figure | 4-29 |

Type that isn't kerned (left) and type that is kerned (right).

Word Spacing

You probably won't be surprised to learn that the term **word spacing** refers to the amount of space between adjacent words in a string or block of text. Word spacing can be wide or narrow. Sometimes designers choose to use no word spacing at all, but this is generally very difficult to read, as illustrated in Figure 4-30.

As with letterspacing, a consistent word spacing of about the advance width of the lowercase letter **i** will generally be the most readable for most fonts, though some sans serifs use a slightly wider default space width, closer to the advance width of a lowercase letter **r**. When word spacing is too wide, readers have to search for the next word in the sentence. When word spacing is too narrow, readers have difficulty recognizing where words begin and end, so reading is slowed and comprehension decreases.

Word   spacing   can   be   wide

Word spacing can be narrow

Wordspacingcanbenonexistant

figure | 4-30 |

Measures of text with wide, narrow, and no word spacing.

Leading

Appropriate **leading** (the space between consecutive lines of

type) is very important to readability. When lines are very far

apart, readers can have difficulty finding the next line of text,

and reading is slowed.

figure | 4-31a |

Text block with extra leading.

When lines of text are too close together, adjacent lines interfere
and distract readers from the words they are trying to read.

figure | 4-31b |

Text block with reduced leading.

If no extra line spacing is added between lines of text, we say
the leading is **solid**.

figure | 4-31c |

Text block with solid leading.

However, most desktop publishing programs automatically add leading at a default value of 20 percent of the typeface's point size, which can then be adjusted manually by the designer.

The interplay between leading, word spacing, and letterspacing is very important. When one is adjusted, the others should be reevaluated because they all must work together. Be careful in long passages of text to be sure that your word spacing is never larger than your leading, if your goal is readability. Notice how awkward an improper ratio looks (Figure 4-32).

figure | 4-32 |

Text block with an improper ratio of leading, word spacing, and letterspacing.

This   shows   an   improper   ratio   between   leading,   word   spacing,   and   letterspacing.   This   shows   an   improper   ratio   between   leading,   word   spacing,   and   letterspacing.   This   shows   an   improper   ratio   between   leading,   word   spacing,   and   letterspacing.

Your Audience

If you want your designs to be highly readable, you must consider the reader. Any design that tires or frustrates the reader is likely to decrease comprehension or completely deter your message from reaching its audience.

Physiology of Reading: Eye Focusing and Reading Gravity

Understanding the physiology of how we read can help designers to create designs that cater to the reader's ergonomic experience. Our eyes read text in a series of sweeps and pauses. As we read across a line of text, we recognize familiarly shaped words and letterforms. Then our eyes pause to refocus while our brains assimilate and interpret the new information. Human eyes can generally sweep about four inches of text before having to refocus.

In addition, people whose first language is a Western language, like English, have learned to read lines of text that go from left to right and top to bottom. They have formed strong body habits of taking in text that way, so any text orientation or layout that contradicts this route will result in diminished readability. This physical habit is very important to whether a reader reads and comprehends a design; we refer to the concept as **reading gravity**.

Spelling

Pleeze chk yrrr spelleg. Readrs' wount taik yoo seriously if yoo mispell werds in yer dezines—and don't rely on your word processing program's spellchecker to correct your spelling. Their our mini words in thee in goulash long which that have multi pal spell links. *Your spellchecker will not catch them!*

In addition to losing credibility with your readers, misspelled words in a design may confuse your readers or even provide them with incorrect information. Each misspelling is likely to cause the reader to pause to decipher the intended meaning of the word, slowing down the reading process and aggravating the reader.

New Vocabulary

kerning: adjusting the letterspace between two adjacent characters of type

leading (line spacing): the space between two consecutive measures of type on a page or layout

letterspace: the space between two letters in a word

letterspacing (tracking): the collective letterspaces within a string or block of text; adjusting the distance between characters in a string or block of text

reading gravity: phenomenon describing how readers' physical reading habits influence their navigational tendencies when encountering a page or layout

solid leading: consecutive measures of type that have no added leading between them

tracking (letterspacing): adjusting the distance between characters in a string or block of text

word spacing: the space between adjacent words in a string or block of text

CHAPTER SUMMARY

Legibility and readability are incredibly important to conveying your intended message to your target audience. If letters are not legible, they cannot be easily recognized, and this slows and frustrates the reader. If a design is not readable, viewers cannot easily find and comprehend the information they seek. Both legibility and readability can be heavily influenced by a designer's choices regarding physical aspects and proximities of letters, words, and lines of text. Backgrounds and negative spaces between and inside text are also very important to legibility and readability issues. Designs must be user-friendly in order to be readable; this means they must be easy to navigate and take into account the experience, the reading habits, and the physiology of the reader.

in review

1. Explain the difference between legibility and readability.

2. Name three factors that affect legibility, and explain how they affect it.

3. Name three factors that affect readability, and explain how they affect it.

4. What is the difference between tracking and kerning?

5. How do color and value affect readability? How does typographic color affect readability? Name a highly readable combination and one with poor readability.

exercises

1. Explore one or more shopping districts with a camera, taking pictures of signs that are examples of poor legibility. Consider what can be done to improve each design.

2. Find three design examples for each type of alignment discussed in this chapter. Consider whether the alignment choices were effective in contributing to the legibility and/or the readability of each layout.

3. Find an advertisement that has poor readability. Make a list of changes that would improve the readability of the design. Then re-create the advertisement, implementing each of the changes you listed.

4. Choose a page from a magazine that includes several areas of text in various sizes/fonts. Choose a page that has only text, no pictures. Determine the appropriate typographic color of each block of text. Using paint or colored pencil, reproduce the layout by representing areas of text with areas of gray values that precisely reproduce the typographic color of each corresponding text block. *Tip: Standing back from the page and squinting will help you to determine an appropriate value match for the typographic colors presented in the original design.*

5. Select a photographic portrait of yourself, of someone you know, or of someone famous. Increase the size of the image (as necessary) so the face is at least six inches wide. Trace the image, dividing it into sections according to typographic color, then cut areas of text from magazines to reproduce the varying levels of gray in your image. Paste them onto bristol paper to produce a new portrait.

Courtesy of Phil Baines for Fuse, issue 1, U.K., 1991.

CHAPTER 5

objectives

- Understand the importance and purposes of layout
- Consider the relationship between form and content
- Learn about and apply the Laws of Gestalt
- Understand the visual hierarchy of design elements
- Learn how emphasis is used to guide an audience through a layout
- Learn how to create designs that comply with reading gravity
- Become familiar with the typographical devices used in layouts

introduction

When you make decisions about where to place text and objects on a page, you are creating a **layout**. How your layout is designed heavily influences whether you will get your message across to your audience.

Effective layouts help your audience to:

- Notice and decide to examine your design
- Find the information they are seeking
- Understand the information you are presenting
- Linger long enough to receive all the pieces of information you wish to convey

Creating a layout that catches and keeps your audience's attention, navigates them effectively through the design, and is easily understood is essential to the designer's ultimate goal of visual communication.

LAYOUT DESIGN ASPECTS

FORM AND CONTENT

Every layout has two competing components that you must juggle to create the most appropriate and effective design: form and content.

A layout's form refers to the way it looks. Balance, unity, contrast, color, value, texture—these are all words that describe different characteristics of a design's form.

A layout's content refers to the message or information that is meant to be conveyed by the design. The content of a layout may be intended to teach, preach, sell, convince, inform, or set a mood. Content can be presented in the form of text, symbols, or images.

Both form and content convey meaning, as seen in Figure 5-1. Even though you may not be able to read the text, you can still get a sense of the light, joyous, whimsical mood of the message.

figure | 5-1 |

Poster for the Tokyo TDC Exhibition, 1997. *Artwork: Fumio Tachibana, Design: Katsunori Aoki.*

Now look at the design pictured in Figure 5-2. Although you may not be able to read the characters, the structured seriousness of the design's presentation conveys a calm, conservative message.

figure | 5-2 |

Poster by Alan Chan. *Courtesy of Alan Chan, Alan Chan Design Co.*

Lastly, look at the design shown in Figure 5-3. In this instance, the design could indicate an angry, violent tone, even to viewers who cannot understand the content of the text. That is because the designer conveyed meaning using both form and content.

figure | 5-3 |

Poster by Koichi Sato of Koichi Sato Design Studio, 1988.

Look at the logos in Figure 5-4. In each example, the designer contrasted the form with the content to try to evoke a reaction from you, the audience. Did it work?

figure | 5-4 |

Logos with typeface designs that contrast with their content. Fonts used: Down Under Heavy, *courtesy of BA Graphics*; Reforma Grotesk Light, *courtesy of Paratype type foundry*, www.paratype.com; Ransahoff CT, *courtesy of CastleType foundry*, www.castletype.com; Bokonon, *courtesy of Cool Fonts type foundry*, www.cool-fonts.com; Viscosity, *courtesy of Fontboy type foundry*, www.fontboy.com; and Prick, *courtesy of Burghal Design type foundry*, www.burghal.com.

The **Skinny** and WIDE LOAD Show

Clean and Tidy Maid Service

| NOTE |

When your client asks you why you made a specific choice about any element of your layout, you always want to be prepared with a well thought out answer. You'll be prepared with these answers if you carefully consider each visual decision you make.

Designers make choices about the relationship between form and content of each component of a layout. Every aspect of a layout should be a conscious decision. Sometimes designers use unity, as in Figure 5-5a, and sometimes they use contrast, as in Figure 5-5b, depending on the reaction they are trying to get from the reader.

figure | 5-5a |

The word's meaning matches its physical quality of being small.

SMALL

figure | 5-5b |

The word's meaning contrasts with its physical quality of being large.

SMALL

The Reader's Interest Level

As the reader's interest in the content of a layout increases, the need for effective form decreases, and vice versa.

For example, if your friend Joe is unemployed, he will probably read the help-wanted classified ads in the newspaper, whether he perceives the layout to be dreary or exciting. He is internally motivated to read that layout because he needs a job.

The designers who lay out those classified ads are aware of this, so they can create layouts that conserve space and save money for the newspaper, knowing that people will read it anyway. On the other hand, a designer must carefully consider the form of the layout when designing an advertisement for a product or service in the same newspaper because viewers are likely to pass it over if it is not visually appealing.

Consider one more example: yourself. You are probably interested in the subject of typography or you wouldn't be reading this book. On the other hand, you probably have many other competing interests and responsibilities. How has the designer who designed the layout for this book made decisions about the relationship between form and content to keep your interest and to help you navigate through this book?

GESTALT PSYCHOLOGY AND LAYOUT ELEMENTS

In the 1920s, a German psychologist named Max Wertheimer developed a set of theories about how we organize and make sense of visual stimuli. He called this set of theories Gestalt psychology; "gestalt" is the German word for "form" or "shape." Wertheimer realized that our eyes see reflections of light waves forming shapes, textures, colors, and values—and it is our brains that interpret those patterns of light into objects and symbols that we can understand.

Understanding Gestalt psychology can be very useful for designers because it provides insights about how viewers will perceive the layouts they see. The Laws of Gestalt are theories proposed by Wertheimer that explain how our brains process visual input by grouping objects in ways that create meaning. These laws grew out of Wertheimer's idea that the groups of objects our brains assemble take on new, more profound meanings, or as Wertheimer put it, "the whole is greater than the sum of its parts."

| NOTE |

Of course, a designer's primary concern must always be communication. Simply being visually pleasing is never enough; a design is only truly successful when it transmits its intended message to the audience effectively.

The Whole is Greater Than the Sum of Its Parts

Suppose you have some eggs, sugar, flour, and butter—you have a group of ingredients; but when you mix them together, they can become a birthday cake. The meaning of the birthday cake to the recipient is greater than just a collection of random ingredients; it holds symbolic, emotional, and social meanings—and is also very tasty!

This is what Wertheimer meant when he said that the whole is greater than the sum of its parts. This idea is central to Gestalt psychology.

Now let's consider a visual example. In Figure 5-6a, you see six triangles. They probably don't hold a lot of meaning for you, aside from the relevant mathematical associations.

figure | 5-6a |

Six triangles in a row.

However, when the triangles are grouped as in Figure 5-6b, we can recognize the group as a star, or a Star of David, or as a contemporary gang symbol, depending on our realm of experience. The same six triangles, when grouped in a specific way, have taken on enormous historical and social meanings.

figure | 5-6b |

Six triangles rearranged to form a Star of David.

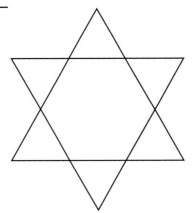

Figure and Ground

Wertheimer also understood that our brains tend to divide perceived objects into two main categories: figure and ground. The figure refers to the object we are looking at; the ground refers to the background behind the object.

We are usually concerned with the figure. If I ask you to draw a picture of a paper clip, you will probably draw the paper clip itself, but you might not also draw the background that you see it against. Designers, however, must be equally concerned with both the figure and the ground of every layout, because the figure and ground fit together like a puzzle—one exists only in relation to the other—and both have an effect on how the audience will perceive a design.

Designers and artists often talk about figure and ground in terms of positive space and negative space—the positive space being the figure, and the negative space being the ground.

Figure 5-7a shows an image of paper clips on a desk. The paper clips shown in Figure 5-7b are the positive space or figure. The desk pictured in Figure 5-7c is the negative space or ground. Each coexists in relation to the other. We may be more interested in the paper clips, but without the desk, the paper clips would be floating in nothingness, as seen in Figure 5-7b.

  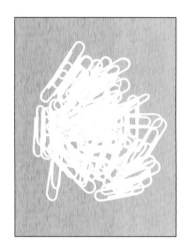

New Vocabulary

layout: the placement of text and objects on a page

figure | 5-7 |

Left (a): Paper clips on a desk.
Middle (b): Positive space, or figure.
Right (c): Negative space, or ground.

Now consider Figure 5-8a. In this case, the text is the positive space, or the figure, as shown in Figure 5-8b, and the background is the negative space, or the ground, as shown in Figure 5-8c. Notice that if we focus alternately on the figure and on the ground, we can evaluate each separately, and make changes accordingly.

Now look at Figure 5-9. First, focus on the white vase as the figure, and consider the black field behind it to be the ground. Then focus on the black silhouettes of two faces kissing as the figures, and consider the white field behind them to be the ground. As your brain shifts its perception of this image, notice that it is very difficult to simultaneously read both the vase and the faces as the figures or to simultaneously consider both the black and white fields to be the ground. Your brain wants to define the figure from the ground, to simplify and more easily make sense of what you are seeing.

figure | 5-8 |

Top (a): Text on a tinted background.
Middle (b): Positive space, or figure.
Bottom (c): Negative space, or ground.

figure | 5-9 |

Optical illusion of faces or a vase.

The Laws of Gestalt

The Laws of Gestalt—theories proposed by Max Wertheimer—explain the different ways that our brains group the shapes, colors, and textures that our eyes perceive, in order to assign meaning to visual stimuli.

The Law of Equilibrium

One such theory of Wertheimer's, the Law of Equilibrium, tells us that our brains prefer simplicity, stability, and cohesion. This means that we prefer to understand the things we see. When our brains can make sense of new stimuli, we can relax and move on to other interests. When our brains cannot make sense of new stimuli, we feel confused, anxious, and stressed out. Since the word "equilibrium" means "at rest" or "balanced," the Law of Equilibrium tells us that we feel more balanced and content when we understand the things we perceive. Therefore, our brains try to make our world seem simpler and easier to understand by grouping objects into familiar and recognizable sets of information.

So, how do our brains group the visual information they receive from our eyes? Gestalt psychology tells us that they do so according to five basic Laws of Gestalt.

- The Law of Similarity
- The Law of Proximity
- The Law of Common Fate
- The Law of Closure
- The Law of Continuation

In the next few pages, we'll examine each of these laws, and learn how they can be applied to working with type.

The Law of Similarity

The Law of Similarity states that our brains group and associate objects that look similar. For example, can you focus on just the circles or just the squares on the left in Figure 5-10? Try it.

figure | 5-10 |

The Law of Similarity causes us to group and associate objects according to shared physical characteristics.

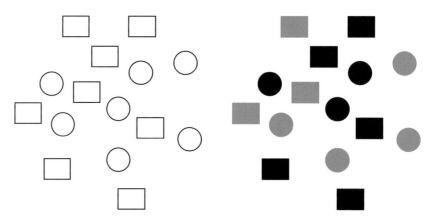

Now try to focus your attention on only the black objects, then only the blue shapes on the right in Figure 5-10b.

In Figure 5-11, you can see that similar visual qualities prompt you to group certain characters or words together. Even though the letters are layered and jumbled, the similarly sized and shaped characters help you organize the information presented in this layout, so that it is possible to read the various passages.

figure | 5-11 |

Overlapping and jumbled lines of text are legible because of the Law of Similarity.

Similar physical characteristics can also give us information about voice. Notice how the similar type styles in Figure 5-12 indicate the repeated voices of individual speakers.

figure | 5-12 |

Similar type styles indicate who is speaking because of the Law of Similarity. Aux Ionesco, *Die Kahle Sangerin*, 1964. *Courtesy of Massin.*

The Law of Similarity tells us that objects can be similar in any visual way for our brains to group them. For example, we might group objects according to size, color, value, texture, or shape.

The Law of Proximity

The Law of Proximity is very closely related to the Law of Similarity.

Since the word "proximity" means "nearness," the Law of Proximity states that our brains group and associate objects that have locations near to each other.

When you look at Figure 5-13, your brain probably groups the five stars on the left together, and the six stars on the right together.

figure | 5-13 |

The Law of Proximity causes us to group and associate objects according to a shared location or nearness.

The Law of Proximity is very important when it comes to typography because the proximity of each letter to the others determines the meaning we will assign to the text, as shown in Figure 5-14.

figure | 5-14 |

How letters are grouped influences how we interpret their meanings.

THEY'VE GONE TO GET HER.
THEY'VE GONE TOGETHER.

In Figure 5-15, text is grouped according to its proximity, or what it's close to. In this case, each blurb of text is assumed to be spoken by the little animal near it.

figure | 5-15 |

Birthday party invitation by Terri Wolfe of Wolfe Design, demonstrating the Law of Proximity.

"He's eighty, you know."

"Will there be a party?"

"With lots of berries and leaves to nibble on?"

"Oh, goody. Are *we* invited?"

Juxtaposing Letterforms

The word **juxtaposition** refers to the placement of objects in relation to one another. For example, when you juxtapose two printed words, you place them near each other, and that creates an inherent relationship between them. If viewers perceive them as a group, they will either combine or contrast the meanings of the elements, but either way, they will understand the meaning of each word in relation to the other. That is why we need only twenty-six letters in our alphabet to convey a whole host of meanings—because we combine letters in different ways to evoke different understandings.

Understanding the Law of Proximity can help a designer avoid unintended associations and miscommunications. Remember that if one object is close to another object, the viewer is likely to associate the two, even if that wasn't the designer's intention. Figure 5-16 is a good example of how otherwise unrelated information might be associated through juxtaposition. If those wooden sticks weren't placed between a torso and legs, you would probably never read them as part of a body.

figure | 5-16 |

This poster demonstrates how juxtaposition can cause viewers to draw a relationship between otherwise unrelated objects. Tyler Weekend Art Workshop poster by Keli Cavanaugh and Steven DeCusatis of Tyler Design Workshop for Tyler Design School of Art, Temple University.

The Law of Common Fate

If you share some quality with another person, you could say you have something in common. Your fate refers to where you will be in the future. So, the Law of Common Fate tells us that our brains will group and associate objects that share a common direction or orientation.

You can probably see how the Law of Common Fate also relates closely to the Law of Similarity—only this time, we are talking about a similarity of direction or orientation.

Notice how your brain groups the objects that point in a similar direction in Figure 5-17.

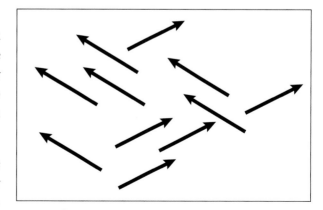

figure | 5-17 |

The Law of Common Fate causes us to group and associate objects according to a shared direction or orientation.

In the photograph of a meteor shower pictured in Figure 5-18, the streaks of light that fall to the left stand out against the ones that fall toward the right. This is because our brains group them according to the direction they seem to travel.

The same phenomenon applies to text, as shown in Figure 5-19.

figure | 5-18 |

This photograph of a meteor shower demonstrates the Law of Common Fate. © *ALI JAREKJI/Reuters/Corbis.*

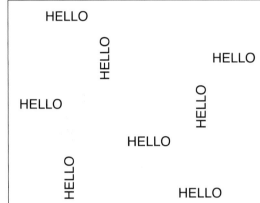

figure | 5-19 |

The Law of Common Fate causes us to group and associate objects according to a shared direction or orientation.

In Figure 5-20, the letters that read right to left stand out against the ones that read left to right. Since the capitals **T**, **H**, **W**, and **Y** are symmetrical and can be read in either direction, their size and color prompt us to group them with the backward **N** and **R**, adding to the confusion. So you see, this designer used a knowledge of both the Law of Common Fate and the Law of Similarity to convey the uncertainty and frustration that students with learning disabilities regularly endure.

figure | 5-20 |

This magazine spread demonstrates both the Law of Common Fate and the Law of Similarity. *Learning the Hard Way*, Art Director: Amanda White-Iseli, Illustration: Isabelle Arsenault, created for *Baltimore* magazine.

The Law of Closure

If you feel a sense of closure when you finish a project, it's because you have completed that project. The word **closure** means completion, and so the Law of Closure tells us that familiar shapes are more readily perceived as complete than as incomplete. Since complete objects are easier to understand, our brain groups the pieces of incomplete objects to create complete recognizable ones. That is why you are able to recognize the object in Figure 5-21 as the letter **B**, and why you are able to read the text in Figure 5-22. Your brain fills in the missing portions to perceive the shapes as ones that you can recognize and understand.

figure | 5-21 |

The Law of Closure causes us to group parts of an incomplete object to perceive a whole, recognizable object.

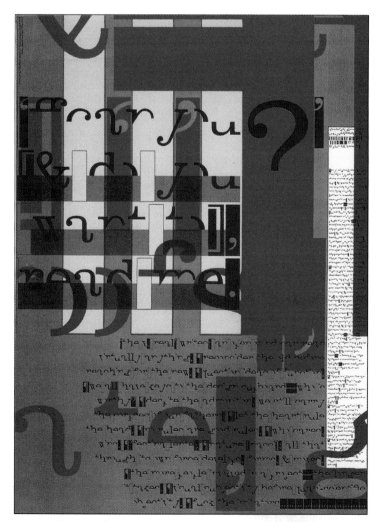

figure | 5-22 |

This poster invokes the Law of Closure. *Can You (Read Me)?* by Phil Baines for *Fuse*, issue 1, U.K., 1991.

The Law of Continuation

The Law of Continuation tells us that our brains will group items that seem to belong to a continuous line. For example, in Figure 5-23, our brains group some of the stars so that we perceive them as a row.

figure | 5-23 |

The Law of Continuation causes us to group objects that can be read as a continuous line.

Have you ever looked up at the stars at night and tried to recognize the constellations? When we group the stars of the universe into constellations, we are applying the Law of Continuation to make sense of visual stimuli. In Figure 5-24, you can make out the shape of the Big Dipper because the brightest stars can be perceived as a continuous line.

figure | 5-24 |

This photograph of Ursa Major, the Big Dipper, demonstrates the Law of Continuation. *Courtesy of Till Credner, AlltheSky.com.*

The Law of Continuation is particularly important to consider when working with type, because we recognize strings of words as sentences, due to this phenomenon. In Figure 5-25, our brains connect the dots to allow us to read the words because of the Law of Continuation, even when the letters aren't directly linked by the lines.

Also, it is this law that can cause us to perceive the distracting white rivers discussed in Chapter 4; when word spaces in adjacent rows of text are too closely aligned, our brains see white rivers that seem to flow down the page. This often occurs in layouts where text alignment is justified.

In Figure 5-26, the designer has applied an understanding of all the Laws of Gestalt. The poster features the image of a tongue near the image of an iron. The designer has purposefully created discomfort in viewers by evoking the thought of a painful burn to the tongue. Even though the images are clearly separate, their proximity suggests the dangerous relationship and possible resulting physical pain—an effective application of the Law of Proximity. The similarity of the shapes of the tongue and the iron, the fact that they point to each other, and the way they seem to form a vertical line across the layout, all work to support this association through the Gestalt Laws of Similarity, Common Fate, and Continuation, respectively. The designer has applied the Law of Closure, as well; we are able to empathize with the pain that tongue will feel because we complete the face in our minds, imagining a real person in that situation, perhaps even ourselves.

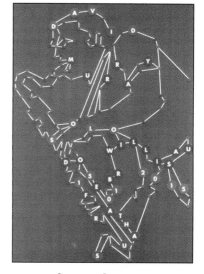

figure | 5-25 |

This poster demonstrates the Law of Continuation. *David Murray* poster by Niklaus Troxler of Niklaus Troxler Graphic Design, for *Jazz in Willisau*, 2001.

figure | 5-26 |

This poster demonstrates a number of the Laws of Gestalt. *Sensation* poster designed by Why Not Associates for the Royal Academy of Arts.

THE *designer* AT WORK

ryan pescatore frisk & catelijne van middelkoop

How did you get started as designers? Tell us about your first jobs in design and the evolution of your careers.

Both of us "Strange Attractors" studied design as undergraduates. We met when we were both invited to attend Cranbrook Academy of Art's 2D department, where we received our MFAs in 2002. In the first year, we found out that "two heads are better than one," and started working together on various projects. Though both of us had experienced the design practice before as freelancers, this was the true beginning of what was to become Strange Attractors. After we completed our master's degrees, we ran our studio from an old car factory in Pontiac, Michigan, and then moved our business to Stockholm. Since September of 2003, Strange Attractors has been operating from the Netherlands, where Ryan recently completed another MFA in type design at The Royal Academy of Art in The Hague.

We made the promise to each other (and to ourselves) that Strange Attractors would make every job or design solution into something to be proud of. We are both very critical and ambitious; now, almost five years later, we still push our limits with each new challenge.

What do you do to get your creative juices flowing when you start a new project? What can you share with us about your design process? What role does technology play in that process?

Our juices are constantly flowing. There simply isn't enough time! We are lucky enough to work on projects that we like very much. Most of our clients have found us, and have kept us busy. The rest of the time we try to spend on our own projects, which we also use to get our name out there and generate other work.

As Strange Attractors, we are trying to be as diverse as possible. We like to be in full control of our projects and therefore try to keep up with all the software that is available—from sound to the Web, from motion to type. Name it, and we'll challenge ourselves to take on the job and prove we can do it well. A new job starts with a discussion about the design problem presented. We do a lot of research using the Internet, real-time libraries, and by going on field trips. In the meantime, we start making tons of notes and, of course, sketches. We always carry around pens and random pieces of paper, from beer coasters to napkins. We ask questions like "who is our audience?" and "how far can we push this?"; we also ask practical questions like "how big is the budget for printing?" and "when is the deadline?" so that we get a better understanding of our possibilities and limitations.

When we work for a client, we plan a first presentation and try to get them to deposit a third of the money before that time so that we can start the work without having to worry about finances. The next step is to start working on at least three different ideas, three different typographic approaches, etc. Our goal is to present one proposal that we feel will be the best, plus two more that are so "out there" that if one of them would be selected, it could be even better. This is definitely the point when we'll start using the computer, so that we can rapidly

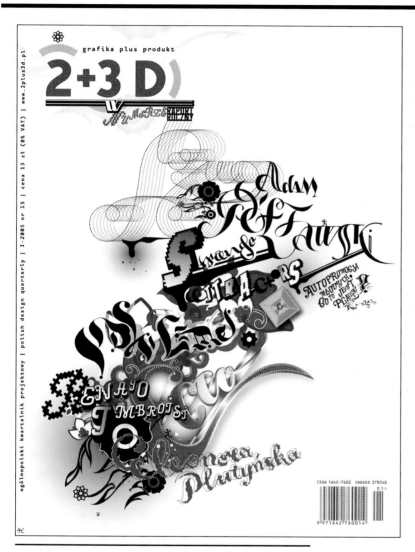

Cover design and lettering by Ryan Pescatore Frisk and Catelijne van Middelkoop for the Polish Design Quarterly, *2+3D Grafika plus Produkt*, 2005. *Courtesy of Strange Attractors, www.strangeattractors.com.*

produce proposals in PDF form, and start communicating with the client. Since Strange Attractors mainly works for clients abroad, full-time access to the Internet is an absolute necessity. When we present our ideas to clients, we never present something we don't like. We have one motto: "Trying to push boundaries."

How has the role of typography in design changed over the last decade? Where do you see it going in the future?

Over the last decade, the computer has influenced the role of typography a great deal. Because anyone with access to a computer can now influence the look of type, many analog "rules" that gave typography its strength have been neglected and forgotten. No longer limited by the lead, type is being tortured and stretched, and used in point sizes that were never seen before. In a way, the whole typographic grid has disappeared.

As you can see in our work, we do not always live by the rules either, but we can only do this successfully because we know the rules and are constantly aware of what we're doing. You can only skillfully break the rules when you know them. That's why we're constantly reading about type, continuing our educations, etc.

People who "design" their own business cards using Word, or their party invitations using other software that came with their PC—people who have not been educated in design—these amateurs have changed today's public image of typography. The common man's favorite typeface is the default Arial, which many don't even recognize as a rip off of the classic typeface Helvetica! Advertisement agencies, cutting their budgets after the Internet bubble burst, have settled for the same easy

3 Four Eyes poster by Ryan Pescatore Frisk and Catelijne van Middelkoop. *Courtesy of Strange Attractors,* www.strangeattractors.com.

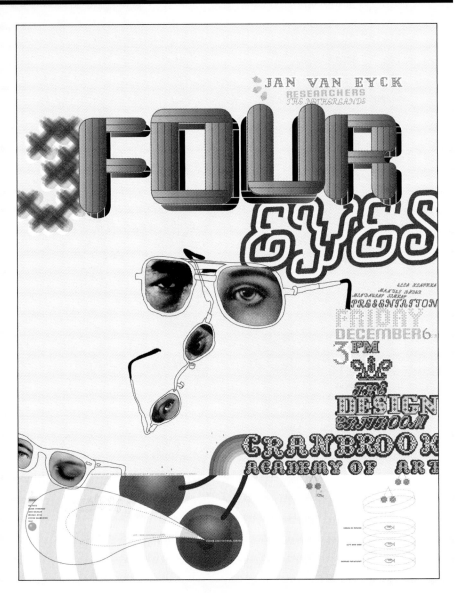

and popular sans serif solutions. All traces of humanity and personality have started to disappear from our everyday type encounters.

Lately, however, something has started to change. Designers seem to be starting to realize that in order to be different and more important—to come up with something new—knowledge of typography's rich history and craftsmanship are of extreme importance. What we would like to see happen to typography is for people to start using a voice of their own again—not the default one we've gotten used to, but a well-considered, clear one. Let there be high-quality alternatives to choose from! The future is rich.

Broadcasting Tongues Lecture and Workshop Series poster by Ryan Pescatore Frisk and Catelijne van Middelkoop. *Courtesy of Strange Attractors,* www.strangeattractors.com *and* www.dialognouveau.com.

What advice do you have for design students and new designers who are just entering the field today?

Be very, very patient, but don't sit around and wait for things to happen. It might work that way for the lucky few, but most of us have to work really hard to get our vision out there. Don't give up too soon; it really can happen! Try to stay on top of your game by reading about design, taking classes, etc., but don't forget about the real world either. It's full of treasures. Never stop questioning what you see. Acknowledge that sometimes two heads ARE better than one. Be critical of yourself, but also believe in yourself. Most important of all: have fun doing what you do.

Ryan Pescatore Frisk & Catelijne Van Middelkoop
www.strangeattractors.com.

CREATING A VISUAL HIERARCHY

By "hierarchy" we mean the order of importance within a group of people, places, or things. For example, when you play cards, there is a hierarchy that you use to determine who wins each hand (Ace, King, Queen, Jack, 10, and so on). At your job, there is probably a hierarchy of authority: president of the company, vice president of the company, regional manager, site manager, assistant manager, and so on.

Applying a **visual hierarchy** to your designs can help lead the viewer from the most important piece of information in your message to the least, in the order that *you* determine. This enhances effective communication because it saves the viewer time and provides clarity. With any design, a viewer may or may not take the time to read the whole message; this is why it is useful to guide your audience to the most important components of your layout first.

The first step in creating an effective visual hierarchy for your layout is to determine the relative importance of each piece of information involved. When you are playing cards, the hierarchy is obvious; it is dictated by the rules of the game. Determining the visual hierarchy for a layout isn't always that simple. The relative importance of any included content may vary, depending on the specific objectives of the client and on the interests and needs of the target audience. Establishing a visual hierarchy that reflects these variables up front will help you to construct your designs more efficiently and effectively.

Figure 5-27 shows examples of two designs, each containing the same content but reflecting different visual hierarchies.

figure | 5-27 |

Two designs with identical content can reflect differing visual hierarchies.

Using Emphasis

Once you've determined an appropriate visual hierarchy, you can translate that into an actual layout by using **emphasis**—that is, by making selected elements more prominent than others to attract attention and to indicate relative importance. Emphasis gives the audience clues about how to navigate through and interpret the presented content. The more an item is emphasized in a layout, the more importance it will be given by the viewer, relative to the other elements in the design. To emphasize any element of a design, you need to make it appear different from the other elements, since our eyes tend to be drawn to visual differences, or elements that **contrast**.

So, if most of the objects in a layout are small, you can emphasize an object by making it big, as in Figure 5-28a.

Or, if most items are big, you can emphasize an object by making it small, as in Figure 5-28b.

figure | 5-28a |

figure | 5-28b |

You can emphasize an object by varying the size.

Varying the size of an object is only one way to emphasize it. We can also use a contrasting color or value, as in Figure 5-28c; a contrasting texture, as in Figure 5-28d; a contrasting shape, as in Figure 5-28e; or a contrasting orientation, as in Figure 5-28f.

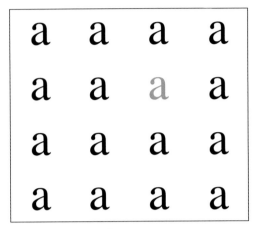

figure | 5-28c |

You can emphasize an object by varying its color or value.

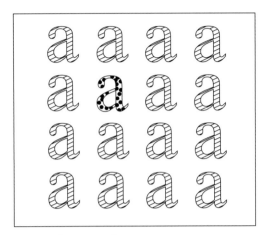

figure | 5-28d |

You can emphasize an object by varying its texture.

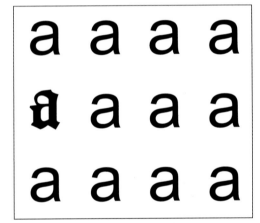

figure | 5-28e |

You can emphasize an object by varying its shape.

figure | 5-28f |

You can emphasize an object by varying its orientation.

Too many contrasting elements can have the same effect as not enough! For example, in Figures 5-29 and 5-30, it is equally difficult to determine a visual hierarchy.

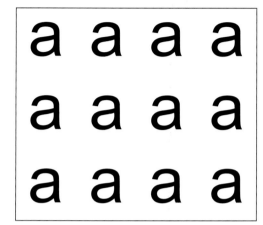

figure | 5-29 |

No object is emphasized over the others.

figure | 5-30 |

No object is emphasized over the others.

Using Reading Gravity

Just as the law of gravity tells us that if we drop an object, it will fall to the ground, the law of reading gravity tells us that we will be naturally inclined to read a layout in the order we are most accustomed to.

So, if your intended audience's first language is English or Spanish, for example, you should assume that your viewers will be in the habit of looking first to the upper left corner of any page, and then reading across and down the page, going from left to right and top to bottom. Of course, if your audience's language is Japanese or Hebrew, their reading gravity will be different.

Habits can be hard to break, so it's very important to keep reading gravity in mind when you are designing any layout.

figure | 5-31a |

A layout that ignores the effect of reading gravity, from *Type & Layout: Are You Communicating or Just Making Pretty Shapes*, by Colin Wheildon, Worsley Press, 2005.

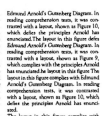

The Headline Goes Here, in the Center

The layout in this figure defies Edmund Arnold's Gutenberg Diagram. In reading comprehension tests, it was contrasted with a layout, shown as Figure 9, which complies the principles Arnold has enunciated. The layout in this figure defies Edmund Arnold's Gutenberg Diagram. In reading comprehension tests, it was contrasted with a layout, shown as Figure 9, which complies with the principles Arnold has enunciated.

The layout in this figure defies Edmund Arnold's Gutenberg Diagram. In reading comprehension tests, it was contrasted with a layout, shown as Figure 9, which complies with the principles Arnold has enunciated.he layout in this figure The layout in this figure complies with Edmund Arnold's Gutenberg Diagram. In reading comprehension tests, it was contrasted with a layout, shown as Figure 10, which defies the principles Arnold has enunciated.

The layout in this figure complies with Edmund Arnold's Gutenberg Diagram. In reading comprehension tests, it was contrasted with a layout, shown as Figure 10, which defies the principles Arnold has enunciated.

The layout in this figure complies with Edmund Arnold's Gutenberg Diagram. In reading comprehension tests, it was contrasted with a layout, shown as Figure 10, which defies the principles Arnold has enunciated.The layout in this figure defies Edmund Arnold's Gutenberg Diagram. In reading comprehension tests, it was contrasted with a layout, shown as Figure 9, which complies with the principles Arnold has enunciated.he layout in this figure The layout in this figure complies with Edmund Arnold's Gutenberg Diagram. In reading comprehension tests, it was contrasted with a layout, shown as Figure 10, which defies the principles Arnold has enunciated.

The layout in this figure complies with Edmund Arnold's Gutenberg Diagram. In reading comprehension tests, it was contrasted with a layout, shown as Figure 10, which defies the principles Arnold has enunciated.

The layout in this figure complies with

Edmund Arnold's Gutenberg Diagram. In reading comprehension tests, it was contrasted with a layout, shown as Figure 10, which defies the principles Arnold has enunciated.The layout in this figure defies Edmund Arnold's Gutenberg Diagram. In reading comprehension tests, it was contrasted with a layout, shown as Figure 9, which complies with the principles Arnold has enunciated.he layout in this figure The layout in this figure complies with Edmund Arnold's Gutenberg Diagram. In reading comprehension tests, it was contrasted with a layout, shown as Figure 10, which defies the principles Arnold has enunciated.

The layout in this figure complies with Edmund Arnold's Gutenberg Diagram. In reading comprehension tests, it was contrasted with a layout, shown as Figure 10, which defies the principles Arnold has enunciated.

The layout in this figure complies with

Edmund Arnold's Gutenberg Diagram. In reading comprehension tests, it was contrasted with a layout, shown as Figure 10, which defies the principles Arnold has enunciated.The layout in this figure defies Edmund Arnold's Gutenberg Diagram. In reading comprehension tests, it was contrasted with a layout, shown as Figure 9, which complies with the principles Arnold has enunciated.he layout in this figure The layout in this figure complies with Edmund Arnold's Gutenberg Diagram. In reading comprehension tests, it was contrasted with a layout, shown as Figure 10, which defies the principles Arnold has enunciated.The layout in this figure complies with Edmund Arnold's Gutenberg Diagram. In reading comprehension tests, it was contrasted with a layout, shown as Figure 10, which defies the principles Arnold has enunciated.The layout in this figure defies Edmund Arnold's Gutenberg Diagram. In reading comprehension tests, it was contrasted with a layout, shown as Figure 9, which complies with the principles Arnold has enunciated.he layout in this figure The layout in this figure complies with Edmund Arnold's Gutenberg Diagram. In reading comprehension tests, it was contrasted with a layout, shown as Figure 10, which defies the principles Arnold has enunciated.The layout in this figure complies with Edmund Arnold's Gutenberg Diagram. In reading comprehension tests, it was contrasted with a layout, shown as Figure 10, which defies the principles Arnold has enunciated.

The layout in this figure complies with Edmund Arnold's Gutenberg Diagram. In reading comprehension tests, it was contrasted with a layout, shown as Figure 10, which defies the principles Arnold has enunciated.

The layout in this figure complies with Edmund Arnold's Gutenberg Diagram. In reading comprehension tests, it was contrasted with a layout, shown as Figure 10, which defies the principles Arnold has enunciated.The layout in this figure defies Edmund Arnold's Gutenberg Diagram. In reading comprehension tests, it was contrasted with a layout, shown as Figure 9, which complies with the principles Arnold has enunciated.he layout in this figure The layout in this figure complies with Edmund Arnold's Gutenberg Diagram. In reading comprehension tests, it was contrasted with a layout, shown as Figure 10, which defies the principles Arnold has enunciated.

The layout in this figure complies with Edmund Arnold's Gutenberg Diagram. In reading comprehension tests, it was contrasted with a layout, shown as Figure 10, which defies the principles Arnold has enunciated.

The layout in this figure complies with Edmund Arnold's Gutenberg Diagram. In reading comprehension tests, it was contrasted with a layout, shown as Figure 10, which defies the principles Arnold has enunciated.The layout in this figure complies with Edmund Arnold's Gutenberg Diagram. In reading comprehension tests, it was contrasted with a layout, shown as Figure 10, which defies the principles Arnold has enunciated.The layout in this figure defies Edmund Arnold's Gutenberg Diagram. In reading comprehension tests, it was contrasted with a layout, shown as Figure 9, which complies with the principles Arnold has enunciated.he layout in this figure The layout in this figure complies with Edmund Arnold's Gutenberg Diagram. In reading comprehension tests, it was contrasted with a layout, shown as Figure 10, which defies the principles Arnold has enunciated.

The layout in this figure complies with Edmund Arnold's Gutenberg Diagram. rasted with a layout, shown as Figure 10, which defies the principles Arnold has enunciated.The layout in this figure complies with Edmund Arnold's Gutenberg Diagram. rasted with a layout, shown as Figure 10, which defies the principles Arnold has enunciated. trasted with a layout, shown as Figure 10, which defies the principles Arnold has enunciated.

Figure 5-31a is a perfect example of the effect of reading gravity; in it, the reader is forced to start reading halfway down the page. Since the viewers are less likely to defy their own reading habits by going back up to the top of the page, there's a good chance that they won't read the top portion of this article.

On the other hand, a design like the one in Figure 5-31b allows the viewers to follow their naturally ingrained habit of reading from top to bottom and left to right.

The Headline Goes Up Here

The text then starts here and continues without interruption in this four-column layout. Text is fully justified. This layout is much favored by readers—and much less so by magazine and newspaper editors, not to mention advertising people. Most layout artists frown on such obvious simplicity. Who's in the right?

The layout in this figure complies with Edmund Arnold's Gutenberg Diagram. In reading comprehension tests, it was contrasted with a layout, shown as Figure 10, which defies the principles Arnold has enunciated. The layout in this figure complies with Edmund Arnold's Gutenberg Diagram. In reading comprehension tests, it was contrasted with a layout, shown as Figure 10, which defies the principles Arnold has enunciated. The text then starts here and continues without interruption in this four-column layout. Text is fully justified. This layout is much favored by readers—and much less so by magazine and newspaper editors, not to mention advertising people. Most layout artists frown on such obvious simplicity. Who's in the right?

The layout in this figure complies with Edmund Arnold's Gutenberg Diagram. In reading comprehension tests, it was contrasted with a layout, shown as Figure 10, which defies the principles Arnold has enunciated. The layout in this figure complies with Edmund Arnold's Gutenberg Diagram. In reading comprehension tests, it was contrasted with a layout, shown as Figure 10, which defies the principles Arnold has enunciated. The text then starts here and continues without interruption in this four-column layout. Text is fully justified. This layout is much favored by readers—and much less so by magazine and newspaper editors, not to mention adver-

tising people. Most layout artists frown on such obvious simplicity. Who's in the right?

The layout in this figure complies with Edmund Arnold's Gutenberg Diagram. In reading comprehension tests, it was contrasted with a layout, shown as Figure 10, which defies the principles Arnold has enunciated. The layout in this figure complies with Edmund Arnold's Gutenberg Diagram. In reading comprehension tests, it was contrasted with a layout, shown as Figure 10, which defies the principles Arnold has enunciated. The text then starts here and continues without interruption in this four-column layout. Text is fully justified. This layout is much favored by readers—and much less so by magazine and newspaper editors, not to mention advertising people. Most layout artists frown on such obvious simplicity. Who's in the right?

The layout in this figure complies with Edmund Arnold's Gutenberg Diagram. In reading comprehension tests, it was contrasted with a layout, shown as Figure 10, which defies the principles Arnold has enunciated. The layout in this figure complies with Edmund Arnold's Gutenberg Diagram. In reading comprehension tests, it was contrasted with a layout, shown as Figure 10, which defies the principles Arnold has enunciated. The text then starts here and continues without interruption in this four-column layout. Text is fully justified. This layout is much favored by readers—and much less so by magazine and newspaper editors, not to mention adver-

reading comprehension tests, it was contrasted with a layout, shown as Figure 10, which defies the principles Arnold has enunciated. The layout in this figure complies with Edmund Arnold's Gutenberg Diagram. In reading comprehension tests, it was contrasted with a layout, shown as Figure 10, which defies the principles Arnold has enunciated. The text then starts here and continues without interruption in this four-column layout. Text is fully justified. This layout is much favored by readers—and much less so by magazine and newspaper editors, not to mention advertising people. Most layout artists frown on such obvious simplicity. Who's in the right?

The layout in this figure complies with Edmund Arnold's Gutenberg Diagram. In reading comprehension tests, it was contrasted with a layout, shown as Figure 10, which defies the principles Arnold has enunciated. The layout in this figure complies with Edmund Arnold's Gutenberg Diagram. In reading comprehension tests, it was contrasted with a layout, shown as Figure 10, which defies the principles Arnold has enunciated. The text then starts here and continues without interruption in this four-column layout. Text is fully justified. This layout is much favored by readers—and much less so by magazine and newspaper editors, not to mention advertising people. Most layout artists frown on such obvious simplicity. Who's in the right?

The layout in this figure complies with Edmund Arnold's Gutenberg Diagram. In reading comprehension tests, it was contrasted with a layout, shown as Figure 10, which defies the principles Arnold has enunciated. The text then starts here and continues without interruption in this four-column layout. Text is fully justified. This layout is much favored by readers—and much less so by magazine and newspaper editors, not to mention advertising people. Most layout artists frown on such obvious simplicity. Who's in the right? The layout in this figure complies with Edmund Arnold's Gutenberg Diagram. In reading comprehension tests, it was contrasted with the layout in Figure 10, which defies Arnold. as Figure 10he principles Arnold has enunciated. Most layout artists frown on such obvious simplicity. Who's in the right? The layout in this figure complies with Edmund Arnold's Gutenberg Diaddafewxxoaagram. In rci-ples Arnold has enunciated.

tising people. Most layout artists frown on such obvious simplicity. Who's in the right?

The layout in this figure complies with Edmund Arnold's Gutenberg Diagram. In reading comprehension tests, it was contrasted with a layout, shown as Figure 10, which defies the principles Arnold has enunciated. The layout in this figure complies with Edmund Arnold's Gutenberg Diagram. In reading comprehension tests, it was contrasted with a layout, shown as Figure 10, which defies the principles Arnold has enunciated. The text then starts here and continues without interruption in this four-column layout. Text is fully justified. This layout is much favored by readers—and much less so by magazine and newspaper editors, not to mention advertising people. Most layout artists frown on such obvious simplicity. Who's in the right?

The layout in this figure complies with Edmund Arnold's Gutenberg Diagram. In reading comprehension tests, it was contrasted with a layout, shown as Figure 10, which defies the principles Arnold has enunciated. The layout in this figure complies with Edmund Arnold's Gutenberg Diagram. In reading comprehension tests, it was contrasted with a layout, shown as Figure 10, which defies the principles Arnold has enunciated. The text then starts here and continues without interruption in this four-column layout. Text is fully justified. This layout is much favored by readers—and much less so by magazine and newspaper editors, not to mention advertising people. Most layout artists frown on such obvious simplicity. Who's in the right?

figure | 5-31b |

A layout that acknowledges reading gravity, from *Type & Layout: Are You Communicating or Just Making Pretty Shapes*, by Colin Wheildon, Worsley Press, 2005.

NOTE

Research has shown that readers are more than twice as likely to read and comprehend a layout that flows according to their reading gravity than one that does not. Keep this in mind every time you develop a new layout.

Typographic Devices

Typographic devices can give us hints about the kind of information to expect from textual items, even before reading them. Such devices help readers draw relationships between page elements and help them to understand how the information is organized. Some of these devices are headlines, subheads, block quotations, headers, tables, captions, **sidebars**, callouts, footers, lists, pull-quotes, and folios, as shown in Figure 5-32.

Headlines

A **headline** is the title of an article or layout. It should be only a few words because its purpose is to draw attention and quickly indicate the topic of the body text. Headlines are usually set at a larger point size than the body text, and can be set in display typefaces without sacrificing reader comprehension.

Subheads

Subheads are secondary headlines that subdivide and organize body text, increasing readability and reader comprehension. Subheads are often darker and larger than body text, but shouldn't be as large as the headline of the layout.

Block quotations

When quotations are longer than a few lines, they are typically designed as **block quotations**, which are set apart with increased spacing before and after. Block quotations are usually indented, single spaced, and often set in a smaller point size than the body text.

Headers

A **header** (or **running head**) is text that runs along the top margin of multiple pages of a publication, and is often used to provide navigational information like titles, dates, or folios.

Tables

A table is an arrangement of data, organized into a grid of rows and columns; it may be bordered or shaded.

Captions

A **caption** is a line or short passage that explains or describes a neighboring image or graphic. Captions are often italicized or set in a smaller point size than body type.

Callouts

A **callout** indicates information about an item in an illustration, using a line, arrow, or pointer.

Sidebars

A **sidebar** is information set apart from the main body text. Often enclosed in a box, sidebars contain text independent of the main passage, though it may be indirectly related. Sidebars are often indicated by a change in background value or color, and are sometimes bordered.

Footers

A **footer** (or **running foot**) is text that runs along the bottom margin of multiple pages of a publication. Like headers, footers are often used to provide navigational information like titles, dates, or folios. Footers can also contain footnotes.

Pull-quotes

A **pull-quote** is a sentence, quoted from the body text of the layout. Its purpose is to draw the attention of readers, promoting interest in the body text. Pull-quotes are usually set in a larger point size and apart from the body text using visual dividers like bars or dingbats.

Lists

Lists indicate a series of related items. Numbering or bulleting lists with dingbats can help readers determine when a new item in the list has begun. They are often indented and have extra spacing added above and below.

Folios

Folios are simply page numbers. Readers usually look for the folio at the top or bottom outside corner of the page, or centered in the footer; however, less traditional folio placements are acceptable as long as they are consistent, and not difficult to find.

figure | 5-32 |

Typographic devices.

New Vocabulary

block quotation: a quotation that is longer than a few lines, and so is set apart with increased spacing before and after and usually indented

callout: the name of an item in illustrations, indicated by a line or arrow

caption: a line or short passage that explains or describes a neighboring image or graphic

contrast: 1. a difference among compared elements; 2. to exhibit dissimilar qualities when compared; 3. to compare differences; and 4. in type, the variation between a character's thickest and thinnest stroke weights

emphasis: a principle of design in which selected elements in a layout are made more prominent than others to attract attention and to indicate relative importance

folio: page number

footer (or **running foot**): text that runs along the bottom margin of multiple pages of a publication, used to provide navigational information like titles, dates, or folios; can also contain footnotes

header (or **running head**): text that runs along the top margin of multiple pages of a publication, used to provide navigational information like titles, dates, or folios

headline: the title of an article or layout used to draw attention

pull-quote: a sentence, quoted from the body text and set apart and in larger point size

sidebar: information that is independent from the body text and is set apart, sometimes enclosed in a box

subhead: secondary headline that subdivides and organizes body text

visual hierarchy: the order of importance of elements within a layout, as indicated by the use of emphasis and typographic elements such as bars, rules, and bullets

NAVIGATION

You always want to keep the viewer's experience in mind when designing layouts. Text and objects must be easy to read and placed in a way that guides the viewer's experience. The visual layout of items must communicate:

- The order in which information should be read

- What objects and text should be grouped together

- The order of importance of this information

Reading and navigating your design must be easy for viewers in order to retain your audience. It should be obvious to readers how to find the information they seek. If a design doesn't effectively lead its audience from the most important piece of information to the least, they are likely to become confused, frustrated, or even irritated.

Usability becomes particularly crucial for layouts that will be interactive. Designers must anticipate the movements of readers through the design, and guide them toward intended messages and necessary information. A few simple rules of thumb can help you to make your interactive designs user-friendly. Although these guidelines are most applicable to digital interactive designs, they can be applied to any interactive experience.

- *Keep it simple.* Navigating a design should be fairly intuitive. The interface should not be so involved that it detracts attention from the content.

- *Make it effortless to use.* Anticipate the needs of your users so you can make elements convenient for them.

- *Let interactions direct future experiences.* Personalizing an environment so that new offerings are based on past selections can be an effective way to create a positive experience for users.

- *Offer choices.* Audiences generally appreciate being able to make decisions about how to allocate their time, pacing, and explorations. In a digital environment, in particular, always provide alternatives for users who wish to end experiences earlier than you'd planned.

- *Be clear.* Users shouldn't have to figure out the components of your design. In a digital environment, this means they shouldn't have to guess which objects are clickable, for instance.

- *Give feedback.* Users will want to know whether they have responded appropriately and whether their participation has been registered. An answer key, the lighting of a flipped switch, or the sound of a clicking button can let the user know whether their action was registered and/or correct.

Layouts designed for a digital environment are likely to be viewed in a nonlinear way, and so they may require some added structures to help the audience find their way around. Incorporating some of the following tools into your designs can help facilitate your audience's experience.

- *Scrolling* will often be necessary for your audience to view your whole layout. Frequently, the opening glimpse of your design will be only a partial view, so make it count. Upon opening a document or web page, the viewers should be able to get their bearings without having to scroll excessively; otherwise, they are likely to become annoyed.

- *Hyperlinks* are text and/or images that access remote locations at the click of a mouse. (Hypertext is a textual hyperlink.) Hyperlinks allow users to navigate a digital environment in a nonlinear fashion. This lets them personalize their experience to best suit their own needs and interests, while helping to preserve their reading flow.

- *Rollovers* trigger visual effects, movements, or variations when the user moves the cursor over the object with the mouse.

- *Spatial zooms* are hyperlinks that allow viewers to increase or decrease the scale of their view or an object by clicking on it.

- *Networks,* or interconnected systems of links within a web site, let users navigate along a nonlinear self-selected path.

- *Linear series* are useful when you want to dictate the order in which information will be viewed, as in a slideshow.

SUMMARY

The term layout refers to the way that a designer places objects and text on a page to create a design. It is important for designers to make conscious decisions about each element of every layout because these decisions will greatly influence whether the audience is able to receive the entire intended message or not. The placement of your text and images will play a major role in whether the audience finds, pays attention to, enjoys, understands, and can navigate through your design.

In creating a layout that visually communicates effectively, the designer must consider the relationship between the form and the content of the layout. Both form and content convey meaning, so the designer must make choices about this relationship. Prioritizing content into a visual hierarchy can also help designers to make good decisions about which elements to emphasize through effective use of contrast. The Laws of Gestalt are theories that explain and predict how our brains will perceive, group, and interpret visual information; understanding them can help designers to apply contrast and emphasis in ways that will effectively manipulate viewers' perceptions. In addition, designers can more than double the chances of their messages being effectively conveyed by applying the concept of reading gravity to designs.

in review

1. What is a layout?

2. How should the audience's expected interest level affect the form of your designs?

3. Name and explain each Law of Gestalt.

4. What is a visual hierarchy? How should the visual hierarchy of design elements influence your layout?

5. Explain the concept of reading gravity.

6. Describe a variety of ways you could emphasize an object or text in a layout.

exercises

1. Look through a newspaper or magazine. Find examples that show different relationships between form and content.

2. Look through some magazines to find examples of text and/or images that illustrate each of the Laws of Gestalt.

3. Select a brochure, business card, advertisement, or magazine layout whose design defies reading gravity. Then select another design that complies with reading gravity. Overlay a piece of tracing paper on top of each design, and chart out a map of arrows, indicating the route a reader would most likely navigate through each design as a result of emphasis and placement of elements.

4. Look through some magazines to find five different examples of ways that designers have emphasized elements of their layouts.

5. Some clients have asked you to create an advertising flyer to be distributed and hung around the neighborhood. The flyer is to include the following text:

"The Association of Bluegrass Music Lovers invites you to attend the Bluegrass Festival and Dance Contest on Friday, August 26, 7pm – 9pm at Grant Park, 2000 York Road, Springfield, California. Tickets are $10 each. All proceeds will be donated to the Young Musicians Scholarship Fund."

The clients include three local organizations which are co-sponsoring this event. Each client, however, has their own objectives, and wants you to design a customized flyer especially for them to distribute. The three client organizations are:

- The Association of Bluegrass Music Lovers—their objective is to promote local interest in Bluegrass music and to gain membership for their organization. They will distribute flyers among their citywide membership.

- The Young Musicians Scholarship Fund—their objective is to promote youth interest in music and to raise money so they can sponsor more young musicians' studies. They will distribute flyers through parent groups and at school-related concerts, dances, and band practices.

- The Grant Park District—their objective is to encourage public use of park facilities and to encourage a sense of neighborhood pride and community. They will distribute flyers among local businesses and community facilities and institutions.

For each sponsoring organization, divide the provided text into a customized list, prioritizing the information from most important to least. Then use each list to create a customized flyer for the corresponding organization. The three flyers must contain exactly the same textual content, but each must typographically reflect its customized visual hierarchy. Consider the relationship between the objectives of each organization, the visual hierarchies you established, and your design choices.

6. Select an advertisement from a magazine. Make a list of each component in the magazine in the order you believe to be the designer's visual hierarchy. Then, make a new list of the same elements, prioritizing them into a different hierarchy. Create a new advertisement that is based on the new visual hierarchy you developed.

7. Create a small book in which each spread includes only text (no images) describing each Law of Gestalt in both its content and its form—this means you'll need to explain each law, and illustrate it using only letterforms.

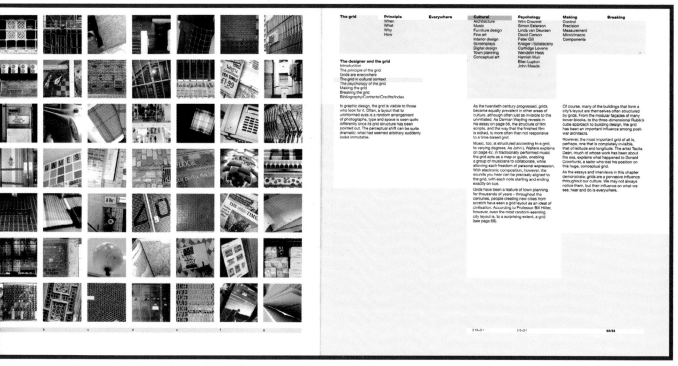

Courtesy of Lucienne Roberts and Bob Wilkinson of sans+baum.

CHAPTER 6

objectives

- Understand why and how to use a grid to add consistency to a document or web site
- Learn the vocabulary associated with grids
- Learn how to align regular and irregular objects to a grid
- Explore a variety of possible grid layouts

introduction

Creating layouts can be made easier by using a **grid**, which is a framework of guidelines that form an underlying structure for the layout of a document or web site. Grids are used by designers to aid in the logical placement of design elements, to maintain consistency among related layouts, and to establish a sense of rhythm throughout a design. Using a grid streamlines the design process because it allows designers to reapply their design decisions to multiple layouts, rather than beginning a new one each time. Grids are especially helpful in saving time on large projects.

USING GRIDS

THE GRID AS A TOOL

If you've ever typed a document using a word processing program on a computer, you have used a grid. You made decisions about the margins and the spacing of your text, and those decisions were then applied to the whole document. For example, if you set the margins at one inch and centered the page numbers in the bottom margin, your page probably looks something like Figure 6-1a. The grid for that page looked like the one shown in Figure 6-1b.

figure | 6-1a |

A page from a typical term paper.

figure | 6-1b |

The grid used to create a typical term paper.

Sometimes you filled the printable area with text, as seen in Figure 6-1c—and sometimes you didn't, as seen in Figure 6-1d. The grid acts as a guide to help you decide where to put your text on the page.

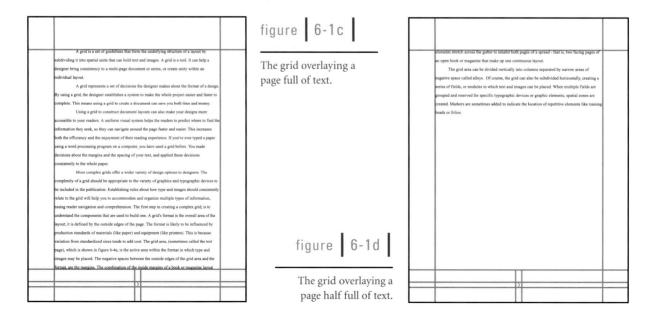

figure | 6-1c |

The grid overlaying a page full of text.

figure | 6-1d |

The grid overlaying a page half full of text.

Suppose your document was to include several block quotations. In this case, your grid would be a bit more complex, as shown in Figure 6-1e. Grids offer a wide variety of design options to designers. The complexity of any grid can be tailored to the kinds of graphics and typographic devices that will be applied to it.

figure | 6-1e |

The slightly more complex grid accommodates an indented block quote.

It is important to always remember, though, that a grid is only a tool. Its purpose is to bring order, unity, and a sense of identity to the layout of a document or digital environment, while making the designer's job easier and faster. In most cases, the grid will not even show in the final publication; it is used only while placing the design elements on the page. The audience will not see the designer's grid—only the unified and well-organized layouts produced by using it. Layouts constructed using grids tend to be more accessible to readers because the uniform visual system helps them predict where to find the information they seek; this increases both the efficiency and the enjoyment of their reading experience.

New Vocabulary

grid: a framework of guidelines that form the underlying structure of a layout by dividing it into spatial units that can hold text, images, or negative space

adventures IN **DESIGN**

THE GOLDEN SECTION

Throughout history, people have been fascinated with the concept of proportion. In ancient Egypt and Greece, philosophers, artists, architects, and mathematicians studied nature to find the spatial relationship that represented the most efficient and harmonious use of space. What was discovered was called "The Golden Section" or "The Divine Proportion."

Examine the rectangle in Figure A.

Figure A: A rectangle with a 5:8 proportion.

A rectangle (or grid) of this proportion (1 to 1.618, or 5:8) is considered by many to be the most harmonious proportion in nature because when it is divided into a square and a rectangle, as in Figure B, the ratio of the rectangular section's width (the shorter side of the tinted area in Figure C) to its length (the longer side of the tinted area in Figure D) is the same as the ratio of the original rectangle's width (the shorter side of the tinted area in Figure E) to its length (the longer side of the tinted area in Figure F).

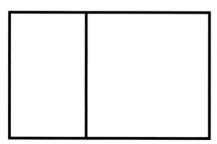

Figure B: A rectangle with a 5:8 proportion can be divided into a square and a rectangle that also has a 5:8 proportion.

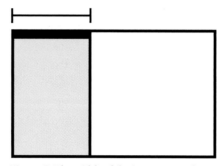

Figure C: The width of the inner rectangle.

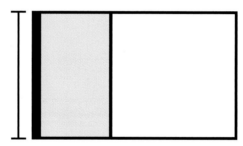

Figure D: The length of the inner rectangle.

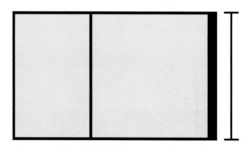

Figure E: The width of the original rectangle.

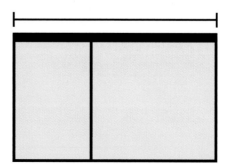

Figure F: The length of the original rectangle.

So, this means that each time a rectangle of this proportion is divided into a square and a rectangle, no space is wasted, and these modules can be efficiently packed together, as can be seen in Figure G. Because this pattern provides an efficient way for cells to grow, it's found again and again in nature, from the shape of this nautilus shell (Figure H) to the double helix that makes up our own DNA (Figure I).

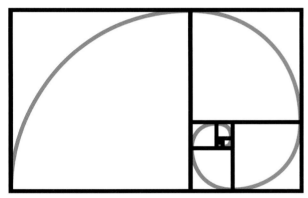

Figure G: The Golden Section.

Figure H: A nautilus seashell, from *Symmetry: A Unifying Concept*, published by Shelter Publications, Inc., Bolinas, CA. *Copyright © 1994 István Hargittai and Magdolna Hargittai.*

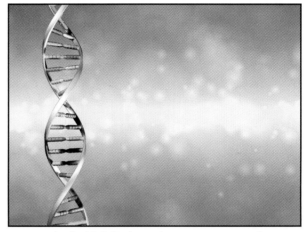

Figure I: The double helix that makes up our DNA. © *Ethan Myerson / iStockphoto.*

Research has shown that human beings tend to have a preference for shapes and compositions of this proportion; that is why the architects of ancient Greece, painters of Renaissance Europe, and many contemporary designers have used the Golden Section to create harmonious layouts and designs. We can even see how the ancient Greek Parthenon's design is guided by the proportions of the Golden Section (Figure J).

Figure J: The Parthenon was built according to the proportions of the Golden Section.

DESIGNING CONSIDERATIONS

To decide what a grid should look like, the designer must consider the needs of the design problem at hand. These considerations can include many things.

Size Requirements

- The amount of information that must be included on each page
- The size of type and objects that will be applied to the grid
- The final size, shape, and orientation of the document

Content Possibilities

- Text and images
- Typographic devices
- Negative spaces

The Design Concept

- The style, mood, and tone of the document or web site
- The specific needs of the target audience
- Consistency with the image of the client

To construct a grid, a designer uses a combination of vertical, horizontal, diagonal, and/or shaped guidelines to divide a layout into spatial units that can hold text and images, or can remain empty. The intended look of the design will dictate the relationships between design elements and the grid.

Production Requirements

A grid's **format** is the overall area of the layout; it is defined by the outside edges of the page. Whether a grid is used to create designs for print or on-screen viewing, its construction should be affected by the standard production sizes applicable to the end medium. For instance, a grid for a web site must accommodate the average computer screen size and proportions, while a grid for a direct mail brochure must accom-

| NOTE |

Negative space is an important part of any layout. Open spaces in a layout can create an air of elegance and simplicity, and can increase readability for viewers. Just as a grid can be used to help organize typographic and graphic elements, it can also be used to help organize and allocate areas to remain empty.

modate standard printing and postal sizes. Variation from standardized sizes tends to add cost, and may risk creating incompatibility with users' needs. For instance, a business card shaped like a star may be a good attention-grabber, but it may also be expensive to produce because it will require a special die-cut, and it won't maximize usage of a standard sheet of cardstock. The fact that the uncommon shape won't fit nicely into clients' wallets (which are designed to hold standard-sized business cards and credit cards) may make the concept counterproductive. The default format for most grid designs will need to conform to production conventions; often this will mean working with a rectangular or square grid. Although deviation from production conventions can certainly be done, this should only be attempted with a specific purpose in mind, and with awareness of possible extra costs and complications.

Establishing a Visual Program

Establishing a **visual program**, or a set of parameters directing how type and images should consistently relate to the grid, can help you accommodate and organize multiple types of information, improving reader navigation and comprehension. For instance, as part of your visual program, you would decide which fields could and could not accommodate text and/or images. You would also decide how various objects should be aligned; text and images can be left-aligned, right-aligned, justified, or centered along one guideline or between two. Deciding how various objects should consistently align to the grid will contribute to the unity of the overall layout.

Grids can be used by designers in different ways. Sometimes grids are used quite strictly according to a rigid visual program. Strict adherence to the grid is particularly useful when working with a series of items; this strategy can establish a strong sense of unity and a compelling impression of brand identity. For instance, if you are designing a set of collectible trading cards, packaging designs for a line of products, or cover designs for a series of books, a rigid visual program can be very useful.

Grids are not always used in a strict manner. Sometimes a grid is established before starting a design, but often the grid emerges and evolves throughout the design process. When using a flexible grid, designers may establish and adapt guidelines to align design elements as needed. Later, they might reuse and continue to adapt the resulting grid to create related designs.

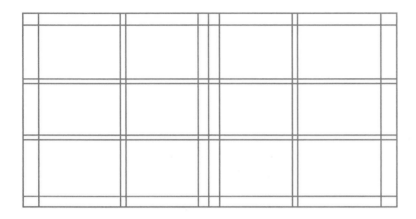

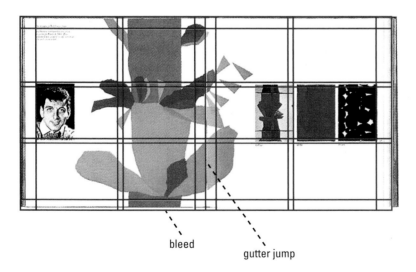

bleed

gutter jump

figure | 6-2 |

The same grid shown overlaying two very different layouts from the *Knoll Design* book by Massimo Vignelli of Vignelli Associates, for Knoll International.

Combining Sections of the Grid

When establishing a visual program, a designer must also decide how fields can (or cannot) be combined. In a very strict use of the grid, text and objects might only begin and end at guidelines; in a more flexible use of the grid, the designer can let text and objects begin at a guideline, and then extend as far as needed, so that the content might not fill a field, or it might extend into other fields, as necessary. Fields can also be combined so that an object or a section of text can begin at one guideline and end several guidelines over. A **gutter jump** happens when typographic or graphic elements stretch across the gutter to inhabit fields on both pages of a spread, as in Figure 6-2. Sometimes an element extends into a neighboring margin, and then extends right past the edge of the page. An element that extends beyond the trim line of a layout is called a **bleed**. **Trim lines** or **trim marks** are sometimes added to the layout to indicate where the guillotine cut will be made after printing. In Figure 6-2, you can see two very different layouts; they were created using the same grid, which is shown overlaying them. Notice that elements don't always fill the fields they inhabit, and that objects sometimes extend across guidelines to occupy multiple fields. Also notice that fields can remain empty, too.

GRID LAYOUTS

Grids lend consistency to multipage documents like books, magazines, newspapers, and brochures. Depending on the needs of the specific project, either a strict or a flexible visual program may be employed in constructing a multipage publication. Although any collection of guidelines can constitute a grid, there are several specific ways that grids have traditionally been applied to multipage documents to establish order, which is maintained through the consistent use of grid components, shown in Figure 6-3.

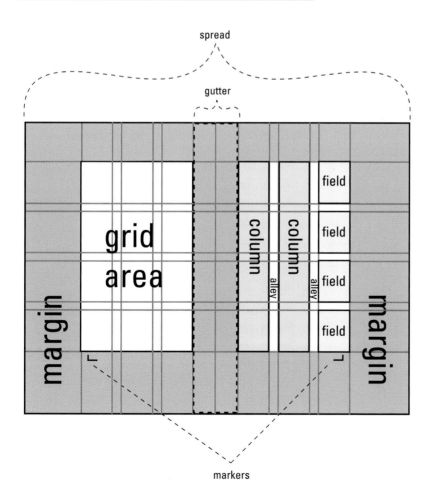

figure | 6-3 |

Grid components.

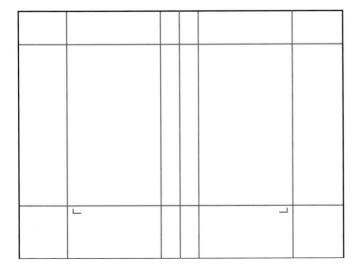

Manuscript Grid

For a multipage publication that includes long spans of continuous text, like a book for instance, you may want to create a manuscript grid—that is, a grid which contains a large area for content, enclosed by **margins**. This large content area is called the **grid area** (also called the **text page** or **text area**). The grid area is the active area within the format where type and images may be placed; the margins are the negative spaces between the outside edges of the grid area and the format. The space formed by the two inside margins of a book or magazine layout closest to the binding is called the **gutter**. When the publication is a book, the manuscript grid will usually be laid out so that the two facing pages that make up one continuous layout, or **spread**, mirror each other. You would also designate specific locations for regularly applied elements (like folios or running heads) to appear by adding **markers** to the grid. Figure 6-4 shows an example of a manuscript grid overlaying a spread from a book.

figure | 6-4 |

A manuscript grid overlaying mirrored facing pages of a book spread from *No. I. Bookbinding* by W. R. Lethaby.

Column Grid

When a layout is to contain a large amount of discontinuous text, like several short articles in a newspaper or magazine, the grid area of a manuscript grid can be divided vertically into columns to create a column grid. A column grid is like a manuscript grid only instead of one large area for content, the grid area is divided into two or more columns, usually separated by narrow areas of negative space called **alleys**, which were shown in Figure 6-3. Figure 6-5 shows an example of a column grid overlaying a spread from a magazine.

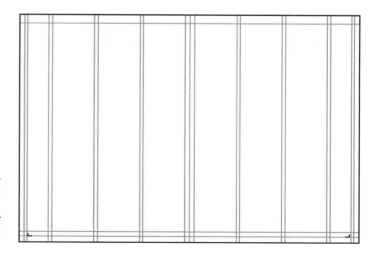

figure | 6-5 |

A column grid overlaying facing pages of a magazine spread from *The Comics Journal* magazine #245, August 2002, designed by Peppy White of Fantagraphics Books.

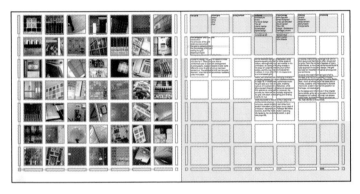

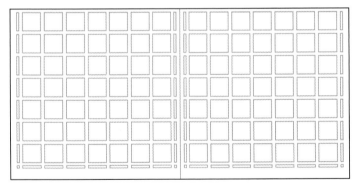

figure | 6-6 |

A modular grid overlaying facing pages of a book spread from *The Designer and the Grid* by Lucienne Roberts and Julia Thrift, designed by Lucienne Roberts and Bob Wilkinson of sans+baum.

Modular Grid

Of course, a grid can also be subdivided horizontally to create a modular grid, as seen in Figure 6-3. The horizontal subdivisions create a series of **fields**, or modules, where text and images can be placed. For layouts that must accommodate many images or graphics, modular grids are extremely useful. A modular grid is usually divided both horizontally and vertically into a series of equally sized fields, sometimes separated by alleys. If you have ever used a piece of graph paper, you have used a modular grid. Often the fields of modular grids are drawn as self-contained boxes instead of a grid of overlapping guidelines, but either approach is acceptable. Figure 6-6 shows an example of a modular grid overlaying a spread from a book.

Baseline Grid

When a design will accommodate a considerable amount of text at a single point size (like in a newspaper), it is useful to establish a baseline grid to make sure the lines of text in neighboring columns line up, and to maximize the use of space in the layout. To create a baseline grid, simply add horizontal guidelines at regularly spaced intervals equal to the point size of your type (including its leading). This will create fields that perfectly accommodate text at the size you have planned for. Unfortunately, changes in point size can look very strange on a baseline grid, because the leading cannot be scaled with the type without violating the grid.

You have used a baseline grid before if you've ever written in a ruled notebook. Just as those light blue lines indicate the baselines for each measure of your handwriting, the guidelines of a baseline grid do the same for type. If you plan to use a standard point size for the body type, a baseline grid can help to ensure that the type will fit easily and that the spacing between paragraphs and around headings will be easy to control. A baseline grid can be combined with the other traditional grid styles to create a very versatile, complex grid, as seen in Figure 6-3. Figure 6-7 shows an example of a baseline grid overlaying a spread from a book.

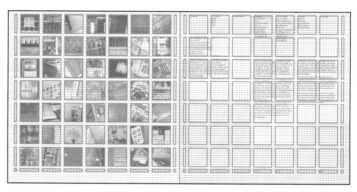

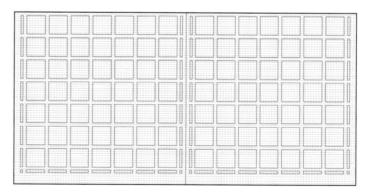

figure | 6-7 |

A baseline grid overlaying the modular grid shown in Figure 6-6.

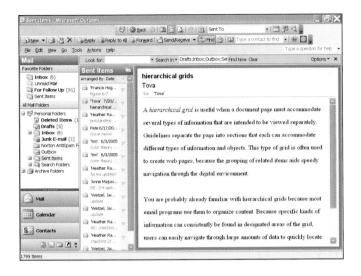

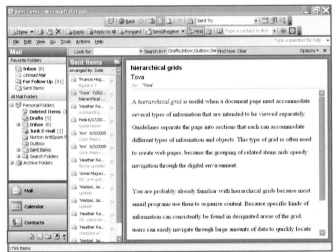

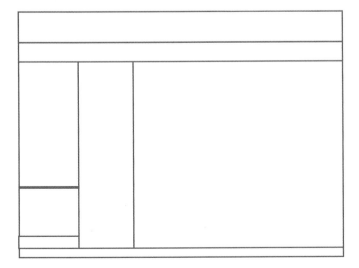

Hierarchical Grid

A hierarchical grid is useful when a document page must accommodate several types of information that are intended to be viewed separately. Guidelines separate the page into sections that can each accommodate different types of information and objects. This type of grid is often used to create web pages, because the grouping of related items aids speedy navigation through the digital environment. You are probably already familiar with hierarchical grids since most e-mail programs use them to organize content. Because specific kinds of information can consistently be found in designated areas of the grid, users can easily navigate through large amounts of data to quickly locate specific content. Figure 6-8 shows an example of a hierarchical grid overlaying a popular e-mail program.

figure | 6-8 |

A hierarchical grid overlaying the popular e-mail program Microsoft Outlook.

Alternative Nontraditional Grids

Although grids are most commonly built of vertical and horizontal lines, diagonal or shaped guides can certainly be incorporated into a grid. For example, Figure 6-9 shows a design based on a grid of concentric circles.

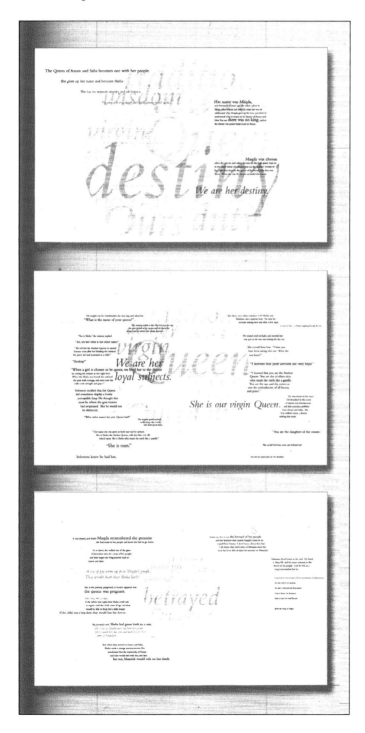

figure | 6-9 |

Pages from a visual essay by Julie Saunders Carlini, "A Broken Promise," built using a grid of concentric circles.

SHAPE AND SIZE CONSIDERATIONS

Sometimes you will need to fit an irregularly shaped object like the one in Figure 6-10a into a grid that looks like the one in Figure 6-10b. The best way to do it is to imagine an invisible **bounding box** around the object that touches each outermost edge, as shown in Figure 6-10c. Use the straight edges and corners of the bounding box to align the image to the grid, as shown in Figure 6-10d.

figure | 6-10a |

An irregularly shaped object.

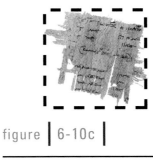

figure | 6-10c |

A bounding box surrounding the irregular image.

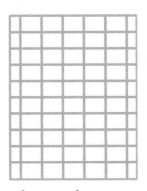

figure | 6-10b |

A grid with vertical and horizontal guidelines.

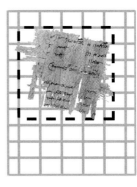

figure | 6-10d |

The bounding box containing the irregular image is aligned to the grid.

New Vocabulary

alley: narrow area of negative space that separates columns

bounding box: an invisible box that surrounds an irregularly shaped object so that the object can be aligned to a grid

field: module of a grid where text and images can be placed

grid area (also called the **text page** or **text area**): the active area within the format where type and images may be placed

gutter: the space formed by the two inside margins of a book or magazine layout closest to the binding

margins: the negative spaces between the outside edges of the grid area and the format

marker: a mark indicating the location of a repetitive element in a layout, like a running head or a folio

spread: two facing pages of an open book or magazine that make up one continuous layout

CHAPTER SUMMARY

Most multipage documents like magazines, books, annual reports, brochures, and newspapers are designed using grids. Grids bring unity and structure to documents and web pages. Using a grid can save designers both time and money because layout decisions can be made one time and then applied to each page of a document, rather than making new decisions for every new page. Using a grid can also make the contents of a document more accessible to readers, since navigation can be enhanced by the grid's consistency.

The layout of a grid must be determined by its function. It should be developed based on the design concept, the content, and the size requirements of the design and its elements. However, it is important to remember that the grid is to be used only as a tool, strictly or flexibly. When harmony or balance can be improved, designers should make exceptions to the grid design.

in review

1. Why would a designer use a grid?

2. Name four types of grids, and describe what kinds of information are best suited to their use.

3. How does a designer use a grid to create a layout?

4. How can an irregularly shaped object be aligned to a grid? What is a bounding box?

5. Is the grid ever seen in the final published design?

6. Must every element of every design always align to the grid?

exercises

1. Look at books, magazines, newspapers, brochures, posters, and web pages to find an example of a manuscript grid, a column grid, a modular grid, and a hierarchical grid.

2. Determine what the designer's grid looked like for each of the examples you found for Exercise 1. You can do this by tracing the evident guidelines of each design onto a piece of tracing paper. Next, examine a multipage document like a book or a magazine to see how a single grid was used to create a number of spreads. Lay a piece of tracing paper over the spread of your choice, and draw guidelines where you think the designer's were. Repeat this process with several spreads from the same publication, using new pieces of tracing paper each time. Finally, try to redraw the designer's original grid by stacking all the tracings, and combining the guidelines from each tracing.

3. Use the information you learned about type families in Chapter 3 to make a small book using a grid. Each spread should name a type family, list its common characteristics, and show at least one example. Be sure to leave enough room in your inner margins to accommodate your binding method of choice.

4. Draw vertical, horizontal, and diagonal guidelines to create a grid that includes at least eight fields. Trace your grid four times onto Bristol paper, to create four separate layouts. Cut pieces of paper from magazines and glue them into the fields of your grid, to create four different compositions, each adhering strictly to the grid you established, each combining fields in different ways.

Frames from animated short *Not My Type II* by Lycette Bros.

CHAPTER 7

objectives

- Understand legibility and readability issues as they pertain to screen typography
- Explain how screen resolution should affect font selection, use, and design
- Become familiar with a variety of font formats
- Find and install fonts on a computer
- Prepare designs containing fonts to be printed
- Create a storyboard for a kinetic type sequence

introduction

Traditionally, typography has been a highly detail-oriented craft in which designers, motivated by a love of letterforms, have labored over each nuance of every stroke and serif of characters. Patience and dedication were key ingredients for designing new typefaces, since a new typeface could take months or even years of intensive work to complete.

Computer technologies have changed all that. Access to the right hardware and software lets any designer or amateur become a type founder quickly and easily. The result has been an overwhelming groundswell of new typefaces, in a full range of both quality and innovativeness.

Many people find computers to be more glamorous and fun than the original graphic design production tools. However, professional designers overwhelmingly agree that the most important key to creating good designs with computer technology is to always remember that the computer is nothing more than a tool. Just like any other tool, a computer is a medium through which designers can make their visions concrete. Although the capabilities of any medium may influence a designer's expressions, it is important that choices be made based on a solid knowledge of design theory, as opposed to being led by the easiest route that a tool might provide. A medium should never command a design nor control a product—only the designer should.

Over hundreds of years, typographic conventions have evolved regarding the proper use of type. These standards have been based mostly on evolving theories about how legibility and readability of printed type could be optimized. These principles have been challenged and tested, both scientifically and over time through use and disuse. Many designers, upon applying these conventions to screen typography, have found them inadequate or inappropriate for the digital environment.

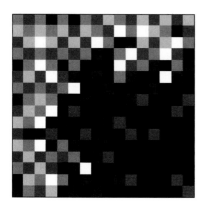

figure | 7-1 |

A bitmap of 16 x 16 pixels. *Courtesy of Mike Kohnke of We Associated. From* A Sense of Type *screen art,* www.weassociated.com/A_Sense_of_Type/2/pixel.html.

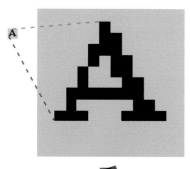

figure | 7-2 |

Close-up of a character rendered in pixels.

SCREEN TYPOGRAPHY

Readers experience typography on a computer screen very differently than in a printed format. For one thing, with printed material, readers focus their eyes on paper with markings on it. In a digital environment, readers focus their eyes on a screen that is emitting light waves. This is inherently much more tiring to the eyes.

In addition, the low resolution of computer screens cannot reproduce the level of detail that the computer is able to generate. This means that even though a computer can understand highly detailed letterforms, only a simplified version of them can be displayed on the computer's monitor.

Display Resolution

A computer monitor displays type and images by lighting up various combinations of **pixels**—tiny squares made up of red, blue, and green dots to form a grid across the screen, as shown in Figure 7-1. The number of dots lit up give a pixel its level of brightness.

Although pixels are small, they are large enough to be noticed by the human eye, so curved and diagonal lines and edges look jagged, as in Figure 7-2. Computer monitors have a resolution of 72 to 96 pixels per square inch (ppi), depending on the size and make of the monitor—much lower than the resolution that computers and printers are capable of producing. Since computer monitors are technologically still very far behind their counterparts, making type look good on-screen becomes a secondary concern to just making it legible at all.

Embedded Fonts

One problem that designers have dealt with for years is that in order to be viewed or printed, a font had to be installed on the hard drive of the viewer's computer. If a specified font was not present on the hard drive, the computer simply made a substitution. This meant that a layout or document designed in a particular font could look completely different when viewed on other computers.

This has been a limiting factor for designers working digitally. Since font files are protected by copyright law, it would be illegal to give a font to the viewers, and it would be impractical to expect viewers to purchase special fonts just to properly view a design—especially if the design is for a web site that is available for public viewing.

So, in order to truly control how their screen designs look to viewers, designers have had to limit themselves to using only the fonts most commonly found on computers, like Times New Roman, Arial, and Courier, for example. For smaller passages of text, another option has been to create a bitmapped image of the text and save it as a *GIF* file. However, this strategy can be impractical because image files are much larger in size than textual data, which translates into longer download times for web pages. To make matters worse, if a viewer's computer can't display the image, the text won't be seen at all. Plus, if the size of the bitmapped text is increased, the text will look pixelated.

Recently, new software capabilities have been developed that allow font data to be embedded into documents and web pages, allowing viewers temporary or limited access to fonts that have not been installed on their computers. Embedded fonts let designers preserve the visual integrity of their designs—and viewers can see and print layouts from any computer, just as they were designed with the original fonts. Embedded fonts also have the benefit of being selectable as type, as you can see from the screenshot in Figure 7-3.

However, there are several problematic issues that diminish the practicality of embedding fonts. For one thing, the Internet Explorer and Netscape browsers have adopted different embedding software standards, so compatibility among web browsers becomes an issue for displaying HTML documents. If the viewer's browser is not compatible, the computer will make default font substitutions. This means that designers

| NOTE |

The word "pixel" comes from the combination of the two words "picture" and "element."

| NOTE |

Type that is converted into a bitmapped image will retain the most clarity when saved as a GIF file. In contrast, photographs will retain their best clarity when saved as JPEGs.

figure | 7-3 |

A web page displaying an embedded font; some of the embedded text has been selected. *Copyright © 2004 Microsoft Corporation. All rights reserved.*

must create designs for HTML pages that will be functional, whether the viewers can see the original fonts or not. The practice of embedding fonts also raises many controversial proprietary issues that have yet to be worked out, though some foundries have answered this issue by offering addendum licenses for embedding fonts.

LEGIBILITY AND READABILITY ON-SCREEN

Screen typography has been evolving for only a few decades, so there's little precedent to help designers make decisions about how to optimize legibility and readability on the screen. However, some design strategies are starting to emerge that may be helpful to designers as they use and develop type that will be read on-screen.

Size

Size is an enormously important factor for on-screen type legibility. For print typography, size is important because reader's eyes have trouble deciphering letters that are too small. In a digital environment, this is exacerbated by the fact that letters degrade at smaller sizes because they are constructed of fewer pixels, and so have cruder shapes, as you can see in Figure 7-4. As a general rule, most digital fonts become difficult to read on-screen at sizes smaller than 10 points.

figure | 7-4 |

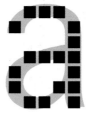 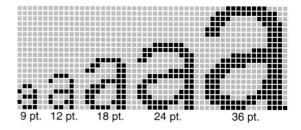

9 pt. 12 pt. 18 pt. 24 pt. 36 pt.

At different point sizes, pixel configurations of a single character vary. *Courtesy of and adapted from Mike Kohnke of We Associated, A Sense of Type screen art from* www.weassociated.com/ A_Sense_of_Type/2/bitmap.html.

Also, keep in mind that when using various sizes of type in the same layout, the smaller and thinner characters may appear less intense than larger and thicker characters. If this optical variance is problematic to your design, you can correct it by adjusting the saturation of the differently sized letters so that they appear to match, as shown in Figure 7-5.

Smaller thinner letters Smaller thinner letters

Larger thicker letters

Smaller thinner letters Smaller thinner letters

Larger thicker letters

Smaller thinner letters Smaller thinner letters

Larger thicker letters

Smaller thinner letters Smaller thinner letters

Larger thicker letters

Typeface

When type needs to be smaller than 10 points, fonts that have been designed specifically for screen use will perform best. These fonts have been designed based on the grid of pixels that make up the computer screen, rather than being designed and then adapted to display onscreen. Some of the first pixel fonts to be designed were Chicago, New York, Monaco, Geneva, Charcoal, and Lucida. Some newer pixel fonts display well at very small sizes, such as Mini 7 and Atom, which are shown in Figure 7-6.

figure | 7-5 |

Left: Both small and large texts are displayed in black and in white. Right: The larger texts have been desaturated to make the letters appear to be the same value as their smaller counterparts.

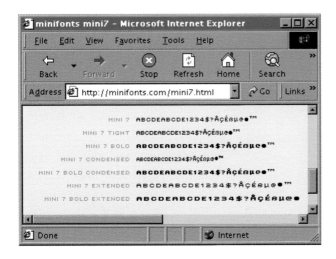

figure | 7-6 |

Screenshots of pixel fonts—Mini 7 designed by Joe Gillespie (left), and Atom designed by Paul Wootton (right). *Courtesy of* MiniFonts.com.

Type Style

If you wish to apply a type style to a font, it's always best to use one that has been created by the font's designer, as opposed to letting your software apply a computer-generated type style. This is because even though the computer can embolden or italicize most fonts, the results

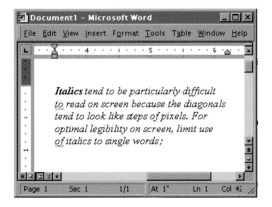

figure | 7-7 |

Screenshot of text set in italics.

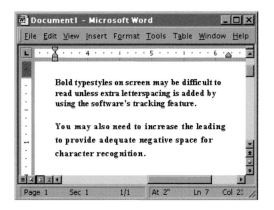

figure | 7-8 |

Screenshot of text set in a bold type style.

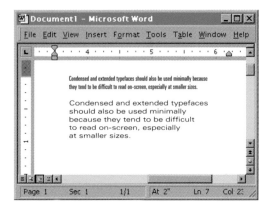

figure | 7-9 |

Screenshot of condensed and extended type.

will look distorted. Some special considerations apply to type styles for the screen:

- Italics can be particularly difficult to read on-screen because the diagonal pixels tend to look like steps (Figure 7-7). For optimal legibility on-screen, limit the use of italics to single words.

- Bold type styles on-screen may be difficult to read unless extra letterspacing is added by using the software's tracking feature. You may also need to increase the leading to provide adequate negative space for character recognition, as shown in Figure 7-8.

- Condensed and extended typefaces should also be used minimally because they tend to be difficult to read on-screen, especially at smaller sizes (Figure 7-9). An alternative to using condensed or extended typefaces would be to alter the tracking to reduce or expand the width of the measure without distorting the actual letterforms. However, keep in mind that reducing the tracking between letters will also diminish legibility.

Spacing

Because experienced readers recognize words by their shapes, the negative space inside and around letterforms is very important to legibility. The low resolution of the computer monitor only adds to legibility and readability problems, so providing extra negative space can be an important strategy to promote letter and word recognition for your readers. Since a lit screen is much more tiring for the eyes, providing adequate negative space around text becomes even more vital to both legibility and readability. Designers must consider the combination of several factors to create a balanced relationship between positive and negative spaces in a composition.

- *Tracking*—For optimal on-screen legibility, set the tracking value of your type anywhere from +5 to +10 units, as shown in Figure 7-10. Larger type sizes may require less tracking, while smaller type sizes may need more.

- *Leading*—Leading needs to be more generously applied to type on-screen than it would be for print in order to optimize legibility. Adding an extra 50 percent to your leading is a good rule of thumb, as you can see in Figure 7-11. So, for example, a line spacing setting of 1.5 generally provides very good legibility.

- *Measure*—The optimal line length on-screen is shorter than it is for print—about 40 characters per line, as compared to an optimal print measure of about 60 characters per line (this is partly to compensate for the added tracking recommended above, as shown in Figure 7-12).

- *Paragraph size*—For optimal readability, paragraphs on-screen should be kept short. Paragraphs should not exceed 10 to 25 lines of text for best on-screen viewing. When type is large, paragraphs may be slightly longer, but when type is small, keep paragraphs as short as possible.

- *Texture*—The overall texture of body copy is particularly relevant for text that will be viewed on-screen because the default spacing of a font may look inconsistent, especially if the designer has not applied hinting techniques to the font file (more about this later in the chapter). When the texture of a passage of text looks inconsistent, you may need to manually kern, or adjust the letterspacing, to manage this issue.

Color

As with print typography, color can be used on-screen to create emphasis, evoke emotions, or set a mood. Colors trigger both physiological reactions and culturally learned psychological associations. Colors that are more intense—and those that are warmer like red, yellow, and orange—tend to trigger a faster heart rate and arouse the senses,

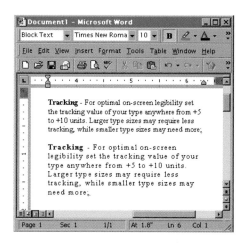

figure | 7-10 |

Screenshot of text without tracking and with added tracking.

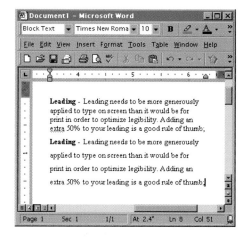

figure | 7-11 |

Screenshot of text without leading and with extra leading.

figure | 7-12 |

Screenshot of text in 60-character measures and 40-character measures.

while less intense and cooler colors tend to have a more calming effect. However, the learned meanings that are associated with colors are just as important to the audience's reaction. These meanings can vary widely from culture to culture. For example, in the United States, red is often associated with anger, while in some Asian countries the same color is associated with celebration.

Color can be used freely in screen designs since cost is not a factor, as it would be with printed colors. However, there is a major pitfall surrounding the use of color in digital environments: a specific color won't look the same when viewed on monitors that are calibrated differently. This severely limits the designer's control over how designs will look to viewers. Colors will also look different when printed than they appeared on-screen. This is because printers mix cyan, magenta, yellow, and black pigments (CMYK) to produce colors, while computer monitors create colors by using combinations of red, blue, and green light waves.

Screen Contrast

Since a lit monitor is much brighter than the reflective light of paper, the contrast between black and white on a monitor is much greater than it is on printed materials. To promote readability, screen typography should have enough contrast to be legible, but not so much contrast as to unnecessarily irritate the viewers' eyes.

When the additive primary colors—red, green, and blue—are all projected at full saturation, the viewer will perceive white; when no light waves are projected, the viewer will see black. The consequence is that a white screen is quite bright and tiring to the eyes, while a black screen, on the other hand, is the least tiring to stare at. Consequently, type set in a light gray value and set against a black background will be the most readable combination for viewers, especially for longer passages. When white type is essential, setting it against a dark gray value can help reduce the contrast and the associated eyestrain.

Also keep in mind that each color has an intrinsic value and brightness, which must be taken into consideration. For instance, a fully saturated yellow will be lighter and brighter than a fully saturated violet. To maximize legibility and readability when setting text against a background, make sure that the contrast between light and dark—and the contrast between bright and dull elements—is sufficient, yet moderate.

| NOTE |

The way a computer monitor generates color can be explained by additive color theory, which describes how light waves of different frequencies combine to make colors. A computer monitor generates color by projecting mixtures of the additive primary colors: red, green, and blue (RGB).

Subtractive color theory, on the other hand, describes how colors are generated when pigments absorb and reflect light waves. The subtractive primaries—cyan, magenta, and yellow, plus black (CMYK)—are used for commercial printing, while the traditional subtractive primary colors—red, yellow, and blue—are used by artists to mix paints.

High levels of contrast can cause an optical dazzle effect. High contrast can also cause type glow, which occurs when the brightness of a background permeates the edges of darker or duller letterforms, making them appear thinner. Type glow can also happen when the brightness of letterforms seems to overflow into a darker or duller background, creating an optical aura that makes the letters seem to glow, as seen in Figure 7-13. Combinations of colors that are opposites (complementary colors) and combinations of colors with similar hues (analogous colors) can also create a dazzle effect, diminishing readability.

Color Temperature

As you make color selections, remember that warm colors (reds, yellows, oranges) appear to advance, and cool colors (blues, greens, violets) appear to recede. Although this means that warmer colors are less appropriate for background colors than cooler colors, keep in mind that color temperature is relative. A background color only needs to be a cooler temperature than the text and objects in order to recede. A warm background will still appear to recede if it is juxtaposed with even warmer text and objects.

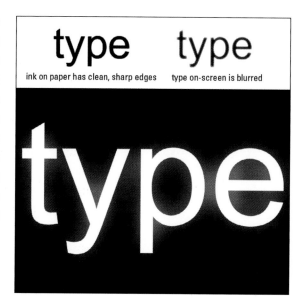

figure | 7-13 |

Type glow. *Courtesy of Mike Kohnke of We Associated. Adapted from* A Sense of Type *screen art,* www.weassociated.com/A_Sense_of_Type/2/pixel.html.

FONT FORMATS

When printing was done primarily by letterpress, fonts (collections of all the characters of specific typefaces necessary for typesetting) were tangible; generally they were made of metal or wood. When typography entered the digital realm, fonts needed to exist in a new format—as electronic files, programmed so that they could be understood and applied by computers to display and print text. Over the years, several digital font formats have been developed, each with its own advantages and limitations. Understanding the differences between these formats can help designers to make good use of fonts in a variety of formats, taking advantage of the benefits and capabilities each has to offer.

figure | 7-14 |

Bitmap font enlarged to show jagged edges.

Bitmap (or Raster) Fonts

The first fonts developed for computers during the early 1980s were **bitmap** (or **raster**) **fonts**. That is, letterforms were constructed by encoding maps that instructed the computers which screen pixels to turn on in order to form a specific **glyph**, or representation of a character. For any font, bitmaps had to be designed in a variety of point sizes, though the computer could use those to generate clumsy versions of characters at intermediary sizes. Because pixels are square, on curves and diagonals their contours appeared jagged. A bitmapped character was understood by the computer just like it would understand an image. Scaling bitmapped fonts was problematic because when a bitmapped character was enlarged, the jagged edges would also be enlarged, as shown in Figure 7-14. This detracted from legibility.

Outline (or Vector) Fonts

The problem of scaling type was addressed with the invention of vector technology. **Outline** (or **vector**) **fonts** are understood by the computer as a series of points that form an outline of the letterform, as shown in Figure 7-15. The outline can be scaled to any size without losing integrity of shape, and can then be **rasterized**, or converted to a bitmapped image, at the selected size. However, if the outlines don't line up properly with the pixels of the screen, the computer makes its best guess of which pixels to turn on. This tends to result in distortion of the letterforms' shapes.

figure | 7-15 |

Vector font showing points and outline.

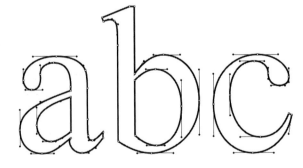

Hinting

The distorted look of vector font characters can be minimized during the design stage through **hinting**, a process in which extra information is encoded into a font file instructing the computer how to modify a character's outlines at different sizes to better align with the screen's grid of pixels. This helps the computer make better choices about which pixels to turn on to best fill a character's outlines at each size. Hinting can greatly improve the look of letterforms on-screen, as you can see in Figure 7-16.

Giant hens ten feet tall
Giant hens ten feet tall

figure | 7-16 |

The font in the top sentence contains hints; the bottom sentence does not.

Anti-aliasing

Some software includes a feature called **anti-aliasing** (also called **font smoothing**), which when enabled by the viewer, can help vector type appear more legible to the human eye. It does this by analyzing the outlines of the glyph and then turning on strategically placed pixels in various shades of gray. This fools the viewer's eyes into perceiving smoother contours, as can be seen in Figure 7-17. Anti-aliasing works very well for larger letterforms, but poorly for small type sizes; because the smoothed letters tend to look blurry, legibility will decrease in smaller letterforms. Also, since anti-aliasing is a preference selected by the viewer, designers cannot count on this feature to be enabled when their designs are viewed.

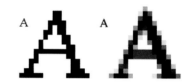

figure | 7-17 |

The letter on the right shows the effect of anti-aliasing when applied to the letter on the left.

PostScript Type 1 Fonts

The PostScript Type 1 font format developed by Adobe was the first vector font format to dominate the market. Type 1 fonts contain two files: one that gives outlining instructions to the computer for screen display, and a second that contains bitmap information for printing. PostScript fonts contain hints, are scalable, and can work cross-platform (on most computers). Type 1 fonts can include up to 256 individual glyphs, but no more. This quantity must include all uppercase and lowercase letters, numbers, fractions, punctuation, symbols, ligatures, small capitals, and accented letters the designer wishes to include in the character set. When a font is designed with more than 256 glyphs, the designer usually creates an expert character set—a separate font file containing the extra glyphs. Because most service bureaus and printers originally invested in Type 1 fonts and expert character sets, this font format remains dominant in the design industry.

TrueType Fonts

A newer font format called TrueType was developed by Apple and promoted by Microsoft as a rival to Type 1 fonts. Also a cross-platform outline font format, TrueType has the added value of superior hinting capabilities. TrueType fonts are stored as a single file, making font management simpler for users, and this format works automatically with the computer's operating system without additional font management software. Apple made the TrueType font specifications publicly available, and so TrueType fonts grew quickly in number and popularity, becoming an industry standard rivaling Type 1 fonts.

OpenType Fonts

OpenType represents a more recent collaboration between Adobe and Microsoft to create a new and superior cross-platform font format that is compatible with various operating systems. Stored as a single font file, the OpenType font format includes the best and most advanced features of both Type 1 and TrueType fonts. It offers greater hinting and kerning capabilities, multilingual typesetting, and it can accommodate extra characters previously only available in expert character sets. Because OpenType coding is based on a standardized international character encoding system called Unicode, this format allows for a simple exchange of texts between a variety of languages by including character sets from multiple languages within a single font.

Unicode

Unicode is the standard international character encoding system for texts written in most of the world's languages. It is not a font format or a software program; it is simply a universal system for encoding the character sets and usage conventions of many languages so they can be stored, processed, displayed, and interchanged. Most newer computer operating systems include Unicode support for about three dozen different languages. Unicode does not have anything to do with the way glyphs are represented in terms of style or size, etc. It only provides information about how the computer should interpret glyphs, not how it should render them. Stylistic information is determined by font files, but fonts must be Unicode-compliant (include Unicode mapping) in order to work with Unicode. The Unicode standard is very useful for programmers who want to create multilingual software applications, and for linguists, business people, and scientists, who deal with multilingual text, mathematical symbols, and other technical characters regularly used in today's global market.

Multiple Master Fonts

There is a Type 1 font extension called the Multiple Master (MM) format, launched by Adobe in 1991. This format allows two variations of a glyph (like large/small or wide/narrow) to be encoded at opposite ends of an axis. Users can specify any point along the axis, and the computer will generate a corresponding glyph. Each variation of the specific glyph is called an instance. A Multiple Master font can include multiple axes, each controlling different design aspects like size, width, weight, and style.

There have, however, been some problems surrounding MM fonts. Many software applications don't support them, and many service bureaus have reported difficulties with their output. Also, although many designers appreciated the added control of MM fonts, most common users just found them confusing and difficult to use. By 1999, Adobe discontinued further development of the technology due to a lack of consumer interest. Figure 7-18 shows several possible variations of a single character created using a Multiple Master font.

figure | 7-18 |

Several instances of a single character set using a Multiple Master font.

ClearType Fonts

ClearType is a new cross-platform outline font format that allows unprecedented precision for screen type on LCD (liquid crystal display) monitors like those included in laptop computers, flat panel monitors, and cellular phones, as well as limited smoothing of type on CRT (cathode-ray tube) monitors. This font format achieves a higher degree of detail by allowing subpixels to be turned on to create a smoother, more refined contour. You see, the pixels that construct LCD screens are different from those that form CRT screens. LCD pixels are subdivided into three stripes of the additive primary colors: red, green, and blue. When all three subpixels are on, the three primary colors are mixed, and white light is emitted from the screen. Different combinations of the subpixels can produce a range of colors and values. The ClearType font format accesses these subpixels to display glyphs at higher resolutions. The pixels of CRT monitors are not subdivided in the same way, and so the full effects of this font format cannot be displayed on them. However, the ClearType format can improve the legibility of CRT screen fonts to some extent because subpixel rendering includes anti-aliasing encoding, which does tend to improve legibility. Figure 7-19 shows close-ups of whole pixel and subpixel renderings of the same glyph.

figure | 7-19 |

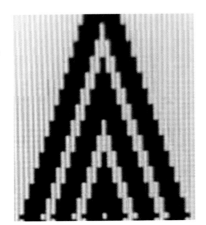 

Left: Whole pixel rendering.
Right: Subpixel rendering.

Building Your Font Library

Fonts to add to your font library are abundantly available for both Mac and PC computers. Some are included when you install specific software programs, others must be installed independently. Many fonts must be purchased, while others are offered at no cost as shareware or freeware. Font files may be purchased on CDs or downloaded online. A quick online search using your favorite search engine will reveal a plethora of web sites offering downloads for a fee or for free. Some are font foundries (which produce their own fonts) and others are font distributors (which offer fonts designed by a variety of foundries). Some sites even allow users to inspect detailed character maps and "test drive" the fonts in a variety of sizes before purchasing.

Downloading from the Internet

Once you find a font you wish to download from the Internet, most web sites will ask you to select between a Mac and a PC version of the font. Usually you can download the font easily with the click of a button. Font files that don't require decompression can be installed by dragging them into the Fonts folder, or by using the Install New Fonts command in the File dropdown menu of the Fonts folder. However, most font files downloaded from the Internet will be compressed, so you'll have to decompress them before installing them. Your computer's software won't be able to access the new fonts until they are decompressed and installed in the Fonts folder. In order to extract the compressed font file(s) to your Fonts folder, you will need decompression software—WinZip or Stuffit Expander, depending on how the file was archived. Both of these utilities are free and can be easily obtained online. If you already have these utilities installed on your computer, double-clicking on the compressed font file will open up the appropriate decompression utility.

Installing New Fonts

In order to use a new font on your computer, you must first install its file(s) onto your hard drive. For some operating systems, it is wise and convenient to install and manage PostScript fonts with type management software, such as Fontbook, Suitcase, Font Reserve, or Adobe Type Manager (ATM). A type utility interprets the information stored in the font files for the computer.

TrueType and OpenType fonts are stored as single files, ending in the extensions .ttf or .otf. PostScript fonts, on the other hand, require installation of two separate files containing instructions for the computer about how to display the font on-screen and how to print it. These files end with the extensions .pfb and .pfm. Both are necessary for proper viewing and printing of a PostScript font. Once a font of any format has been installed, you may need to restart applications that were open during the installation, in order to activate the new font's availability to the software.

> ## New Vocabulary

anti-aliasing (or **font smoothing**): the optical smoothing of the jagged edges of a character on a computer screen accomplished by analyzing the outlines of the glyph and then turning on strategically placed pixels in various shades of gray along its edges

bitmap (or **raster**) **fonts**: letterforms that are constructed by encoding maps that instruct computers on which screen pixels to turn on in order to form a specific glyph

glyph: a representation of a character

hinting: a process in which extra information is encoded into a font file instructing the computer how to modify a character's outlines at different sizes to better align with the screen's grid of pixels

outline (or **vector**) **fonts**: letterforms that are understood by the computer as a series of points forming an outline of the letterform; the outline can be scaled to any size without losing integrity of shape

rasterize: to convert an outline font to a bitmapped image, at a selected size

THE *designer* AT WORK

nick curtis

How did you get started as a designer? Tell us about your first job in design and the evolution of your career.

The die was cast at a very early age for me. One evening when I was three, after seeing an episode of the 1930s Flash Gordon serial on TV, I picked up a red crayon and drew a mural of my impressions of that episode on the wall next to my bed. Needless to say, my parents were not thrilled and debated a suitable punishment. Fortunately for me, they hadn't finished their debate by the next day, when my mother's father dropped by for a visit. He was an artist by training and ran a professional scenery shop in Chicago. He had always been rather disappointed that none of his five children, nor any of *their* children, had followed in his footsteps. When Grandpa saw the "mess" I had made of the wall, he sent forth shouts of joy, proclaiming "The boy has talent!" When our family moved from that house the next year, my father carefully cut out that section of wallboard, and it has remained in the family ever since.

I received some formal training in drawing, with art lessons at a local weekend academy during my grade school years. The summer between grade school and high school, I worked for a neighbor who was an architect, and learned how to work a T-square and ruling pen. In high school, I worked on the school newspaper and yearbook, and saw my first work in print. In college, I did the news-

paper and yearbook thing again, and got my first taste of freelancing, designing and lettering concert and event posters. So, the transition from part-time designer to full-time designer was a fairly seamless process.

Once I turned pro, my career path followed an interesting trajectory: I began working as a designer in a print shop, then moved into an ad agency, then a multimedia agency, then a couple of television stations, then into a prepress shop, and finally back into a print shop. Over the course of those years, virtually every skill set that I had learned previously became obsolete; the T-squares and ruling pens disappeared, desktop publishing was born, and the computer took over the design world. I'm really curious to see what's next.

What do you do to get your creative juices flowing when you start a new project? What can you share with us about your design process? What role does technology play in that process?

It really depends on the project. My favorite projects are the revival fonts that I develop. Since typefaces of a particular time are, in a sense, reflections of the times in which they were originally created, I find it helpful to acquaint myself with those times by looking at ads, posters, and other pop cultural items of the day. Then I usually forget about the project for a time and do some work on another task, or do something entirely unrelated (read a book, listen to music, etc.). I read some time ago that, if you bundle up all the elements of a problem and drop them into your subconscious mind, your subconscious will do all the heavy lifting in the background and eventually present you with a neatly packaged solution. Whether or not it's true in all cases, I can't say, but quite often it works for me. When I resume work on a project that I've allowed to percolate by itself for awhile, things just seem to flow smoothly with very little effort. So, sometimes it works.

Then again, sometimes it doesn't, and sometimes you don't have the luxury of postponing a project until it works

Gasoline Alley NF
abcdefghijklmnopqrstuvwxyz
ABCDEFGHIJKLMNOPQRSTU
VWXYZ (1234567890$%&*@!?.;)

Gasoline Alley NF typeface by Nick Curtis of Nick's Fonts,
www.nicksfonts.com.

itself out. At those times, technology is a fantastic time-saver and option-expander. In the olden days—the dark ages of T squares and ruling pens that I referred to earlier—there were no "Undo" or "Revert to Saved" commands. Laying ink on paper is thermodynamically irreversible, so doing multiple versions of any project involved starting back at the beginning, repeating exactly what you had done before to get to your point of departure, then doing something different to create an alternate version. Today, the drafting instruments I purchased along the way—some of them quite expensive—have become quaint semi-antiques gathering dust but, frankly, I'll take the new tools any day.

How has the role of typography in design changed over the last decade? Where do you see it going in the future?

Perhaps the most dramatic change has been an exponential increase in the choices of typefaces available. When I started working professionally in the design business in the 1970s, it was possible to know by sight and name virtually every typeface available. Most type was set in metal or by phototypesetters, and the range of available faces was limited. The major exception was dry-transfer lettering. Letraset, which was the leading supplier, came out with a new catalog every six months or so, offering a couple dozen new typefaces.

When type composition moved to the desktop in the early 1980s, the early Macs had a whopping fourteen fonts, so

the choices were still very limited. But once FontStudio and Fontographer came on the scene, the game changed, and it continues to change at an ever-increasing pace. Right now as I write these words, there are not a few hundred typefaces available to designers; there are tens of thousands. Also, there are even "robotic fonts" available, which mutate their letterforms ever so slightly each time you use them.

The only prediction about the future of typography that I can make with any confidence is that the choices will continue to multiply; beyond that, the possibilities are limited only by the imagination and creativity of programmers. Perhaps we'll see "mood-ring fonts," which discern your mood as you write, then alter the design of their letterforms to suit that mood. Is it likely? Who knows, but it is possible.

What role should social responsibility play in design? What can designers contribute to our society?

At its best, graphic design functions as glass: it can be a window through which we see someone or something else, or it can be a mirror, in which we see ourselves. In either case, we are unaware of the glass itself, so it appears to be neutral, but it never really is.

Design influences us on several levels; we are most aware of it when it stimulates us intellectually, or delights us aesthetically. But it can also affect us unconsciously, at the "lizard-brain" level and, despite our wishing it otherwise, this is the level that motivates much of our behavior and actions. At this level, two of the most powerful motivators are empathy and antipathy.

From a general point of view, design that inspires empathy—that is, an emotional connection with a wider community—is socially responsible, but it *can be* socially irresponsible if that particular wider community has misguided, dangerous, or destructive beliefs. Design which inspires antipathy is socially irresponsible if that antipathy is directed against individuals or groups and manifests itself as hatred or bigotry. On the other hand, antipathy toward detestable actions or attitudes—for example, the very same hatred or bigotry, or criminal or self-destructive behavior—is socially responsible. So, the issue is complicated.

The best advice I could offer designers revolves around the glass analogy: whether the glass is a window or a mirror, make sure that it's not distorted.

What advice do you have for design students and new designers who are just entering the field today?

First and foremost, be aware that learning is a lifelong process, especially in the field of design. A large—and growing—proportion of the skills and knowledge you acquire today will likely be obsolete in the very near future, so be prepared and open to the changes that will inevitably come.

Second, don't pigeonhole yourself as this or that particular kind of designer, or as an expert in one particular kind of software. Expand your horizons at every available opportunity.

Finally, avail yourself of every opportunity to learn the practical side of applying your designs. If you're a print designer, learn as much as you can about how the ink actually ends up on the paper. If you're a multimedia designer, learn as much as you can about the capabilities

and limitations of the media you're designing for. If you're a web designer, learn how to optimize your work so that it loads fast and correctly for as many people as possible. And so on . . .

Nick Curtis, Nick's Fonts, Gaithersburg, Maryland
www.nicksfonts.com

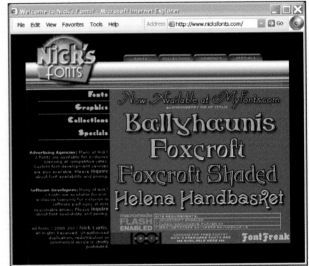

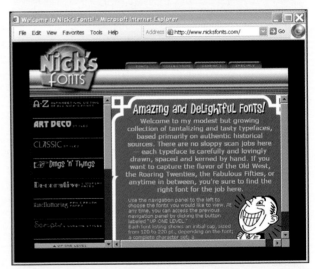

Screenshots of Nick's Fonts web site. *Courtesy of Nick's Fonts,* www.nicksfonts.com.

PRINTING FONTS

If you send your digital designs to an output service for printing, you must send along the font files for every font that is included in your designs. This is legal, as long as the output service only uses the font files for your job and then returns the files to you.

For most designs that incorporate type, it's best to create them using page layout software, like Adobe InDesign, QuarkXPress, or PageMaker. These programs easily integrate outline fonts with bitmapped imagery to create high-quality output. If you use a photo manipulation program like Photoshop to create your design, the fonts you include will be rasterized. Once that happens, they will not be editable, and will give a poor result if scaled.

If you plan to use many fonts in one design, you may want to use a drawing software program like Adobe Illustrator so that you can take advantage of the "create outlines" feature. This lets you select letters and convert them into outlined shapes. (Even though you may be using outline fonts like PostScript, TrueType, or OpenType, the computer still recognizes them as glyphs, and unless you convert them from glyphs to outlined shapes, any output device will require the font file to be installed.) Once the text has been converted to outline shapes, the computer will read the shapes simply as vector art, and any output device will be able to print them without needing to access any font files. This will save you the trouble of organizing and sending along all those font files to the output service.

Print Resolution

Resolution issues can be confusing because the units of measurement that are used to describe different kinds of resolution are often incorrectly interchanged. As we've already discussed, display resolution is measured in ppi (pixels per inch). Printer resolution, on the other hand, is measured in dots per inch (dpi), or lines per inch (lpi) for halftone printing.

Most printers can print in a range of resolutions. The higher the resolution, the smoother and more detailed the printed character will look, and the slower the printing time. Generally, print resolutions of 600 dpi or 133 lpi are considered standard professional print quality. Even though text and images on a computer screen can only be viewed at 72 to 96 ppi, if they are to be printed they will need a higher display resolution. The standard display resolution setting for type and images for professionally printed materials is 300 ppi. At this display resolution, a printer will be able to render layouts very nicely at 600 dpi. Most ink-jet and laser printers can print at a resolution of 300 to 600 dpi, while imagesetters can print at resolutions up to 4,000 dpi.

The quality of printed work is also dependent on the type of output device used. For instance, a single image printed at 600 dpi will look different depending on the output device. As you can see from Figure 7-20, laser printers have the ability to produce cleaner images than ink-jet printers, and imagesetters are even more precise—even if they are all printing at the same number of dots per inch. This is because different kinds of devices apply the ink in different ways.

ink-jet printer   laser printer   imagesetter

An ink-jet print, a laser print, and an imagesetter print of the same text.

The quality of reproduction from ink-jet printers is getting better, and in many instances can equal that of laser printers.

Imagesetters, which image onto photographic materials, or direct-to-plate, create the most accurate images, particularly of letterforms at small sizes.

At very low print resolutions, hinting data encoded into the font files can help the printer to optimally render a range of type sizes. The computer uses this information to rasterize outline fonts according to the scale and resolution at which they will be printed. The printer then reads a bitmap of the glyph, and applies dots of ink or toner to the paper according to the bitmap. You can see the difference hinting can make in Figure 7-21. However, at higher print resolutions, hints will not make a discernable difference.

Rasterize

without hints

Rasterize

with hints

Close-up of printed text without hints and with hints, from *Pocket Guide to Digital Printing* by Frank Cost.

If the printing surface is at all porous, there will be some bleeding of the ink, which may make the letters appear slightly thicker and slightly obscured. Figure 7-22 illustrates how ink bleeding can affect the shapes of printed type and objects.

Simulated bleeding of printed ink on a porous surface, adapted from *Pocket Guide to Digital Printing* by Frank Cost.

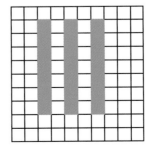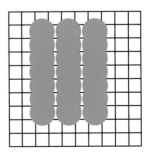

Trapping and Knockouts

If your design will be printed using the four-color printing process, you may need to account for **misregistration** (the misalignment of color separations and/or adjacent colors in printed materials). One method of dealing with misregistration is by using a technique called **trapping**. Trapping is done by slightly enlarging the lighter of two touching shapes so that it overlaps the darker color a little bit, as shown in Figure 7-23. That way, if objects aren't printed in their precise places, the color of the paper won't show through around their edges. When printing text, trapping is particularly important because misregistration can decrease legibility. Another approach to ensuring legibility against misregistration in the four-color printing process is to avoid placing printed text against colored objects or backgrounds when creating layouts. Instead, text in those locations can be created by using knockouts, as shown in Figure 7-24. A **knockout** is text that is not actually printed, but instead is cut out from a solid area of printed color. The shapes of the letters are formed by the printed negative spaces that surround the letterforms, but the text itself remains the color of the paper.

figure | 7-23 |

Trapping.

figure | 7-24 |

Knockout.

KINETIC TYPE

Kinetic type refers to type that moves; it is appropriate for use in film titles, television openers, commercials, and digital environments. Kinetic type was used expressively in television and film throughout the 1960s, when designers were frequently hired to create inventive title sequences. These openers were clever, funny, and intriguing, and they were structured as little narratives that extended the main narratives they introduced. They were graphically daring—artistic techniques of integration and distortion were employed that would have been considered too avant-garde for the body of the films.

> ### New Vocabulary

knockout: text that is not actually printed, but instead is cut out from a solid area of printed color; the shapes of the letters are formed by the printed negative spaces that surround the letterforms, but the text itself remains the color of the paper

misregistration: the misalignment of color separations and/or adjacent colors in printed materials

trapping: a way of dealing with misregistration, by slightly enlarging the lighter of two touching shapes so that it overlaps the darker color a little bit

figure | 7-25 |

Kinetic montage, series of screenshots from the short animated film *Little Yellow Writing Hood* by Ryan Pescatore Frisk and Catelijne van Middelkoop of Strange Attractors Design for FSI FontShop International.

Designers created these sequences using line art animation (cartooning), stop-action filming techniques like claymation, rotoscoping (drawing onto film to combine illustrative and photographic elements), and a range of other cinematographic techniques. Smaller budgets for film and television during the 1970s recession caused an industrywide shift to less expensive and less dynamic titling styles.

Only recently, with the entrance of computers onto the scene, are we beginning to see a rebirth of thoughtfully designed kinetic type. New digital capabilities offer widespread opportunities for kinetic typographic experimentation. In addition, the World Wide Web offers a low-budget venue for sharing these explorations.

The territory of digital kinetic type is widely considered to be mostly uncharted, and its potential far from reached. Although traditional film theory and typography offer some basis for a kinetic type methodology, philosophies and structures are only beginning to emerge to guide those designers who are creating kinetic type in digital environments.

Purpose

Adding motion adapts type's form over time, releasing new expressive qualities. Determining the specific purpose for putting type into motion is important so that all design decisions will support that purpose. Designers must be careful not to let the novelty of entertaining elements distract from or obscure their messages. Some reasons to add the element of motion to type might be to:

- Reinforce or illustrate the text's content
- Extend the text's meaning beyond its content
- Negate or challenge the text's content

Structure

Kinetic type can be structured as a montage or a collage. A montage is a linear arrangement of type and images that together create a narrative—that is, they tell a story that has a beginning, a middle, and an end. Figure 7-25 shows a sequence from an animated montage called *Little Yellow Writing Hood*, which showcases over three hundred of a foundry's fonts by dynamically telling a typographic adaptation of the classic fairy tale *Little Red Riding Hood*.

A collage, on the other hand, is a nonlinear collection of type and images that together suggest or explore a theme. While a montage must be viewed in sequence to be fully understood, a collage can convey meaning when viewed in any order. The collage in Figure 7-26 shows a sequence that uses a Russian Constructivist visual theme to present up-and-coming directors and their films by drawing a tongue-in-cheek comparison between film directors and political dictators.

Any kinetic montage or collage will be composed of frames, shots, scenes, and sequences. A frame is a single still image, the smallest component of a sequence. A shot is a combination of frames that contains a continuous action. Juxtaposition of groups of related shots composes a scene. Finally, scenes can be assembled in a specific order to create a sequence that expresses a narrative or a theme.

Designers of kinetic type need to make decisions about the compositional proximity of the text and objects, both in relation to each other and to the edges of the frame. In an open frame, actions take place both within the frame and outside of it—as if the viewer were looking out of a window, as seen in Figure 7-27. In a closed frame, all actions take place within the borders of the screen—much as if the frame were a room, like in Figure 7-28.

figure | 7-26 |

Kinetic collage, series of screenshots from *IFC: Ten New Titans* by TWOTHOUSANDSTRONG for the Independent Film Channel.

figure | 7-27 |

Open frame.

figure | 7-28 |

Closed frame.

Storyboarding

A **storyboard** is a set of sketched or rendered frames that demonstrates the layout, actions, and timing for a time-based or interactive design. Storyboarding helps designers to plan layouts and timing of shots and scenes for sequenced narratives, and to devise functional design aspects like navigational controls for interactive tutorials, games, and web sites. Storyboards are useful for developing and implementing any design that will unfold over time because they provide the chance to test out and evaluate ideas about how design elements should function—before actually going into production.

A storyboard is also an important communication tool. A designer can use a storyboard to help explain and market new designs to clients. A storyboard can also serve as a blueprint for the design, communicating important directions to everyone involved in the project's production. Storyboards can start as a series of very simple sketches with notes and arrows indicating motions and directions, like the set pictured in Figure 7-29. They can be developed to any level of refinement, depending on the needs of the project, as you can see from the highly polished storyboard pictured in Figure 7-30.

figures | 7-29 (top) and 7-30 (bottom) |

Rough and polished storyboards for *Little Yellow Writing Hood* by Ryan Pescatore Frisk and Catelijne van Middelkoop of Strange Attractors Design for FSI FontShop International.

Time

When time is a component of a design, the added movement, rhythm, sequence, and transformation of form can be literal rather than implied, as they must be in static designs. Of course applying the dimension of time to typography poses some new opportunities, challenges, and considerations for designers. Conveying a message using type over time can mimic the sequenced delivery of the spoken word. Typographic characters can be storytellers and/or cast members in narratives that support, negate, or ignore the innate content of what they spell. Type can be physically active, and can dynamically transform its characteristics, or even shift its identity by morphing into other characters or objects.

An innovative font called Beowolf is best viewed over time. Beowolf's designers wanted to challenge the precept that a font is defined by the reproducibility of its specifically shaped characters. Posing the example of handwriting, they assert that such sameness is not only unnecessary to readability, but that slight variances are "quite pleasing to the eye." So, they created a font by encoding the glyphs to randomize their shapes and colors, within specified boundaries. Within those boundaries, the glyphs shift freely so that they appear to wiggle and dance. The font's glyphs aren't recognizable by identification of static shapes, as is the case with other typefaces. Instead, Beowolf is recognized by its rhythm and style of transformation. When printed, repeated characters of Beowolf look different from each other, as you can see in Figure 7-31.

figure | 7-31 |

Beowolf typeface by Erik van Blokland and Just van Rossum of LettError Type foundry.

Motion

The movements that take place in a kinetic design help to tell the story. They also help to express a tone of voice, or assign personalities to elements. Some variables of motion type that must be considered by designers are well illustrated by the web site of a design firm called 13thFloor (*www.13thfloordesign.com*), pictured in Figure 7-32.

- *Proximity* refers to the location of the text in relation to other elements and in relation to the edges of the frame; text can converge, retract, and overlap. In the first frame of Figure 7-32 (left), the numbers are slowly stacked, each above the last from L to 12 to simulate the experience of riding an elevator going up.

- *Rotation* of elements takes place around a center point or axis; text can be flat or spatial, clockwise or counterclockwise. In the same sequence, once we pass the 12th floor, an elevator button for the 13th floor appears. When clicked, or "pressed," the button begins to rotate. The button's rotation increases in speed until it emits a spiral that grows to fill the screen. When the spiral recedes, we see we have been transported through a portal into a new dimension, a strange landscape of giant rotating 13s. The effect is the feeling of being a captive audience at a carnival funhouse.
- *Direction* describes the way in which the type moves; it can be horizontal, vertical, diagonal, advancing, receding, or random. Once we arrive in the field of 13s in Figure 7-32 (left), a creepy clown bursts from behind the elevator button, and rotating words describing the design firm's services seem to advance and recede. The last service to advance doesn't recede, but simply falls down. Then the clown begins to spin and advance. A zoom into the clown's eye, which is actually a number 13, provides a transition to the next scene.
- *Orientation* refers to the reading direction of the text, which can be horizontal, vertical, diagonal, or curved. When we enter the clown's eye in Figure 7-32 (right), we find ourselves in what one could assume to be the clown's fiery iris. Against his pupil, testimonials about the design firm appear and disappear in a variety of orientations.

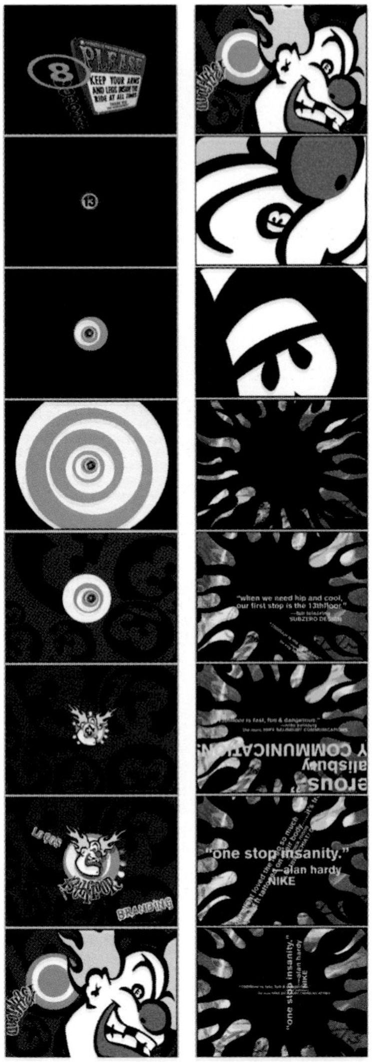

figure | 7-32 |

Series of screenshots from web site animation by Dave Parmley and Eric Ruffing of 13thFloor depict type in motion.

Voice and Personality

Type can be personified or anthropomorphized by assigning it human or animal-like behaviors. A tone of voice, an emotion, or a personality can be instilled into type through its form and movements. A good way to encourage the audience's suspension of disbelief is by applying the same laws of physics to your animated characters that we normally live by. Easing in and out of movements can help simulate the physics of an environment subject to gravity.

In the inventive short film series "Not My Type," which is pictured in Figure 7-33, every aspect of the imagery is built of animated letterforms. In this narrative film, no words are written or spoken. Instead, a variety of typefaces, symbols, and characters are animated to convey the emotions and behaviors of its characters.

figure | 7-33 |

Frames from animated short *Not My Type II* by Lycette Bros.

Rhythm and Pace

Rhythm in traditional typography is created through spatial repetition of characters or their traits. In kinetic typography, both regular and irregular rhythms can also be created by repetition of motions. A general rule of thumb in the filmmaking industry has been to display text for a duration of twice the time needed to read it. This allows the audience adequate time to read and assimilate the information being presented.

The pace of a kinetic design describes how fast or slow the rhythm is. The pace is set by a succession of durations and intervals, separated by transitions. A duration is the amount of time an object is shown or an action takes place. Intervals provide resting places between actions. Transitions lead viewers from one shot or scene to the next. The most commonly used transitional techniques are cuts, dissolves, fades, and wipes.

- *Cuts* are straight transitions from one image to another. In Figure 7-34a, you can see how a designer cut from one shot to the next in a commercial.

- *Dissolves* are transitions in which one image dissolves into another. Figure 7-34b shows how the sequence in Figure 7-34a would have looked if the designer had used a dissolve instead of a cut to make the transition between the shots.

- *Fades* are transitions in which one image fades away to nothing before the next image appears. Figure 7-34c shows the same sequence only with a fade transition applied.

- W*ipes* are transitions in which a new image is exposed in a horizontal, vertical, angled, or radial sweep across the screen. Figure 7-34d shows how a horizontal wipe would look if applied to this sequence,

There are additional transitions available on most editing software, but overuse of these novelty transitions is generally considered to be amateurish by professional designers and filmmakers. Many designers select only one or two transitional styles to apply consistently throughout a film, in order to minimize confusion for the viewer.

When editing a kinetic design, be careful to monitor the pace of the piece; if durations, intervals, or transitions are too long, viewers may become impatient and lose interest.

figure | 7-34a |

Frames showing a cut transition from *Foggie Bummer*, a commercial by Jonathan Barnbrook of Barnbrook Design for BBC Radio Scotland.

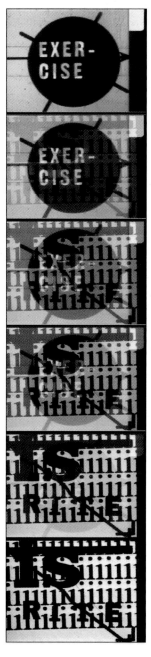

figure | 7-34b |

A dissolve transition between the same frames shown in Figure 7-34a.

figure | 7-34c |

A fade transition between the same frames shown in Figure 7-34a.

figure | 7-34d |

A wipe transition between the same frames shown in Figure 7-34a.

SUMMARY

Computers have changed the very nature of type. The highly detail-oriented nature of traditional typographic design is wasted on computer screens because the poor resolution cannot reproduce the intricate nuances of type designs. Instead, legibility and readability have become paramount to screen typography, always keeping the reader's comfort, comprehension, and ease of viewing in mind. The result is that traditional typographic conventions don't always work well in a digital environment. A whole different set of "rules" for maximizing screen legibility and readability is only now beginning to emerge.

The form that written content takes goes a long way in communicating the design's meaning and voice to the audience. Of course, as with traditional typography, meanings can be portrayed through selection of typeface, type style, size, character width, stroke weight, color, etc. Emphasis can highlight content through contrast, repetition, and distortion of recognizable letterforms. With the added elements of time and motion, viewers can witness or even participate in the process of transformation. The events they encounter and choose along the way give added dimension to the themes and narratives.

Digital typography also offers many new capabilities that let designers create dramatic and dynamic designs. No longer held to the rigid grid of the printing press, designers can easily incorporate experimental compositional techniques and strategies that push the boundaries of how viewers read, assimilate, navigate, and interact with text. No longer does type have to be static or unchanging. Designers are only just beginning to pioneer explorations into dynamic use of type in the digital realm and redefine the boundaries of what type can be and how it can be used as a vehicle for communication.

> ### New Vocabulary
>
> **storyboard:** a set of sketched or rendered frames that demonstrates the layout, actions, and timing for a time-based or interactive design

> ### It's all an illusion!
>
> The illusion of movement in film, video, and digital environments results from the sequencing of still images at a rate that is faster than the eye can register each one individually. The human brain continues to perceive what the eye sees for an instant longer than the eye actually sees it. This physiological phenomenon is called Persistence of Vision. Paired with Gestalt's psychological Law of Closure, Persistence of Vision allows the brain to fill in the missing positions to create the perception of a continuous flowing movement. A rate of 24 frames per second is sufficient to trick the human eye into perceiving a sequence of still images as one single moving image.

in review

1. What are some differences between screen and traditional typography? How do these differences impact legibility and readability issues?

2. What are pixel fonts?

3. What are the pros and cons of using embedded fonts in your designs?

4. Explain how legibility and readability can be improved in digital environments by adjusting the following variables: size, type style, tracking, leading, paragraph size, measure, and texture.

5. What is type glow, and how can you avoid it in your designs?

6. Explain the difference between bitmap (or raster) fonts and outline (or vector) fonts.

7. What is hinting?

8. What is anti-aliasing?

9. When a design will be printed using the four-color printing process, what are two ways to prevent misregistration from eroding legibility?

exercises

1. Search the Web for sites that use type in innovative ways. Consider the typographic strategies the designers used, and why they were effective.

2. Search the Web for sites that use type poorly. Determine what isn't working, and how the designer could make typographic improvements.

3. Find, download, and install any free font of your choice onto your computer.

4. Design a web page that explains how to use type in a digital environment for optimal legibility and readability. Divide the layout vertically, and repeat the same text on both sides. Apply what you know about color, contrast, size, type style, tracking, leading, paragraph size, measure, and texture to make one side highly legible, and the other side hard to read.

5. Create a storyboard for an expressive interactive e-card that uses only type to convey its message. The e-card can explore any common greeting card theme or honor any holiday.

6. Your client is making a spin-off television show based on a character from your favorite program. Create a text-dominant storyboard for the show's 30-second opener, which must include the name of the program, the title of the episode, and the names of the director, actors, and screenplay writer.

7. Create a design for a web page or PowerPoint presentation that teaches the audience how to play your favorite card game, using only typographic characters and symbols—no images. As you design your layout, consider how you will help your viewer navigate through the digital environment and how you will emphasize important elements for on-screen viewing. Consider how elements like line length, leading, word spacing, typeface, font size, and font color will affect the legibility and readability of your design in a digital environment. Consider how your decisions might have differed for a printed presentation.

Magnet type specimens created by Joe Freedman of Sarabande in
1993, based on original designs by Lucien Bernhard for American
Type Foundry, circa 1940. *Courtesy of Sarabande.*

CHAPTER 8

objectives

- Explain the purpose of a proposed font design
- Establish guidelines for the design of a new font
- Make informed decisions about contrast, angle of stress, and terminals to ensure consistency within a character set
- Create an original typeface
- Understand copyright law as it applies to type design
- Develop a full character set
- Add adequate spacing to characters
- Create a specimen to display and market an original font

introduction

If you're going to design an original typeface, the first question that comes to mind is, why? After all, there is a plethora of available typefaces out there—more than ever before. The digital revolution's ensuing boom in new typeface designs has surpassed the typeface explosion of the industrial revolution considerably. Yet, just as there is always room in the world for one more painting, so it is with typefaces. People create new typefaces for many of the same reasons they create new paintings—to express themselves, to make personal statements about the world they live in, to fulfill a specific design or illustrative need, or to create a distinctive corporate image.

So, if you are interested in designing a typeface, you'll need to decide what your reasons are, and what purpose the end-product will serve. Ask yourself who will use this typeface, and how and where will they use it. Will it be primarily viewed on-screen or in print—at large sizes or small? Will it be viewed at close range or from a distance? For what sorts of messages and documents will people want to use your font? What mood or spirit or kind of meaning should it convey; what will its personality be like?

DESIGNING TYPE

GETTING STARTED

A good way to begin your typeface design is to write a short description of the project. Describe your intended meanings, moods, and feel of the typeface, how it will be used, who will use it, etc. This will take some research, especially if you are creating a design for a client. Ask the questions who, what, where, when, why, and how.

- *Who* will use this font, and who will read it?

- *What* characters will be included in this font? Uppercase? Lowercase? Will you include numerals, punctuation, ligatures? What symbols will be included? Will you create any accompanying type styles? Is this to be a single font or an entire font family? All this should be decided up front, based on the planned usage of the font. If you intend to license your font through a foundry, they may require a specific range of characters to be included.

- *Where* will this font be viewed? On-screen? In print? On a large billboard? In a cramped telephone book? In long passages, or will it only be used for display?

- *When* (what time period) should this font evoke or reflect?

- *Why* create this new font; what purpose will it serve? What meanings and/or emotions should this font express? What associations should it elicit?

- *How* will this font be rendered? Will it be printed on high-quality paper using an image-setter that can catch every detail? Will it be printed on low-quality paper with low-quality inks that will blob and run? Will it be viewed at very small or large sizes?

Your answers to these questions will help you make specific decisions along the way about which design elements and strategies to choose and use. Referring back to your initial description throughout your process will keep you on track during the time it takes to complete the design of a whole font.

Keep a Log

As you proceed through the font design process, you should keep very good records. There will be a lot of details—probably too many to keep track of by memory alone. Keep a notebook handy, and log all the specifics of what you designed, what worked, and what didn't work. Keep a record for every step of the process and for every character you work on, so that you will be able to easily access the information later.

Finding Inspiration

Before starting your design, you should view and study as many typefaces as possible, so that you can know what is already out there and what is being used to serve similar purposes to yours. This knowledge will help you to differentiate your typeface from the others, while learning from other designers' mistakes and successes. Specimen books (type sample catalogs), published by foundries (font manufacturers) old and new, are a great source of inspiration. Many foundries will send you free or inexpensive type specimens upon request. Also, libraries that feature collections on printing are likely to have many old specimen books from a range of historical periods. Of course, you can view hundreds of fonts online, and this can be very helpful. However, because of the computer's poor screen resolution, you'd do better to view the typefaces in print so you can appreciate the detailed nuances that make each typeface unique.

Scrapbooking can be another good source of ideas. When you see examples of type that interest you, collect and/or record them in your scrapbook, and write notes to yourself about what interested you in particular about each design. This will help with your brainstorming later.

Designing for Legibility

As you are designing glyphs, keep in mind that the upper halves and the right sides of the English alphabet are most crucial to character recognition. That's because most of the variations that provide distinctive visual cues are found in those areas, as you can see from Figure 8-1.

figure | 8-1 |

Upper and lower and right and left portions of glyphs.

PREPARATIONS

A good typeface is consistent enough that it doesn't interrupt the reading of the content. This means that when you look at a page of body text, no one letter should stand out from the others, allowing a smooth reading flow. Because of the varying shapes of letters, several optical illusions can take effect, which make consistent letterforms appear to be inconsistent. In these situations, it is necessary to make adjustments to create optical consistency, even at the expense of actual consistency. Many of these illusions and their solutions are discussed in this chapter, but the most important thing to remember is to trust your eyes.

There are several key decisions that you must make at the onset of designing your font to ensure consistency. These selections will steer the course for the entire design and form the essence of your font's style. These essential elements can be divided into four categories: guidelines, contrast, angle of stress, and terminals.

Guidelines

You are already familiar with the terms baseline, x-height, cap height, ascender line, and descender line from Chapter 2. These guidelines don't just help designers lay out type, they are also essential to designing type. They compose a grid that lets the designer make sure that all the characters of a font are proportioned consistently; you will need to establish those guidelines to create a new font.

To do this, you will start with an em square; that is, an imaginary bounding box that is used to size and align glyphs. The size of the em square is always the same as the typeface's point size. It must accommodate each character in full—everything has to fit inside, even **diacritical (accent) marks** that might be applied to letters later. It must also contain some extra space on the sides and top of the glyph so adjacent characters don't bump into each other. The em square is generally divided by the baseline into two areas—the **ascent**, which is the area above the baseline, and the **descent**, which is the area below (Figure 8-2).

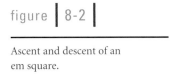

figure | 8-2 |

Ascent and descent of an em square.

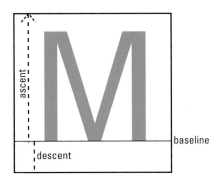

Most PostScript fonts are designed with an em square that has been divided into 1000 units, and TrueType fonts are designed with an em square of 1024 units, shown in Figure 8-3. However, it is up to the designer to decide how many em square units to work with. The more finely the em square is divided, the higher the resolution. The maximum em square that most font editing software can accommodate is 4000 units; however, since the average printer cannot reproduce much more detail than the average 1000 to 1024 units, this level of detail is generally excessive. Even fonts developed for output on high-quality imagesetters are adequate when based on a doubled em square divided into 2000 units for PostScript or 2048 units for TrueType.

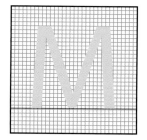

em square divided into 1024 units   em square divided into 2048 units

figure | 8-3 |

An em square divided into 1024 units and 2048 units.

The proportions at which you divide the em square, and thus set your guideline measurements to, are up to you. However, it will help to be aware of standard guideline proportions, so that you can make educated decisions about deviating from tradition.

- The baseline traditionally divides the em square at about 20 percent up from the bottom (Figure 8-4). For an em square of 1000 units, this would mean an ascent of about 800 units and a descent of about 200 units.

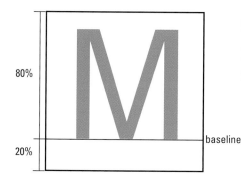

figure | 8-4 |

The baseline of this em square is 20 percent up from the bottom.

- The cap height is generally about 75 percent to 85 percent of the height of the ascent, starting at the baseline (Figure 8-5). This means that for an em square of 1000 units with an 800 unit ascent, the cap height would be around 600 to 700 em units above the baseline.

figure | 8-5 |

The cap height of this em square is about 75 percent to 85 percent of the height of the ascent.

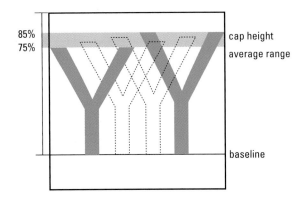

- The x-height is traditionally sized at around 50 percent to 80 percent of the cap height. So, for our em square of 1000 units with an 800 unit ascent and a 600–700 unit cap height, a traditional x-height would be somewhere between 300 and 560 em units above the baseline, as seen in Figure 8-6. There is a lot of flexibility here, so remember as you select an x-height that a low x-height will make your type appear smaller than a tall x-height at the same point size. If the x-height is too short, the letters may become too small to read at smaller point sizes. On the other hand, if the x-height of the font is too tall, legibility will be decreased because short ascenders can become difficult to recognize. For instance, an **h** with a very short ascender might be hard to distinguish from an **n**.

figure | 8-6 |

The x-height of an em square is usually about 50 percent to 80 percent of the cap height.

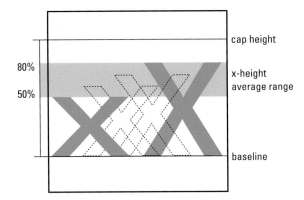

- The ascender line should be either the same height or slightly taller than the cap height.

- The descender line can be the full descent size (in this case, 200 em units), as shown in Figure 8-7, or it can be slightly shorter.

figure | 8-7 |

Ascender and descender lines of an em square.

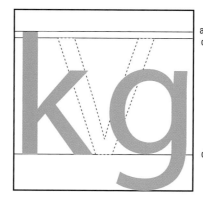

ascender line
cap height

descender line

- You may also need to establish letter connector guidelines, as shown by the gray bar in Figure 8-8. This is only necessary if your font will be a cursive script in which letters will connect to each other. In this case, you'll need to select a height where all the connecting strokes will make contact with adjacent letters.

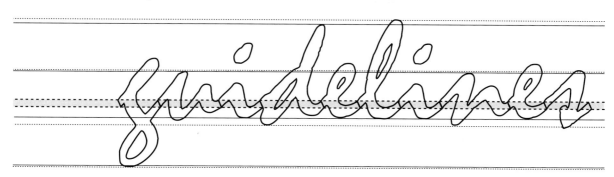

Before deciding upon the proportions of your font, you should examine many typeface examples with a variety of proportions to get a sense of what will work best for your design.

figure | 8-8 |

Letter connector guidelines.

Unfortunately, the guidelines we've discussed so far won't satisfy the needs of every character. Rounded and pointed letters look slightly smaller than other letters of the same size because they have so much extra negative space surrounding them in the areas where they meet the guidelines. To compensate for this, you will need to create the optical illusion that they are the same size as the other letters by making them slightly bigger. The way to do this is to let them slightly overshoot the standard guidelines. You will need to establish a set of **overshoot guide-lines** so that your round and pointed letters maintain optical consistency with the other characters, as shown in Figure 8-9. The overshoot guide-lines include the baseline overshoot, the x-height overshoot, the cap height overshoot, the ascender line overshoot, and the descender line overshoot (optional).

figure | 8-9 |

Overshoot guidelines.

Standard overshoot amounts range between 10 to 20 em units for a 1000 unit em square. That's an extra 1 to 2 percent above (or below) each guideline.

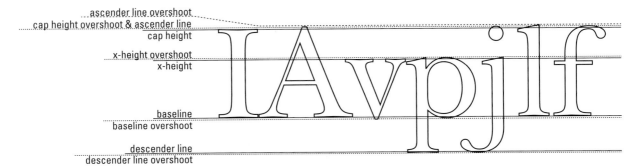

ascender line overshoot
cap height overshoot & ascender line
cap height
x-height overshoot
x-height
baseline
baseline overshoot
descender line
descender line overshoot

Determining the width of characters within the em square tends to be a bit more subjective, unless you are creating a monospaced font in which all characters have the same width. A good traditional strategy is to start out by establishing three basic widths: a narrow width (for letters like **i**, **j**, **l**, and **t**), a wide width (for letters like **M** and **w**), and a medium width for all other characters. Then vary the width when needed, as you design each letter; those with strong horizontals may need narrowing, since horizontals create an optical illusion of added character width, as illustrated by Figure 8-10. Trust your eyes as you make adjustments for optical consistency.

figure | 8-10 |

Characters with strong horizontals may need narrowing, since horizontals create an optical illusion of added character width.

Contrast

As you remember from previous chapters, contrast in typography refers to the variance between the thick and thin letter parts; that is, the difference between the widths of the stem and hairline strokes and between the thick and thin parts of curved strokes. Extremely low-contrast fonts may look dull and detract from the legibility of body texts by robbing letterforms of their distinctive uniqueness. Extremely high-contrast fonts may detract from the legibility of body texts by dazzling the eyes and by distorting letterforms past easy recognition. Again, you should study real examples to get a sense of what sort of contrast you want to establish.

For a traditional-looking font, you can base your stroke weights on the cap height you've already established by using the following percentages:

- Vertical capital stem stroke: 13 to 18 percent of the cap height
- Vertical capital hairline stroke: 5 to 8 percent of the cap height

You can then select your vertical lowercase stroke measurements based on your vertical capital stroke weights.

- Vertical lowercase stem stroke: 80 to 90 percent of the vertical capital stem stroke
- Vertical lowercase hairline stroke: 70 to 80 percent of the capital hairline stroke (note: crossbars are often thicker)

You can then determine the curved and diagonal stem widths based on your vertical stroke measurements. Curved and diagonal stems will need to be slightly wider to optically match their straight counterparts; this is because curved and diagonal lines look narrower than straight lines of the same width, as you can see in Figure 8-11.

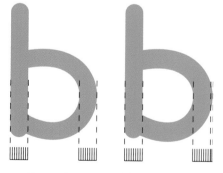

figure | 8-11 |

Optical illusion—curved lines look narrower than straight lines of the same width.

- Curved stem widths: approximately 10 percent wider than their corresponding vertical counterparts

It's a good idea to make templates of each stroke weight, like the ones shown in Figure 8-12, so that you can easily and consistently apply them to appropriate strokes.

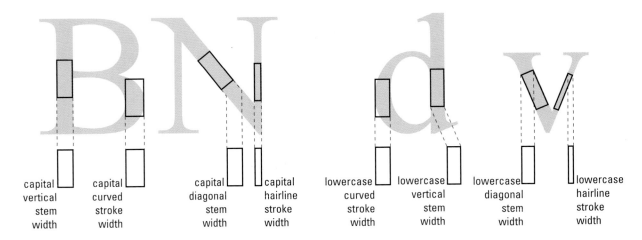

figure | 8-12 |

Sample stroke templates.

Angle of Stress

The angle of stress is another factor that should be optically consistent in a font. Although fonts have become somewhat removed from their calligraphic heritage, the consistent distribution of thick and thin letter parts still adds grace and distinctiveness to many fonts. A typical font has an angle of stress anywhere between 60 to 90 degrees, relative to the baseline, as shown by Figure 8-13.

figure | 8-13 |

The average angle of stress is 60 to 90 degrees, relative to the baseline.

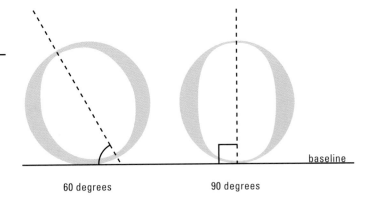

Terminals

Finally, you must consider the nature of your font's terminals; that is, the ends of the characters' strokes. Sometimes terminals have serifs; sometimes they don't. If a font does have serifs, they might be bracketed or they may not be. Whether you are designing a serif or sans-serif font, it is likely that there will be some variation in terminal shape and size depending on position, and you will need to make some decisions about these variations up front, to ensure overall consistency for the font.

For fonts that have serifs, you will need to determine the shapes and sizes of both uppercase and lowercase serifs, barbs, and beaks. You will also need to decide on the slope and height of the brackets that connect the serifs to the stems. Brackets, which ease the transition from the stem to the serif, can be short or tall, wide or narrow, and lightly or heavily sloped, as shown in Figure 8-14.

figure | 8-14 |

Bracketed serifs.

For all fonts, you will need to apply consistent shapes and sizes for terminals including tails, ears, apexes, vertexes, and swashes, as applicable.

New Vocabulary

ascent: the area of the em square that is above the baseline

descent: the area of the em square that is below the baseline

diacritical (accent) mark: a mark, point, or sign—such as a cedilla, tilde, circumflex, or macron—added or attached to a letter to indicate pronunciation

overshoot guidelines: a set of guidelines that overshoot the standard guidelines, for the design of letterforms that require optical adjustments to compensate for the optical illusion that rounded and pointed letters appear smaller than other letters of the same size

CHOOSING A RENDERING METHOD

How you begin creating your designs will depend upon your intended look and feel for the font, and also upon how you plan for it to be viewed.

If your font's style will be based on a hand-rendered technique like calligraphy, handwriting, rubber stamping, stenciling, or block printing, you'll want to start out by making originals in your selected medium to scan and use as digitized drawing templates. When rendering original characters manually, don't just write or produce each character once; produce each one a number of times, so that you can select the best example of each to use to create your template, as shown in Figure 8-15. You should also render a full character set of originals at once, because if you have to backtrack later to create originals for missing characters, you may compromise the consistency of your font's look and feel.

figure | 8-15 |

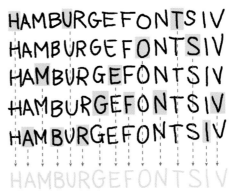

Produce each character multiple times.

Construction of Components

The Latin alphabet is comprised of a limited number of shapes including vertical, horizontal, and diagonal lines, and circles. One method of font design is to first design the components, and then assemble them in different ways to construct each glyph. Your parts inventory should include each character element that was discussed in Chapter 2. If you choose to use this method, you will need to create some or all of the following components, according to your established guidelines, contrast, angle of stress, and terminals.

- *Stems:* the width and the angle of vertical stem strokes
- *Hairlines:* the width and the angle of vertical hairline strokes
- *Crossbars:* thickness, angle, and height of horizontal and diagonal hairline strokes that connect on both ends; keep in mind that to look centered, a crossbar will need to be placed slightly above center, and that horizontal lines create the illusion of added width, so characters with strong horizontals may need to be slightly shortened for optical consistency
- *Cross strokes:* thickness, angle, and height of horizontal and diagonal hairline strokes that cross a stem

- *Arms:* thickness, angle, and lengths of strokes that extend horizontally or upwards diagonally from the stem of a letter and end freely
- *Legs:* width and angle of diagonal strokes that extend downward from the stem to the baseline and end freely
- *Bowls:* width and thickness of large and small bowls
- *Counters:* shapes and widths for counters of both large and small bowls
- *Eyes:* shapes and width of the closed counter in the lowercase **e**
- *Shoulders:* thickness and slope of the areas where curved strokes meet straight strokes
- *Terminals:* shapes of terminals that do not have serifs
- *Serifs:* shapes and sizes of serifs (if applicable)
- *Dots:* shapes and sizes of dots for **i** and **j**

Once you create these components, you can assemble them according to your guidelines, using your judgment and trusting your eyes.

Drawing Outline Glyphs

Most designers start by sketching their ideas, and then redrawing them as outline glyphs on the computer. Some people scan and trace their sketches, while others just look at their sketches while redrawing them on the computer. Some designers even begin drawing outline fonts right on the computer, though this approach isn't widely advocated because that method can lead to a design governed by the computer's easiest capabilities.

It is possible to draw glyphs directly into most font editing programs, but most designers find it easier to draw their designs in a drawing program like Adobe Illustrator or CorelDRAW, and then import their glyphs into a font editor for fine-tuning. This is because vector-based drawing programs provide a bit more flexibility and control than most font editors. It's a good idea to check your curves after you import each glyph into the font editor, because translation between programs isn't always perfect.

There are two good strategies that work well when drawing vector-based glyphs on the computer. The first is to start out by creating shapes using the shape tool, and then add, subtract, and manipulate points and curves to mold the shape into a glyph. The second strategy is to use the pen, pencil, or brush tool to draw the glyph as a combination of strokes, and then assign the desired stroke weights and convert the strokes into shapes, as shown in Figure 8-16. The shapes can then be united into a

| NOTE |

Here's a useful tip! To convert strokes into shapes, use the Outline Stroke function if you used the pen or pencil tools to draw the glyph; use the Expand Appearance function if you drew it using a brush tool.

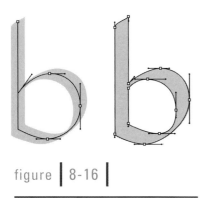

figure | 8-16 |

A glyph, drawn as a combination of strokes, then converted into shapes.

single glyph, if necessary, and areas that exceed your guidelines can be trimmed away or adjusted. This technique will give you a basic shape that you can then refine to suit your design goals.

Drawing with Bézier Curves

There's a good possibility that your character shapes will require you to work with **Bézier curves**, which are mathematically defined rounded shapes created by setting endpoints (or anchor points) and then re-shaped by moving control points (or handles). When using Bézier curves to create glyphs, there are a few important tips that will help you to create glyphs with smooth curves and small file sizes.

- Use as few points as possible to draw your glyph, as shown in Figure 8-17.

figure | 8-17 |

Use as few points as possible to draw your glyphs.

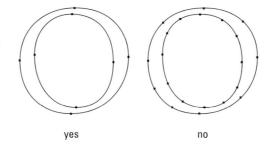

- Handles should not cross each other, as shown in Figure 8-18.

figure | 8-18 |

Handles should not cross each other.

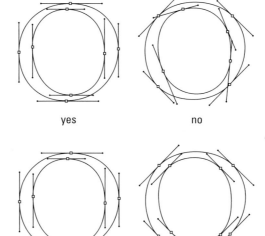

figure | 8-19 |

Points should be placed orthogonally.

- Points should be placed orthogonally (parallel to the axes) to create curves; that is, they should be at the outermost point on the curve so that the handles extend vertically or horizontally, as shown in Figure 8-19.

- The handles of a point along a smooth curve should be straight across from each other at a 180-degree angle, as illustrated in Figure 8-20.

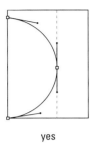 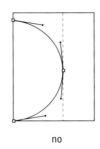

yes   no

figure | 8-20 |

The handles of a point along a smooth curve should be straight across from each other at a 180-degree angle.

- At a point where a curve becomes straight, the handles should project straight out in the same direction as the straight line. Don't let the handle overshoot the beginning of the curve, or it will look bloated, as seen in Figure 8-21.

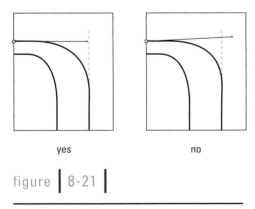

yes   no

figure | 8-21 |

Where curves become straight, the handles should project straight out in the same direction as the straight line without overshooting the curve.

New Vocabulary

Bézier curves: mathematically defined rounded shapes created by setting endpoints (or anchor points) and then reshaped by moving control points (or handles)

Building Pixel Fonts

If you will be creating a font to be viewed on a CRT or LCD screen, it's a good idea to create your character designs based on a pixel grid because the grid represents the most detail that you'll be able to achieve on-screen. Letterforms that are designed based on the pixel grid will show less distortion on-screen, and will adapt to a variety of point sizes more easily on-screen, too. Some pixel font designers begin on graph paper and then translate their designs to the screen. Others begin right on the computer, selecting individual pixels one at a time. This can be done in most photo and painting programs, or you can use software developed specifically for designing pixel fonts. The pencil tool in most painting programs will color a single pixel, and with a zoom level of around 800 percent, you should be able to view it well enough.

Reviving or Modifying Existing Fonts

Sometimes designers simply revive an old existing typeface, or modify an existing digitized font. On one hand, this approach can be easier because the decisions regarding proportions and shapes have already been made. However, this approach can also be a bit sticky because there are legal and ethical issues involved.

Reviving an Existing Font

If you wish your font to be true to the original design, you'll first need to find clean printed samples to work from—the larger the samples, the better. Scan these at a high resolution, at least 300 dpi, so you can capture as much detail as possible. Once scanned, you can trace the glyphs. As you trace, you may want to compensate for the bleeding of the ink in your sample by tightening the forms.

You may decide to use your software's autotrace feature, but keep in mind that this function is likely to assign too many points to the shape, and may not trace the glyph perfectly. If you do use autotrace, you'll definitely need to go back and clean up the results by hand, removing extra points and repairing incorrectly traced areas.

Once the original glyphs have been traced, you can eliminate your templates and perfect the glyphs. You may want to reproduce a true revival of the font, or create a derivative work by adding your own modifications. If you do this, make sure that your changes represent consistent and purposeful improvements. Also, if the typeface designer of the original font is known, credit should most certainly be given.

Modifying Digitized Fonts

It is possible to import a font into your font editing software that has already been digitized, and then trace the glyphs. However, unless you plan to modify the glyphs enough that they could be reasonably considered an original work, you should be wary of this technique for legal, if not ethical, reasons.

Copyright and Patent Issues

Designing a typeface is quite a time-consuming and detail-oriented creative process. European legislatures have recognized this by granting copyrights for original font designs. Because President Clinton signed the World Intellectual Property Organization (WIPO) Copyright Treaty of 1998, Americans must also legally obtain licenses to work with fonts owned by European foundries. However, the United States legislature takes a different position on copyright of domestic font designs.

United States copyright law protects the authors of "original works of authorship," granting them exclusive rights to reproduce, distribute copies, publicize, publicly display, and prepare derivative works from the copyrighted work. Although this includes protection for "pictorial, graphic, and sculptural works," font designs (the actual shapes of the glyphs) are not currently copyrightable in the United States. Congress and the courts have upheld the United States Copyright Office's policy that "familiar symbols or designs; mere variations of typographic ornamentation, [and] lettering…" are not eligible for copyright. The courts have ruled that since alphanumerical glyphs must recognizably adhere to preexisting basic forms in order to be functional, they cannot contain the required level of originality to qualify for a copyright.

However, font programs *are* eligible for copyright. The name and coding of a computer program or file that creates glyphs *is* copyrightable because it constitutes a "literary work," an expressive form that is protected by copyright law.

Furthermore, copyrighting of an original work is automatic. Whether the author has registered the work with the United States Copyright Office or not, it is still protected by law. Registration of such is simply a formality, whose purpose is to create a public record of the details of a specific copyright, like the author's name and the copyright date.

So, it is legally considered unlawful piracy to trace existing digitized glyphs, and, with only minimal modifications to the coding, to rename the font and sell it as original work.

Fonts may also be protected by patents. Patents grant inventors the right to exclude others from making, using, or selling their inventions. Design patents are issued by the United States Patent and Trademark Office for a term of fourteen years. The law states that design patents may only be issued to "whoever invents any new, original, and ornamental design for an article of manufacture." This means that in order to qualify for a design patent, a font must be sufficiently novel and original.

It's pretty hard to obtain a patent for a font; one must provide drawings which clearly show the originality of the artwork, disclose any prior art that could have influenced the design, and pay a fee. Also, the application for the patent must be submitted within one year of first public use. Once issued, however, the patent protects the aesthetic appearance of the font, as opposed to the digital encoding that is protected by copyright law.

DESIGN STRATEGY

Having made all the preparations, you are ready to actually begin designing your glyphs. This is a big project! Each individual character is an artwork unto itself, and there will be a minimum of twenty-six. Where to begin?

It's good to start with the uppercase letters, and then create the punctuation marks and numbers. That way, you'll have an incomplete, but usable, character set by the time you're ready to start your lowercase letterforms.

A common strategy for font design is to begin with a few letters whose structures are repeated throughout the alphabet. Letters can be categorized into groups that share similarly shaped strokes and approximate character widths. Designing one from each category will make it faster and easier to develop the other letters in each group. When letterforms are derived from each other, that doesn't mean their features will be exactly the same, only that they will be similar. Making a chart like the one in Figure 8-22 can help you to determine relationships between letters.

figure | 8-22 |

Chart categorizing glyphs by intended shapes and widths.

	Narrow Width	Between Narrow and Medium Width	Medium Width	Between Medium and Wide Width	Wide Width
Curvilinear strokes			S	C, G, O, Q	
Rectilinear strokes	I,	E, F, L	H, T		
Angular strokes		Y, Z	A, K, N, V, X		M, W
Rectangular / Rounded combination	J	B, P	U	D, R	
Curvilinear strokes		s		a, c, e, g, o	
Rectilinear strokes	i, l				
Angular strokes			k, v, x, y, z		w
Rectangular / Rounded combination	f, j, r, t	h, n, u		b, d, p, q	m

The way the letters have been categorized in this example is not absolute—you should distribute the letters to best suit your particular design. Also keep in mind that once you have constructed any letterform based on another, you'll need to adapt it for optical balance. Pay special care to the letterform's distinctive features—these elements are most essential to quick and easy recognition. First designing **I**, **H**, **O**, and **V** will speed up the process of designing almost all the other letters.

Testing is Important!

It is wise to start with **I**, and then derive **H** from it, and then immediately begin testing how the letters look in relation to one another. You may find you need to make some adjustments to one or all of them before proceeding. Once you are satisfied with the **H**, next create **O** using the same testing process, and then the **V**.

Building up to a string of letters is common practice. A standard test string of characters to start with is **HAMBURGEFONTSIV** (and **hamburgefontsiv**). This string of characters includes letters representing a range of shapes and widths. The advantage of working with a representative string of letters is that you begin to see how they function in relation to one another. That way you can identify problems or mistakes, and correct them early on. You should also try squinting at your test string, and viewing it as reversed type (white on black). As you can see from Figure 8-23, these techniques will help you to identify problematic areas.

| NOTE |

You should test each new letter in combination with the other letters, and make necessary adjustments EVERY time you add a new glyph to your character set!

hamburgefontsiv
hamburgefontsiv
hamburgefontsiv

figure | 8-23 |

Squint or view your test string as reversed type (white on black) to identify mistakes.

Capital Glyphs with Vertical Stems

All letters with vertical stems are based on the letter **I**, so this is a good place to start. The capital **I** can be slightly thicker than the stems of other characters, to compensate for its innate narrowness. The practice of adding cross strokes to the top and bottom of the letter **I** is based on an attempt to adapt the alphabet to a monospace format. However, technically it is incorrect—those are serifs, not cross strokes.

From **I**, you can derive **J**, **T**, and **H**.

• To make **J**, start with **I** and add a tail.

• To make **T**, add a cross stroke to **I**.

• To make **H**, use two slightly narrowed **I**s and a crossbar. To make the crossbar appear centered optically, you'll need to place it slightly above center, as shown in Figure 8-24, or you may want to simply place it at your x-height. The placement of the crossbar will be applied to many other letters later. Also, remember that the horizontal thrust of the **H** will make it look a bit wider than it really is, so the character may need to be slightly narrowed. This phenomenon applies to all the letters with strong horizontal strokes including **B**, **E**, **F**, **H**, **L**, **P**, **T**, **U**, and **Z**.

figure | 8-24 |

Optical illusion—to make the crossbar appear centered optically, place it slightly above center.

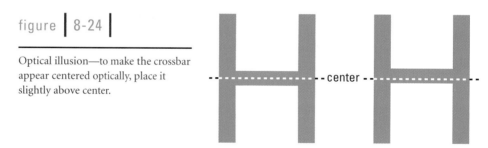

From **H**, you can derive **U**, **K**, and **E**.

• To make **U** from **H**, remove the crossbar and connect the bottoms of the vertical strokes with a rounded stroke. **U** is sometimes slightly narrower than **H**.

• To make **K** from **H**, eliminate the crossbar and right vertical stem. Then project an arm and a leg from where the crossbar would have been. The arm and the leg of the **K** generally form an approximate 90-degree angle, usually meeting slightly above center, as with the crossbar of the **H**. The leg is sometimes longer than the arm, and is often thicker.

• To make **E**, remove the right stem from the **H**. Then add arms to the top and bottom of stem. Adapt the crossbar as needed to form the middle arm of the **E**, which is usually the shortest of the three. The bottom arm is usually the longest of the three. Horizontal strokes appear thicker than vertical strokes of the same width. To counteract this optical illusion, slightly narrow the thicker horizontal strokes until they look optically consistent with their vertical counterparts, as shown in Figure 8-25.

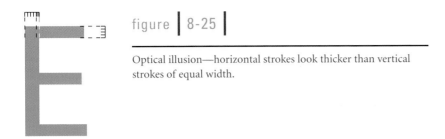

figure | 8-25 |

Optical illusion—horizontal strokes look thicker than vertical strokes of equal width.

From **E**, you can derive **F**, **L**, and **B**.

- To make **F**, remove the bottom arm from **E**. You may need to lower the middle arm slightly to decrease the large lower open counter.

- To make **L**, remove the two upper arms from **E**.

- To make **B**, connect the arms with curved strokes. You may need to shorten the top arm, since the upper bowl is usually smaller than the lower bowl.

From **B**, you can derive **R** and **P**.

- To make **R**, remove the lower bowl from the **B**, and extend a leg from the bottom of the remaining bowl. The leg can extend past the bowl or align with its outermost edge. The leg can be straight or slightly curved. Also, sometimes the bowl of the **R** is larger than the upper bowl of the **B**.

- To make **P**, remove the lower bowl from the **B**. The bowl of the **P** is often larger than the corresponding bowls of the **R** and **B**, so you'll probably want to increase its size.

Capital Glyphs with Curved Strokes

When you are ready to begin designing curved letterforms, it is best to start with the letter **O**. That's because the other curved letters are all based on the form of the **O**.

Several optical illusions affect our perceptions of the letter **O**, so to attain optical consistency you will need to make some adjustments.

- Circles look smaller than squares of the same size, so it is necessary to slightly enlarge the **O**, causing the letterform to overshoot the baseline and the cap height slightly. This is also true for triangles, as you can see from Figure 8-26.

figure | 8-26 |

Optical illusion—circles and triangles look smaller than squares of the same size.

- Perfectly round circles also appear to be wider than they are tall—another optical illusion, as pictured in Figure 8-27. If you want the **O** to look optically round, you'll need to narrow it slightly, as you did with the **H**.

Optical illusion—perfectly round circles appear to be wider than they are tall, so compensate by narrowing them slightly.

- Since curved lines appear to be thinner than straight lines, so you'll need to compensate by making the thick strokes of the **O** slightly thicker than their vertical counterparts, as shown in Figure 8-28.

figure | 8-28 |

Make curved strokes slightly thicker than straight lines to compensate for the optical illusion that curves appear to be thinner than straight strokes of equal width.

- To combat a fourth optical illusion affecting the **O**, round strokes should always be slightly thinner at the top and bottom, as shown in Figure 8-29. This is to compensate for the optical illusion that causes horizontals to appear thicker than verticals of the same width. This compensation should be administered, even for a font that otherwise has no contrast.

figure | 8-29 |

Optical illusion—horizontals appear thicker than verticals of the same width.

From **O**, you can derive **D**, **Q**, **C**, and **G**.

- To make **D**, use **I** and half of an **O**.
- To make **Q**, add a tail to **O**.
- To make **C**, adapt **O**.
- **G** can actually be adapted from **C** by adding a crossbar and a spur, as needed.

Capital Glyphs with Diagonal Strokes

Triangular shaped letters may need to overshoot their guidelines slightly, just as the round letters did. Diagonal strokes should be slightly wider than their vertical counterparts, and taper down toward the crotch of the vertex, in order to achieve optical consistency, as shown in Figure 8-30. The strokes can even be slightly notched at their inner junction, to prevent ink clog. This concept applies to all junctures that create tight counters. Figure 8-31 shows an extreme example of a typeface designed for the publication of cheap phone books, so that text printed at small sizes onto porous paper would be legible.

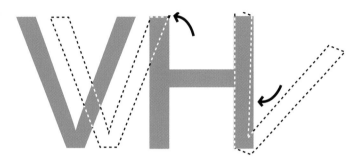

figure | 8-30 |

Optical illusion—diagonal strokes look narrower than vertical strokes of equal width, but they look wider at junctions.

figure | 8-31 |

Matthew Carter designed Bell Centennial Bold to prevent ink clog at small sizes on cheap paper. *Courtesy of Linotype type foundry, Linotype Library GmbH,* www.linotype.com.

The **V** is generally comparable in character width to the **H**. To make **V**, join a downward sloping diagonal stem with an upward sloping diagonal hairline stroke, so that the angle between them is approximately 38 to 55 degrees.

From **V**, you can derive **A, N, M, W, Y,** and **Z**.

- To make **A**, turn **V** upside down and add a crossbar. Take care that the crossbar is low enough that the counter is not obscured, and will not fill with ink upon printing. The crossbar of the **A** is often lower than that of the **H**.

- To make **N**, rotate **V** slightly counter clockwise, add an extra hairline stroke to the left side, and make adjustments as needed. Note that the diagonal stroke is the stem of the letter **N**, and the vertical strokes are hairlines.

- To make **M**, start by inverting two **V**s, and place them next to each other so that they touch. Adjust the angle of the outer strokes, making them vertical or only slightly splayed. The center point usually, but not always, meets the baseline. **M** is usually the second widest letter of the alphabet.

- To construct the **W**, you can align two **V**s. The inside strokes of the **W** can cross or they can join at the cap height. **W** is usually the widest letter of the alphabet.

- The **Y** can be constructed by combining the bottom of **I** with a scaled down **V**.

- To make **Z**, rotate the stem of **V** clockwise, and combine it with the top and bottom arms of **E**.

From **Z**, you can derive **X**.

- To make **X**, flip the stem of **Z**, and add a cross stroke. Often, the top of the **X** is slightly narrower than the bottom, and the stem and hairline strokes usually meet slightly above center, as with the **H**, for optical balance. Also bear in mind that when two diagonal lines cross, an optical illusion can cause one or both to look slightly misaligned. If this is the case with your **X**, make the necessary adjustments to achieve optical balance, as shown in Figure 8-32.

figure | 8-32 |

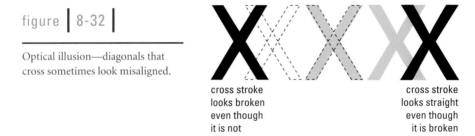

Optical illusion—diagonals that cross sometimes look misaligned.

cross stroke
looks broken
even though
it is not

cross stroke
looks straight
even though
it is broken

This leaves only **S**, an anomaly. The spine of the **S** is not only unique among the letters, but it is considered by many to be the most difficult shape to perfect. One useful approach is to make a guide by stacking two circles at the desired proportion and tracing the curves to create the spine. As you are determining the proportions of the **S**, remember that the optical center of the **S** is slightly above center, just as it was with previous letterforms.

Special Characters and Extended Character Sets

You will want to consider including special characters in your character set. These commonly include numerals, punctuation marks, and ligatures (letter pairs that have been joined into a single character), but can also include monetary symbols, math characters, fractions, accented characters, initial capitals, small capitals, and swash characters. Sometimes designers create an extended character set to accommodate the seldom used characters of a typeface.

Numerals

If your font is to include numerals, you'll need to decide whether to create lining numerals, old-style numerals, or both. **Lining numerals** optically sit on the baseline and extend up to the cap height; **old-style numerals**, on the other hand, include several characters (**3**, **4**, **5**, **7**, and **9**) that drop below the baseline to the descender line and extend only up to the x-height. Both lining and old-style numerals are pictured in Figure 8-33.

lining numerals 0123456789

old-style numerals 0123456789

figure | 8-33 |

Lining numerals and old-style numerals.

You will also need to decide whether to apply capital or lowercase stroke weights to your numerals. Although use of a lowercase stroke weight is most common to numerals, there are many examples that follow the capital stroke weights instead.

When you are creating numerals or mathematical and monetary symbols, it is important that they all have the same advance width. This is so that they will line up properly on a spreadsheet or in an equation. Of course, the number **1** will be naturally narrower than the other numerals, but you'll be able to add extra spacing to its sides. In general, numerical character widths are based upon the lowercase rather than the uppercase dimension of the font. This strategy eases the disparity between the widths of the **1** and the other figures.

Punctuation Marks

The period and the comma are probably the most frequently used punctuation marks, and many other marks are based on their shapes. Punctuation marks that tend to be used mid-sentence are particularly important to the reader's flow, in that they must be especially unobtrusive so as not to interrupt reading. The following tips regarding punctuation marks should get you started and help you to avoid some common errors.

- A period can be the same size as the dot that tops the **i** and **j**, or slightly larger, as shown in Figure 8-34.

- The comma should look like a period with a tail that extends below the baseline (Figure 8-35).

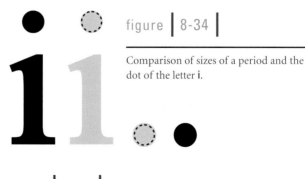

figure | 8-34 |

Comparison of sizes of a period and the dot of the letter **i**.

figure | 8-35 |

Period and comma.

Apostrophe, comma, and foot mark.

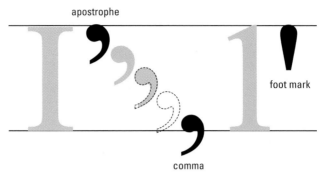

- The apostrophe should look like a comma that aligns with the cap height. Sometimes the tail of the apostrophe is shorter than a comma's tail, as seen in Figure 8-36. Don't confuse a foot mark for an apostrophe—this is a common error.

- Quotation marks can be made using two inverted apostrophes to open, and two regular apostrophes to close, as shown in Figure 8-37. Don't confuse an inch mark for quotation marks.

figure │ 8-37 │

Apostrophe, quotation marks, and inch mark.

Hyphens are generally about half as high as the x-height (Figure 8-38).

- Dashes are usually the same height as hyphens, or they are slightly higher. There are two kinds of dashes: the em dash, which is generally the full length of the advance width of the letter **M** (Figure 8-39); and the en dash, which is generally the full length of the advance width of the letter **n**, or one half the length of the em dash (Figure 8-40).

figure │ 8-38 │

Vertical placement of hyphen.

figure │ 8-39 │

Placement and length of the em dash in relation to the letter **M**.

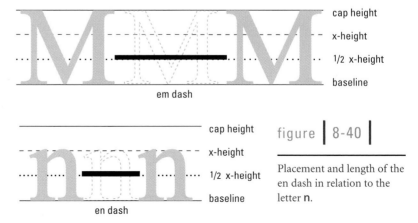

figure │ 8-40 │

Placement and length of the en dash in relation to the letter **n**.

Ligatures

Ligatures are letter pairs that have been joined to form a single character, as shown in Figure 8-41. Originally, ligatures were useful space-saving devices for scribes. Later, printers used them to replace letter pairs that couldn't be kerned closely enough together. There are a few instances when ligatures can improve the look of modern-day type, but unless two adjacent letters are colliding, they are nonessential to the English language. (However, they are not obsolete—other languages, like German, do still rely on them.) The most commonly used ligatures are combinations of **fi** and **fl**, which are the pairs most likely to collide with one another.

Ligatures come with their own problems, though. Connected letters are not standard to the English language, and tend to be less legible than freestanding letters. Also, ligatures can cause spacing difficulties since their components cannot be kerned or tracked in relation to one another.

Nonetheless, ligatures are often included in character sets, and many designers continue to combine letter pairs in new and dynamic ways, as seen in Figure 8-42.

first flight

figure | 8-41 |

Common ligatures, **fi** and **fl**, set in the typeface Classica Normal Expert, designed by Thierry Puyfoulhoux of Présence Type in 1998/2001. *Courtesy of Présence Type*, www.presencetypo.com.

figure | 8-42 |

Dynamic ligature combinations set in the typeface Classica Prestige C, designed by Thierry Puyfoulhoux of Présence Type in 2003. *Courtesy of Présence Type*, www.presencetypo.com.

Lowercase Glyphs

As with the uppercase letters, lowercase letters also can be derived from one another.

- From **o**, you can create **c** and **e**.
- From **h**, you can create **l** and **n**.
  - From **l**, you can create **i**, **j**, **f**, and **t**.
  - From **n**, you can create **u**, **m**, and **r**.
- From **p**, you can create **b**, **q**, and **d**.
  - From **q**, you can create **g**.
  - From **d**, you can create **a**.
- From **v**, you can create **y**, **w**, **z**, and **x**.
  - From **x**, you can create **k**.
- Again, **s** is an anomaly; scale and adapt the capital **S**, if possible.

As with the uppercase letters, each glyph should be tested next to the other characters before you progress to the design of a new glyph.

The Space

When the spacebar is tapped on a keyboard, most average roman fonts advance a distance approximately the same as the advance width of a lowercase **i**. San-serif fonts sometimes have a slightly larger space that is closer in width to a lowercase **r** shown in Figure 8-43. When creating a font, the default width of the space must be specified, just as with any actual character.

figure | 8-43 |
_____
Advance width of a space.

Hinting

Once the characters of your font have been designed, it will be necessary to add hints to your font, to optimize display of your font at a range of point sizes. As you remember from the previous chapter, hints are instructions that the designer encodes into a font to tell the computer how to best interpret glyphs at different sizes. For an outline font to look good on-screen at a variety of sizes, it will need to be hinted. Most font editing programs have autohinting functions, which can make the process much easier. However, you may not be satisfied with the results of autohinting, and may need to make some adjustments manually.

Fonts that don't contain hints tend to suffer in two ways when resized: their stroke widths tend to become distorted and inconsistent, and their components tend to become mis-aligned. To tackle these problems, you can set up two kinds of parameters in your font editor.

- Alignment zones define acceptable spatial ranges for the locations of letter parts; these can prevent glyph components from becoming misaligned, as seen in Figure 8-44.

An inspired calligrapher can create pages of beauty using stick ink, buzz saw, or even strawberry jam.
An inspired calligrapher can create pages of beauty using stick ink, buzz saw, or even strawberry jam.
An inspired calligrapher can create pages of beauty using stick ink, buzz saw
An inspired calligrapher can create pages of beauty using stick ink, buzz saw

- Stem values define acceptable values for the thickness of strokes and serifs; these can prevent stroke widths from distorting and becoming inconsistent.

figure | 8-44 |

Top: a font with incorrectly set alignment zones.

Bottom: a font with corrected zones.

Since you want your parameters to be consistent throughout the whole character set, it is advisable to delay hinting until you are completely finished designing your glyphs, and then do them all at once.

SPACING

Many font designers will tell you that the most important factor in the quality of a font is its spacing. Though not difficult, high-quality spacing of a font is quite time consuming. This is because proper spacing can only be done by eye. The autospacing function is about as reliable as the autotrace function—it can be used to get you started, but it will not be able to make the superior visual judgments that you can. Decisions about the letterspacing should not be rushed. The legibility of your font is dependent on its letterspacing, and so this step should be handled with great care and patience. As you space your font, keep in mind the rhythm of the negative spaces. The relative sizes of letterspaces and counters should create a consistent flowing visual rhythm, as shown in Figure 8-45.

> ### New Vocabulary
>
> **ligature:** a letter pair that has been joined to form a single character
>
> **lining numerals:** numeral characters that optically sit on the baseline and extend up to the cap height
>
> **old-style numerals:** numeral characters that include several characters (3, 4, 5, 7, and 9) that drop below the baseline to the descender line and extend only up to the x-height

figure │ 8-45 │

Negative spaces inside and between letters should be relatively consistent.

numeric nu
space matches counters

numeric nu
spacing too crowded

numeric nu
space matches counters

figure │ 8-46 │

Sidebearings. *Photograph courtesy of Elizabeth Nevin of the Briar Press.*

│ NOTE │

If letters are meant to touch, as in some script fonts, the sidebearings will have a value of zero.

Sidebearings

In Figure 8-46, you see a lead letterpress sort. The sort is rectangular so it can be lined up with other sorts into measures. The letterform does not take up the whole width of the sort—some space is left on each side so that when used to form a word, the letter won't touch adjacent ones. These spaces to the left and right of each letterform are called **sidebearings**.

When two sorts are placed next to each other, the combination of their two adjacent sidebearings forms a letterspace, as you can see in Figure 8-47. Letterspaces should look consistent, but because of the variation in glyph shapes they will need to be *inconsistent* to create the optical illusion of consistency. This means that the sidebearings of each glyph will need to vary depending on its unique shape.

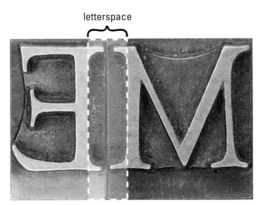

figure │ 8-47 │

Letterspace. *Photograph courtesy of Elizabeth Nevin of the Briar Press.*

We use a similar, though less tangible, model with digital fonts. Instead of existing physically on a rectangular sort, digital fonts exist virtually in a rectangular box like the one in the Fontographer Character Edit Window pictured in Figure 8-48. At this point, you have already determined the full height of the box—that's the height of the em square. Now it's time to consider the width of the box, or the advance width. This is the amount of space that the cursor will advance when you tap the letter's key on a keyboard. It will vary from letter to letter, since all glyph widths and shapes vary. The full advance width will be the widths of the letter and the left and right sidebearings combined.

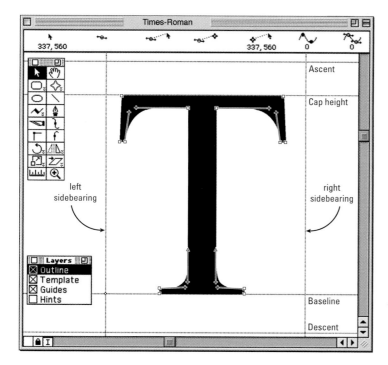

figure | 8-48 |

Character Edit Window from the font editing software Fontographer.

Sidebearings for Uppercase Letters

Although you will need to rely on your eyes and good judgment in determining sidebearing values, there are a few tricks that can help you to get started. By using a chart like the one in Figure 8-49, you can estimate the sidebearing values of most uppercase letters, based on only a few. The common approach is to begin by determining the spacing for **H** and **O**. Once these have been established, you'll be able to fill in much of the chart. Keep in mind that your sidebearing measurements begin and end with the outermost strokes of the glyphs, as opposed to their serifs.

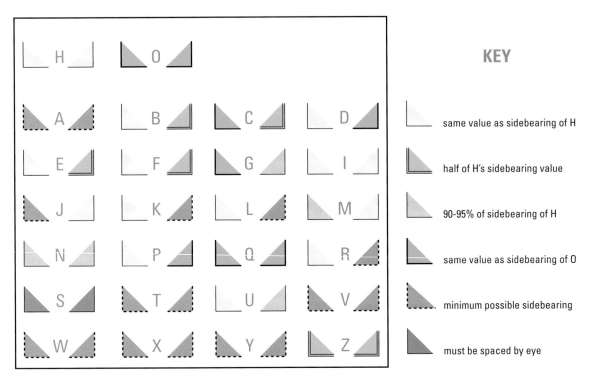

KEY

same value as sidebearing of H

half of H's sidebearing value

90-95% of sidebearing of H

same value as sidebearing of O

minimum possible sidebearing

must be spaced by eye

figure | 8-49 |

Sample chart for estimating uppercase letter sidebearing values.

To get a sidebearing measurement for the letter **H**, you'll have to experiment.

1. Print five rows of **H**s, varying the letterspacing from row to row, from very narrow to very wide, as shown in Figure 8-50.

figure | 8-50 |

Finding a sidebearing measurement for the letter **H**.

2. Pick the two best adjacent rows, and create three new rows with intermediary letterspace values.

3. Repeat step 2 until you are satisfied.

4. Divide the space between two **H**s in half. The result is your preliminary value for each sidebearing of **H**.

Next, establish a sidebearing measurement for the letter **O**. Again, you'll need to experiment. Repeat the same process you used to determine the sidebearing values for **H**, only this time use **O**, as shown in Figure 8-51.

figure | 8-51 |

Finding a sidebearing measurement for the letter **O**.

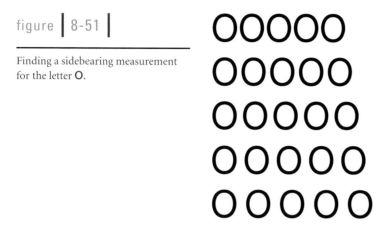

Once you have chosen sidebearing values for **H** and **O**, try them out together.

1. Print this string of letters: **HOHOHHOOHH**.

2. Carefully examine the spacing. You may have to adjust the sidebearings of one or both letters so that they look natural next to each other and when repeated. Remember, the letterspaces must be optically consistent. This means that mathematically, you'd want a consistent area of negative space between letters, rather than a consistent distance between letters. Try to imagine if you were filling in the letterspaces with tiles, spacing the letters so that it would take the same number of tiles to fill each letterspace, as shown in Figure 8-52.

figure | 8-52 |

Maintain a consistent area of negative space between letters.

3. Repeat steps 1 and 2 until you are satisfied.

Now it is time to note the values of **H** and **O** in your chart. You can apply the **H** and **O** sidebearing values to letters with similar shapes.

• **H**'s sidebearing value can be applied to the left sidebearings of **B**, **D**, **E**, **F**, **K**, **L**, **P**, **R**, and **U**; to the right sidebearings of **J** and **M** (note that the left sidebearing of **M** will be different); and to both sidebearings of **I**.

• **O**'s sidebearing value can be applied to the left sidebearings of **C** and **G**, to the right sidebearings of **D** and **P**, and to both sidebearings of the letter **Q**.

- Half of **H**'s sidebearing value can be applied to the right sidebearings of **B**, **C**, **E**, and **F**; and to both sidebearings of **Z**.

- 90 to 95 percent of **H**'s sidebearing value can be applied to the left sidebearing of **M**, to the right sidebearings of **G** and **U**, and to both sidebearings of **N**.

- The narrowest possible sidebearing value should be applied to the left sidebearing of **J**; to the right sidebearings of **K**, **L**, and **R**; and to both sidebearings of **A**, **T**, **V**, **W**, **X**, and **Y**.

This leaves only **S**, whose spacing, like its design, is an anomaly. To determine the sidebearings for **S**, juxtapose it between **H** and **O**.

1. Print the string of letters **OHHSOSSHOO** five times, as shown in Figure 8-53. Use your predetermined sidebearing values for **H** and **O**, but vary the sidebearings of the **S** from row to row, from narrow to wide.

figure | 8-53 |

_____

Finding sidebearing measurements for the letter **S**.

OHHSOSSHOO

OHHSOSSHOO

OHHSOSSHOO

OHHSOSSHOO

OHHSOSSHOO

2. Pick the two best adjacent rows, and create three new rows with intermediary letter-space values.

3. Repeat step 2 until you are satisfied.

Sidebearings for Lowercase Letters

A similar process can be used to deduce the sidebearing values for lowercase letters. Just as you based the uppercase sidebearing values on **H** and **O**, you will base the lowercase sidebearing values on **n** and **o**. Please note that since **n** is not perfectly symmetrical, its left and right sidebearing values will be slightly different. A modified chart like the one in Figure 8-54 can help you estimate the sidebearing values of most lowercase letters.

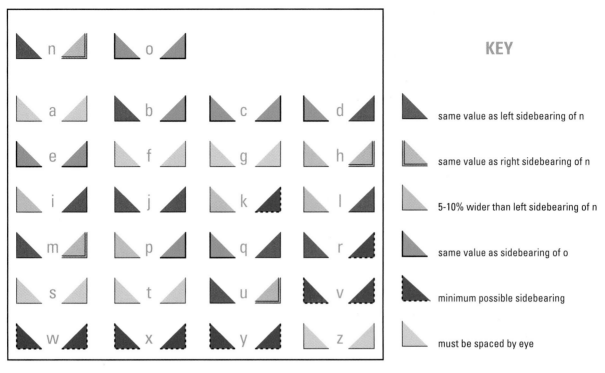

same value as left sidebearing of n

same value as right sidebearing of n

5-10% wider than left sidebearing of n

same value as sidebearing of o

minimum possible sidebearing

must be spaced by eye

- n's left sidebearing value can be applied to the left sidebearings of **r**, **b**, and **j**; n's right sidebearing value can be applied to the right sidebearing of **h**; and both sidebearings of **m** and **u** will match those of **n**.

- n's left sidebearing value can also be applied to the right sidebearings of **d**, **i**, **j**, **l**, and **q**.

- The left sidebearings of **h**, **i**, **k**, **l**, and **p** should be about 5 to 10 percent wider than the left sidebearing of **n**.

- o's sidebearing value can be applied to the left sidebearings of **d** and **q**; to the right sidebearings of **b** and **p**; and to both sidebearings of **c** and **e** (or the right sidebearings of **c** and **e** can be slightly smaller).

- The narrowest possible sidebearing value should be applied to the right sidebearings of **k** and **r**, and to both sidebearings of **v**, **w**, **x**, and **y**.

As with the uppercase **S**, the lowercase **s** must be spaced by eye. Also, the sidebearings of **a**, **f**, **g**, **t**, and **z** will have to be spaced visually. For each of these letters, to determine the sidebearings, juxtapose them between **n** and **o**. For example:

figure | 8-54 |

Sample chart for estimating lowercase letter sidebearing values.

1. Print the string of letters **nsossn** five times, with variable spacing, as you did to space the uppercase **S**. Use your predetermined sidebearing values for **n** and **o**, but vary the sidebearings of the **s** from row to row, from narrow to wide.

2. Pick the two best adjacent rows, and create three new rows with intermediary letter-space values.

3. Repeat step 2 until you are satisfied.

4. Repeat steps 1-3 with **naoaan**, **nfoffn**, **ngoggn**, **ntottn**, and **nzozzn**.

Once you have assigned preliminary values to the sidebearings of your letters, you'll have to go through the character set, glyph by glyph, to make any necessary adjustments to perfect the sidebearings values. Test each glyph in combination with **H**, **O**, and with itself. For instance, for **A**, you'd use a string of letters like **HAAHAOAAO**. Make adjustments to each letter's sidebearings, as needed.

Using the prior analogy of filling the letterspaces with an equal number of imaginary tiles, your eventual goal will be to make the same number of tiles fill the letterspaces between every letter combination. Unfortunately, this won't always be achievable because some letter pairs have open shapes that create unusually large areas of negative space between them. Just do your best to make the letterspacing as optically consistent as possible. Problem pairs can be individually kerned later, but first you must optimize the letterspacing of the font by choosing appropriate sidebearing values for each glyph. After all, the better the quality of a font's letterspacing, the fewer kerning pairs it will need in the long run.

Kerning

Once you are completely satisfied with your letterspacing, it's time to start kerning. Kerning is necessary because even with optimal sidebearing values, some letter pairs will still look awkward. Remember, the goal of kerning is to make letter pairs look natural, not necessarily to minimize letterspaces.

When you kern a letter pair using a font editing program, you are telling the computer to pretend that a specific pair of letters has alternate sidebearing values when they appear next to each other in the order specified. This information is coded into the font, so that when users apply your font to their body text, the overall texture will appear smooth. For instance, the letters **T** and **o** have specific sidebearing values, but when a user types **To**, the right sidebearing of the **T** and the left sidebearing of the **o** would be automatically reduced for improved optical balance according to the letter pair's encoded kerning information. You can apply the autokerning function in your font editing program, but as with other automated functions, it is not completely reliable. Again, you will need to trust your eyes.

Font editing programs allow designers to create thousands of kerning pairs, and it is common for fonts to have anywhere from 100 to 1,500 kerning pairs; 100 is usually a bit low, and 1,500 is bordering on excessive. Some designers choose to kern all the letter pairs of their fonts, but most find that between 300 and 800 letter pairs must be kerned to make the letterspacing of a font look optically consistent.

On the charts in Figures 8-55a, b, and c, the most frequently kerned letter pairs are highlighted. These charts can serve as a guide to help you decide how to prioritize your kerning process. However, the final decision about which pairs need to be kerned will be yours to make, based on how the pairs actually look when set in your font.

Uppercase kerning pairs

	A	B	C	D	E	F	G	H	I	J	K	L	M	N	O	P	Q	R	S	T	U	V	W	X	Y	Z	.	,	;	:	'
A	AA	AB	**AC**	AD	AE	AF	**AG**	AH	AI	AJ	AK	AL	AM	AN	**AO**	AP	**AQ**	AR	AS	**AT**	**AU**	**AV**	**AW**	AX	**AY**	AZ	A.	A,	A;	A:	**A'**
B	**BA**	BB	BC	BD	**BE**	BF	BG	BH	BI	BJ	BK	**BL**	BM	BN	BO	**BP**	BQ	**BR**	BS	BT	**BU**	**BV**	**BW**	BX	**BY**	BZ	**B.**	**B,**	B;	B:	B'
C	**CA**	CB	CC	CD	CE	CF	CG	CH	CI	CJ	CK	CL	CM	CN	**CO**	CP	CQ	**CR**	CS	**CT**	CU	**CV**	**CW**	CX	**CY**	CZ	**C.**	**C,**	C;	C:	C'
D	**DA**	DB	DC	**DD**	**DE**	DF	DG	DH	**DI**	**DJ**	DK	**DL**	**DM**	**DN**	**DO**	DP	DQ	**DR**	DS	DT	**DU**	**DV**	**DW**	DX	**DY**	DZ	**D.**	**D,**	D;	D:	D'
E	EA	EB	**EC**	ED	EE	EF	EG	EH	EI	EJ	EK	EL	EM	EN	**EO**	EP	EQ	ER	ES	ET	EU	EV	EW	EX	EY	EZ	E.	E,	E;	E:	E'
F	**FA**	FB	**FC**	FD	FE	FF	**FG**	FH	FI	**FJ**	FK	FL	FM	FN	**FO**	FP	FQ	FR	FS	FT	FU	FV	FW	FX	FY	FZ	**F.**	**F,**	**F;**	**F:**	F'
G	GA	GB	GC	GD	**GE**	GF	GG	GH	GI	GJ	GK	GL	GM	GN	**GO**	GP	GQ	**GR**	GS	GT	**GU**	GV	GW	GX	**GY**	GZ	G.	G,	G;	G:	G'
H	HA	HB	HC	HD	HE	HF	HG	HH	HI	HJ	HK	HL	HM	HN	HO	HP	HQ	HR	HS	HT	HU	HV	HW	HX	HY	HZ	H.	H,	H;	H:	H'
I	IA	IB	IC	ID	IE	IF	**IG**	IH	II	IJ	IK	IL	IM	IN	**IO**	IP	IQ	IR	IS	IT	IU	IV	IW	IX	IY	IZ	I.	I,	I;	I:	I'
J	**JA**	JB	JC	JD	JE	JF	JG	JH	JI	JJ	JK	JL	JM	JN	**JO**	JP	JQ	JR	JS	JT	JU	JV	JW	JX	JY	JZ	**J.**	**J,**	J;	J:	J'
K	KA	KB	**KC**	KD	KE	KF	**KG**	KH	KI	KJ	KK	KL	KM	KN	**KO**	KP	KQ	KR	KS	KT	KU	**KV**	KW	KX	KY	KZ	K.	K,	K;	K:	K'
L	LA	LB	**LC**	LD	LE	LF	**LG**	LH	LI	LJ	LK	LL	LM	LN	LO	LP	LQ	LR	LS	**LT**	**LU**	**LV**	**LW**	LX	**LY**	LZ	L.	L,	L;	L:	**L'**
M	MA	MB	**MC**	MD	ME	MF	**MG**	MH	MI	MJ	MK	ML	MM	MN	**MO**	MP	MQ	MR	MS	MT	MU	MV	MW	MX	MY	MZ	M.	M,	M;	M:	M'
N	NA	NB	**NC**	ND	NE	NF	**NG**	NH	NI	NJ	NK	NL	NM	NN	**NO**	NP	NQ	NR	NS	NT	NU	NV	NW	NX	NY	NZ	**N.**	**N,**	N;	N:	N'
O	**OA**	**OB**	OC	**OD**	**OE**	**OF**	OG	OH	**OI**	OJ	**OK**	**OL**	**OM**	**ON**	OO	**OP**	OQ	OR	OS	**OT**	**OU**	**OV**	**OW**	**OX**	**OY**	OZ	**O.**	**O,**	O;	O:	O'
P	**PA**	PB	PC	PD	**PE**	PF	PG	PH	PI	PJ	PK	**PL**	PM	PN	**PO**	**PP**	PQ	PR	PS	**PT**	**PU**	**PV**	**PW**	PX	**PY**	PZ	**P.**	**P,**	**P;**	**P:**	P'
Q	QA	QB	QC	QD	QE	QF	QG	QH	QI	QJ	QK	QL	QM	QN	QO	QP	QQ	QR	QS	QT	**QU**	QV	QW	QX	QY	QZ	Q.	Q,	Q;	Q:	Q'
R	RA	RB	**RC**	RD	RE	RF	**RG**	RH	RI	RJ	RK	RL	RM	RN	RO	RP	RQ	RR	RS	**RT**	**RU**	**RV**	**RW**	RX	**RY**	RZ	R.	R,	R;	R:	R'
S	SA	SB	SC	SD	SE	SF	SG	SH	SI	SJ	SK	SL	**SM**	SN	SO	SP	SQ	SR	**SS**	**ST**	**SU**	**SV**	**SW**	SX	**SY**	SZ	**S.**	**S,**	S;	S:	S'
T	**TA**	TB	**TC**	TD	TE	TF	**TG**	TH	TI	TJ	TK	TL	TM	TN	**TO**	TP	TQ	TR	TS	TT	TU	TV	TW	TX	TY	TZ	**T.**	**T,**	T;	T:	T'
U	**UA**	UB	**UC**	UD	UE	UF	**UG**	UH	UI	UJ	UK	UL	UM	UN	**UO**	UP	UQ	UR	**US**	UT	UU	UV	UW	UX	UY	UZ	**U.**	**U,**	U;	U:	U'
V	**VA**	VB	**VC**	VD	VE	VF	**VG**	VH	VI	VJ	VK	VL	VM	VN	**VO**	VP	VQ	VR	**VS**	VT	VU	VV	VW	VX	VY	VZ	**V.**	**V,**	**V;**	**V:**	V'
W	**WA**	WB	**WC**	WD	WE	WF	**WG**	WH	WI	WJ	WK	WL	WM	WN	**WO**	WP	WQ	WR	WS	WT	WU	WV	WW	WX	WY	WZ	**W.**	**W,**	**W;**	**W:**	W'
X	XA	XB	XC	XD	XE	XF	XG	XH	XI	XJ	XK	XL	XM	XN	**XO**	XP	XQ	XR	XS	XT	XU	XV	XW	XX	XY	XZ	X.	X,	X;	X:	X'
Y	**YA**	YB	**YC**	YD	YE	YF	**YG**	YH	YI	YJ	YK	YL	YM	YN	**YO**	YP	YQ	YR	**YS**	YT	YU	YV	YW	YX	YY	YZ	**Y.**	**Y,**	**Y;**	**Y:**	Y'
Z	ZA	ZB	ZC	ZD	ZE	ZF	ZG	ZH	ZI	ZJ	ZK	ZL	ZM	ZN	**ZO**	ZP	ZQ	ZR	ZS	ZT	ZU	ZV	ZW	ZX	ZY	ZZ	Z.	Z,	Z;	Z:	Z'

figure | 8-55a |

The most frequently kerned uppercase character pairs.

Some font editing programs also allow designers to create kerning classes, in which the kerning value of a selected letter pair can be assigned to a group of similarly shaped letter pairs. For example, using this function, a designer could automatically assign the value for the kerning pair **yo** to other kerning pairs **yc**, **yd**, and **ye**. Kerning classes can save a lot of time, but as with autokerning, this function should be used with caution and much overseeing and testing.

Uppercase/lowercase kerning pairs

	a	b	c	d	e	f	g	h	i	j	k	l	m	n	o	p	q	r	s	t	u	v	w	x	y	z
A	Aa	Ab	Ac	Ad	Ae	Af	Ag	Ah	Ai	Aj	Ak	Al	Am	An	Ao	Ap	Aq	Ar	As	At	Au	Av	Aw	Ax	Ay	Az
B	Ba	Bb	Bc	Bd	Be	Bf	Bg	Bh	Bi	Bj	Bk	Bl	Bm	Bn	Bo	Bp	Bq	Br	Bs	Bt	Bu	Bv	Bw	Bx	By	Bz
C	Ca	Cb	Cc	Cd	Ce	Cf	Cg	Ch	Ci	Cj	Ck	Cl	Cm	Cn	Co	Cp	Cq	Cr	Cs	Ct	Cu	Cv	Cw	Cx	Cy	Cz
D	Da	Db	Dc	Dd	De	Df	Dg	Dh	Di	Dj	Dk	Dl	Dm	Dn	Do	Dp	Dq	Dr	Ds	Dt	Du	Dv	Dw	Dx	Dy	Dz
E	Ea	Eb	Ec	Ed	Ee	Ef	Eg	Eh	Ei	Ej	Ek	El	Em	En	Eo	Ep	Eq	Er	Es	Et	Eu	Ev	Ew	Ex	Ey	Ez
F	Fa	Fb	Fc	Fd	Fe	Ff	Fg	Fh	Fi	Fj	Fk	Fl	Fm	Fn	Fo	Fp	Fq	Fr	Fs	Ft	Fu	Fv	Fw	Fx	Fy	Fz
G	Ga	Gb	Gc	Gd	Ge	Gf	Gg	Gh	Gi	Gj	Gk	Gl	Gm	Gn	Go	Gp	Gq	Gr	Gs	Gt	Gu	Gv	Gw	Gx	Gy	Gz
H	Ha	Hb	Hc	Hd	He	Hf	Hg	Hh	Hi	Hj	Hk	Hl	Hm	Hn	Ho	Hp	Hq	Hr	Hs	Ht	Hu	Hv	Hw	Hx	Hy	Hz
I	Ia	Ib	Ic	Id	Ie	If	Ig	Ih	Ii	Ij	Ik	Il	Im	In	Io	Ip	Iq	Ir	Is	It	Iu	Iv	Iw	Ix	Iy	Iz
J	Ja	Jb	Jc	Jd	Je	Jf	Jg	Jh	Ji	Jj	Jk	Jl	Jm	Jn	Jo	Jp	Jq	Jr	Js	Jt	Ju	Jv	Jw	Jx	Jy	Jz
K	Ka	Kb	Kc	Kd	Ke	Kf	Kg	Kh	Ki	Kj	Kk	Kl	Km	Kn	Ko	Kp	Kq	Kr	Ks	Kt	Ku	Kv	Kw	Kx	Ky	Kz
L	La	Lb	Lc	Ld	Le	Lf	Lg	Lh	Li	Lj	Lk	Ll	Lm	Ln	Lo	IL	IL	Lr	Ls	Lt	Lu	Lv	Lw	Lx	Ly	Lz
M	Ma	Mb	Mc	Md	Me	Mf	Mg	Mh	Mi	Mj	Mk	Ml	Mm	Mn	Mo	Mp	Mq	Mr	Ms	Mt	Mu	Mv	Mw	Mx	My	Mz
N	Na	Nb	Nc	Nd	Ne	Nf	Ng	Nh	Ni	Nj	Nk	Nl	Nm	Nn	No	Np	Nq	Nr	Ns	Nt	Nu	Nv	Nw	Nx	Ny	Nz
O	Oa	Ob	Oc	Od	Oe	Of	Og	Oh	Oi	Oj	Ok	Ol	Om	On	Oo	Op	Oq	Or	Os	Ot	Ou	Ov	Ow	Ox	Oy	Oz
P	Pa	Pb	Pc	Pd	Pe	Pf	Pg	Ph	Pi	Pj	Pk	Pl	Pm	Pn	Po	Pp	Pq	Pr	Ps	Pt	Pu	Pv	Pw	Px	Py	Pz
Q	Qa	Qb	Qc	Qd	Qe	Qf	Qg	Qh	Qi	Qj	Qk	Ql	Qm	Qn	Qo	Qp	Qq	Qr	Qs	Qt	Qu	Qv	Qw	Qx	Qy	Qz
R	Ra	Rb	Rc	Rd	Re	Rf	Rg	Rh	Ri	Rj	Rk	Rl	Rm	Rn	Ro	Rp	Rq	Rr	Rs	Rt	Ru	Rv	Rw	Rx	Ry	Rz
S	Sa	Sb	Sc	Sd	Se	Sf	Sg	Sh	Si	Sj	Sk	Sl	Sm	Sn	So	Sp	Sq	Sr	Ss	St	Su	Sv	Sw	Sx	Sy	Sz
T	Ta	Tb	Tc	Td	Te	Tf	Tg	Th	Ti	Tj	Tk	Tl	Tm	Tn	To	Tp	Tq	Tr	Ts	Tt	Tu	Tv	Tw	Tx	Ty	Tz
U	Ua	Ub	Uc	Ud	Ue	Uf	Ug	Uh	Ui	Uj	Uk	Ul	Um	Un	Uo	Up	Uq	Ur	Us	Ut	Uu	Uv	Uw	Ux	Uy	Uz
V	Va	Vb	Vc	Vd	Ve	Vf	Vg	Vh	Vi	Vj	Vk	Vl	Vm	Vn	Vo	Vp	Vq	Vr	Vs	Vt	Vu	Vv	Vw	Vx	Vy	Vz
W	Wa	Wb	Wc	Wd	We	Wf	Wg	Wh	Wi	Wj	Wk	Wl	Wm	Wn	Wo	Wp	Wq	Wr	Ws	Wt	Wu	Wv	Ww	Wx	Wy	Wz
X	Xa	Xb	Xc	Xd	Xe	Xf	Xg	Xh	Xi	Xj	Xk	Xl	Xm	Xn	Xo	Xp	Xq	Xr	Xs	Xt	Xu	Xv	Xw	Xx	Xy	Xz
Y	Ya	Yb	Yc	Yd	Ye	Yf	Yg	Yh	Yi	Yj	Yk	Yl	Ym	Yn	Yo	Yp	Yq	Yr	Ys	Yt	Yu	Yv	Yw	Yx	Yy	Yz
Z	Za	Zb	Zc	Zd	Ze	Zf	Zg	Zh	Zi	Zj	Zk	Zl	Zm	Zn	Zo	Zp	Zq	Zr	Zs	Zt	Zu	Zv	Zw	Zx	Zy	Zz

figure | 8-55b |

The most frequently kerned uppercase/lowercase character pairs.

Throughout the kerning process, you'll need to test your letter pairs. Since letters are usually read as word shapes in passages of text, this is the best place to test your letterspacing. Generate a preliminary version of your font, and set blocks of real (or nonsensical) text in a variety of sizes. Make sure to include words with typically problematic letter pairs. Print the blocks of text, and examine them closely for any spaces that disrupt your reading rhythm. Mark all problematic combinations. Some helpful tricks for finding trouble areas include looking at the text upside down,

Lowercase kerning pairs

	a	b	c	d	e	f	g	h	i	j	k	l	m	n	o	p	q	r	s	t	u	v	w	x	y	z	.	,	;	:	'
a	aa	ab	ac	ad	ae	af	ag	ah	ai	aj	ak	al	am	an	ao	ap	aq	ar	as	at	au	av	aw	ax	ay	az	a.	a,	a;	a:	a'
b	ba	bb	bc	bd	be	bf	bg	bh	bi	bj	bk	bl	bm	bn	bo	bp	bq	br	bs	bt	bu	bv	bw	bx	by	bz	b.	b,	b;	b:	b'
c	ca	cb	cc	cd	ce	cf	cg	ch	ci	cj	ck	cl	cm	cn	co	cp	cq	cr	cs	ct	cu	cv	cw	cx	cy	cz	c.	c,	c;	c:	c'
d	da	db	dc	dd	de	df	dg	dh	di	dj	dk	dl	dm	dn	do	dp	dq	dr	ds	dt	du	dv	dw	dx	dy	dz	d.	d,	d;	d:	d'
e	ea	eb	ec	ed	ee	ef	eg	eh	ei	ej	ek	el	em	en	eo	ep	eq	er	es	et	eu	ev	ew	ex	ey	ez	e.	e,	e;	e:	e'
f	fa	fb	fc	fd	fe	ff	fg	fh	fi	fj	fk	fl	fm	fn	fo	fp	fq	fr	fs	ft	fu	fv	fw	fx	fy	fz	f.	f,	f;	f:	f'
g	ga	gb	gc	gd	ge	gf	gg	gh	gi	gj	gk	gl	gm	gn	go	gp	gq	gr	gs	gt	gu	gv	gw	gx	gy	gz	g.	g,	g;	g:	g'
h	ha	hb	hc	hd	he	hf	hg	hh	hi	hj	hk	hl	hm	hn	ho	hp	hq	hr	hs	ht	hu	hv	hw	hx	hy	hz	h.	h,	h;	h:	h'
i	ia	ib	ic	id	ie	if	ig	ih	ii	ij	ik	il	im	in	io	ip	iq	ir	is	it	iu	iv	iw	ix	iy	iz	i.	i,	i;	i:	i'
j	ja	jb	jc	jd	je	jf	jg	jh	ji	jj	jk	jl	jm	jn	jo	jp	jq	jr	js	jt	ju	jv	jw	jx	jy	jz	j.	j,	j;	j:	j'
k	ka	kb	kc	kd	ke	kf	kg	kh	ki	kj	kk	kl	km	kn	ko	kp	kq	kr	ks	kt	ku	kv	kw	kx	ky	kz	k.	k,	k;	k:	k'
l	la	lb	lc	ld	le	lf	lg	lh	li	lj	lk	ll	lm	ln	lo	lp	lq	lr	ls	lt	lu	lv	lw	lx	ly	lz	l.	l,	l;	l:	l'
m	ma	mb	mc	md	me	mf	mg	mh	mi	mj	mk	ml	mm	mn	mo	mp	mq	mr	ms	mt	mu	mv	mw	mx	my	mz	m.	m,	m;	m:	m'
n	na	nb	nc	nd	ne	nf	ng	nh	ni	nj	nk	nl	nm	nn	no	np	nq	nr	ns	nt	nu	nv	nw	nx	ny	nz	n.	n,	n;	n:	n'
o	oa	ob	oc	od	oe	of	og	oh	oi	oj	ok	ol	om	on	oo	op	oq	or	os	ot	ou	ov	ow	ox	oy	oz	o.	o,	o;	o:	o'
p	pa	pb	pc	pd	pe	pf	pg	ph	pi	pj	pk	pl	pm	pn	po	pp	pq	pr	ps	pt	pu	pv	pw	px	py	pz	p.	p,	p;	p:	p'
q	qa	qb	qc	qd	qe	qf	qg	qh	qi	qj	qk	ql	qm	qn	qo	qp	qq	qr	qs	qt	qu	qv	qw	qx	qy	qz	q.	q,	q;	q:	q'
r	ra	rb	rc	rd	re	rf	rg	rh	ri	rj	rk	rl	rm	rn	ro	rp	rq	rr	rs	rt	ru	rv	rw	rx	ry	rz	r.	r,	r;	r:	r'
s	sa	sb	sc	sd	se	sf	sg	sh	si	sj	sk	sl	sm	sn	so	sp	sq	sr	ss	st	su	sv	sw	sx	sy	sz	s.	s,	s;	s:	s'
t	ta	tb	tc	td	te	tf	tg	th	ti	tj	tk	tl	tm	tn	to	tp	tq	tr	ts	tt	tu	tv	tw	tx	ty	tz	t.	t,	t;	t:	t'
u	ua	ub	uc	ud	ue	uf	ug	uh	ui	uj	uk	ul	um	un	uo	up	uq	ur	us	ut	uu	uv	uw	ux	uy	uz	u.	u,	u;	u:	u'
v	va	vb	vc	vd	ve	vf	vg	vh	vi	vj	vk	vl	vm	vn	vo	vp	vq	vr	vs	vt	vu	vv	vw	vx	vy	vz	v.	v,	v;	v:	v'
w	wa	wb	wc	wd	we	wf	wg	wh	wi	wj	wk	wl	wm	wn	wo	wp	wq	wr	ws	wt	wu	wv	ww	wx	wy	wz	w.	w,	w;	w:	w'
x	xa	xb	xc	xd	xe	xf	xg	xh	xi	xj	xk	xl	xm	xn	xo	xp	xq	xr	xs	xt	xu	xv	xw	xx	xy	xz	x.	x,	x;	x:	x'
y	ya	yb	yc	yd	ye	yf	yg	yh	yi	yj	yk	yl	ym	yn	yo	yp	yq	yr	ys	yt	yu	yv	yw	yx	yy	yz	y.	ly,	y;	y:	y'
z	za	zb	zc	zd	ze	zf	zg	zh	zi	zj	zk	zl	zm	zn	zo	zp	zq	zr	zs	zt	zu	zv	zw	zx	zy	zz	z.	z,	z;	mz	z'

squinting at the page so it turns to a gray blur, and reversing the text so that the letters are white and the background is printed black. These techniques can help you to spot inconsistencies in the texture and overall color of the passages. Once you have identified necessary changes, make repairs and retest. Repeat this process several times until you are completely satisfied with all letter combinations.

figure | 8-55c

The most frequently kerned lowercase character pairs.

New Vocabulary

sidebearings: the empty spaces to the left and right of the letterform on a sort or its digital equivalent

SPECIMENS

Soon after the invention of movable type in Europe, printers and type founders began to produce type specimen sheets to show off their typeface selections and printing qualities. In the 1920s, it became a common practice to produce specimen books, which at first were usually catalogs displaying single lines of each available typeface, accompanied by their names. Over the years, specimen books became more decorative and more informative. Fonts were sometimes displayed as full alphabets including any combination of measurements, magnified details, additional type styles, and even samples for suggested uses. Eventually, whole books were even produced that were dedicated to individual font families.

Today, designers and foundries continue the tradition of making type specimens to market their font designs. The format of these specimens varies widely, ranging from a short line of text in a catalog to a whole book dedicated to the variations of a single font, and from an artistic poster or brochure to an online interactive catalog.

Now that you have created your own font, you'll want to select a design strategy for showing it off. If you plan to submit your font to an existing foundry, they will have their own specific guidelines regarding what sort of sample they need to see to consider it for adoption. However, if you plan to market the font yourself, or present it in your portfolio, you will need to produce a font specimen in a format that suits your purposes.

As with any design, the best way to begin is by doing research. Visit the web sites of existing foundries to view their online catalogs and to order their printed catalogs. Go to a library with a good printing collection, and view historical examples. Also, do some brainstorming about what you want your font's presentation to tell people about it. What sorts of associations and uses might your presentation suggest? Who will see the specimen once produced? What sorts of information about the font will be relevant to them? Are you presenting a single font or a whole type family? How will you distribute your specimen? Does your distribution method lead to any size or weight requirements? What are your cost and time limitations?

Historical Models

People have been creating type specimens for over 400 years, so historical models can be a rich and diverse source of ideas about ways to display your font.

Line Specimens

Figure 8-56 shows a line specimen from 1822, which was printed by James Ronaldson of Philadelphia. He and his partner Archibald Binny started the first enduring type foundry in America, and they were the first to publish a specimen book in America, too.

figure | 8-56 |

Line specimen printed in 1822 by James Ronaldson of Binny & Ronaldson, the first enduring American type foundry. *Typeface design by Richard Ronaldson, courtesy of University of Delaware Library, Newark, DE.*

Line specimens can be composed of any number of measures of type. They can display type style or size variations, or both. Sometimes the letters appear alphabetically. Other times they are arranged to spell words in English, Latin, or other languages. Content of text might change from line to line, or the same text might be repeated a number of times, as shown in Figure 8-57. Sometimes text is displayed as a series of headlines, as shown in Figure 8-58.

figure | 8-57 |

Line specimens, page from specimen booklet by Font Bureau, *1-Line Specimens*, 2nd ed., 2004. Typefaces Amplitude (Christian Schwartz, 2002), Anisette (Adolphe Mouron Cassandre, Jean François Porchez, 1997), Antique Condensed (Jim Parkinson, 1995), and Armada (Tobias Frere-Jones, 1994). *Courtesy of Font Bureau.*

figure | 8-58 |

Line specimens, page from specimen book by Font Bureau, *Font Bureau Type Specimens*, 3rd ed., 2004. Typeface FB Century created by Greg Thompson and Font Bureau in 1992, based on original designs by Morris Fuller Benton, 1906.

Text Block Specimens

Another way that your font can be displayed is in text blocks. In this format, whole blocks of text are set in a variety of sizes and type styles, to give a better sense of how they would compare with each other as body text. Some of the earliest specimen sheets were printed using the text block specimen format. For example, Figure 8-59 is a specimen sheet from 1592 displaying blocks of text set in two type styles at various sizes. Figure 8-60 shows an example of a more recent text block style specimen.

figure | 8-59 |

Text block specimen from 1592, from *Printing Types* by Alexander Lawson. *Copyright ©1971 by Alexander Lawson, and reprinted by permission of Beacon Press, Boston.*

figure | 8-60 |

Text block specimens, page from specimen book by Font Bureau, *Font Bureau Type Specimens*, 3rd ed., 2004. Typeface Griffith Gothic created by Tobias Frere-Jones in 1997, based on original designs by G. H. Griffith, 1937.

Analytical Specimens

An analytical specimen is one that conveys multiple kinds of information in a single layout. When William Caslon produced his first specimen sheet in 1734 (see Figure 1-27), his goal was to include as much information as possible about the font. He presented it in alphabet form, as lines of text, and text blocks at a variety of sizes and type styles. Figure 8-61 shows a more recently created analytical specimen, in which the designer has referenced Caslon's historically significant one.

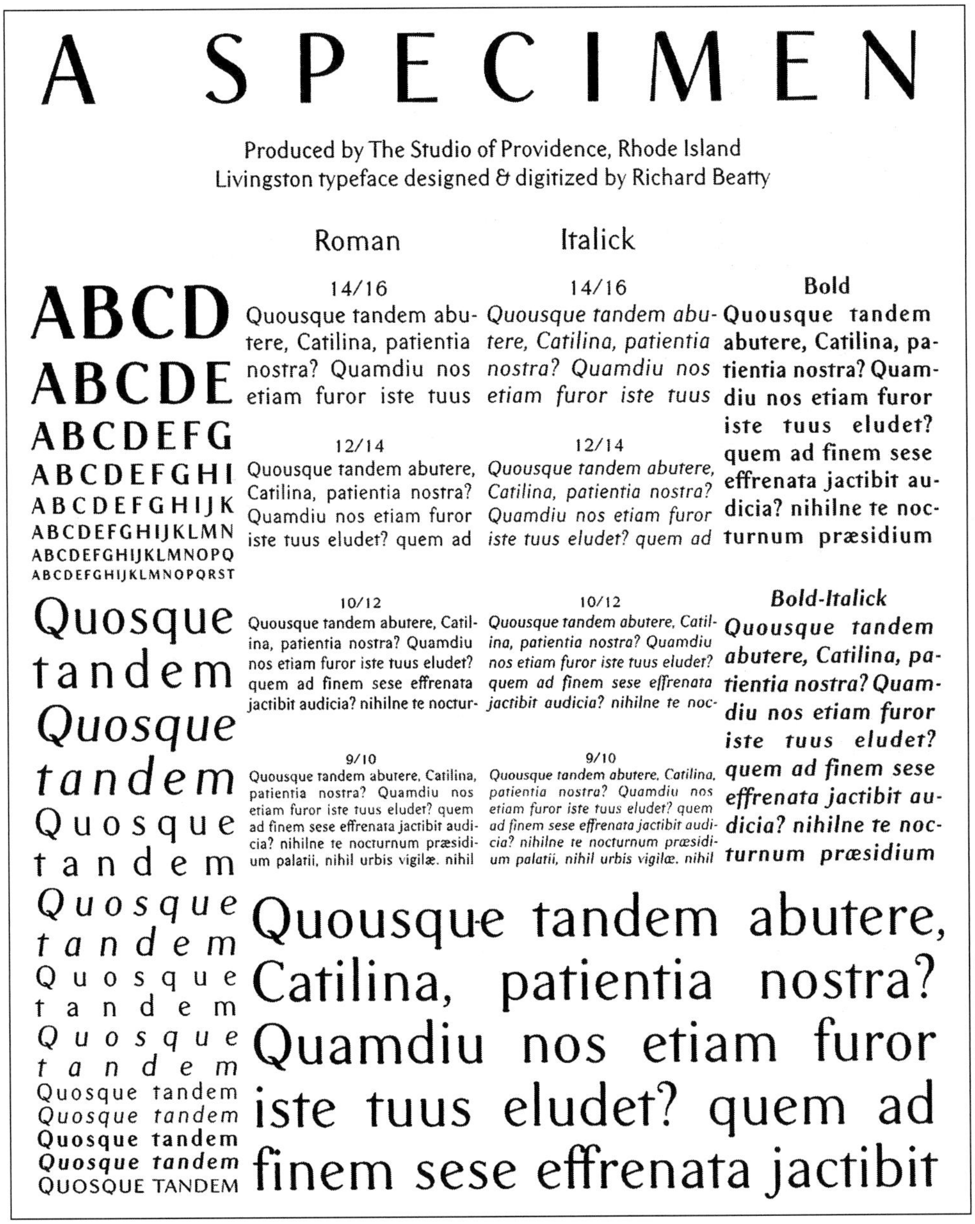

figure | 8-61 |

Analytical specimen for typeface Phillips, designed and digitized by Richard W. Beatty (reduced in size). Richard W. Beatty fonts are available from *www.will-harris.com* or *www.fontshop.com*.

Figure 8-62 shows a more modernistic approach to creating an analytical specimen. This poster is both graceful and concise, while conveying several different kinds of information about this font. The unusually large letterform commands attention and invites the kind of inspection not typical of a viewer's experience with body text. Magnifying just a few letterforms to a grand scale can reveal the graceful nuances of the glyphs' forms, while making a bold stylistic statement. The specimen pictured in Figure 8-63 takes this approach one step further, focusing on just sections of a few selected characters in order to highlight stylistic characteristics typical to the font.

figure | 8-62 |

Analytical specimen poster of the typeface Présence, designed by Thierry Puyfoulhoux of Présence Typo in 2000.

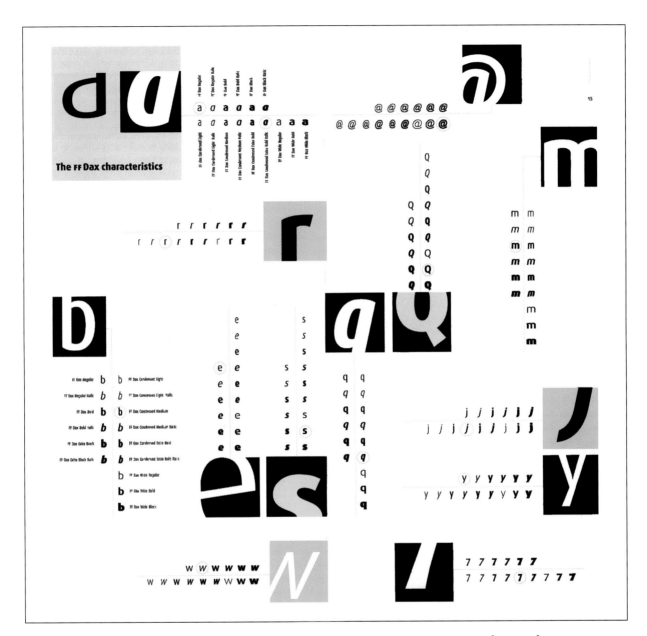

Type in Use

Since fonts are usually purchased for their utilitarian value, displaying specimens of your font in use can be a good marketing technique. Not only can it give potential customers ideas about how to use your font, it can also reinforce any cultural or emotional associations you are hoping will be assigned to your font by viewers.

figure | 8-63 |

Artistic specimen of the typeface FF Dax, designed by Hans Reichel in 1995/1997, layout by Wim Westerveld of NEON, for FontFont, FSI FontShop International, 2004.

The font specimens in Figure 8-64 were originally issued in the 1940s as part of a specimen book of typefaces by Lucien Bernhard. Each specimen displays a collage of fictional signage, each with a distinctive personality. When the fonts were digitally revived in the 1990s, these specimens were also.

A more recent example showing a similar strategy is pictured in Figure 8-65. In each of these specimens, a distinctive personality has been affiliated with a font by incorporating it into a cleverly familiar vernacular format. In this way, the designer engages each viewer who feels nostalgia for the cultural reference, providing a sense of inclusion to those who recognize them.

figure | 8-64 |

Magnet type specimens simulating possible uses of the revived typefaces Tradition, Buckeye, and Touraine, created by Joe Freedman of Sarabande in 1993, based on original designs by Lucien Bernhard for American Type Foundry, circa 1940. *Courtesy of Sarabande.*

figure | 8-65 |

Type specimens simulating possible uses of the typefaces Keystoned, Total Disorder, and Prints Charming, by Lloyd Springer of The TypeArt Foundry Inc.

Artistic Specimens

Sometimes designers incorporate type into a more artistic format to emphasize the font's expressive qualities, and to associate a marketable image with the typeface. Figure 8-66 shows an artistic type specimen design from 1933, in which the Art Deco layout enhances the elegant upbeat persona of the typeface.

Today, designers continue to create specimens that demonstrate the emotive capabilities of their fonts in artistic formats. For instance, the designer of the font featured in Figure 8-67 used characters as compositional elements to create this abstracted artistic specimen poster.

Many times, designers create powerful artistic type specimens by incorporating imagery into their designs. For instance, the contrasting dainty and grungy qualities of the typeface showcased in Figure 8-68 are reconciled by imagery that suggests nostalgia for glories past and a sense of refinement that has become shabby with age.

figure | 8-66 |

Artistic type specimen for the typeface Stygian Black No. 25, by Ludlow Typograph Company, 1933. *Courtesy of Steven Heller and Louise Fiji.*

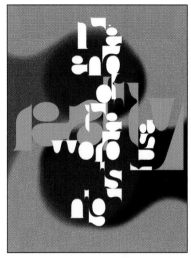

figure | 8-67 |

Artistic type specimen of the typeface Auto Suggestion, designed by Neville Brody of Research Studios in 1993.

figure | 8-68 |

Artistic type specimens of the typefaces Memory Lapses, Diesel, Nars, and Carimbo, by Eduardo Recife of Misprinted Type.

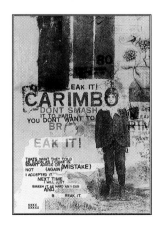
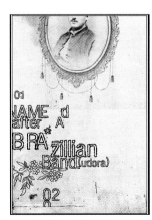

Specimen Book

The form of a specimen book can range from a short pamphlet to a bound hardcover book. Its content can focus on the details of a particular font family, or it can catalog all the offerings of a foundry. Any combination of the specimen formats discussed here can be incorporated into a specimen book.

Figure 8-69 shows some pages from the catalog of a small foundry that took a unique approach to showcasing their fonts. They invited designers to render texts of their own choosing, using the foundry's fonts. The resulting designs were compiled into a catalog of artistic specimen posters.

figure | 8-69 |

Type specimens designed by Gabriel Martínez Meave, Rares Malureanu, and Jean-François Porchez for the typefaces Rayuela, Borges, and Quimera, designed by Alejandro Lo Celso of PampaType in 2002.

Online Specimens

Before the digital revolution, printed specimen books were the most common and essential marketing tools for fonts. However, the introduction of computers to the design scene has not only influenced the way that fonts are generated and printed, it has also changed the way they are marketed and sold. Now, many foundries have web sites where they display their wares.

Digital font specimens have some different limitations and capabilities, compared to their printed counterparts. On one hand, the low resolution can rarely do justice to the detailed designs of typefaces, so printed specimens are still considered necessary by many foundries and their customers. On the other hand, a digital specimen is much cheaper to produce than a printed one, and consumers can purchase and download the fonts directly from web sites without having to wait. The elements of time and motion can add interest to the specimen's layout, and can aid user navigation. Since online formats can be interactive, specimens showing alternative views of a font can be linked, and rollovers can allow users to toggle between views. Some online specimen formats even allow users to "test drive" fonts using a digital typesetter like the one shown in Figure 8-70.

figure | 8-70 |

Online digital typesetter lets users "test drive" fonts; screenshot of MyFonts.com Test Drive at *www.myfonts.com. Courtesy of Bitstream, Inc.*

Figures 8-71a and 8-71b picture screenshots from one foundry's web site, in which all the foundry's offered fonts are displayed. When the cursor is rolled over any cell, it is highlighted, and a larger specimen appears that includes letters from each of the font's type styles. When the cell is clicked, a new screen displays sample alphabets in all the font's available type styles. A printable specimen can also be downloaded from the site in a PDF format (8-71c).

figures | 8-71a and 8-71b |

Online type specimens at *www.psyops.com*, featuring the typeface Oculus, designed by Rodrigo X. Cavazos of PSY/OPS Type SF in 1996.

figure | 8-71c |

A page from the PDF document of type specimens, PSY/OPS Lineguide, from *www.psyops.com*, featuring the typefaces Oculus by Rodrigo X. Cavazos, Inégalé by Matthijs van Leeuwen, Aperto by Paul Veres, and Reform by Anuthin Wongsunkakon. *Courtesy of PSY/OPS Type SF, 2003.*

Innovative Approaches

Of course, the creativity you can apply to creating font specimens is limitless. Any format that suits the purpose of informing customers about the features of your font might be viable. Figure 8-72 shows a particularly innovative approach taken by one foundry in creating font specimens; the foundry produced a promotional pack of cards, each bearing a unique specimen of a particular font offering.

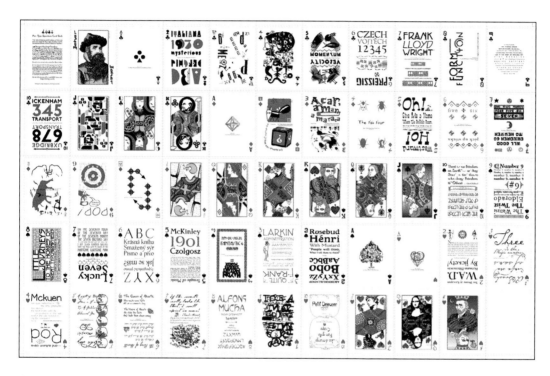

figure | 8-72 |

Type specimens printed on playing cards designed by Richard Kegler of P-22 Type Foundry.

CHAPTER SUMMARY

Designing a font well is a long, arduous, and painstaking task. People seem to either love it or hate it, depending on their preferences for detail-oriented work and their feelings about type. Those who wish to try their hand at designing a font can make their task much easier by keeping good records, conducting a significant amount of research, selecting an appropriate design strategy, and making well-planned decisions about the font's design elements. The quality of a font is often judged by its optical consistency, its legibility, and its readability. Since appropriate spacing is incredibly important to the legibility and readability of a font, assigning sidebearing and kerning values should be done with great care and extensive testing and retesting. Once completed, designers and foundries produce type specimens to market their fonts to the public, using a wide variety of formats.

> *in review*

1. What questions should you consider when planning a new font design?

2. What kind of research should you conduct before beginning to design a font?

3. What preliminary decisions will help to ensure consistency in the design of your character set?

4. Why would you choose one rendering method over another? Explain an appropriate use for each method discussed.

5. What are overshoot guidelines, and what is their use?

6. Discuss the legal and moral implications of reviving or modifying an existing font.

7. Which letterforms can be derived from which other letterforms?

8. Describe three optical illusions that will influence the way you design specific letters.

9. How can you test the characters and spacing of your font? When should you perform these tests?

10. Why is kerning important to font design?

11. Describe three specimen formats and their most appropriate uses.

► *exercises*

1. Create a type scrapbook of characters, words, or text blocks that attract you. Search printed materials and web sites for text to photocopy, clip, or print. Compile at least forty examples into your scrapbook. Write notes in the scrapbook about what interests you about each selection.

2. Collect examples of printed type specimens. Online specimens might be available for download in PDF format, or you can take photographs or make scans of printed matter. Printed specimens might be found in libraries and used bookstores, or can be ordered from foundries.

3. Visit the web sites of several foundries. Compare and contrast how each displays their fonts.

4. Write a plan to design a font that describes "who, what, where, when, why, and how."

   a. Describe and defend the rendering method you plan to use to create your font.

   b. Make decisions about the guideline proportions, contrast, angle of stress, and terminals of the font you plan to design. Draw diagrams to illustrate your choices.

   c. Organize your character set into a chart according to planned similarities of shape and width. Using the information in this chapter as a guide, decide which characters will be derived from others for your particular font.

   d. Design the letters I, H, O, and V of your font.

   e. Design all the letters of your font that are necessary to create a type specimen reading HAMBURGEFONTSIV or hamburgefontsiv.

5. Practice spacing letterforms by eye, manually. Cut one hundred letters from a page in an old magazine. Draw guidelines on a piece of white paper, and use tweezers and glue to attach the letters in a new order, creating five rows of twenty letters, plus wordspaces, so that the spacing looks natural, and the text block's texture looks smooth.

6. Design a type specimen sheet, poster, or web site to market one or more fonts of your choice.

7. Go to an online font archive like *www.myfonts.com*, or a similar web site. Select any typeface that interests you. Make note of the font's title, and the foundry that owns it. Open the character map for the typeface you have selected. Select any three capital letters, one at a time, and copy the JPEG file of each to your hard drive. Next, print the images of the three letters you selected. Without referring back to your original source, or to other similar fonts, use the three letters you printed as a basis for designing ten of the remaining twenty-three characters of the alphabet. After you have completed your designs, go back to your original source, and print the font's versions of the same characters you designed, for comparison. Consider your design choices and compare them to the original designer's design choices.

AIGA Literacy Campaign poster designed by Charles Anderson of
Charles S. Anderson Design Company for AIGA/Colorado.

CHAPTER 9

objectives

- Understand communication theory
- Understand the responsibility of designing visual communications
- Enhance personal creativity through active brainstorming and visual collecting
- Create graphic resonance in a design
- Match (and mismatch) the form to the message in purposeful ways
- Investigate and analyze a variety of ways and reasons that designers choose to either follow or break typographic "rules"

introduction

The written word is an extension of the spoken word; however, the written word bypasses all the verbal and gestural cues that normally help us interpret the meanings of words we hear. For instance, facial expressions, tonal inflections, and hand gestures can help us to understand the same word or sentence as funny, affectionate, friendly, rude, sarcastic, or mean. Someone loudly yelling the word "stop!" with her hand extended and her palm facing you is probably trying to communicate a different meaning than a person who laughs coyly and waves her hand as she says the same word.

For this reason, it is important that designers create effective visual forms. After all, a designer's primary concern must always be communicating the message in question. Creating layouts that are visually pleasing is not enough—a design's purpose is to communicate.

That is the difference between creating a design and creating art: while art is an expression created by an artist to please him or herself, a designer uses the same tools and vocabulary, but to communicate a message to an intended audience while expressing the vision of a client. The message may be social, political, or economic; the intended outcome might be for the audience to make a purchase, support a cause, vote for a candidate, watch a television program, or learn about a social concern.

The first step in communicating effectively using type is to determine exactly what you want to communicate. What type must accomplish in any design depends heavily on the audience and on the message. Designers set specific design goals, taking into consideration the specific needs and tastes of their audiences, as well as the content, meaning, and mood of the design's message.

History has shown us that design carries the power to influence people's beliefs about themselves, their communities, and their environments. Creating designs that might influence values and economics is a serious responsibility. Designers must understand how to communicate effectively in order to create designs that successfully convey deliberate messages to intended audiences.

COMMUNICATION THEORY

Understanding how to communicate effectively is based on the principle that *all learning is active*. That is, every audience actively chooses which messages to pay attention to, every audience actively interprets the meaning of messages according to their own knowledge base and set of experiences, and every audience actively decides how to react to received messages. The implication of this is that designers cannot assume that an intended message will reach, be understood by, or evoke the intended reaction from its intended audience.

However, designers are not powerless to effect the likelihood of successful transmission of their messages. Understanding how communication works, and where it is most vulnerable, can help designers to visually communicate more effectively.

The Sender, the Receiver, and the Message

Any design begins when an individual or organization wants to communicate a message to an intended audience. The message might be social, political, medical, religious, or economic in nature. We'll call the individual or organization that wants to send the message the *sender*, and we'll call the intended audience the *receiver*. Figure 9-1 illustrates this relationship.

figure | 9-1 |

Communication chart: sender, receiver, and message.

Now let's imagine three specific senders who want to send messages to three specific receivers, so that we can trace the path of the transmission of the messages.

Example 1: An organization called the National Association of Librarians (NAL) wants to send a message to the schoolchildren of America, telling them that "Reading is cool!" In this case, NAL is the sender. The schoolchildren of America are the receivers, and "Reading is cool!" is the message.

Example 2: Ms. Frank, the owner of the Juicyburger Diner in Baltimore, wants to tell the people of Baltimore to eat at her restaurant. In this case, Ms. Frank is the sender. The people of Baltimore are the receivers. The message is "Eat at the Juicyburger Diner."

Example 3: The Big Bad Wolf wants to lure Little Red Riding Hood to Grandma's house so he can eat her for dinner. In this case, the wolf is the sender, Little Red Riding Hood is the receiver, and the message is "Come to Grandma's house."

The Source

Now, you may have noticed that some of these senders might be rather unconvincing spokespeople for their audiences. NAL seems a bit too stuffy to interest schoolchildren, Ms. Frank doesn't look too healthy, and the Big Bad Wolf is not exactly Little Red Riding Hood's trusted friend!

Each sender, for their own reasons, decides to use a *source* to communicate their message. The source will be the person or organization that the audience will *perceive* to be the sender.

NAL has decided to adopt a fun mascot—Libby the Bookworm—to send the message to the children of America. Ms. Frank is choosing to remain anonymous, and send her messages from "the folks at the Juicyburger Diner." The wolf will pretend to be Grandma in order to make his message seem credible to Little Red Riding Hood. Libby the Bookworm, the folks at the Juicyburger Diner, and Grandma are all sources. The receivers will perceive them to be the senders, whether they truly are or not. Figure 9-2 updates our illustration of the communication process.

figure | 9-2 |

Communication chart: source.

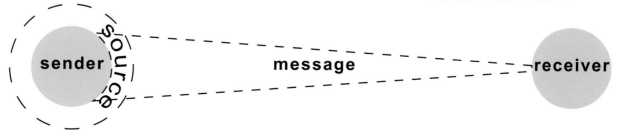

The Sociocultural Environment

Each sender must somehow encode the message by selecting and combining words and symbols to create the message. However, each sender will naturally make selections according to his or her own understanding about the meanings of language and symbols, because each sender has his or her own realm of experience to draw upon. Encoding of the message will be filtered through the sender's sociocultural environment—the social and cultural realities perceived by the sender in relation to the world. The receiver also exists within a sociocultural environment and will decode the message according to his or her own understanding of language and symbols.

So you can see that the sender can increase the likelihood of successful transmission of the message by selecting language and symbols that will communicate effectively with the specific intended audience. In Figure 9-3, we add the encoding and decoding steps to our communication process.

figure | 9-3 |

Communication chart: encoding and decoding.

The Medium

The sender must also select a *medium* by which to send the message. For example, the sender might print the message in a brochure, flyer, magazine, or on a billboard. The sender might also buy a commercial on television or radio or send printed materials through the mail.

Continuing with our example, perhaps the NAL board of directors votes to advertise in a children's magazine, Ms. Frank has take-out menu flyers printed to give out to established and potential customers, and the Big Bad Wolf sends a dinner invitation through the mail. In these cases, the magazine, the flyers, and the invitation each represent the mediums that the senders use to carry their messages to the intended audiences. Figure 9-4 shows the addition of the medium to the communication process. Notice that the medium carries the message.

figure | 9-4 |

Communication chart: medium.

Noise

Unfortunately for the senders, there are a number of obstacles that might interfere with successful transmission of their intended messages. We call these obstacles *noise*, named for the sound of static that we hear on the radio when the signal experiences interference. Noise that interrupts visual communication tends to happen in three key places along the communication route we have established.

Semantics

The first place where a designer must be wary of noise is in the selection of language and symbols for the message. The designer must be sure to understand what message the client (or sender) wishes to transmit, and who the intended audience is. It is the designer's job to select words and symbols that will convey the appropriate meaning to the intended receivers. The designer must learn enough about the receivers' sociocultural environment to select symbols and language that will be meaningful and appropriate to convey the message.

For example, if NAL creates an ad using graduate-level vocabulary, the schoolchildren may not understand the advertisement. If Ms. Frank chooses symbols that are unappetizing or offensive to her customers, they may not want to visit her restaurant. If the wolf uses pawprints instead of letters to write out his message, Little Red Riding Hood won't be able to read his invitation. In Figure 9-5, we have added semantic noise to the illustration of the communication process.

figure | 9-5 |

Communication chart: semantic noise.

Internal Noise

The next place where noise can occur is in the medium that carries the message. Just as a radio might have static that obscures the announcer's voice, a message might be overlooked because of competing messages or distractions within the medium, or because of poor layout or location. For example, NAL might choose a magazine for teens instead of one for children, or the ad might be buried in the back of the magazine where children rarely look. Ms. Frank's menu-flyer might have a confusing layout that drives customers to order from a competing restaurant. The layout of the wolf's dinner invitation might look more like a holiday card to put on the mantle, and Little Red may never realize it's actually an invitation. In Figure 9-6, you can see that internal noise happens within the medium that carries the message.

figure | 9-6 |

Communication chart: internal noise.

External Noise

A third source of noise comes from other messages outside the medium that compete for the receiver's attention. Other magazines on the newsstand might distract schoolchildren from buying the one with NAL's advertisement in it. Other restaurants on the way to the Juicyburger Diner might look equally enticing and more convenient to potential customers. Other mail in the mailbox might distract Little Red Riding Hood from even opening the invitation to Grandma's house. In addition, the receivers might get phone calls or e-mail or turn on television programs or have homework, jobs, or visitors—all of which might prevent them from ever seeing, reading, or understanding the senders' messages. An enormous amount of information floods our senses daily, each item competing for our attention, and we cannot possibly assimilate all of these messages. Every receiver selects which messages to focus on, and which ones to ignore. It is a designer's job to get the receiver's attention, communicate the message effectively in a way the receiver can understand, and make an impression that causes the receiver to remember and act on the message. In Figure 9-7, external noise has been introduced into the communication process.

figure | 9-7 |

Communication chart: external noise.

Feedback

One last step in the communication process is *feedback*. Sometimes receivers will provide feedback about messages by sending their own messages to the source or to the medium. For instance, a child might write a letter to the source Libby the Bookworm, telling her about a book he enjoyed. A parent might send an e-mail to the editor of a magazine, thanking them for printing NAL's advertisement. Little Red Riding Hood might call Grandma on the phone to tell her that she can't come to visit. Sometimes senders solicit feedback from receivers, since this is an effective way to learn about how effectively the communication process is working. For example, Ms. Frank might leave questionnaires on the tables, asking customers to rate the service and the food they received. Figure 9-8 demonstrates the final phase of the communication process: feedback. Notice that just like the sender's message, the receiver's feedback must also travel through semantic, internal, and external noise to reach its intended audience.

figure | 9-8 |

Communication chart: feedback.

Implications of Communication Theory

Understanding communication theory gives designers useful insights about designing for an audience. The first is that receivers are active participants in the communication process—not just passive receivers of unquestioned information. Receivers will choose whether or not to act on the new information, according to their own sociocultural backgrounds.

Another implication is that any message may or may not be received correctly or in full by its audience, due to the distortions and distractions of noise. Understanding this helps designers to create concise designs that navigate readers from the most important information to the least. This understanding also helps designers to consider their designs holistically—taking into account that they must contend with both predictable and unpredictable competing messages.

A third important point is that senders can increase the effectiveness of transmission of their messages by requesting feedback early and often. This is why as designers, we critique our work before it is finished—so that we can hone our messages throughout the design process in order to promote effective communication while maximizing our use of time.

A last implication is one that should affect us all as consumers. Realizing that the source isn't always necessarily the true sender of the messages we receive can inspire us to practice a healthy amount of skepticism and critical thinking as receivers of information in the communication process.

GRAPHIC RESONANCE

An important concept that helps designers enhance the communicative nature of their designs is **graphic resonance**. Graphic resonance refers to the underlying tone of a design. The designer sets the tone by utilizing **connotative elements** in the design; that is, elements that evoke emotions or suggest associations with familiar experiences and memories. The secondary messages that connotations can convey can be very powerful, and so must be applied with great thought.

When we speak, we set the tone of our messages by using tonal inflections, gestures, and facial expressions. Since printed type bypasses these communicative devices, designers must use other techniques to create graphic resonance. As you will see in the examples that follow, designers can select, place, and manipulate text in ways that match type to its message to create emphasis, reiteration, or harmony; or they can intentionally mismatch them to create irony, surprise, or dissonance. Creatively used, type can physically suggest a mood, a time period, a familiar experience, a cultural phenomenon, or an action.

Graphic resonance is as important as legibility to the conveyance of a message. Some designers argue that it is even more important. The layout in Figure 9-9 warns designers against relying too heavily on legibility to communicate effectively. For each design you create, you will need to weigh the demands of legibility and style to create an effective balance. You will need to determine the most appropriate combination of graphic resonance and legibility, for each specific design challenge, in order to optimize communication. The correct balance for any design will depend on your intended audience, the demands of the medium that will carry your message, and the wishes of your client.

MIS- DON'T
LEGI- TAKE
FOR BILITY
ICATION. COMMUN

figure | 9-9 |

Legibility vs. Communication designed by David Carson of David Carson Design, Inc., 1997.

Defining Creativity

A creative person is someone who can imagine an array of alternate solutions to one problem or challenge. Simply using the most obvious "tried and true" solutions may sometimes be appropriate, but might not offer the most creative results. To express creativity, a designer must be willing to apply time and energy to inventing and considering new and different strategies for achieving goals. Sometimes new creative solutions are better than the commonly accepted ones, other times they are not.

Designers are constantly challenged to use creativity to bring out the most connotative and expressive qualities of type; that is, qualities that will evoke emotions and associations. The braver designers try using type in new ways, and some become trendsetters. However, as designers imagine the vast possibilities of how to communicate their client's messages, they must also be bound by the vision and limitations of their clients. Finding creative ways to express the client's vision to the intended audience—within the boundaries of the client's fiscal limitations, tastes, and preconceived ideas—gives structure to each design challenge.

Sources of Creative Inspiration

How can a designer evoke his or her own creativity? Particularly creative designers will tell you that they are able to come up with interesting creative ideas because they are willing to brainstorm and consider the wide range of ideas that brainstorming brings. When you brainstorm, it's best not to reject or fall in love with any one idea immediately. Remember that there is more than one correct solution to any design problem; be open to considering a variety of solutions. Think about the graphic resonance you hope to achieve in your design; what visual cues could you incorporate into the design that would suggest the ideas and moods you want to convey to your target audience? This may mean researching the tastes and symbols that are meaningful to your audience. It may also include researching and evaluating how other contemporary and historical designers have solved similar design problems.

Creative designers also keep their eyes open, constantly evaluating and enjoying the things they see. They aren't afraid to deconstruct visual ideas and recombine them to form new ones. Just noticing visual stimuli can help boost creativity. Keeping a scrapbook of the images and uses of type that appeal to you can help you to analyze and organize your ideas. Jotting down your impressions about the images you collect can help you to better understand your own preferences and reactions to what you see. Don't limit yourself to established sources for designers, like books, magazines, and web sites about design. Look all around you at both fabricated and natural objects, consider arts that tempt all the senses, and relate your own experiences to visual expressions. In this way, you will heighten your awareness of your surroundings, and find more ideas at your disposal.

Following and Breaking the "Rules"

In previous chapters, we discussed a number of "rules" about how to use type. Most of these rules are meant to promote legibility or cater to prevailing cultural preferences and traditions. Typographic rules have some important functions. Using type in traditional ways can prevent the physical form of type from competing with the content of the message it carries. The predictability of using type in conventional ways can increase readability and therefore can increase reader comprehension. In addition, a shared understanding about how type should function can streamline the printing process, since specifications can be easily communicated and errors can be easily recognized and corrected.

New Vocabulary

connotative elements: evoking emotions or suggesting associations with familiar experiences or memories

graphic resonance: the underlying tone of a design, set by utilizing connotative elements in the design

However, designers who have boldly experimented with type by breaking traditional rules have forged new channels for design, and have started new traditions and trends. A designer who understands the "rules" of typography can make educated decisions about how and when to break them for a most effective outcome. Breaking these rules should always be done as a conscious decision, driven by defensible reasoning and strategies. More than likely, if your design breaks commonly accepted typographic rules, you will be asked to defend your deviation from tradition from a design standpoint—to your clients and to other designers—so be prepared to explain your choices.

CREATIVE STRATEGIES

An enormous selection of typefaces is available to designers; many of these typefaces can be downloaded for free from the Internet. Some are better designed than others, but regardless of structural integrity, consistency, and legibility, many typefaces can evoke desired emotive qualities when carefully applied.

Designers use a wide variety of strategies to creatively apply text in ways that produce graphic resonance. As always, designers work to balance the needs of legibility and style to convey their messages most effectively. Sometimes they use their knowledge of typographic standards to guide their designs, and sometimes they use that knowledge to forge paths around the traditional "rules" of typography. Some of the tools that designers use to establish graphic resonance are visual correspondence, visual irony, visual exaggeration, visual rhythm, and visual distortion.

Visual Correspondence

When a typeface visually reinforces the content of text by creating associations with familiar experiences, time periods, or cultural phenomenon, this is called **visual correspondence**. For example, the nineteenth-century wood type fonts used in the political poster pictured in Figure 9-10 evoke a patriotic "old time" graphic resonance that makes the candidate seem accessible, likeable, traditional, and devoted to his cause, while the textual content proves he has a sense of humor. In Figure 9-11, the fingerprint patterning of the typeface subtly suggests that "art is . . ." about individuality of expression. This association is based on the fact that our culture recognizes fingerprints as marks of personal identity.

figure | 9-10 |

Leslie Davis poster designed by Glenn Gray of Clarity Coverdale Fury for the *Leslie Davis for Governor* campaign, 2003.

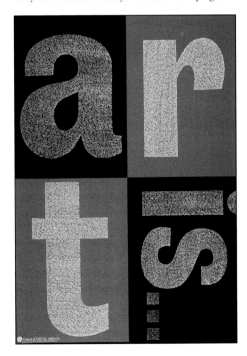

figure | 9-11 |

Art Is poster designed by Paula Scher of Pentagram Design for the School of Visual Arts.

Visual Irony

Sometimes designers use **visual irony**, injecting satire and surprise to propel their messages by selecting typefaces that contrast with the text's content. In Figure 9-12, Linotype type foundry purposefully mismatched the typeface with the message to emphasize their wide selection of typefaces. The image displays an inappropriately whimsical and girly font, spelling the words "NYPD POLICE" on the side of a police car. The byline reads "More than 5,500 original typefaces – also the right one!"

In Figure 9-13, the designer has created a sense of visual irony by juxtaposing contrasting themes of nature and technology—turning the kernels of corn into a computer keyboard, right there on the cob!

Police Car advertisement, 2004. *Courtesy of Linotype Library GmbH.*

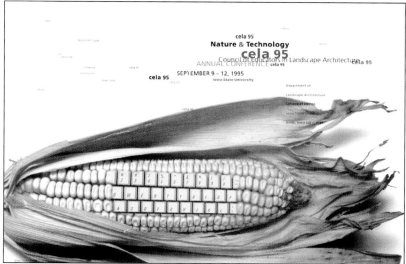

Cela95 Nature & Technology Council of Educators poster by Paula J. Curran of Iowa State University Department of Art and Design for the Council of Educators in Landscape Architecture, 1995.

Visual Exaggeration

Content can also be reinforced through **visual exaggeration** of type by placing text in ways that seem to act out the content of the text, or attempt to simulate the experience being described. In Figure 9-14, the letters are arranged so that the word "Twisted" seems to twist and contort.

Visual Rhythm

Designers use rhythmic devices to create graphic resonance in their designs. **Visual rhythm** can be achieved through the creative use of repetition, overlap, movement, alignment, spacing, reading gravity, and contrast to produce interesting and refreshing results.

Figure 9-15 uses repetition, overlapping, and emotive type styles to visually simulate the experience of scratching a persistent itch.

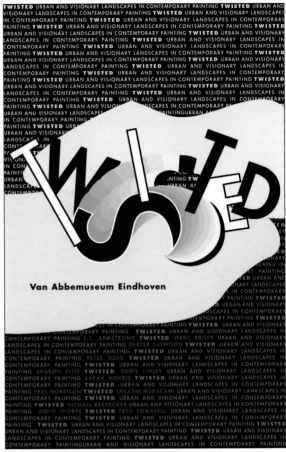

figure | 9-14 |

Book cover for *Twisted*, designed by Arlette Brouwers & Koos van der Meer of Studio de pal, Netherlands, for NAI Publishers, 2001.

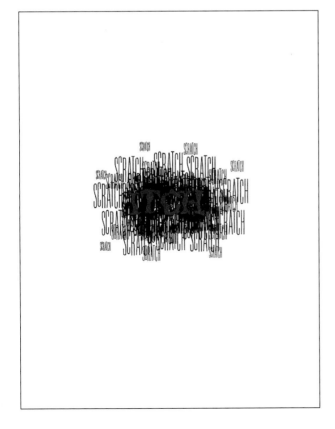

figure | 9-15 |

Self-promotional holiday card, *Scratch and Itch*, by Chris Froeter of Froeter Design Company, Inc., 1996.

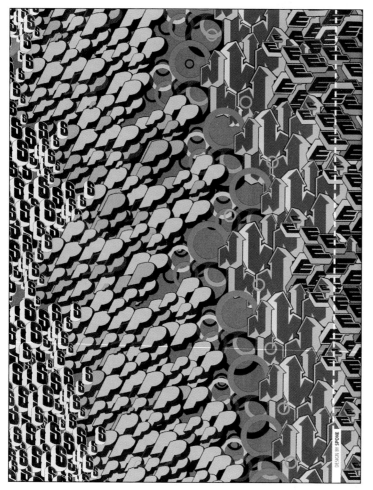

figure | 9-16 |

Self-promotional wrapping paper design
by Greg Lamarche of SPONE, 2003.

Repetition

In Figure 9-16, the designer has created
an innovative wrapping paper design by
using repetition. Repeated characters are
collaged to create an effervescent sensation. Each letter grouping is clearly defined from the others through the use of
contrasting color, shape, direction, and
dimensionality, so that each letter grouping clearly reads as one letter. Despite the
hundreds of characters present, the
reader easily identifies the word SPONE.
This is effective self-promotion because
the graphic resonance in the design con-
notes active dynamism and confident
daring of the designer, SPONE.

In Figure 9-17, the repetitive patterning
of the large and small white and orange
lines of text create a syncopated rhythm
that establishes an upbeat and sassy
graphic resonance. The doubling of the
lines of text also correlates with the content of the accompanying headline "Twin
Peek," which refers to a typeface design
project honoring the Twin Cities.

figure | 9-17 |

Twin Peek magazine spread designed by
Tricia Bateman for *HOW* magazine, 2004.

Overlap

The poster shown in Figure 9-18 presents a much darker graphic resonance. The awkwardly spaced overlapping letterforms, angry scribbles, and unclear imagery combine to create a disturbing, sporadic rhythm that expresses a dissonant, confused, and fearful tone—emphasizing the disturbing nature of social injustices that Amnesty International exists to combat and the urgency of their mission.

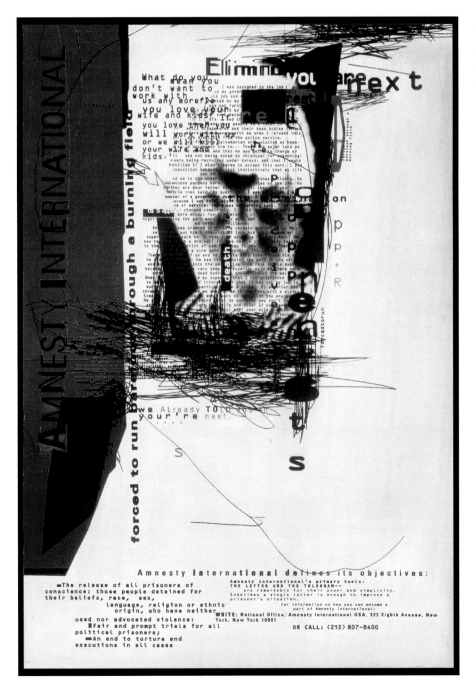

figure | 9-18 |

Poster by Joan Dobkin for Amnesty International, 1991.

Movement

The designer of the poster shown in Figure 9-19 used a variety of techniques to integrate the text with the imagery in ways that create a sense of motion and an energetic, fun graphic resonance. The figure juggles the characters that spell "Bumbershoot 1989"—their movements are indicated by the motion lines of text that stream behind them. The repetitive arms and faces indicate the movements of the juggler over time. The overlapping rotated logo on the barrel he balances on indicates that it is rolling, and that the feat he performs in front of the amazed crowd is both thrilling and astounding.

Digital media allows designers to add the dimension of time to their designs so that motion can be literal. In Erykah Badu's web site about her music (*www.erykahbadu.com*), handwriting and drawings are sketched onto the layout in front of the viewer's eyes, creating a flowing, rhythmic welcoming graphic resonance. Rollovers reveal additional handwritten words, doodles, and splatters of color that easily integrate into the collage-style design. Arrows appear and disappear, indicating the navigational structure. Small and oddly shaped pop-up windows with hand-drawn outlines seamlessly become a part of the layout, adding new information while keeping the viewer from feeling like they've left the original home page (Figure 9-20).

figure | 9-19 |

Bumbershoot poster by Art Chantry for One Reel and the Seattle Arts Commission, 1989.

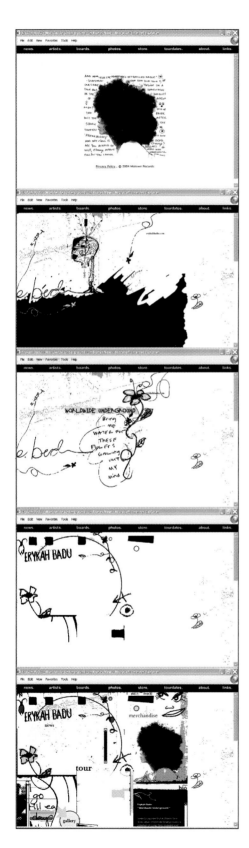

figure | 9-20 |

Screenshots from web site containing artwork and photos by Erykah Badu, *www.erykahbadu.com*, produced by Dan Petruzzi and Afra Amir Sanjari and designed by Kirsten O'Loughlin and Chris Ro of *Okayplayer.com. Used by permission of Motown Records, a division of UMG Recordings, Inc, 2004.*

Alignment

Sometimes designers vary text alignments for stylistic ends. When used effectively, the diminished legibility of alternative alignments can be made up for by increased readability, stemming from the graphic resonance that's been established. For example, the right-aligned runaround text in Figure 9-21 seems to mold around the smoothly gyrating Italian word "forma," meaning "form." The design feels almost malleable. The graceful graphic resonance of the layout brings elegance to the right-aligned text passage.

figure | 9-21 |

A spread of *Per Lui* magazine published by Edizioni Condé Nast S.p.A. in 1990. Art director Neville Brody.

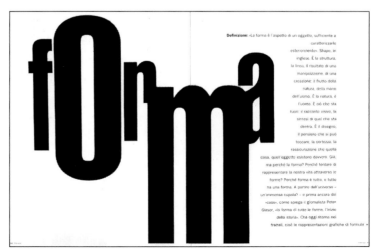

In Figure 9-22, the designer has created a sinister theatrical graphic resonance using a variety of techniques. The blurbs of slightly rounded and centered body type echo the shape of the rounded den-like room, and emphasize the strangeness of the characters and their interactions. The symmetrical layout of the body type is also suggestive of a stage, each text block representing an anonymous audience member. The pink serif body type against the black cloudy shadows seems quiet and creepy. By contrast, the harsher sans-serif typeface set in all caps, and also centered, suggests the characters' voices to be raspy and unearthly. The hand-drawn letters that form the words "Dr. Bombay's" seem to drip along the muddy walls, adding to the overall eeriness.

figure | 9-22 |

Dr. Bombay's by Camille Rose Garcia, from *Blab* magazine 13, Autumn 2002. *Courtesy of Fantagraphics Books.*

The designs pictured in Figure 9-23 use asymmetrical alignment to mimic and exaggerate the movements of the simple machines that the text describes. The simple, clever designs imply a user-friendly trustworthiness for the company they represent.

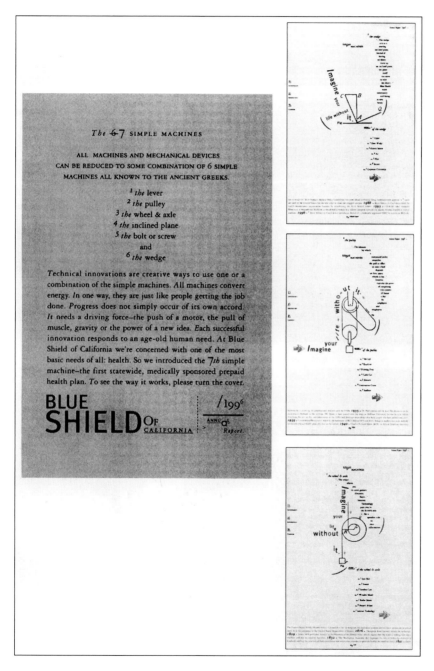

figure | 9-23 |

Annual report by Jennifer Sterling of Jennifer Sterling Design for Blue Shield of California, 1996.

Spacing

Using unusual spacing can create an interesting texture or emphasis in a layout. The interplay of the varying positive and negative spaces in Figure 9-24 creates a wavy, uneven textured page color that gives the piece an almost musical quality.

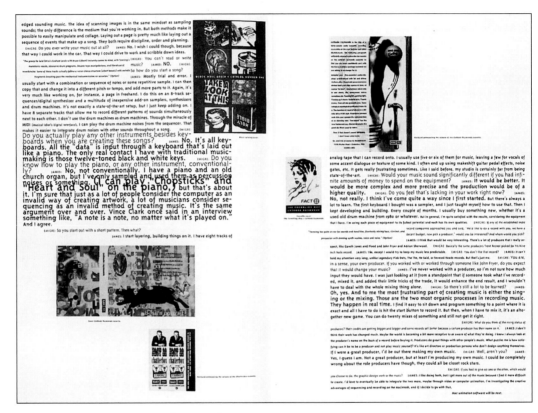

figure | 9-24 |

Emigre magazine spread designed by
Rudy VanderLans of Émigre, Inc., 1990.

The prominent white rivers in Figure 9-25 add a choppy, fragmented horizontal rhythm and a strong vertical flow to the reading experience, ending with the widow on the bottom line.

In Figure 9-26, the designer has purposefully broken a number of typographic "rules" in order to convey the idea that the product it advertises is innovative, individualistic, and not confined by convention. The nontraditional choices concerning letter case, word division, letterspacing, and leading all work to support this portrayal, creating a new and exciting unconventional rhythm. The text *"the new CAMARO. What else would you expect from the country that invented rock 'n roll"* equates the rhythm of the strangely spaced letters to the beat of a rock 'n roll song, suggesting an association between the music and the product.

figure | 9-25 |

Page from Avital Ronell's
The Telephone Book, 1989, designed
by Richard Eckersley of University
of Nebraska Press.

figure | 9-26 |

Advertisement by David Carson of
David Carson Design, Inc., for Chevy
Camaro, 1997.

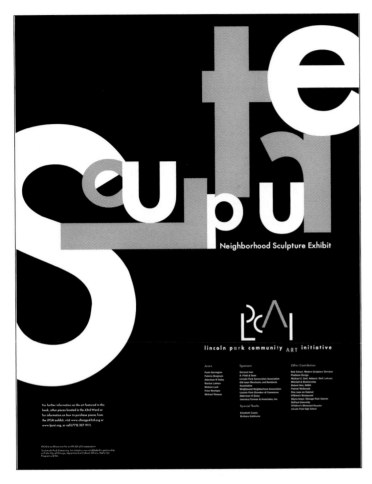

figure | 9-27 |

Poster designed by Stephanie Harte of
Spacetacular for Lincoln Park
Community Art Initiative.

Reading Gravity

The design in Figure 9-27 creates a snaky rhythm by defying reading gravity. Viewers are drawn into the layout at the large letter **S** on the left and follow the meandering word across and up the page to the top right corner of the layout. However, the roundness of the letter **e** and the backward letter **r** both help to lead the viewer's eye back into the page, where the strong vertical **t** catches it, leading straight down to the logo and supporting blurb of information.

Contrast

Another way that designers can establish rhythm in their layouts is through effective use of contrast. Contrasting design elements can also add interest and emphasis to a design. To use contrast in typography, designers can make use of contrasting typefaces, point sizes, set widths, stroke weights, colors, values, textures, orientations, and negative/positive relationships.

In Figure 9-28, the designer has played with the negative and positive relationships of the letterforms and imagery to create a busy, lively layout full of surprises and a rhythmic buzz. The letters shift from black to the page color playfully, right in the middle of words. The solidly set measures of text create a jumbled effect, leaving no leading to provide a resting place for viewers' eyes. The figures also alter between black and the page color, each serving as both foreground and background depending on where the viewer focuses. The solid black **O**s throughout the text mimic the solid buttons and polka dots in the image above, adding some unity and a bubbly sense of fun to this high-contrast design.

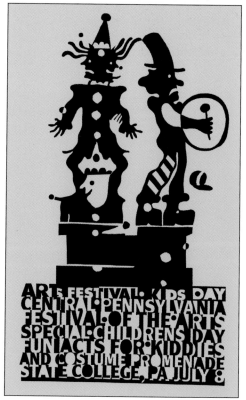

figure | 9-28 |

Pennsylvania Festival of the Arts: Kids Day posters by Lanny Sommese of Sommese Design for the Central Pennsylvania Festival of the Arts, 1997.

figure | 9-29 |

Table of contents from *Blab* magazine 13, Autumn 2002, designed by Monte Beauchamp of Fantagraphics Books.

In the table of contents page pictured in Figure 9-29, the designer has used contrasting stroke weights and values to create a festive blinking rhythm. The maniacally grinning clown face peering straight at the viewer brings to mind the flashing lights of a carnival, enforcing the intermittent rhythm of the text.

Students are warned again and again not to use too many typefaces in a design. However, designers sometimes purposefully break this rule of thumb to create a festive carnival type atmosphere for their designs. Figure 9-30 shows a poster in which the designer used the contrasting shapes of varied typefaces to create a clattering, excited rhythm for the layout of a poster promoting a literacy campaign.

Visual Distortion

Altering or deforming letterforms to cause graphic resonance through the use of **visual distortion** can be a creative way to manipulate the message that the words send. For example, in Figure 9-31, the letterforms are stretched to resemble a sku code; the correlation is enhanced by placement of the recognizable sku number at the bottom. The implication of this piece is that if we, the viewers, aren't careful, we too are in danger of being transformed into mindless consumers and victims of deindividualization.

figure | 9-30 |

AIGA Literacy Campaign poster designed by Charles Anderson of Charles S. Anderson Design Company for AIGA/Colorado, 1995.

figure | 9-31 |

Print ad/poster by Eric Tilford of Pyro/Core11 for Dr. Martens, 1995.

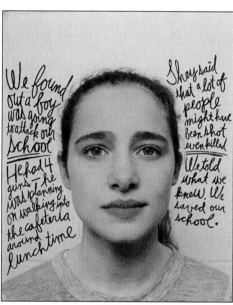

Hand-Rendered Type

When using type in a layout, developing or using a specific font with its own standards and consistencies generally adds a sense of professionalism and uniformity to a layout. However, there are times when a message or story is most effectively told in the more personal human voice of hand-rendered type.

Figure 9-32 provides a good example of this. The poster seeks to convince teenagers, who are often distrustful of confiding in adults, to share any information they know that might prevent violence in schools. The young girl pictured looks kind, healthy, and innocent—her whole life is ahead of her. Her eyes connect with the viewer's, and the handwritten words that surround her are presumed to be *her* voice, implying that sharing information could mean saving *her* life. The result is powerful, personal, and very persuasive.

figure | 9-32 |

Michelle ad created by Talmage Cooley, Daniel Gross, and Ian Toombs of PAX—Real Solutions to Gun Violence.

Another example of effective use of hand-rendered type is exhibited in Figure 9-33. The magazine *Adbusters* uses a variety of techniques—including handwritten type, highlighting, collage, finger-smudging, and drilling a hole through the center of the magazine—to make a social and political statement about the media. The designer emphasized the individualistic separateness of this magazine from larger, more powerful corporate media sources by using handwritten text on a finger-smudged background for the cover. The hole through the middle of the head, combined with the caption "Systematically Distorted Information," implies that misinformation is being violently poured into our consciousnesses without our consent. However, the finger-smudges and the bold outlining and coloring imply that we, as media consumers, can be empowered to resist mindless submission.

In the spread shown in Figure 9-33, typed and hand-rendered text are collaged to create an active grass-roots feel and an empowering do-it-yourself attitude. An image of a handwritten sticky note highlights the prominent message of the spread.

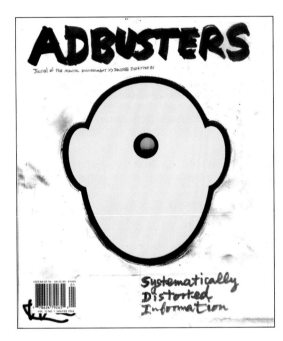

figure │ 9-33 │

Magazine cover and spread from *Adbusters* magazine, No. 51, Jan/Feb 2004, *www.adbusters.org.*

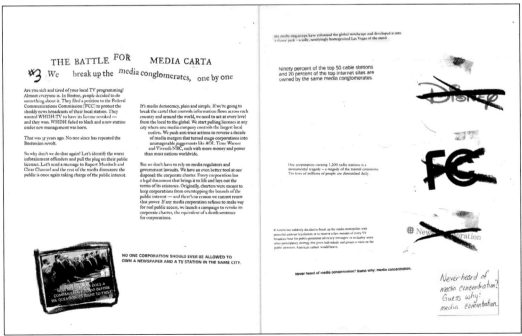

Dimensionality

Adding depth cues that imply dimensionality can draw viewers into a design, and create a sense of place. Designers can give letters the illusion of dimensionality by using depth cues—visual triggers that remind us of how we perceive the world in three dimensions. Depending on how these cues are used together, they can strengthen or contradict each other to create a clear sense of place, or confusion and ambiguity.

- *Overlap or layering:* closer forms may block the view of objects behind them; layers can be transparent (see-through) or translucent (semi-transparent) as in Figure 9-37, or opaque (solid) as in Figure 9-36.

- *Size:* objects appear to grow smaller as their distance increases, as in Figure 9-37.

- *Linear perspective:* parallel lines seem to converge as they move farther away, as in Figures 9-34, 9-35, and 9-37.

- *Foreshortening:* objects viewed in extreme linear perspective look distorted, as in Figures 9-34 and 9-35.

- *Vertical location:* because we see three-dimensional objects in linear perspective, everything in our environment appears to diminish in size and shift in vertical location toward the horizon, which is always at eye level. This means farther objects look closer in vertical location to the horizon line. Below eye level, objects appear higher as they diminish toward their vanishing point on the horizon. Above eye level, the opposite is true: objects appear lower as they get farther away from us, and closer to the horizon, as in Figure 9-37.

- *Surface simulation:* the surface of a virtual object can be made to look as if it has the texture of a recognizable surface like metal, glass, water, wood, paper, or plastic, as in Figures 9-35 and 9-36.

- *Shade and shadow:* a shadow is a dark area of the background, cast when an object blocks a directional light, while shade describes the dark part of the object that faces away from the light source, as in Figures 9-34 and 9-36.

- *Color:* brighter tones appear closer, while duller tones seem farther away; this is because when we view faraway objects, they are dulled and darkened by the atmosphere through which we see them, as in Figure 9-37.

- *Depth of field:* refers to the distance range that appears in focus; a shallow depth of field only displays a short span clearly. For instance, the foreground might be perfectly focused, while the middle ground and background look blurry, as in Figure 9-37. When the depth of field is deep, all elements appear in crisp focus.

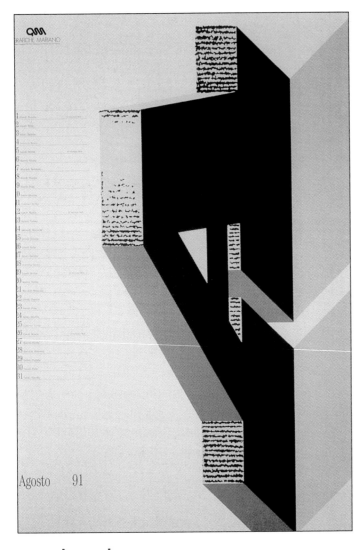

figure | 9-34 |

1991 Grafiche Mariano Calendar by Italo Lupi of Studio Lupi for Grafiche Mariano Tipografia.

In Figure 9-34, the designer uses foreshortening, shadow, and perspective to make the letter **A** seem to jut out toward the viewers, drawing them into the layout.

In the advertisement shown in Figure 9-35, type has been physically distorted using linear perspective, foreshortening, and surface simulation to mimic the three-dimensional look of folded paper.

The designer of the letterhead pictured in Figure 9-36 uses a dramatically lit still shot from the company's film footage to create an identity system that suggests that the company's films are as sophisticated, cinematic, artistic, and multidimensional as their logo. Depth cues include shade and shadow, surface simulation, and overlap of the letterforms above the shadows that are cast behind them.

In Figure 9-37, the designer has used the visual depth cues of size, overlap, linear perspective, color, vertical location, and a shallow depth of field to convince the viewer to perceive the timeline's text as hanging in space. In doing so, the viewer equates the dimensions of time and space and understands the layout as a three-dimensional timeline.

figure | 9-35 |

Promotion by Robert Bergman of Bergman Associates, NYC, for *Das Papier* magazine, 1998.

figure | 9-37 |

3-D Interactive Timeline by Earl Rennison of Perspecta and Lisa Strausfeld of Perspecta and Pentagram Design for the *Millennium Project: Constructing a Dynamic 3+D Virtual Environment for Exploring Geographically, Temporally and Categorically Organized Historical Information*, 1995. *Courtesy of Pentagram Design.*

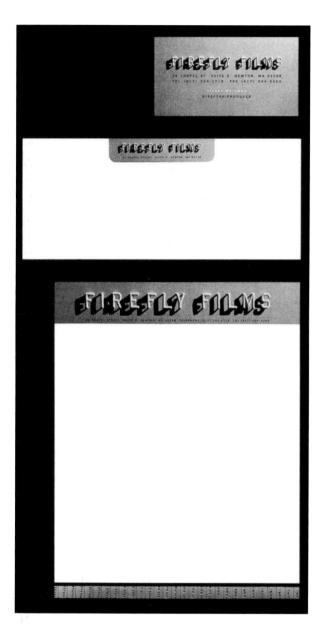

figure | 9-36 |

Stationery designed by Fritz Klaetke of Visual Dialogue for Firefly Films, 1995.

New Vocabulary

visual correspondence: reiteration of a message through the use of a typeface that visually relates to the content of the text

visual distortion: alteration or deformation of letterforms to manipulate the message that the words send

visual exaggeration: to amplify a message by manipulating and placing text in ways that seem to act out the content or simulate the experience being described

visual irony: using satire and surprise to communicate a message by purposefully selecting typefaces that contrast with the content of the text

visual rhythm: rhythm that is visually suggested through use of repetition, overlap, movement, alignment, spacing, reading gravity, and contrast

THE *designer* AT WORK

eduardo recife

How did you get started as a designer? Tell us about your first job in design and the evolution of your career.

I used to draw since I was very young. Later on, I got really into graffiti, and that lead me into type. When I first got hooked with the Internet, I found such great people working on personal images, experimental typefaces, etc.—it was something that just hypnotized me. My first jobs were creating posters for local bands and exhibitions. Later on I worked in a design agency here in Brazil for two years. Since then I've been freelancing.

What do you do to get your creative juices flowing when you start a new project? What can you share with us about your design process? What role does technology play in that process?

Mostly, my state of mind is what influences me the most in creating, but another piece of art, music, or even people can also be very inspiring. My process is simple. First, I get an idea in my head, then I start to collect images and work on drawings and textures to go with it. Once I have all the material, I start to actually decide where everything is going to be put using Photoshop, and the final result just appears. I like it to be as spontaneous as it can be.

What advice do you have for design students and new designers who are just entering the field today?

Find good resources and references, keep practicing, accept criticisms, and do it all with love.

Eduardo Recife of Misprinted Type, Belo Horizonte, Brazil
www.misprintedtype.com

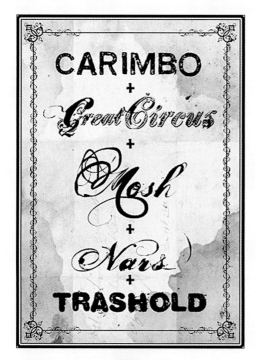

Artwork and type specimens by Eduardo Recife of Misprinted Type, *www.misprintedtype.com.*

INTERPLAY OF TYPE AND IMAGE

Traditionally, the role of image in its relationship with type has been a supportive one. From the time that illuminations first illustrated biblical passages, images were primarily used to recap and extend the content of the accompanying text. This tradition continued largely unchallenged for centuries, until the invention of photography in the twentieth century redefined this relationship. Designers quickly discovered that information and emotions could be powerfully conveyed through the selection, cropping, juxtaposition, and manipulation of photographic images. They realized that when used together, text and images each have the power to manipulate the viewer's interpretation of the other. Experimentation with the interplay of text and imagery became widespread, and continues today. Some designers have challenged the text-dominant standard by creating designs that are image-dominant or in which text and images share or compete for hierarchical status. Designers have also challenged the traditional separateness of text and imagery, by combining them and manipulating their relationships in a variety of ways.

figure | 9-38 |

CD cover by Christopher Eichenseer of Some Odd Pilot for Contact Records, 2004.

Type into Image

Although the text-dominant approach remains popular, it is no longer the standard. Creating new and interesting relationships between text and imagery has become a challenge that has led to many creative approaches and solutions. Figure 9-38 shows one example in which the text and imagery have been integrated in an interesting way—the text invades the space of the image as a reverse drop-out—and the shape of the sun's glare on the camera lens echoes the shape of the text, breaking down the boundaries between the text and the image.

When text and images invade each other's spaces, new and powerful relationships and stories can emerge. In the poster art pictured in Figure 9-39, the text and imagery have been combined to create a moving farewell to the designer's homeland, Yugoslavia. The handwritten text reading "despair, pain, hope, anger" are placed on the palm along the lines which are believed by many to reflect a person's experiences and identity. The missile being shot from the fingertip brings to mind both the violence of war that the protagonist has fled, and the isolation he feels as he is jettisoned from his homeland. The words creating the flight trail of the missile translate into English as "Goodbye Yugo" (short for Yugoslavia).

In the children's book *The Day I Swapped My Dad for Two Goldfish,* drawings and photographs are collaged with digital and found type to create a dreamlike atmosphere in which a surreal storyline becomes believable. The story is told from the perspective of a boy, his voice indicated by a childlike typeface, with hand-drawn speech bubbles indicating conversation. The father's face is always obscured by a newspaper, which he constantly reads, ignoring his children. News clippings are collaged around him and appear wherever his presence is felt. In Figure 9-40a the boy sits in his dad's chair in a faint cloud of newsprint, feeling his dad's absence after trading him to a friend for two goldfish. In Figure 9-40b, when the children are reunited with their father, the cloud of newsprint surrounds him and separates him from his children, symbolizing his continued inattention toward them.

figure | 9-39 |

Political poster, *Goodbye Yugo*, designed by Alexander Kneselac of The Collective Design, 2001.

figures | 9-40a and 9-40b |

Illustrations by Dave McKean of Hourglass from Neil Gaiman's book *The Day I Swapped My Dad for Two Goldfish* for HarperCollins, 1997.

The text in the poster pictured in Figure 9-41 illustrates a sound. Words seem to reverberate as they emanate from the throat of the performer, filling the space as she belts out her song.

Figure 9-42 displays another way in which type can be integrated into an image. In this example, the type is set within the background image of a map. The designer has filled the map of the world to capacity with text to illustrate the problem of overpopulation.

figure | 9-41 |

Kansas City Event poster designed by John Muller of Muller and Company for Kansas City Events.

figure | 9-42 |

World Word Map painted by Paula Scher of Pentagram Design, 1998.

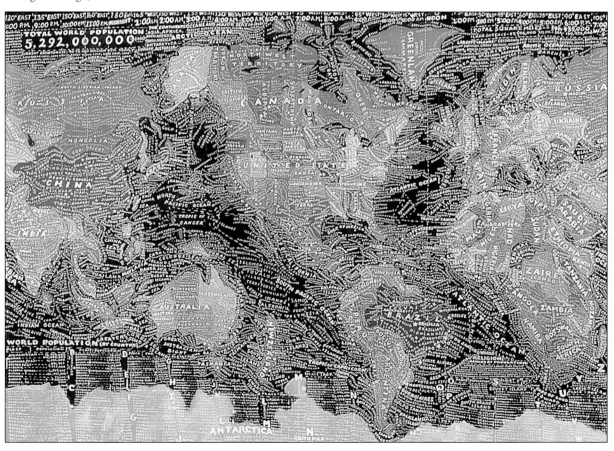

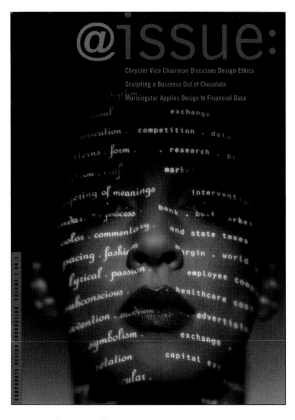

figure | 9-43 |

@*issue* magazine cover designed by Kit Hinrichs of Pentagram Design for the Corporate Design Foundation, photograph by Michelle Clement.

There are other ways that designers can blur the line between type and image. In the magazine cover pictured in Figure 9-43, text has actually been projected onto the face of the model, who was then photographed, integrating the text into the imagery in a very physical way.

Type As Image

In Figure 9-44, type is used illustratively instead of images. Objects are indicated in space by printed words that float where the objects should be. Some words don't replace objects, but rather actions and moods. By reading the text, we learn that two friends are sitting on chairs at the pictured table. We guess that one is a man and one is a woman, from the masculine and feminine typefaces that spell "Friend," and from the shoes that each wears; the friend on the left wears "loafers," while the "friend" on the right wears "pumps." We see that the couple are eating and sipping wine and giggling, and we learn of the joyful atmosphere from the words "glow" and "mirth."

figure | 9-44 |

Mirth postcard designed by Marlene McCarty and Tibor Kalman of M&Co for Restaurant Florent, 1989.

figure | 9-45 |

Advertising campaign designed by Carlos Segura of
Segura, Inc. for Hewitt.

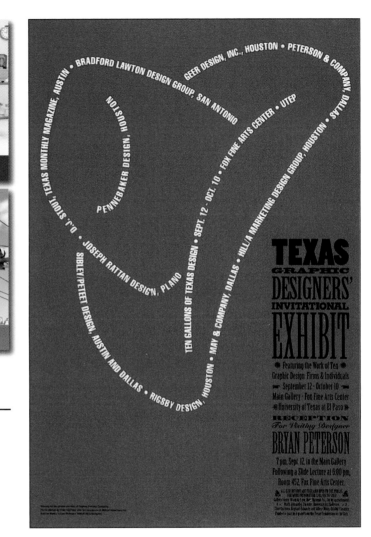

In Figure 9-45, the designer has applied contoured text alignment to
body text, creating ghosts of people at work. The anonymity of the figures lets viewers picture themselves filling the roles, making the advertisement feel more personalized.

In Figure 9-46, the designer has used shaped text alignment to form imagery by drawing the outline of a cowboy hat with text. This design appropriately advertises an event that takes place at the University of Texas,
a state famous for its cowboys.

figure | 9-46 |

Texas Designers poster designed by Clive
Cochran of Mithoff Advertising, Inc.,
for the University of Texas at El Paso
Department of Art, 1996.

figure | 9-47 |

Promotional poster designed by Keith Novicki of Design Equals More for the arts collective, 5 Minds, photography by Will Shively of Shively Photography, 1995.

Image into Type

Images can also invade type's realm. In Figure 9-47, people dance among the letterforms. The type has literally become the setting for the imagery. Notice that the models are both in front and in back of the type, giving it a sense of dimension that it wouldn't otherwise have.

In Figure 9-48, the designer has injected image into type by filling the letterforms with images. In this way, the designer has added a sense of transparency to the design—the viewer must look through the letters to focus on the imagery.

Images can also be transformed into letters—even into whole alphabets. In Figure 9-49, naturally appearing vein lines that resemble letters in stones have been photographed to assemble an alphabet. Figure 9-50 shows an example of another way a designer has used found objects to create alphabets. The letterforms in this image were assembled from collected studio materials.

figure | 9-48 |

Catalog cover designed by Andy Cruz, Allen Mercer, and Jeremy Dean of House Industries, 1995.

figure | 9-49 |

Poster designed by Italo Lupi for De Pedrini, 1991.

figure | 9-50 |

Alphabet using found studio objects, *Kurlansky Kaps* by Mervyn Kurlansky of Pentagram Design for Preston Polytechnic, 1983.

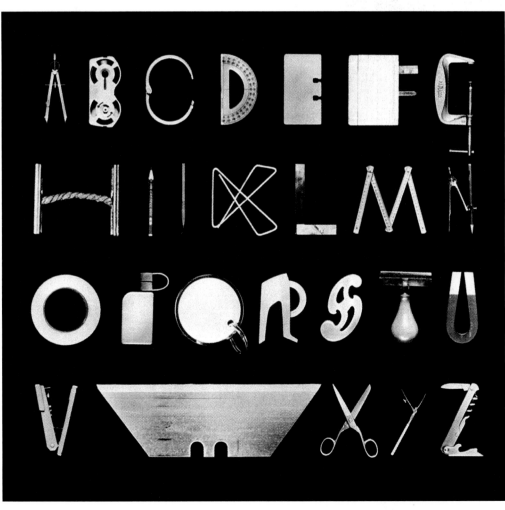

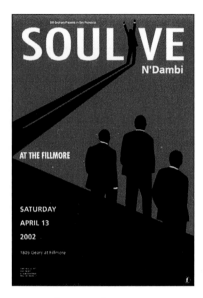

figure | 9-51 |

Soulive poster designed by Jed Morfit of Jed Morfit Illustration for Bill Graham Presents, art directed by Arlene Owseichik of Bill Graham Presents, 2002.

Image As Type

Sometimes designers use an image to replace only one letter or word in a text that is otherwise formed by traditional type. This technique is called **substitution**. Figure 9-51 shows an example of substitution: the figure of a man is substituted for the letter I in the word "SOULIVE," his shadow simultaneously placing him in relation to the other figures pictured.

Decorative Typographic Elements

Designers can also create relationships between type and symbols, dingbats, rules, and/or directionals to create innovative designs. For example, on the book cover pictured in Figure 9-52, the designer's abundant use of rules, directionals, text boxes, dingbats, and symbols provides an active and fun navigational path, reminiscent of running around a basketball court. Figure 9-53 shows a book cover in which the designer has creatively manipulated numbers to form the letters that spell out the book's title, *Searching for a New Visual Language*. The nontraditional use of recognizable symbols reiterates the title's meaning.

figure | 9-52 |

Book cover designed by Carlos Segura of Segura, Inc., for Gatorade, 2002.

figure | 9-53 |

Searching for a New Visual Language poster, designed by Duane King, creative director Todd Hart, of focus2 Brand Development, 1999.

Interactivity

Interactivity, when used creatively, can be a very engaging and fun element for viewers. Recent growth in computer technologies has created opportunities for new typographic experimentation. One very interesting experiment in interactive typography that can be toyed with by visitors is found at *www.ni9e.com* (Figure 9-54), a web site whose mission is "typoactive experience exploration" and "creating for the sake of art/design"; it showcases a series of interactive typographic poems and experiences that utilize type, sound, movement, and interactivity to evoke associations and emotions, and to inspire imagination and critical thinking. The web site is a good example of how one designer has explored the boundaries of typographic interactivity.

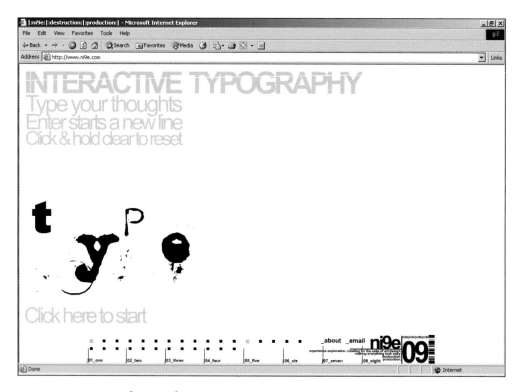

figure | 9-54 |

Screenshot of *"Typopactive Interactive Typography,"* web page from *www.ni9e.com*, designed by Max Asare of ni9e, 2001.

Another particularly beautiful interactive typographic web site that floods the senses with creativity, movement, and sound can be found at *www.daxo.de*, where the font FF Dax is playfully presented to visitors. Viewers become collaborators as they are led through an entertainingly interactive analytical type specimen featuring a series of vignettes in which the font's characteristics can be explored at a self-determined pace.

One such exploration follows the format of a "lesson" called "How to make an FF Dax from a Helvetica," pictured in Figure 9-55. In this humorous sketch, users trigger hammers that strike Helvetica letters like a blacksmith might pound steel, transforming them into members of the FF Dax character set. After each transformation, an affirming "Done!" rewards participants, and then an enticing "Do it again" invites them to play some more.

figure | 9-55 |

Screenshots of interactive typographic web page from *www.daxo.de*, designed by Hans Reichel of Daxo, 1997.

figure | 9-56 |

Typographic public art, *Eric Morecambe Memorial*, designed by Gordon Young & Why Not Associates, for the TERN Project, Lancaster City Council, completed in 1999.

As new technologies are developed, the possibilities for computerized interactivity continue to expand. However, interactivity doesn't have to be a computer-related phenomenon only. Figure 9-56 shows an example in which designers have created a physically interactive typographic piece. The audience interacts with the type as a part of their environment. They walk on the words, and move about them. The intimacy of the interaction between the design and the audience generates an enveloping graphic resonance that creates a powerful and moving experience for viewers.

New Vocabulary

substitution: using an image to replace a letter or word in a layout

CHAPTER SUMMARY

Because the written word bypasses verbal and gestural cues, designers add graphic resonance to their designs by using type expressively to effectively communicate tone and mood, to evoke emotions, and to suggest associations with familiar experiences, memories, cultural phenomenon, emotions, or time periods. Graphic resonance is as important as legibility to the conveyance of a message because by infusing type with connotative qualities, a designer can enhance the communicative capabilities of a design. Designers intentionally match or mismatch type to its message in creative ways to generate emphasis, reiteration, harmony, irony, surprise, or dissonance.

To create graphic resonance, designers use a variety of techniques and devices including visual correspondence, visual irony, visual exaggeration, visual rhythm, and visual distortion, along with the use of decorative typographic elements and interactivity. Some of the rhythmic devices designers can use include repetition, overlap, movement, alignment, spacing, contrast, and toying with the viewer's reading gravity. Designers can also create graphic resonance by creating relationships between type and images that manipulate the viewer's perceptions about each one. Designers attempt to optimize communication by determining an appropriate combination of graphic resonance and legibility to suit each design challenge. The correct balance can vary depending on the demands of the message, the intended audience, the requirements of the medium, and the goals of the client.

Understanding how communication works can help designers to become effective visual communicators. In studying the communication process, some very useful strategies are revealed about how designers can increase the chances that their messages will be effectively communicated.

Designers invent creative design solutions by imagining an array of alternate solutions to any given design problem or challenge; they evoke their own creativity by becoming more alert and receptive to visual stimuli, brainstorming, and considering the possibilities from a wide range of ideas.

in review

1. Explain the communication process.

2. Discuss your thoughts on a designer's social responsibility, as a participant in the communication process.

3. What does it mean to be creative?

4. What is graphic resonance?

5. What is visual correspondence?

6. What is visual irony?

7. What is visual exaggeration?

8. What are some ways that designers can integrate type and imagery?

exercises

1. Go through magazines and find an example of each of the following concepts: visual correspondence, visual irony, visual exaggeration, and substitution. Consider the differences.

2. Find a published example (in a book, magazine, etc.) of a design in which a traditional typographic "rule" was broken. Consider whether the piece communicates successfully, and why or why not.

3. Visit web sites that offer free font downloads. Select fonts that express the connotative qualities of each of the following words:

   - joyous
   - complex
   - envious
   - thrilling
   - sophisticated
   - unbalanced
   - mean
   - compassionate

exercises

4. Download the free fonts you found in the previous exercise, and then print the listed words in the selected fonts. Next to each word, note the elements of the font that contribute to or create its connotative qualities.

5. Make a type scrapbook. Collect a minimum of twenty examples of found type that impress you (imagery is optional). Collage them into a scrapbook. Make notes next to each item, specifying your thoughts about each piece. Your scrapbook should reflect your personal way of seeing as a designer; treat the layout of each page as a new design challenge.

6. Create an alphabet from found fabricated or natural objects and/or photographic images. Determine what types of objects will be used, and whether to work with uppercase or low-ercase letters, so that your alphabet will be cohesive. Establish both thematic and structural guidelines to give consistency to your new typeface, including subject matter, stroke weight, contrast, angle of stress, terminals, serifs, x-height, materials, textures, etc. Once your alphabet is completed, create a type specimen sheet for the new alphabet.

7. Collage found type and images to create a typographic narrative that illustrates a scene from a dream you've had. Integrate type and images in any way you wish to create graphic resonance.

8. Select a historical event, a social phenomenon, or a proverb. Create a layout using text that successfully conveys the message of your selection while openly defying a rule of design discussed in earlier chapters. You might choose to ignore reading gravity, use many differ-ent typefaces, place text against backgrounds that make it hard to read, distort text so that it is difficult to read, or use awkward negative spaces in your layout. Consider your strate-gies for using the broken rule to the design's advantage.

Courtesy of Elizabeth Nevin of the Briar Press.

GLOSSARY

alignment: refers to how text on a page relates to its margins

alley: narrow area of negative space that separates columns

angle of stress: the angle to which the main strokes of a typeface aim, in relation to their baseline

anti-aliasing (or **font smoothing**): the optical smoothing of the jagged edges of a character on a computer screen accomplished by analyzing the outlines of the glyph and then turning on strategically placed pixels in various shades of gray along its edges

apex: the point at which two upward slanting strokes of a letterform meet

arm: a secondary stroke, extending horizontally or upward from a stem stroke and ending freely

ascender: the portion of a lowercase character that extends above the x-height

ascender line: a real or imaginary line that marks the proper height for the tall lowercase letters of a typeface like **b**, **d**, **f**, **h**, **k**, and **l**; for some typefaces, this line is the same as the cap height

ascent: the area of the em square that is above the baseline

asymmetrical text alignment: text that is not aligned to either margin

barb: a serif that is shorter on one end, found on the terminal of a curved stroke

baseline: a real or imaginary horizontal line upon which the letters of a word rest so that the characters appear to line up evenly

beak: a half-serif on the terminal of a straight stroke

Bézier curves: mathematically defined rounded shapes created by setting endpoints (or anchor points) and then reshaped by moving control points (or handles)

bitmap (or **raster**) **fonts:** letterforms that are constructed by encoding maps that instruct computers on which screen pixels to turn on in order to form a specific glyph

bleed: a typographic or graphic element that extends beyond the trim line of a layout

block quotation: a quotation that is longer than a few lines, and so is set apart with increased spacing before and after and usually indented

body size: the height of the face of a type sort, or its digital equivalent

body type (**text type, body text**): type used for longer passages or the main body of a text

bounding box: an invisible box that surrounds an irregularly shaped object so that the object can be aligned to a grid

bowl: a curved stroke that encloses a counter

bracketed serif: a serif that has a curved wedge connecting the serif to the stem stroke, easing the transition between them

callout: the name of an item in illustrations, indicated by a line or arrow

cap height: a real or imaginary horizontal line that marks the height of the capital letters of a typeface

caption: a line or short passage that explains or describes a neighboring image or graphic

centered text alignment: aligns evenly between the left and right margins of the text block

closure: completion

concrete text alignment: text shaped to illustrate the idea or word that the text describes

connotative elements: elements which evoke emotions or suggest associations with familiar experiences or memories

contoured text alignment: text placed so that it creates or fills a specific shape

contrast: 1. a difference among compared elements; 2. to exhibit dissimilar qualities when compared; 3. to compare differences; and 4. in type, the variation between a character's thickest and thinnest stroke weights

counter: area where space is contained or enclosed by a letterform

counterforms: the negative spaces inside and around letterforms

cross stroke: a secondary stroke that intersects a stem stroke

crossbar: a horizontal secondary stroke that connects two main strokes

crotch: the pointed counter where two strokes of a character meet

descender: the portion of a character that falls below the baseline

descender line: a real or imaginary horizontal line that marks the proper length for the lowercase g, j, p, q, and y of a typeface

descent: the area of the em square that is below the baseline

diacritical (accent) mark: a mark, point, or sign—such as a cedilla, tilde, circumflex, or macron—added or attached to a letter to indicate pronunciation

display type: larger and/or decorative type used to attract attention; generally used for titles, headings, or headlines

ear: a small stroke that sometimes extends from the top of a lowercase letter g

em or em square: a relative unit of measurement used for making comparisons between sizes of characters and spaces within a typeface of a particular point size; an em is always a square unit equal in height and in width to the point size of a given typeface

emphasis: a principle of design in which selected elements in a layout are made more prominent than others to attract attention and to indicate relative importance

en or en square: a relative unit of measurement used for making comparisons between sizes of characters and spaces within a typeface of a particular point size; an en is always half the width of the em

eye: the small counter of a lowercase letter e

field: module of a grid where text and images can be placed

folio: page number

font: a collection of all the characters of a specific typeface that are necessary for typesetting

footer (or running foot): text that runs along the bottom margin of multiple pages of a publication, used to provide navigational information like titles, dates, or folios; can also contain footnotes

format: the overall area of the layout, as defined by the outside edges of the page

glyph: a representation of a character

graphic resonance: the underlying tone of a design, set by utilizing connotative elements in the design

grid: a framework of guidelines that form the underlying structure of a layout by dividing it into spatial units that can hold text, images, or negative space

grid area (also called the **text page** or **text area**): the active area within the format where type and images may be placed

gutter: the space formed by the two inside margins of a book or magazine layout closest to the binding

gutter jump: a typographic or graphic element that stretches across the gutter to inhabit fields on both pages of a spread

hairline stroke: a secondary stroke of a character, often is thinner than the stem

header (or running head): text that runs along the top margin of multiple pages of a publication, used to provide navigational information like titles, dates, or folios

headline: the title of an article or layout used to draw attention

hinting: a process in which extra information is encoded into a font file instructing the computer how to modify a character's outlines at different sizes to better align with the screen's grid of pixels

ideogram: an image that stands for a concept or idea

incunabula: term for books produced during the shift from handwritten manuscripts to printed books; Latin for "cradle" or "swaddling cloth"

intaglio: any printing process in which the ink sits below the surface of the plate

justified text: aligns flush against the left and right margins of the text block

juxtaposition: the placement of objects in relation to one another

kerning: adjusting the letterspace between two adjacent characters of type

knockout: text that is not actually printed, but instead is cut out from a solid area of printed color; the shapes of the letters are formed by the printed negative spaces that surround the letterforms, but the text itself remains the color of the paper

layout: the placement of text and objects on a page

leading (line spacing): (pronounced led-ing) 1. thin strips of lead placed between lines of type in letterpress printing; 2. the space between two consecutive measures of type on a page or layout (line spacing)

left-aligned text (flush left/ragged right): aligns flush against the left margin of the text block, but is uneven on the right

leg: a secondary stroke that extends downward from a stem to the baseline and ends freely

legibility: the ease with which a reader can recognize and differentiate between letterforms

letterspace: the space between two letters in a word

letterspacing (tracking): 1. the collective letterspaces within a string or block of text; 2. adjusting the distance between characters in a string or block of text (tracking)

ligature: a letter pair that has been joined to form a single character

lining numerals: numeral characters that optically sit on the baseline and extend up to the cap height

link: a small connecting stroke between the loop and the upper bowl of a lowercase letter **g**

lithography: a planographic printing process which is based on treating a limestone to attract ink in some places and repel it in others

logogram: a symbol that represents a whole word, like @ or $ or #

loop: lower curved stroke or bowl of a lowercase **g**

margins: the negative spaces between the outside edges of the grid area and the format

marker: a mark indicating the location of a repetitive element in a layout, like a running head or a folio

measure (line length): the length of a line of text

misregistration: the misalignment of color separations and/or adjacent colors in printed materials

old-style numerals: numeral characters that include several characters (3, 4, 5, 7, and 9) that drop below the baseline to the descender line and extend only up to the x-height

orphan: the first line of a paragraph, isolated at the bottom of a column or page

outline (or **vector**) **fonts:** letterforms that are understood by the computer as a series of points forming an outline of the letterform; the outline can be scaled to any size without losing integrity of shape

overshoot guidelines: a set of guidelines that overshoot the standard guidelines, for the design of letterforms that require optical adjustments to compensate for the optical illusion that rounded and pointed letters appear smaller than other letters of the same size

petroglyph: a rock engraving

phonogram: a symbol that represents a spoken sound

pica: measurement of type that equals ⅙ of an inch

pictogram: a simplified image illustrating a specific word

pictograph: a prehistoric rock painting; also known as a pictogram

pixels: the smallest grid units of graphical information that can be manipulated to display a specific color or value on a CRT computer monitor

planography: any printing process in which the ink sits on top of a smooth surface

point: measurement of type that equals 1/72 of an inch

pull-quote: a sentence, quoted from the body text and set apart and in larger point size

rasterize: to convert an outline font to a bitmapped image, at a selected size

readability: how easily a page of text can be read and navigated

reading gravity: phenomenon describing how readers' physical reading habits influence their navigational tendencies when encountering a page or layout

relief printing: any printing process in which the ink sits on a raised surface

right-aligned text (flush right/ragged left): aligns flush against the right margin of the text block, but is uneven on the left

roman: an upright, non-italic typeface with serifs

runaround text alignment: text wraps around graphics or textual elements in a layout

sans serif: a typeface that has no serifs (often used in the adjective form: sans-serif)

serif: an extension at a terminal of a letterform; also refers to a typeface that has serifs

set width: the width of a character, relative to its cap height

shaped text alignment: text flows along a curved or irregular line or shape

shoulder: the transitional area of a stroke that goes from curved to straight

sidebar: information that is independent from the body text and is set apart, sometimes enclosed in a box

sidebearings: the empty spaces to the left and right of the letterform on a sort or its digital equivalent

solid leading: consecutive measures of type that have no added leading between them

sort: a rectangular metal piece of type for use in letterpress printing

spine: the curved main stroke of a letter **S**

spread: two facing pages of an open book or magazine that make up one continuous layout

spur: a small stroke sometimes found on the right side of the base of a capital letter **G**

stem stroke: a character's main vertical, diagonal, or curved stroke, which is often thicker than the other strokes of the letter

storyboard: a set of sketched or rendered frames that demonstrates the layout, actions, and timing for a time-based or interactive design

stroke: an individual straight or curved line that is used to build a character

stroke weight: the thickness of the individual strokes of a character

subhead: secondary headline that subdivides and organizes body text

substitution: using an image to replace a letter or word in a layout

swash: a decorative extended stroke that sometimes projects from a terminal, often found on script letterforms

tail: the small stroke at the base of a capital **Q** that differentiates it from a capital **O**; the descenders on lowercase **j**, **p**, **q**, and **y** are sometimes also called tails

terminal: an endpoint of a stroke, which may or may not have a serif

tracking (letterspacing): adjusting the distance between characters in a string or block of text

trapping: a way of dealing with misregistration, by slightly enlarging the lighter of two touching shapes so that it overlaps the darker color a little bit

trim line or **trim mark:** line or mark that indicates where the guillotine cut will be made after printing

type: 1. metal sorts used for printing letterforms; 2. typeset text; and 3. printed characters

type family: 1. a collection of type that includes a specific typeface and all the type styles of that typeface; or 2. a category that type is classified into, based on the historical origin and physical characteristics of the letterforms

type style: a modified version of a typeface

typeface: a collection of letterforms that have been especially designed to go together

typographic color: the overall tonal value of a block of type on a page, as perceived when the eye combines the positive and negative shapes of the layout

typography: the study, use, and design of type

vertex: the point at which two downward slanting strokes of a letterform meet

visual correspondence: reiteration of a message through the use of a typeface that visually relates to the content of the text

visual distortion: alteration or deformation of letterforms to manipulate the message that the words send

visual exaggeration: to amplify a message by manipulating and placing text in ways that seem to act out the content or simulate the experience being described

visual hierarchy: the order of importance of elements within a layout, as indicated by the use of emphasis and typographic elements such as bars, rules, and bullets

visual irony: using satire and surprise to communicate a message by purposefully selecting typefaces that contrast with the content of the text

visual program: a set of parameters directing how type and images should consistently relate to the grid

visual rhythm: rhythm that is visually suggested through use of repetition, overlap, movement, alignment, spacing, reading gravity, and contrast

waistline: a real or imaginary horizontal line that marks the height of the body of a tall lowercase letter (often is the same as the x-height)

watermark: a kind of trademark that is built into fine papers by including raised designs in the paper molds; these marks are visible when the paper is held up to the light

white rivers: negative white space seeming to flow down a page within a block of text, usually due to inconsistent word spacing

widow: the last one or two words of a paragraph, isolated at the bottom of a page or at the top of a new column or page

word spacing: the space between adjacent words in a string or block of text

x-height: a real or imaginary horizontal line that shows how tall to make the lowercase letters of a typeface

x-height ratio: the height of regular lowercase letters of a typeface (those without ascenders) in relation to the typeface's cap height, generally measured using the lowercase **x** as a standard

xylography: a relief printing process in which raised images and calligraphy are cut onto wooden slabs and then inked

Courtesy of Elizabeth Nevin of the Briar Press.

BIBLIOGRAPHY B

Adbusters: Journal of the Mental Environment 51, vol. 12, no. 1 (Jan/Feb 2004).

Ashwin, Clive. *History of Graphic Design and Communication, A Source Book.* London: Pembridge Press, 1983.

Baines, Phil, and Andrew Haslam. *Type and Typography.* New York: Watson-Guptill Publications, 2002.

Beauchamp, Monte. *Blab 13* (autumn 2002).

Bellantoni, Jeff, and Matt Woolman. *Moving Type: Designing for Time and Space.* Switzerland: RotoVision, 2000.

————. *Type in Motion.* New York: Rizzoli International Publications, Inc., 1999.

Berry, W. Turner, and H. Edmund Poole. *Annals of Printing: A Chronological Encyclopaedia from the Earliest Times to 1950.* London: Blandford Press, 1966.

Booth-Clibborn, Edward, and Daniele Baroni. *The Language of Graphics.* New York: Harry N. Abrams, Inc., 1979.

Bosshard, Hans Rudolf. *The Typographic Grid.* Switzerland: Niggli Verlag AG, 2002.

Cabarga, Leslie. *Logo, Font & Lettering Bible.* Cincinnati, OH: How Design Books, 2004.

Carlson, Jeff; Toby Malina; and Glenn Fleishman. *Typography: The Best Work from the Web.* Gloucester, MA: Rockport, 1999.

Carter, Harry, and H. D. L. Vervliet. *Civilité Types.* Great Britain: Oxford University Press, 1966.

Carter, Rob. *Digital Color and Type.* Switzerland: RotoVision, 2002.

Carter, Rob; Ben Day; and Philip Meggs. *Typographic Design: Form and Communication.* New Jersey: John Wiley & Sons, Inc., 2002.

Chappell, Warren, and Robert Bringhurst. *A Short History of the Printed Word.* Point Roberts, WA: Hartley & Marks Publishers Inc., 1999.

Clair, Colin. *A Chronology of Printing.* New York: Frederick A. Praeger, 1969.

Clair, Kate. *A Typographic Workbook.* New York: John Wiley & Sons, Inc., 1999.

Cleaver, Wilbur Fisk. *Five Centuries of Printing: A Compilation of Important Events in the History of Typography.* Johnstown, PA: High School Print Shop, 1932.

Cost, Frank. *Pocket Guide to Digital Printing.* New York: Thomson Delmar Learning, 1997.

Craig, James. *Designing with Type: A Basic Course in Typography.* New York: Watson-Guptill Publications, 1999.

Craig, James, and Bruce Barton. *Thirty Centuries of Graphic Design.* New York: Watson-Guptill Publications, 1987.

Cullen, Cheryl Dangel. *The Best of Brochure Design 6.* Gloucester, MA: Rockport Publishers, Inc., 2001.

Darling, Harold. *From Mother Goose to Dr. Seuss.* San Francisco: Chronicle Books, 1995.

Davis, Susan, ed. *Typography 23: The Annual of the Type Directors Club.* Hong Kong: HBI Publishers, 2002.

Earls, David. *Designing Typefaces.* Switzerland: RotoVision, 2002.

Eason, Ron, and Sarah Rookledge. *Rookledge's International Handbook of Type Designers: A Biographical Directory.* U.K.: Sarema Press Ltd., 1991.

Elam, Kimberly. *Geometry of Design.* New York: Princeton Architectural Press, 2001.

Ernst, Sandra B. *The ABC's of Typography.* New York: Art Direction Book Company, 1984.

Felici, James. *The Complete Manual of Typography.* Berkley, CA: Adobe Press, 2002.

Fishel, Catharine. *Minimal Graphics.* Gloucester, MA: Rockport Publishers, Inc., 1999.

Foges, Chris, ed. *Magazine Design.* Switzerland: RotoVision, 1999.

Friedl, Friedrich; Nicolaus Ott; and Bernard Stein. *Typography: An Encyclopedic Survey of Type Design and Techniques Throughout History.* New York: Black Dog & Leventhal Publishers, Inc., 1998.

Gale, Nathan. *Type 1: Digital Typeface Design.* New York: Universe Publishing, 2002.

Garrett, Jesse James. *The Elements of User Experience.* New York: AIGA, New Riders Press, 2003.

Goodman, Allison. *The 7 Essentials of Graphic Design.* Cincinnati, OH: How Design Books, 2001.

Gordon, Bob. *Making Digital Type Look Good.* New York: Watson-Guptill Publications, 2001.

Götz, Veruschka. *Color & Type for the Screen.* Switzerland: RotoVision, 1998.

Goudy, Frederic W. *The Alphabet and Elements of Lettering.* New York: Dorset Press, 1989.

Gress, Edmund G. *Fashions in American Typography.* New York: Harper & Brothers Publishers, 1931.

Groth, Gary, ed. *The Comics Journal* 245 (August 2002).

Haller, Lynn. *Creative Edge Type.* Cincinnati, OH: North Light Books, 1999.

Harvey, Michael. *Creative Lettering Today.* New York: Design Books, 1996.

Hayden, Clare, and Heinke Jenssen, eds. *Corporate Identity 3.* New York: Graphis, 1998.

Haynes, Merritt Way. *The Student's History of Printing.* New York: McGraw-Hill, 1930.

Heller, Steven, and Seymour Chwast. *Graphic Style: From Victorian to Digital.* New York: Harry N. Abrams, Inc., 1988.

Heller, Steven, and Louise Fili. *British Modern.* San Francisco: Chronicle Books, 1998.

———. *Design Connoisseur.* New York: Allworth Press, 2000.

———. *Streamline.* San Francisco: Chronicle Books, 1995.

———. *Typology: Type Design from the Victorian Era to the Digital Age.* San Francisco: Chronicle Books, 1999.

Heller, Steven, and Elinor Pettit. *Graphic Design Time Line: A Century of Design Milestones.* New York: Allworth Press, 2000.

Heller, Steven, and Christine Thompson. *Letterforms: Bawdy Bad & Beautiful.* New York: Watson-Guptill Publications, 2000.

Hoe, Robert. *A Short History of the Printing Press.* New York: Robert Hoe, 1902.

Hollis, Richard. *Graphic Design: A Concise History.* New York: Thames and Hudson, 1994.

HOW magazine (February 2004).

Hurlburt, Allen. *The Design Concept.* New York: Watson-Guptill, 1981.

———. *The Grid.* New York: John Wiley & Sons, Inc., 1978.

———. *Layout: The Design of the Printed Page.* New York: Watson-Guptill, 1977.

Johnson, A. F. "Fat Faces: Their History, Forms and Use." *Alphabet and Image: A Quarterly of Typography and Graphic Arts,* vol. 5 (September 1947).

Jury, David. *About Face: Reviving the Rules of Typography.* UK: RotoVision, 2002.

Kane, John. *A Type Primer.* New Jersey: Prentice Hall, 2003.

Kristof, Ray, and Amy Satran. *Interactivity by Design.* Mountain View, CA: Adobe Press, 1995.

Kubler, George A. *A New History of Stereotyping.* New York: J. J. Little & Ives Company, 1941.

Lawson, Alexander. *Anatomy of a Typeface.* Boston: David R. Godine, Publisher, 1990.

———. *Printing Types: An Introduction.* Boston: Beacon Press, 1971.

Lehmann-Haupt, Hellmut. *Gutenberg and the Master of the Playing Cards.* New Haven, CT: Yale University Press, 1966.

Lester, Paul Martin. *Visual Communication: Images with Messages.* Belmont, CA: Wadsworth/Thomson Learning, 2000.

Lewis, John. *Typography: Design and Practice.* New York: Taplinger Publishing Co., 1978.

Lieberman, Ben J. *Types of Typefaces.* New York: Sterling Publishing Company, Inc., 1967.

Livio, Mario. "The Golden Number." *Natural History* 112, no. 2 (March 2003): 64-69.

Lupton, Ellen, and J. Abbott Miller. *Design Writing Research: Writing on Graphic Design.* New York: Princeton Architectural Press, 1996.

Mass Appeal Magazine, no. 25 (2003).

Meggs, Philip B. *A History of Graphic Design.* New York: John Wiley & Sons, Inc., 1998.

————. *Type and Image: The Language of Graphic Design.* New York: John Wiley & Sons, Inc., 1992.

Metzl, Ervine. *The Poster.* New York: Watson-Guptill Publications, 1963.

Moran, James. *Printing in the 20th Century.* New York: Hastings House, Publishers, Inc., 1974.

————. *Printing Presses, History and Development from the Fifteenth Century to Modern Times.* Berkeley, CA: University of California Press, 1973.

Moye, Stephen. *Fontographer: Type by Design.* New York: MIS:Press, 1995.

Müller-Brockmann, Josef. *Grid Systems.* Switzerland: Verlag Niggli AG, 1996.

Neuenschwander, Brody. *Letterwork: Creative Letterforms in Graphic Design.* London: Phaidon Press, 1993.

Orcutt, William Dana. *Master Makers of the Book.* New York: Doubleday, Doran & Company, Inc., 1928.

Owen, William. *Modern Magazine Design.* Dubuque, IA: Wm. C. Brown Publishers, 1992.

Park, Mimi, and Francesca Messina. *The Society of Publication Designers 37th Publication Design Annual.* Gloucester, MA: Rockport Publishers, Inc., 2002.

Perfect, Christopher, and Jeremy Austen. *The Complete Typographer.* New Jersey: Prentice Hall, 1992.

Perfect, Christopher, and Gordon Rookledge. *Rookledge's International Type Finder.* Boston: Serema Press Ltd, 1991.

Poynor, Rick. *Typographica.* London: Laurence King Publishing, 2001.

Poynor, Rick, and Edward Booth-Clibborn. *Typography Now: The Next Wave.* London: Edward Booth-Clibborn, 1991.

Print's Regional Design Annual. 57, no. 6 (2003).

Richards, G. Tilghman. *The History and Development of Typewriters.* London: Her Majesty's Stationary Office, 1964.

Richardson, Margaret E. *Type Graphics: The Power of Type in Graphic Design.* Gloucester, MA: Rockport Publishers, Inc., 2000.

Roberts, Lucienne, and Julia Thrift. *The Designer and the Grid.* East Sussex, UK: RotoVision, 2002.

Samara, Timothy. *Making and Breaking the Grid: A Graphic Design Layout Workshop.* Gloucester, MA: Rockport Publishers, Inc., 2002.

Shedroff, Nathan. *Experience Design 1.* Indianapolis, IN: New Riders, 2001.

Sidles, Constance J. *Great Production by Design*. Cincinnati, OH: North Light Books, 1998.

Silver, Linda, ed. *Print's Best Typography 2*. New York: RC Publications, 1995.

Spencer, Herbert. *Pioneers of Modern Typography*. Cambridge, MA: The MIT Press, 1982.

Strizver, Ilene. *Type Rules: The Designer's Guide to Professional Typography*. Cincinatti, OH: North Light Books, 2001.

The Times, Printing Number: Reprinted from the 401,000th Issue of The Times, Tuesday, September 10, 1912, London: The Times, 1912.

Thorpe, James. "The Posters of the Beggarstaff Brothers." *Alphabet and Image: A Quarterly of Typography and Graphic Arts*, vol. 4 (April 1947).

Timmers, Margaret, ed. *The Power of the Poster*. London: V&A Publications, 2003.

Toulouze, Michel. *L'art et Instruction de Bien Dancer: A Facsimile of the Only Recorded Copy with a Bibliographical Note by Victor Scholderer*. London: The Royal College of Physicians, Emery Walker Ltd., 1936.

Tracy, Walter. *Letters of Credit: A View of Type Design*. Boston: David R. Godine, Publisher, 2003.

Triggs, Teal. *Type Design: Radical Innovations and Experimentation*. New York: Harper Design International, 2003.

Turnbull, Arthur, and Russell N. Baird. *The Graphics of Communication*. New York: Hold, Rinehart and Winston, 1980.

Twemlow, Alice, ed. *365: AIGA Year in Design 23*. New York: AIGA, 2002.

Twyman, Michael. *The British Library Guide to Printing History and Techniques*. Toronto: University of Toronto Press, Inc., 1999.

————. *Henry Bankes's Treatise on Lithography*. London: Printing Historical Society, 1976.

————. *Early Lithographed Books*. London: Farrand Press & Private Libraries Association, 1990.

Twyman, Michael; Gary Kurutz; George Fox; and Curtiss Taylor. *Bicentennial of Lithography*. San Franscisco: Book Club of California, 1999.

VanderLans, Rudi, and Zuzana Licko. *Emigre: Graphic Design into the Digital Realm*. New York: Van Nostrand Reinhold, 1993.

Walton, Roger, ed. *Big Type*. New York: HBI, 2002.

Wheildon, Colin. *Type & Layout*. Berkeley, CA: Strathmoor Press, 1996.

Wildbur, Peter. *Information Graphics*. New York: Van Nostrand Reinhold, 1989.

Wolpe, Berthold. *Vincent Figgins Type Specimens 1801 and 1815; Reproduced in Facsimile*. London: Printing Historical Society, John Roberts Press, 1967.

INTERNET ARTICLES AND GENERAL RESOURCES

"About Points and Pixels as Units." <*http://www.hut.fi/u/hsivonen/units.html*>.

Adams, Peter C. S. "PageMaker Past, Present and Future." March 16, 2004. <*http://www.makingpages.org/pagemaker/history/*>.

AIGA. "Symbol Signs." <*http://www.aiga.org/content.cfm?ContentAlias=symbolsigns*>.

Apple Computer, Inc. "Advanced Typography with Mac OS X: Using and Managing Fonts." July 2004. <*http://images.apple.com/pro/pdf/L303878B_Font_TT_v4.pdf*>.

"The Arabic Language Script." <*http://www.indiana.edu/~arabic/arabic_script.htm*>.

Archer, Caroline. "Printers Once Promoted Themselves through their Knowledge of Type." *Eye Magazine*, 2001. <*http://www.eyemagazine.com/feature.php?id=85&fid=448*>.

"Bauhaus Manifesto 1919." <*http://www.architetturamoderna.com/pdf/Bauhausmanifesto.pdf*>.

Bellis, Mary. "Inventors: A Brief History of Writing Instruments." <*http://inventors.about.com/library/weekly/aa100197.htm*>.

Bellis, Mary. "Inventors: The History of Phototypesetting." <*http://inventors.about.com/library/inventors/blphototypesetting.htm*>.

BitLaw. "Design Patents." <*http://www.bitlaw.com/patent/design.html*>.

Book Information Website. "Book History Timetable." 1998. <*http://www.xs4all.nl/~knops/timetab.html*>.

Briem, Gunnlaugur. "Notes on Type Design." August 2001. <*http://briem.ismennt.is/2/2.3.1a/2.3.1.01.notes.htm*>.

The British Library. "Concise History of the British Newspaper in the Nineteenth Century." <*http://www.bl.uk/collections/brit19th.html*>.

The British Library: Digital Catalogue of Illuminated Manuscripts. "An Introduction to Illuminated Manuscripts." <*http://prodigi.bl.uk/illcat/TourIntro1.asp*>.

Brown, R. J. "History Buff: A Capsule History of Typesetting." <http://www.historybuff.com/library/reftype.html>.

"Capital and Labour—The Invention of the Steam-Engine: Watt's Early Inventions."
<http://www.history.rochester.edu/steam/lord/4-1.htm>.

Chernov, F. "Bourgeois Cosmopolitanism and Its Reactionary Role." October 30, 2003.
<http://www.cyberussr.com/rus/chernov/chernov-patriotizm-e.html>.

Chinaknowledge.org. "Chinese Art—Graphic Art."
<http://www.chinaknowledge.de/Art/Printing/printing.html>.

Computerhope.com. "Computer History. History for 2000 to Today."
<http://www.computerhope.com/history/2000.htm>.

"Confusion Over Sub-Pixels and CRTs." March 15, 2005. <http://grc.com/ctdialog.htm>.

"Dada." <http://www.jahsonic.com/Dada.html>.

Every, David, K. "What is the History of TrueType?" November 9, 2002.
<http://www.mackido.com/History/History_TT.html>.

Fabian, Nicholas. "The Master of Univers, Adrian Frutiger."
<http://web.archive.org/web/20000823071215/webcom.net/~nfhome/frutiger.htm>.

FluxEuropa. "The Art and Ideas of Wyndham Lewis." January 7, 1999.
<http://www.fluxeuropa.com/wyndhamlewis-art_and_ideas.htm>.

Foam Train Fonts. "History of Type." <http://www.owlsoup.com/foamtrain/history.html>.

"Futurism: Manifestos and Other Resources." June 14, 2002.
<http://www.unknown.nu/futurism/>.

Georgia Tech, Institute of Paper Science and Technology. "Watermarks." March 21, 2005.
<http://www.ipst.gatech.edu/amp/collection/museum_watermark.htm>.

Gibson, Steve. "Sub-Pixel Font Rendering Technology." 2003. <http://grc.com/cleartype.htm>.

Hamilton Wood Type and Printing Museum. "About Wood Type."
<http://www.woodtype.org/museum_information_about.shtml>.

"IBM Archives: 1976." <http://www-1.ibm.com/ibm/history/history/year_1976.html>.

inkPlus. "CG Fundamentals."
<http://inkplus.syste.ms/Academy/Fundamentals/CGFundamental-Resolution.htm>.

International Poster Gallery Online. "The New Economic Policy (1921-1927)." *Revolution by Design: The Soviet Poster.* <http://www.internationalposter.com/ru-text.cfm#NEP>.

"Lithography in the Victorian Age."
<http://www.bl.uk/collections/early/victorian/lithogra/lithog10.html>.

MacGregor, Chris. "The TypeRight Guide to Ethical Type Design."
<http://www.typeright.org/ethicsguide.html>.

Madden, Mary, and Lee Rainee. "America's Online Pursuits: The Changing Picture of Who's Online and What They Do." December 22, 2003.
<http://www.pewinternet.org/reports/reports.asp?Report=106&Section=ReportLevel1&Field=Level1ID&ID=463<http://www.prepressure.com/ps/history/history.htm>.

Met Special Topics Page. "Gothic Art."
<http://www.metmuseum.org/toah/hd/mgot/hd_mgot.htm>.

Met Special Topics Page. "Romanesque Art."
<http://www.metmuseum.org/toah/hd/rmsq/hd_rmsq.htm>.

Microsoft. "Microsoft Typography—A Brief History of TrueType." June 30, 1997.
<http://www.microsoft.com/typography/history/history.htm>.

Microsoft Research. "Gary Starkweather Profile."
<http://research.microsoft.com/aboutmsr/jobs/garys.aspx>.

Musée de l'imprimerie de Lyon.
<http://www.imprimerie.lyon.fr/imprimerie/sections/fr/une/une>.

O'Hanlon, Charlene. "Gary Starkweather: Laser Printer Inventor." November 13, 2002.
<http://www.crn.com/sections/special/hof/hof02.asp?ArticleID=38521>.

Old and Sold Antique Digest. "Lithography—Phototypesetting." Originally published 1963.
<http://www.oldandsold.com/articles09/lithography-6.shtml>.

"On the Goodness of Unicode." April 6, 2003.
<http://www.tbray.org/ongoing/When/200x/2003/04/06/Unicode>.

Otten, Liam. "A Rare Acquisition." *Washington University in St. Louis Magazine,* Spring 2001. *<http://magazine.wustl.edu/Spring01/LibraryAcquisition.html>.*

Parkin, Simon. "Visual Energy." June 21, 2000. *<http://www.hyperreal.org/raves/database/visuale/ve2.htm>.*

Phinney, Thomas W. "A Brief History of Type." *<http://www.redsun.com/type/abriefhistoryoftype/>.*

Pinkus, Karen. "Futurism: Proto Punk?" *<http://www.unknown.nu/futurism/protopunk.html>.*

Sewell, J. "Aquatint." *<http://www.collectorsprints.com/glossary/aquatint.asp>.*

SSi. "Font Foundry Myths." July 16, 1997. *<http://ssifonts.com/Myths.htm>.*

SSi. "SSi Foundry Myths #15—If Copyright Does Not Provide Font Protection, Patents Can Protect Most Fonts." *<http://ssifonts.com/Patents1.HTM>.*

Tom Chao's Paper Money Gallery. June 13, 2005. *<http://www.tomchao.com/>.*

TrueType Typography. "A History of TrueType." *<http://www.truetype.demon.co.uk/tthist.htm>.*

United States Copyright Office, The Library of Congress. "Copyright." June 6, 2005. *<http://www.copyright.gov/>.*

United States Patent and Trademark Office. "General Information Concerning Patents." January 2005. *<http://www.uspto.gov/web/offices/pac/doc/general/index.html#laws>.*

U.S. Census Bureau. "Home Computers and Internet Use in the United States: August 2000." *<http://www.census.gov/prod/2001pubs/p23-207.pdf>.*

Xerox. "Online Fact Book." *<http://www.xerox.com/go/xrx/template/019d.jsp?view=Factbook&id=Historical&Xcntry=USA&Xlang=en_US>.*

Courtesy of Elizabeth Nevin of the Briar Press.

CONTRIBUTORS

13thFloor; Dave Parmley and Eric Ruffing; *www.13thfloordesign.com*

Adbusters magazine; Chris Sauvé; *www.adbusters.org*

Adobe Systems Inc.; *www.adobe.com/type*

Alan Chan Design Co.; Alan Chan; *www.alanchandesign.com*

AlltheSky.com; Till Credner and Sven Kohle; *www.allthesky.com*

American Airlines Publishing; J. R. Arebalo, Jr.; *www.americanwaymag.com*

American Type Founders; *www.columbia.edu/cu/lweb/data/indiv/rare/type-exhibit/atf.htm*

Apple; Todd Wilder; *http://developer.apple.com/fonts*

Arnika; Michael Ashley; *www.arnikans.com*

Art 270, Inc.; Carl Mill, Diane Zotter-Mill, and Nicole Lombardo Ganz; *www.art270.com*

Art Chantry Design; Art Chantry; *www.artchantry.com*

Artists Rights Society (ARS); *www.arsny.com*

Astigmatic One Eye Typographic Institute; Brian J. Bonislawsky; *www.astigmatic.com*

Atomic Media; Matthew Bardram; *www.atomicmedia.net*

BA Graphics; Bob Alonso; *www.myfonts.com*

Baltimore Magazine; Amanda White-Iseli and Isabelle Arsenault; *www.baltimoremagazine.net*

Bannigan Artworks; Todd and Linda Hallock; *www.celticartworks.com*

Barnbrook Design; Jonathan Barnbrook; *www.barnbrook.net*

Basel Fair; Wolfgang Weingart; *www.weingartarchive.com*

Beacon Press; *www.beacon.org*

Bergman Associates; Robert Bergman; *http://bergassociates.com*

Berthold Types Limited; Melissa M. Hunt; *www.bertholdtypes.com*

Berthold Wolpe Estate

Bill Graham Presents; Thomas Scott and Arlene Owseichik; *www.bgp.com*

Bite It!; Trevor Jackson; *www.outputrecordings.com*

Bitstream Inc.; Bob Thomas; *www.myfonts.com*

Blambot; Nate Piekos; *www.blambot.com*

Blue Vinyl Fonts; Jess Latham; *www.bvfonts.com*

Briar Press; Elizabeth Nevin; *www.briarpress.org*

The British Library; *www.bl.uk*

Burghal Design; Kate Peters; *www.burghal.com*

Butterfly Stroke Inc.; Fumio Tachibana and Katsunori Aoki; *www.butterfly-stroke.com*

Camille Rose Garcia; Camille Rose Garcia; *www.camillerosegarcia.com*

Campbell Fisher Design; Mike Campbell; *www.thinkcfd.com*

CastleType; Jason Castle; *www.castletype.com*

Centre for Ephemera Studies, Department of Typography & Graphic Communication, The University of Reading; Michael Twyman; *www.rdg.ac.uk/AcaDepts/lt*

Charles S. Anderson Design Company; Charles Anderson; *www.csadesign.com*

Clarity Coverdale Fury; Jac Coverdale and Glenn Gray; *www.claritycoverdalefury.com*

The Collective Design; Alexander Kneselac; *www.collective.dreamhost.com*

Cool Fonts; Todd Dever; *www.cool-fonts.com*

Cranbrook Academy of Art; Gerri Craig; *www.cranbrook.edu*

Crookeder; Dylan Nelson; *www.crookeder.com*

David Carson Design, Inc.; David Carson; *www.davidcarsondesign.com*

David King Collection, London

Daxo; Hans Reichel; *www.daxo.de*

Design Equals More; Keith Novicki

Duke University Rare Book, Manuscript, and Special Collections Library; Linda McCurdy; *http://library.duke.edu/specialcollections*

Elsner + Flake; Veronika Elsner and Gunther Flake; *www.elsner-flake.com*

Emigre, Inc.; Rudy VanderLans and Zuzana Licko; *www.emigre.com*

Family Dog Productions; Chet Helms

Fantagraphics Books; Eric Reynolds, Monte Beauchamp, and Peppy White; *www.fantagraphics.com*

focus2 brand development; Duane King and Todd Hart; *www.focus2.com*

Font Bureau Inc.; Robb Ogle and Sam Berlow; *www.fontbureau.com*

fontBoy; Bob Aufuldish and Kathy Warinner; *www.fontboy.com, www.aufwar.com*

FontFabrik; Wim Westerveld of Neon

FontFont, FSI FontShop International; Manfred Klein and Veronica Hamer; *www.fontfont.com, www.fontshop.com*

Fox Ash; David Jury

Froeter Design Company, Inc.; Chris Froeter; *www.froeterdesign.com*

Glasgow City Council (Museums)

The Herb Lubalin Study Center of Design and Typography at The Cooper Union School of Art; *www.cooper.edu/art/lubalin*

The Hoefler Type Foundry, Inc., Hoefler & Frere-Jones, Enschede; Jonathan Hoefler; *www.typography.com*

Hourglass; Dave McKean

House Industries; Andy Cruz, Allen Mercer, and Jeremy Dean; *http://houseind.com*

HOW magazine; Bryn Mooth and Tricia Bateman; *www.howdesign.com*

The Independent Film Channel; Christine Lubrano; *www.ifctv.com*

Ingrimayne Type; Robert Schenk; *http://ingrimayne.saintjoe.edu/fonts*

Iowa State University Department of Art and Design for the Council of Educators in Landscape Architecture; Paula J. Curran

István Hargittai and Magdolna Hargittai; István Hargittai and Magdolna Hargittai

Jed Morfit Illustration; Jed Morfit; *www.jedmorfit.com*

Jennifer Sterling Design; Jennifer Sterling; *www.jennifersterling.com*

Joan Dobkin; Joan Dobkin; *www.joandobkin.com*

Julie Saunders Carlini; Julie Saunders Carlini

Karanya Aksornkoae and Panya Chittaratlert; Karanya Aksornkoae and Panya Chittaratlert

Karma Group; Brad Knapp; *www.attainkarma.com*

Koichi Sato Design Studio; Koichi Sato

Koninklijke Bibliotheek; Jan Maarten de Booij; *www.kb.nl/index-en.html*

LettError; Erik van Blokland and Just van Rossum; *www.letterror.com*

Library of Congress, Washington, D.C.; *www.loc.gov*

Linotype, Linotype Library GmbH; Fabrice Ruth Dissieux; *www.linotype.com*

Louviere + Vanessa; Jeff Louviere; *www.louviereandvanessa.com*

Lycette Bros.; John and Mark Lycette; *www.lycettebros.com*

M&Co; Maira Kalman; *www.mairakalman.com*

Made in Space; April Greiman; *www.madeinspace.la*

Massin; Robert Massin

Microsoft Corporation; Simon Daniels; *www.microsoft.com*

MiniFonts.com; Joe Gillespie and Paul Wootton; *http://minifonts.com*

Miscellaneous Man: Rare original Posters and vintage Graphics; George Theofiles; *www.miscman.com*

Misprinted Type; Eduardo Recife; *www.misprintedtype.com*

Mithoff Advertising, Inc.; Clive Cochran; *www.mithoffburton.com*

Monotype Imaging Ltd, UK; *www.monotypefonts.com*

Motown Records, a division of UMG Recordings, Inc.; Erykah Badu; *www.erykahbadu.com*

Muller and Company; John Muller; *www.mullerco.com*

NAI Publishers; *www.naipublishers.nl*

Neko Studios; Su. Suttle; *NekoStudios.com*

ni9e; Max Asare; *www.ni9e.com*

Nick's Fonts; Nick Curtis; *www.nicksfonts.com*

Niklaus Troxler Graphic Design; Niklaus Troxler; *www.troxlerart.ch*

Okayplayer; Dan Petruzzi, Afra Amir Sanjari, Kirsten O'Loughlin, and Chris Ro; *http://okayplayer.com*

One Reel; Heather Smith; *http://onereel.org*

Otto & Marie Neurath Isotype Collection, Department of Typography & Graphic Communication, University of Reading; *www.rdg.ac.uk/AcaDepts/lt*

Outside The Line Design; Rae Kaiser; *www.outside-the-line.com*

P22 Type Foundry, Inc.; Richard Kegler; *www.p22.com*

PampaType; Alejandro Lo Celso; *www.pampatype.com/English.html*

Paratype, Ltd.; Sergey Kochin; *www.paratype.com*

Patent Pending Industries; Jeff Kleinsmith; *www.patentpendingindustries.com*

PAX—Real Solutions to Gun Violence; Douglas Flores, Talmage Cooley, Daniel Gross, and Ian Toombs; *www.pax.com/speakup/adsandpress.html*

Pentagram Design; Kit Hinrichs, Paula Scher, Steven Bateman, and Mervyn Kurlansky; *www.pentagram.com*

Phil Baines; Phil Baines; *http://philbaines.co.uk*

The Pierpont Morgan Library; *www.morganlibrary.org*

Présence Typo; Thierry Puyfoulhoux; *www.presencetypo.com*

PSY/OPS Type SF; Rodrigo X. Cavazos; *http://psyops.com*

Push Pin Studios; Seymour Chwast; *www.pushpininc.com*

Pyro/Core11; Eric Tilford; *www.core11.com*

Research Studios; Neville Brody; *www.researchstudios.com*

Richard Beatty Designs; Richard W. Beatty

Rikuyosha Co., Ltd.; www.rikuyosha.co.jp

St. John's College in the University of Oxford; Catherine Hilliard and James Allen; *http://image.ox.ac.uk/list?collection=stj*

sans+baum; Julia Thrift, Lucienne Roberts, and Bob Wilkinson

Sarabande; Joe Freedman; *www.sarabande.com*

Saul Bass Estate

Segura, Inc. / T-26.; Carlos Segura; *www.segura-inc.com*, *www.t26.com*

Shelter Publications, Inc.; Lloyd Kahn; *www.shelterpub.com*

Shively Photography; Will Shively

Some Odd Pilot; Christopher Eichenseer; *www.someoddpilot.com*

Sommese Design; Lanny Sommese

Spacetacular; Stephanie Harte; *www.spacetacular.com*

Special Collections Research Center, University of Chicago Library; Daniel Meyer; *http://century.lib.uchicago.edu*

Special Collections, University of Delaware Library; Iris Snyder; *www.lib.udel.edu*

SPONE; Greg Lamarche

Staatsbibliothek, Bamberg; *www.staatsbibliothek-bamberg.de*

StereoMC's; N. Hallam; *www.stereomcs.com*

Steven Heller; Steven Heller

Strange Attractors Design; Ryan Pescatore Frisk and Catelijne van Middelkoop; *www.strangeattractors.com*

Studio de pal, Netherlands; Arlette Brouwers and Koos van der Meer

Studio Lupi; Italo Lupi

twothousandstrong; Douglas R. Marshall; *www.2000strong.com*

Tyler Design Workshop, Temple University; Keli Cavanaugh and Steven DeCusatis; *www.temple.edu/tyler*

TypeArt Foundry Inc.; Lloyd Springer; *www.typeart.com*

University of Nebraska Press; Richard Eckersley; *http://unp.unl.edu*

URW++ Design & Development; Peter Rosenfeld; *www.urwpp.de/english/home.htm*

V&A Images / Victoria and Albert Museum; *www.vam.ac.uk*

Victor Moscoso; Victor Moscoso; *www.victormoscoso.com*

Vignelli Associates; Massimo Vignelli; *http://vignelli.com*

Visual Dialogue; Fritz Klaetke; *www.visualdialogue.com*

Von Zezschwitz: Art and Design Auctions of Munich; Dr. Graham Dry; *www.von-zezschwitz.de/impressum.php*

We Associated; Mike Kohnke; *www.weassociated.com*

Why Not Associates; *www.whynotassociates.com*

Wolfe Design; Terri Wolfe; *http://tswolfedesign.com*

Worsley Press; Colin Wheildon; *www.worsleypress.com*

Zentralbibliothek Zürich; *www-zb.unizh.ch*

Courtesy of Elizabeth Nevin of the Briar Press.

INDEX I